M000310534

The Institutions Curse

The "resource curse" is the view that countries with abundant natural resources suffer from a host of maladies, including weak state capacity, authoritarianism, the underprovision of public goods, and corruption and economic stagnation. This book debunks this view, arguing that there is an "institutions curse" rather than a resource curse. Legacies endemic to the developing world have impelled many countries to develop natural resources as a default sector in lieu of cultivating modern and diversified economies, and bad institutions have also condemned nations to suffer from ills unduly attributed to minerals and oil. Victor Menaldo also argues that natural resources can actually play an integral role in stimulating state capacity, capitalism, industrialization, and democracy, even if resources are themselves often a symptom of underdevelopment. Despite being cursed by their institutions, weak states are blessed by their resources: greater oil means more development, both historically and across countries today.

VICTOR MENALDO is Associate Professor of Political Science at the University of Washington and an affiliated faculty of the Center for Statistics and the Social Sciences, Near and Middle Eastern Studies, and the Center for Environmental Politics.

Business and Public Policy

Series editor

ASEEM PRAKASH, University of Washington

Series board

Vinod K. Aggarwal, University of California, Berkeley
Tanja A. Börzel, Freie Universität Berlin
David Coen, University College London
Peter Gourevitch, University of California, San Diego
Neil Gunningham, The Australian National University
Witold J. Henisz, University of Pennsylvania
Adrienne Héritier, European University Institute
Chung-in Moon, Yonsei University
Sarah A. Soule, Stanford University
David Vogel, University of California, Berkeley

This series aims to play a pioneering role in shaping the emerging field of business and public policy. *Business and Public Policy* focuses on two central questions. First, how does public policy influence business strategy, operations, organization, and governance, and with what consequences for both business and society? Second, how do businesses themselves influence policy institutions, policy processes, and other policy actors and with what outcomes?

Other books in the series

TIMOTHY WERNER, *Public Forces and Private Politics in American Big Business*

HEVINA S. DASHWOOD, *The Rise of Global Corporate Social Responsibility: Mining and the Spread of Global Norms*

LLEWELYN HUGHES, *Globalizing Oil: Firms and Oil Market Governance in France, Japan, and the United States*

EDWARD T. WALKER, *Grassroots for Hire: Public Affairs Consultants in American Democracy*

CHRISTIAN R. THAUER, *The Managerial Sources of Corporate Social Responsibility: The Spread of Global Standards*

KIYOTERU TSUTSUI & ALWYN LIM (Editors), *Corporate Social Responsibility in a Globalizing World*

ASEEMA SINHA, *Globalizing India: How Global Rules and Markets are Shaping India's Rise to Power*

The Institutions Curse

Natural Resources, Politics, and Development

VICTOR MENALDO

University of Washington

CAMBRIDGE
UNIVERSITY PRESS

CAMBRIDGE
UNIVERSITY PRESS

University Printing House, Cambridge CB2 8BS, United Kingdom

Cambridge University Press is part of the University of Cambridge.

It furthers the University's mission by disseminating knowledge in the pursuit of education, learning and research at the highest international levels of excellence.

www.cambridge.org
Information on this title: www.cambridge.org/9781316503362

© Victor Menaldo 2016

First published 2016

Printed in the United States of America by Sheridan Books, Inc.

A catalogue record for this publication is available from the British Library

Library of Congress Cataloging-in-Publication data
Menaldo, Victor, 1977– author.
The institutions curse : natural resources, politics, and development / Victor Menaldo, University of Washington.
Cambridge, U.K. ; New York : Cambridge University Press, 2016.
LCCN 2016010374 | ISBN 9781107138605 (hardback)
LCSH: Economic development – Developing countries. | Institution building – Developing countries. | Natural resources – Developing countries. | Developing countries – Politics and government. | BISAC: POLITICAL SCIENCE / Economic Conditions.
LCC HC59.7 .M435 2016 | DDC 338.9009172/4–dc23
LC record available at https://lccn.loc.gov/2016010374

ISBN 978-1-107-13860-5 Hardback
ISBN 978-1-316-50336-2 Paperback

For my parents

Contents

Figures

Maps

Tables

Acknowledgments

I would like to take this opportunity to pay homage to many of my teachers, mentors, and fellow researchers, as well as my parents. It might be cliché to say this, but this book is in many respects a conduit; it conveys many insights and ideas I have picked up along the way.

I owe a special debt of gratitude to Stephen Haber. He was a superb advisor and mentor to me in graduate school, has been really fun to work with as a coauthor, and is a good friend. His work on the political economy of finance, industrialization, natural resources, democracy, and authoritarianism has profoundly shaped my own views; they made an indelible mark on this book. Most concretely, the first half of Chapter 4, on the institutions curse and institutions blessing, is inspired by much of his work and the work of his coauthors. And the second half of that chapter, on institutional origins, draws very closely on joint work with Steve on the relationship between rainfall and democracy. There, we first deployed the data on factor endowments that I used in Chapters 4 and 5. I thank both him and Roy Ellis for their lead role in conceptualizing and constructing that data, as well as some of the tribalism indexes used in Chapter 7.

I have also drawn on other coauthored works throughout the book. Chapters 2, 3, and 6 build on two papers co-written with Steve; "A Reevaluation of the Resource Curse: Does Oil Fuel Authoritarianism?" and "Natural Resources in Latin America: Neither Curse Nor Blessing." Chapters 3 and 4 draw on several papers co-written with Michael Albertus. These include "Dictators as Founding Fathers: The Role of Constitutions in Autocracies" and "If You're Against Them You're With Us: The Effect of Expropriation on Autocratic Survival."

I also benefited greatly from several conferences. During presentations and conversations at those conferences, I learned a lot from several experts working in the energy industry. Two conferences stand out. The first, hosted by the RAND Corporation in Washington, D.C., in which I presented an earlier version of Chapter 5, exposed me to very insightful knowledge about the hydrocarbon industry. In particular, Chris Perry, Energy Analyst at the U.S. Defense Intelligence Agency and Mohamed Badissy, at the Office of the General Counsel at the U.S. Department of Commerce, provided me with a welter of helpful information. The second was sponsored by Anand Rajaram, at the World Bank. Along with Paasha Mahdavi, I helped to organize this conference and presented several topics from the book. I owe Paasha, in particular, a debt of gratitude. As we jointly prepared for the conference, I learned a lot of great stuff from him about national oil companies and other aspects of the global oil industry. After the conference, he continued to provide me with helpful feedback on the book itself.

There are many others I am grateful to. For providing comments on different aspects of the book during conferences, or during presentations, or electronically, I would like to thank Chris Adolph, Yuen Yuen Ang, Jim Caporaso, Alexander Cooley, Thad Dunning, Jeff Frankel, Ellis Goldberg, Benjamin Graham, Daniel Hirsty, Jean Lachapelle, David Laitin, Margaret Levi, James Long, Pauline Jones Luong, Kai Kaiser, Edgar Kiser, Francisco Flores-Macías, Edward Maleski, Nimah Mazaheri, Joel Migdal, Francisco Monaldi, Kevin Morrison, Gerardo Munck, Paul Musgrave, Jeff Nugent, Jack Paine, Maggie Peters, Steve Pfaff, Brian Rathbun, William Reno, Michael Ross, Daniel Slater, Lucan Way, Jessica Weeks, Erik Wibbles, Joe Wright, and Dwayne Woods. I also thank Jesse Carah, Jennifer Noveck, and Nora Webb Williams for invaluable research assistance. Nora and Kendra Dupuy read earlier drafts of the book and provided valuable feedback. This helped me to greatly improve the manuscript. Finally, I would like to thank Kevin Tsui for sharing his datasets with me.

I would also like to thank my parents. My father rose from nothing to become a petroleum engineer. He always wanted me to follow in his footsteps; I was never particularly good at chemistry, and hope this book comes close enough to satisfying that dream. My mother, who does not have a college degree, raised four boys, all the while helping my dad sell goods and services from our dining room to oilfield service companies and refineries. I learned a lot about the oil industry, and how politics actually works, from both of them – most of it through osmosis.

Finally, I would like to thank my wife, Nicola, and son, Sebastian. Without them, and their love, none of the sacrifices associated with writing this book would have been worth it. Believe me!

1 | Introduction

The world is richer, more democratic, and healthier than ever before. The trajectory traced by the world's Gross Domestic Product (GDP) is an upward sloping line. The frequency of free and fair elections obeys this pattern too, as do measures of human well-being, such as average lifespans. Despite the unprecedented progress that our species has achieved over the last two centuries, however, development still varies widely across space. It has skipped over some places entirely.

What explains why some countries are more developed than others? Why do Denmark, South Korea, and New Zealand have a thriving economy, a stable and democratic political system, and public policies that benefit the majority of citizens? Why are Congo, Myanmar, and Ecuador poor, unstable, authoritarian, and a hotbed of patronage politics, rent-seeking, and virulent civil strife?

These questions matter greatly. Liberal democracies that are governed by the rule of law, and that generate consistent economic growth, are blessed with smarter, healthier, and happier citizens. They tend to live beyond hardscrabble subsistence, and their children grow up to be statesmen, scientists, and respected businesswomen. They also enjoy the personal security and leisure time required to indulge in artistic expression and engage in philanthropy. Of course, they might live perfectly ordinary lives, with weekend barbeques as the pinnacle of middle-class life. Whatever the case, they probably do not live in constant fear of starvation, violence, or persecution. Their children will probably not become warlords.

While "what determines development?" is among the most important question in social science, many hypotheses that have been put forth to answer it are quite bizarre. For example, some researchers argue that the key to development is warfare and the constant preparation for war (Morris 2014). Others maintain that it is the quality of a nation's genetic stock (Wade 2014) – despite the fact that places such as China and India have experienced big reversals of fortune that were not preceded by any

1

obvious changes in their gene pools (see, e.g., Chanda and Putterman 2007). Perhaps the most perplexing answer that has been put forth so far to explain political and economic underdevelopment, however, is that a country's oil, coal, natural gas, and minerals are a curse.

For decades, parallel literatures in political science and economics have blamed natural resources for several pathologies. The extraction, transportation, and export of hydrocarbons and minerals are believed to vitiate the rule of law and jeopardize property rights. They therefore hinder economic diversification and retard economic growth. Instead, they stimulate unproductive rent-seeking and foment corruption. This fuels civil strife, promotes authoritarianism, and exacerbates gender inequality.[1]

Why would this be? The resource curse view postulates that natural resource exports – and especially oil – constitute an external, unearned, and "easily capturable" source of rents. This severs the fiscal link between rulers and the ruled and renders the former unaccountable to the latter. Once rulers are freed from taxing their citizens, they are freed from having to solicit their consent or input. Natural resource revenues therefore bolster the power of executives and the bureaucracy and create countless opportunities for rent-seeking and corruption. Paradoxically, although these rents may prolong the tenure of tyrants, they might also catalyze civil wars in a bid to capture this valuable prize.[2]

For these reasons, the appellation *petro-state* has become an epithet. To compare a country to Saudi Arabia or Angola is to deride it and imply that its political economy is pathological, its politics dysfunctional, and its society hopelessly corrupt. Therefore, the default reaction by researchers, policymakers, journalists, and activists to a major new discovery of oil or minerals is to shower the news with opprobrium. At best, stakeholders and concerned publics in the Global North enact nostrums to help the unfortunate victim best cope with its impending disease.[3] At worst, countries such as Equatorial Guinea and Congo are forsaken after being branded as reviled pariahs.

---

[1] For two recent reviews that enumerate these findings, see Frankel (2010) and Van Der Ploeg (2011).

[2] Chapter 2 reviews the literature on the resource curse and provides citations for these claims.

[3] One popular intervention is for Western NGOs to monitor and audit resource rich countries' budgets and treasuries. See Weinthal and Luong (2006, p. 41) and Chapter 8 of this book.

In disagreeing with the prevailing consensus, this book hypothesizes that the effect of oil and minerals is not negative. There is no resource curse and oil is not the devil's excrement.[4] Rather, I adduce ample evidence for a resource blessing. Not only do oil and other natural resources create immediate benefits such as an infusion of foreign capital and foreign exchange, as well as technical expertise – which can quickly spill over into the larger economy – but these also create sizable investments in infrastructure. They also generate public revenues, many upfront, which are often spent on education and health. And, as this book will demonstrate, natural resources, and especially oil, help improve the quality of political and economic institutions, strengthening the state, democracy, and the rule of law.

Readers versed in world affairs might summon some important anecdotes to protest this contrarianism. Despite Hugo Chavez's so-called Bolivarian Revolution, oil dependent Venezuela remains mired in intractable poverty exacerbated by an economic crisis and beset by political and social unrest. Oil-dependent Nigeria is afflicted by environmental degradation, corruption, and political violence. Oil- and gas-dependent Russia has slid back into dictatorship, if not imperialism. And Saudi Arabia, the world's largest oil producer and exporter, is ruled as a quasi-theocracy; one of the few places on earth where citizens have no say over their political destiny and women are treated as second-class citizens. And let's not even get started on the basket cases that are Congo and Equatorial Guinea.

Readers might also point to the authoritative, if not stentorian, exhortations voiced by pundits and policymakers. The consensus that resources are a curse has endowed anecdotes and correlations with law-like qualities usually reserved for findings in the natural sciences. The resource curse is taken as a self-evident truth at multilateral aid organizations, presented as a robust fact in popular books, and disseminated widely in the media. While magazines such as *The Economist* and *Foreign Policy* continue to publish special reports on the resource curse on a regular basis, *New York Times* columnist Thomas Friedman has decreed a "first law of petro-politics": oil and political freedom are totally incompatible.

---

[4] This term was coined by Juan Pablo Pérez Alfonzo, Venezuela's oil minister during the 1960s, and a founder of the Organization of Petroleum Exporting Countries (OPEC).

If taken to its logical conclusion, the view that resources are a curse entails that countries should abstain from extracting and exporting their oil, natural gas, industrial metals, and gemstones. Indeed, in the recent past some researchers and policymakers did just that: recommended that developing countries dedicated to exporting commodities and importing manufactured goods change course. In other words, that they make cars and refrigerators, not extract oil and copper, thus ending their "dependency" on the Global North.[5] Even if the price of freeing themselves from the international economic order is the forfeiting of their comparative advantage and the millions, if not billions, of dollars in foreign exchange that pay for food, medicine, and computers.

The global trade in resources

Hydrocarbons and minerals are largely responsible for modern life as we know it. Ours is a world powered by uranium, gold, silver, copper, iron, zinc, nickel, chromium, coal, natural gas, and, of course, oil. The large-scale, commercial conversion of minerals and petroleum into fuel and industrial applications helps explain why we are wealthier and healthier than our ancestors. Readily available fossil fuels and industrial metals have drastically reduced the price of transportation, fertilizers, and the chemicals and plastics that allow us to produce almost every modern good around us. They have also helped fuel globalization; a global division of labor centered on international trade and investments has reduced the price of food, medicine, clothing, technology, and services.

Calomiris and Haber (2014), citing Morris (2010), articulate it best when they write that:

[C]oal ... could be burned to produce steam, providing reliable and seemingly endless amounts of power. The use of fossil fuels gave rise to a number of developments that changed the relationship between states and their populations. First, it gave rise to a revolution in transportation and communications, particularly the steam-powered ship, the railroad, and the electrical telegraph. These changes enabled people and goods to be moved on a massive scale, accelerating and expanding trade [...] people who had

---

[5] See Haber (2014) on the literature about the development strategy perspective and dependency theory.

been trapped by poverty [...] could now move to more productive areas of the globe and thus improve their standard of living. (pp. 76–77)

While about two billion dollars' worth of oil is traded daily, petroleum constitutes the biggest share of the energy consumed by both exporters and importers. It is for this reason that the oil price affects countries' balance of payments, savings, inflation, and growth. While large, unexpected spikes in the price can bring importers' economies crashing to the ground, sharp reductions can stimulate economic activity and tame price increases across the economy.[6] They can even make politicians more popular.[7]

The early twenty-first century's historic boom

For a book about the causes and consequences of natural resources published in 2016, it is fitting that, between 2000 and 2014, an impressive – and in many ways historically unparalleled – commodity boom occurred. Propelled by the blistering pace of economic development in China, India, and other developing countries, the consumption of oil and minerals grew exponentially during this time period. To satisfy this roaring demand, numerous extractive firms, governments, and state-run firms participated in a natural resource boom that reached nearly every corner of the world, including the Arctic.

Consider some numbers. In 2011, National oil companies (NOCs) that include Saudi Aramco, Gazprom, NIOC (Iran), PetroChina, Kuwait Petroleum, and Pemex invested over US$5 billion in research and development alone. In 2012, ExxonMobil, Shell, British Petroleum (BP), and Chevron – the international oil companies (IOCs) known as the supermajors – spent over US$100 billion on oil exploration and production (*The Economist*, August 3, 2013, online edition). Between 2013 and 2015, annual hydrocarbon investments topped US$1 trillion (International Energy Agency 2014). Precious metals and other minerals experienced a similar investment boom.

More than anywhere else, the developing world played host to this boom. While resource endowments per square kilometer in 2000 were

---

[6] See Engemann, Owyang, and Wall (2014) for evidence from the United States.
[7] To give one example, on the relationship between gas prices and presidential approval ratings for George W. Bush, see Beck, Jackman, and Rosenthal (2006).

worth US$114,000 in the Organization for Economic Cooperation and Development (OECD) countries, they were worth only US$23,000 in Africa (Collier 2010). Since then, however, mining and hydrocarbon firms and oil importers have looked to emerging markets, including previously neglected countries in Africa and the Pacific. China has been at the forefront of many of these new ventures, investing quite heavily in upstream and downstream extractive projects across the developing world. While Chinese outward investment in energy and minerals surpassed US$77 billion in 2011, Russia and India tallied impressive numbers around that time as well (see Rostoum 2014).

Many developing countries therefore became new explorers, producers, and exporters of natural resources. In Afghanistan, Liberia, and Kenya, geologists discovered trillions of dollars in untapped stocks of copper, gold, cobalt, lithium, and other rare earths. Kenya won the double jackpot. It, along with Tanzania, Uganda, and Ethiopia, became home to quite promising hydrocarbon discoveries. So did Vietnam, Mozambique, and Papua New Guinea. Unsurprisingly, between 2000 and 2012, average rents from natural resources grew by over 30 percent in the average Sub-Saharan African country. And they grew by over 10 percent in the average Asian country.[8]

Older natural resource producers in the developing world also experienced revivals. They include Angola, Azerbaijan, Botswana, Ghana, Indonesia, Kurdistan, Niger, Russia, and South Africa. They also include major Middle Eastern producers. Between 2007 and 2013, over US$340 billion was invested in the region's hydrocarbon sector, the lion's share of its GDP. Latin America's pedigreed oil and mineral producers were not far behind either. From 2004 to 2007, Foreign Direct Investment (FDI) dedicated to hydrocarbons grew by 223 percent in Brazil and 623 percent in Colombia; and FDI allocated to mining grew by 458 percent in Brazil, 502 percent in Bolivia, and 550 percent in Mexico (see Bebbington and Bury 2013, p. 16).

Besides being one of the most capital-intensive sectors of the world economy, hydrocarbons, mining, and timber produced reliable sources of income for developing countries during the boom. For the 165 nations that obtain any amount of rents from natural resources, in 2012 the average value of those rents totaled 11 percent of GDP; the

---

[8] I calculated these figures using the World Bank Development Indicators; Asia includes East Asia, Southeast Asia, and South Asia.

median 5 percent.[9] This represents hundreds of billions of dollars of foreign exchange and huge amounts of public revenues that governments in the developing world heavily rely on.

But why emphasize the developing world? After all, it is also the case that between 2000 and 2015 a huge boom in unconventional hydrocarbons, often extracted after the hydraulic fracturing of shale rock, or retrieved from oil sands, also occurred in North America. It is no wonder, therefore, that the United States and Canada are among the world's top destinations for oil and gas investment. Yet, further ahead I will demonstrate that this achievement is misleading. Other mature producers, such as Russia and China, also top the charts. What both sets of hydrocarbon producers share in common is that they have long depleted their easiest-to-extract reserves and have resorted to sophisticated, and expensive, techniques, including hydraulic fracturing or secondary recovery. Conversely, some mature producers in the developing world such as Saudi Arabia still have massive oil fields that they have not yet drilled, and/or the lion's share of their stocks can be extracted at quite low marginal cost, which drives down their capital investment costs. In Chapter 5, I demonstrate that after holding other things constant, such as a country's surface area and the age of its extant oil wells, total capital allocated to hydrocarbons – both foreign and domestic – is greater in developing countries than in the developed ones.[10]

Moreover, this book does not totally neglect the developed world. To the contrary, it draws several lessons about the causes and consequences of natural resources from the historical trajectory of developed countries. This is for several reasons. Long before tales of resource curses sprang up in countries across the developing world, it is in the developed world where many of the world's most notable mining and oil booms began. Countries such as Sweden, England, Canada, the United States, and Australia make clear that, while natural resources are not exogenous, randomly assigned variables, their effects

---

[9] I calculated these figures using the World Bank's World Development Indicators.

[10] Conventional FDI data on hydrocarbons are not adjusted for purchasing power parity, thus lowballing countries with cheap land and labor; neither does it include domestic sources of capital, such as the profits of nationalized oil companies that are reinvested, or the value of shares owned by domestic investors.

are, on the whole, salutary for political and economic development. This is true for both the current boom and past boom periods.

The 2014–16 oil bust and worries about climate change

Why focus on natural resources, and especially oil, if it's yesterday's news? As of late, commodity exporting countries and the mining and hydrocarbon firms that do business there have faced several serious challenges, some of them potentially existential. These days it is not uncommon to hear that fossil fuels are doomed to – forgive the bad joke – go the way of the dinosaurs: extinct.

A historic collapse in the international oil price began in June of 2014. By November of 2015, crude petroleum had lost more than half its value. Similar collapses in other fossil fuels and the prices of key industrial metals, especially copper, occurred simultaneously. There are several reasons for this unprecedented bust.

On the supply side, commodity stockpiles mushroomed in anticipation of high future demand. In regards to hydrocarbons, these gluts were exacerbated by historically high levels of oil and gas production in the United States. Further downward pressure on the price of oil ensued. Saudi Arabia, the world's swing producer, and thus the ultimate stabilizer of prices, decided to abstain from cutting back on the production of crude. Other oil producers, such as Russia, continued to pump oil at record levels to compete for market share.

On the demand side, in regards to the price of tradable commodities in general, demand for oil and other raw commodities in the developed world peaked around 2005. Over the last decade Americans, in particular, have tended to drive fewer miles than they once did. Moreover, an economic downturn gripped China beginning in early 2015 and led to a notable decline in Chinese demand for fossil fuels and industrial metals; since China accounts for about half of the world's consumption of raw commodities, this helps explain a significant share of the 2014–16 reduction in commodity prices.

Finally, there are signs that both developed and developing countries are beginning to craft plans to limit greenhouse gas emissions in a serious way. This has led many market analysts to fret about the fact that many hydrocarbon firms, whether they are privately held multinationals or state-owned and – run, will be faced with the prospect of writing down billions of dollars in "stranded assets." This would entail that the quantity of capital allocated to fossil fuels will be sharply reduced in the future in order to adjust to reductions in demand associated with new taxes, bans, carbon trading markets, or changes in the price of substitutes. Before the 2014–15 oil price collapse, oil consumption was projected to increase from 90 million barrels per day (bbl/d) in 2013 to 104 million bbl/d in 2030 and 113 million bbl/d by 2040 (see *The Economist*, August 3, 2013, online edition). Now it is unclear if these projections will hold.

In the more immediate term, the situation appears mixed. On the one hand, many multinational oil and mining companies' profits have taken a huge hit; firms that became highly leveraged in the wake of record low interest rates after the 2008 Global Financial Crises have been especially affected. In turn, firms have reduced their exposure to the exploration and extraction of natural resources in the most risky projects – for oil, this means they have curtailed their investments in the Artic, the North Sea, and the Atlantic Ocean.[11] On the other hand, only a handful of American fracking firms have gone bankrupt in the wake of the 2014–16 oil price collapse. While the number of drilling rigs in operation has plummeted, and thousands of oilfield workers have lost their jobs, most of these small, nibble fracking firms have found ways to continue to break even at rock bottom oil prices. They have cut costs to the bone, ramped up the production of oil from existing wells to continue to compete for market share, and some, amazingly, have even raised new rounds of capital.[12]

Ironically, the most recent commodity bust has perhaps set the stage for another boom down the road. Reductions in exploration and extraction will inevitably map onto a reduced supply of natural resources in the future, thus fueling higher prices, which should incentivize yet another

[11] Global investment in upstream oil and gas was reduced by over 100 billion dollars in 2015 compared to 2014 (see *The Economist*, November 14, 2015, online edition).

[12] Innovations include substantially increasing the amount of sand pumped into oil and gas wells, improving the propping of the shale rock after fracturing it to remove more hydrocarbons, protracting the length of horizontal oil drills, swiftly reallocating rigs to locations to the oil and gas can be extracted more efficiently, and dramatically reducing the time it takes to drill a well (see Olson and Ailworth 2015, p. A2). Whether many of the smaller, highly leveraged fracking firms will survive seems especially doubtful in light of the fact that the junk bond market that underwrites their financing has taken a huge hit since late 2015, driving up yields and drying up credit. Indeed, between January 2015 and June 2016, over seventy-five energy firms declared bankruptcy

big round of investment, exploration, and production down the line. Even if concerns about climate change continue to intensify and translate into tighter regulations on carbon emissions, and a shift away from oil, this may mean that natural gas, which produces far less carbon dioxide than oil, will increasingly pick up the energy supply slack. The next big energy boom may be centered on gas and feature much more fracking.

Similarly, even if we will soon be able to extract all of the minerals we will ever need from nearby asteroids, countries cannot simply wave a magic wand and conjure a modern industrial economy – a point that will be made clearer further ahead. Therefore, it is not a surprise that developing nations have ignored pleas by academics and think tanks to leave the big bills associated with natural resources on the sidewalk. While the halls of the World Bank and Non-governmental organizations (NGOs) may be festooned with posters that read "just say no to blood diamonds," this is certainly not the case in Kinshasa's presidential palace.

The bottom line is that identifying the underlying causes and consequences of hydrocarbons and other natural resource production remains imperative. If hydrocarbons and minerals in fact cause political, economic, and social underdevelopment, then the global commodity trade is harming billions, and it will continue to do so into the foreseeable future. If there is a resource curse, it is among the most perverse and large-scale tragedies in history. Minerals, oil, natural gas, and coal, which bankroll prosperity for so many by making modern life possible, might be condemning many more to doom and despair.

This book's contributions

This book makes several contributions. First, in its attempt to contribute to the literature on the causes and consequences of natural resources, it reaches a host of new conclusions that strongly challenge received wisdom. Second, it contributes to the literature on comparative political economy in general, situating natural resource sectors in a greater institutional and policy infrastructure, at both the global and national level. Third, it offers insights into political and economic history.

This book attempts to make sense of the cross-national correlation between natural resources and underdevelopment in a new way. While I acknowledge many of the anecdotes that paint the extractive industry in a bad light, I do not resort to the resource curse as their cause. As documented in my previous work on this topic and elsewhere, natural resource stocks and flows are not exogenous, randomly assigned variables.[13] Instead, they are a function of legal systems, regulation, and market forces. What is less appreciated, and which I demonstrate in this book, is that this insight generates implications that undermine much of the empirical literature that concludes that there is a natural resource curse. Once the institutions that are responsible for natural resources in the first place are controlled for, oil and minerals have a positive effect on development. This is because, after holding geology constant, natural resources are much more likely to be explored for and extracted in weak, dysfunctional states.

Because of oil's potential to generate sizable revenues and hard currency, its exploration is rarely left to chance or the market alone. The same holds for hard rock minerals; the difference between geological potential and a usable ore does not merely reflect commodity prices, technology, and extraction costs, but deliberate government policies that influence their exploration and extraction rates. Oil and mineral stocks are ultimately determined by policymakers' choices about subsoil rights, fiscal and monetary policies, and labor, safety, and environmental regulations.

A natural resource-based economy and the pathologies attributed to a country's endowments are jointly determined by weak state capacity and low-quality institutions. Hydrocarbon extraction and mining are often default economic sectors that arise and persist in countries cursed by their institutions. Sometimes they are the only capital-intensive sectors that see daylight in countries where rulers face high fiscal transaction costs and they cannot make credible promises. While weak states with low-quality institutions cannot curate vibrant and diversified economies, because they fail to provide incentives that encourage broad physical and capital investments, specialization, and exchange, they can turn to natural resources to generate substantial revenues. These revenues can be collected by the weakest of states, years before the first drop of oil is actually produced or the first ore is mined.[14]

---

[13] I review much of this literature in Chapter 3 and provide relevant citations there.

[14] To give but one example, investor countries often shower their hosts with generous bilateral aid, FDI, and other perks in advance of extracting minerals. The Chinese government has used this practice widely.

This book makes sense of why and how financially strapped countries with few alternative ways of generating revenues and foreign exchange undertake natural resource exploration and production – often in cases where their geological potential is wanting, the oil price is low, or their production costs are high. Revenue starved states that have a difficult time making believable promises are more likely to launch oil exploration efforts, goose the production of extant wells, export oil, and tax it.

Countless examples of desperate governments that have had a disproportionate influence on the ultimate size of a country's resource stocks and flows raise this point into high relief.

Consider Australia, before it was the prosperous, liberal, nation we now know. Throughout its history, gold mining has experienced several revivals. One of the most famous of these booms originated in Queensland in 1866, and then spread to Kimberly and Kalgoorlie. What is often overlooked about it is that it was explicitly triggered by the federal government. Australia found itself facing a severe balance of payments crisis, and sought to generate foreign exchange to pay for imports. Given a sharp economic downturn, the federal government was also preoccupied with bolstering investment and generating jobs to avoid social unrest and shore up its finances. So it actively stimulated greater mineral prospecting and production.

Bolivia is a more extreme example. Since the 1950s, state-owned tin mines have always sought to maximize output, irrespective of market conditions, even during periods when prices are depressed (see CEMYD 1990).

Oil extraction is not an exception. Sudden accelerations in depletion rates have been quite common in Russia, Iran, Venezuela, and, as this book will clearly show in Chapter 5, Azerbaijan. When these countries have found themselves in a fiscal pinch, governments have loosened the oil spigot (see Matsen, Natvik, and Torvik 2012), a pattern that, unsurprisingly, is repeating itself in 2016 Russia, at record levels.

Sometimes, this can go terribly wrong. Take what happened to Syria's Omar/Omar North oil field, which began production in February 1989, initially generating 55,000 bbl/d. "Shortly thereafter, operator Shell was pressed by the cash-strapped Syrian government to step up production (against Shell's advice) to 100,000 bbl/d. The result was serious reservoir damage, and in April 1989, output plummeted to 30,000 bbl/d" (Cordesman 2004, p. 81). Although production eventually recovered to 45,000 bbl/d, much of the pressure needed to extract the oil had to be provided by water injection.

A similar phenomenon occurred in Western Siberia during the 1970s. The Soviets sought to maximize the production of crude in the short run by increasing infill drilling and exploiting similar techniques to deplete Siberian oil at a faster rate in order to meet increasingly ambitious industrial goals. The upshot was severe damage to oil wells and, overall, the very inefficient production of crude.

If petroleum engineering textbooks were the sole guide to policy-makers' decisions about resource extraction, follies such as Syria's and Siberia's would never occur. In theory, every oil well has a unique extraction profile that maximizes the wealth that can be obtained from it, and which can be expressed in terms of net present value. In practice, however, political exigency often trumps concerns about economic efficiency. Weak states lack the luxury of pursuing optimal extraction paths.

Moreover, contrary to popular folklore, foreign capitalists involved in extractive industries don't fear weak states. Even petrostates with the worst reputations can raise capital for oil exploration and production with relative ease – even if they have expropriated oil firms in the past.[15] IOCs are able to import the knowledge and expertise they need from their home countries. They have evolved a host of mechanisms to hedge against all manner of risks – geological, price, commercial, and political – endemic to the developing world. Sometimes, they have strong armed or coopted quiescent host governments to protect their rights and interests. Other times, they have used neocolonial strategies such as Gunboat Diplomacy or bilateral investment treaties (BITs). They have also put together diversified global portfolios, so that no single oil field in the developing world, or any one emerging market, can drive their profitability or threaten their solvency. As a last

---

[15] Consider two recent examples from Latin America. Argentina effectively expropriated Repsol's 57.4 percent stake in Yacimientos Petrolíferos Fiscales (YPF) in 2012. Yet, this has not deterred interest by both Argentine and foreign oil firms in partnering with YPF to exploit the country's promising offshore oil plays. These firms include China National Offshore Oil, Norway's Statoil, and Chevron, which have been enticed by generous concessions. In Venezuela, China continues to dedicate billions of dollars in capital to the oil industry, as well as finance infrastructure and development projects in exchange for oil, despite the fact that Hugo Chavez expropriated assets worth almost $2 billion from ExxonMobil.

line of defense, they have purchased billions of dollars in political risk insurance. Even when their assets have been expropriated by host countries, they have been more than adequately compensated (see Maurer 2013).[16]

Perhaps most importantly, Saudi Arabia, working in concert with OPEC, has stabilized the global oil market for decades. It has used its unparalleled spare production capacity to smooth volatility around a reasonable price band. In turn, this has underpinned relative predictability. In particular, the kingdom's willingness to uphold a firm floor for oil prices – tacitly aided by the United States ban on oil exports – has steadied planning and investment horizons among IOCs and NOCs. Ironically, the result is billions of dollars in capital needed to unlock oil in hard-to-reach, risky places outside of Saudi Arabia, including the North Sea, Canada's oil sands, the Mexican Gulf, and the deep waters off of Angola and Brazil.[17]

For several reasons, many multinational mining and oil firms increasingly prefer to do business in developing countries. Oil and mining companies have been put off by escalating fiscal, labor, and production costs in the developed world.[18] Tough environmental, labor, and safety regulations also threaten their profits. The extraction and transportation of minerals and oil unleashes deforestation, forest fragmentation, erosion, sedimentation, sinkhole formation, and the destruction of ecosystems. It pollutes waterways and groundwater with arsenic, aluminum, magnesium, iron, mercury, and brine. This poisons drinking water and ruins agriculture. Pipelines leak. Railroads transporting oil derail, catch fire, and kill. Drilling rigs explode and spill oil. They also kill.

Indeed, across the developed world negligence and harm wrought by extractive firms is exposed by savvy media and publics and is ultimately

---

[16] Consider recent cases such as Argentina, Russia, and Venezuela. Courts and arbitration tribunals have ruled against these host governments, compelling them to compensate private oil firms that were expropriated in the recent past. These states have either begun to comply with these decisions or have seen their assets seized by foreign governments acting to enforce these orders.

[17] Indeed, many pundits aver that Saudi Arabia has now lost its ability, or at least desire, to play this stabilizing role because it has surrendered considerable market share to new oil producers, especially American shale oil firms.

[18] For example, steep tax increases on oil and minerals in Scotland and Australia, respectively, have deterred new investments in their exploration and production in those countries.

punished. Regulations, fines, and payouts from class action lawsuits meted out to address damages are costly.[19] They harm reputations and crimp profits. Environmental disasters and fallouts may even tip firms into insolvency.[20]

Moreover, in the Global North policymakers have been increasingly eager to avert the negative spillovers associated with natural resources. They have made it more expensive for firms to operate or barred them from operating entirely. Consider two recent examples from the United States.

First, in September of 2015, Royal Dutch Shell walked away from an almost decade long, multibillion dollar search for hydrocarbons off the coast of Alaska in the Arctic Ocean. This project had become infamous after anti-fossil fuel advocates – who had assembled in the Puget Sound off of Seattle in kayaks and were therefore christened kayactivists – picketed the Polar Pioneer, an offshore drilling rig bound for the Chukchi Sea. While Shell was partially driven to write down over US$4 billion in losses after they failed to find enough initial evidence of oil and gas to justify prohibitive costs and risks, perhaps the biggest impediment they faced was regulatory. It was unsurprising that Shell blamed the U.S. Federal government for sowing considerable regulatory uncertainty; the company experienced several false starts that cost them millions of dollars when breaking through the polar ice and conducting exploratory drilling because they repeatedly failed to properly comply with a host of measures meant to protect the environment and wildlife.

Second, in November of 2015 the Obama Administration rejected the application by TransCanada, a Canadian company, to build and operate the Keystone XL oil pipeline, which was submitted in September of 2008. The plan called for transporting crude oil from the Alberta oil

---

[19] This is not to say that NGOs and other stakeholders do not identify ecological disasters and human rights violations caused by international firms, including extractives, in the developing world. They often do, but have not met with uniform success. For every successful attempt at restitution, such as after the Bhopal gas leak in India in 1984, which killed 20,000 people, there have been many more failures to hold governments and corporations accountable for accidents, disasters, and damage.

[20] For example, the total costs incurred by BP related to the damages caused by the 2010 Deepwater Horizon oil spill in the Gulf of Mexico is US$54 billion. In the wake of the disaster, the company's stock price took a huge hit, losing almost half of its value.

sands in Western Canada to refineries in Texas and Louisiana across a 1,200-mile long pipeline that would have traversed through, among other states, Nebraska and Oklahoma. Among the reasons given by the federal government for its rejection of TransCanada's proposal were the environmental risks associated with potential oil spills and political symbolism: a signal that the United States was willing to get serious about climate change in the lead-up to the 2015 Paris Climate Summit.[21]

Meanwhile, mining and hydrocarbon firms have continued to get away with environmental degradation, negligence, and catastrophes in the Global South. Consider that, in November of 2015 – ironically, during the same week in which the Obama administration had rejected the XL Keystone oil pipeline – two dams collapsed in Brazil's Minas Gerais state, causing massive damage. The dams, operated by Australia's BHP Billiton and Brazil's Vale under the auspices of a joint venture to mine iron ore, were used to store wastewater. After their collapse, a torrent of contaminated water and mud completely engulfed the town of Mariana; the toxic sludge wrought widespread environmental havoc, severely damaged the local economy, and killed several people. While state and local officials accused the mining companies of negligence in the wake of the disaster, years earlier those same officials had, to no avail, voiced serious concerns about the structural integrity of the dams.

These contrasting stories offer several lessons. While OECD governments have the will and capacity to enforce laws that protect their environments and human health and safety, their counterparts in the developing world do not. By contrast, developing countries have laxer environmental policies and safety standards, fewer regulations of all types, and lower tax burdens. In addition, weak states often allow extractive firms to buy massive tracts of land on the cheap and to participate in the drafting of mining and land tenure laws that vouchsafe their rights and interests (see Krishnan 2014). They are also much

---

[21] To be sure, cynics can claim that mothballing Keystone is a moot point: the lion's share of the oil in the Canadian tar sands is too cost prohibitive at the moment to produce; and whatever oil is commercially viable is already transported through existing pipelines and railroads. However, increasingly stringent environmental and safety regulations presage significant increases in the costs associated with these alternative delivery routes; to give just one example: new rules governing the transportation of flammable materials over rail issued the same week that Keystone was rejected mean that trains transporting oil are required to install expensive new brakes.

worse at protecting the rights and interests of the indigenous people that make conflicting claims over land and water. Finally, increased trade liberalization and capital mobility has allowed firms to shift their operations to the developing world.

For these reasons, regulatory arbitrage makes a whole lot of sense. Whatever the underlying geological conditions, it is often better for hydrocarbon and mining firms to do business in the Global South. Speaking of how difficult it is to look for oil and natural gas by drilling exploratory wells in the United States, Halbouty (1993, n.p.) remarks that "the restrictions and regulations imposed on wildcatting are so severe that the large operators have gone overseas to explore and the independents have been so decimated that there are no incentives left for them to 'wildcat.'" Despite a noticeable boom in shale-based oil production, stringent regulations on, and fines levied against, frackers have spread throughout the United States, as well as England, France, and Germany, stalling the industry's spread.[22]

Rare earths are perhaps the quintessential example of how regulatory arbitrage has shaped the international mining industry.[23] China's recent rise to dominance in the production of these metals is as much a story about its status as a pollution haven as it is a reflection of its geological potential. While the United States once dominated the production of lanthanides – which have valuable commercial, medical, and military applications – their extraction was eventually eschewed by voters and politicians, primarily because it releases radioactive agents such as uranium and thorium. Unhindered by concerns about leaching, China prioritized the rare earths industry, subsidizing production and turning a blind eye to heavy environmental degradation. The upshot is that the United States now imports close to 100 percent of these minerals from China, even though it was self-sufficient not too long ago.

Fleshing out the institutions curse

Another one of this book's major contributions is to focus on the big picture. I posit that overreliance on natural resources is simply one symptom of a deeper, underlying disease that afflicts developing

[22] Many state and local governments in the United States have banned fracking or use red tape and other measures to deter new wells from being installed. A notable example is New York.
[23] This section draws heavily on Humphries (2013).

countries. This book labels that disorder the institutions curse. Other symptoms include fiscal monopolies that represent hyper-regressive forms of taxation, urban bias that ruins farmers, crony capitalism that erodes consumer surplus, and politicized finance that rations already scarce credit.

Countries cursed by their institutions fail to provide the type of political, legal, and infrastructural ecosystem that fosters broad-based economic development. Most investors outside of extractive industries tend to stay away. Governments therefore lack a revenue base that can be taxed at low cost. While they tend to suffer from a dearth of modern firms with readily taxable assets, income streams, and payrolls, they also lack the administrative wherewithal required to levy regular revenues, let alone tax income and payrolls. This renders moot any attempt to adequately tax the formal sector, if it exists at all. Moreover, weak states suffer from a scarcity of foreign exchange needed to pay for vital imports and face onerous costs of borrowing. The government's inability to credibly commit to repaying its debts, exacerbated by a genuine lack of economic growth, domestic revenues, and foreign currency, heightens political risk.

There are other, more prosaic, yet perhaps more pressing, knock-on effects. Investors stay away, in general, when central banks take their marching orders from the state and are therefore forced to finance budget deficits with inflationary taxation. They stay away from participating in export-based manufacturing, in particular, because they lack access to reliable electricity, roads, and ports. Or they are deterred because of the onerous costs of securing licenses and permits to operate, buying or leasing property, getting their machinery and goods in and outside of the country, and hiring and firing workers.

When governments cannot make credible commitments to inclusive property rights, and they face steep transaction costs to taxing the economy, they turn to peculiar ways of generating revenues and consolidating their political support. Weak states cursed by their institutions may erect fiscal monopolies on inelastic goods and turn to financial repression. Or they may create marketing boards that siphon money away from the countryside by paying farmers below market prices for the food they produce and then re-exporting it at a substantial profit. They may also indulge in industrialization via crony capitalism and inflationary taxation. Finally, they may erect natural resource sectors from scratch since, unlike their counterparts in industries centered on intangible goods and services, such as intellectual property, foreign investors operating in extractive industries do not really fear political risk. They are too shrewd, powerful, and wealthy to be stopped from striking it rich in the developing world's mines and oil basins.

The politicized generation and distribution of rents across all of these possibilities allows equally shrewd politicians trying to survive in weak states to kill two birds with one stone. On the one hand, they create a revenue base where one is entirely absent due to high fiscal transaction costs. On the other hand, they help cultivate loyal political supporters who come to rely on politicians for their livelihood.

In this book, I therefore explore the critical role played by commitment problems and transaction costs in conditioning elites' strategies of power acquisition and maintenance. When commitment problems are particularly thorny and fiscal transaction costs too high, incumbents turn to strategies that can generate both rents for private actors in ways that procure political loyalty and easy-to-tax revenues – revenues that can finance the state. These rents and revenues are produced by firms that receive selective commitments to their property rights and economic interests that are credible. And often they are rendered credible not despite state weakness but because of it; multinational firms with market values that are sometimes greater than the GDP of the countries they operate in are quite able to enforce these rights.

This can come at a steep, long-run cost, however. It may further promote the cartelization of property rights at the expense of the majority. It may further enervate state capacity. It may exacerbate underdevelopment. In other words, these strategies cultivate investments with perverse side effects. They are both caused by and culminate in future fiscal transaction costs and reduced levels of state capacity.

Yet, this book also argues and shows that natural resources can play an integral part in stimulating state capacity, capitalism, industrialization, and democracy, even if the oil and minerals are themselves often a symptom of underdevelopment. On average, oil rents do not displace ordinary government revenues, nor are they causally associated with the under-provision of public goods and similar welfare enhancing policies. Instead, once we neutralize the confounding effect of a country's underlying institutions, the impact of oil on ordinary government revenues, regime type, institutional quality, and capitalism is positive. Despite being cursed by their institutions, weak states are blessed by their natural resources. In other words, natural resources can help countries escape a development trap.

This book also makes some other theoretical and empirical contributions that are worth noting. I try to account for the striking fact that there is a high correlation between the rule of law, democracy, and economic development – in other words, why Western Europe and several of their colonial offshoots, such as Australia and Canada, are more similar than they are different. I also try to account for why the Middle Eastern monarchies are relatively better off than the non-monarchies after holding oil constant.

I draw on the work of several intrepid researchers to argue that differences in factor endowments explain the variation in the world's contemporary institutions. The enduring organization of society and politics is ultimately rooted in climate and agricultural legacies. Good institutions in Western Europe and its settler colonies are linked to moderate rainfall and fertile soils that favored cultivating cereal agriculture on a relatively small scale – usually on family farms. This provided a social and economic structure that favored liberalism and democracy. It also favored broad-based economic development.

In the Middle East, things are a bit more complicated. Extreme aridity and pastoral nomadism centered on camel herding sustained tribal social structures and a traditionalist political culture. Today, that infrastructure maps onto monarchical forms of governments. Meanwhile, in some Middle Eastern countries the climate was a bit less harsh and allowed for settled agriculture to blossom; but this occurred only sporadically, was practiced on a relatively large scale, was centered on irrigation, and gave birth to feudal social structures. This legacy now maps onto the region's non-monarchies. Differences between monarchies and non-monarchies endure despite millennia of imperialism, the spread of Islam, and European colonialism. They also endured despite the discovery of oil across both regime types.

Roadmap to the rest of the book

The next chapter begins by outlining a series of puzzles that challenge the resource curse. Although these puzzles have been documented elsewhere as well, in Chapter 2, I use original datasets developed by myself and Stephen Haber, along with several new insights, to hammer home their contours and implications (see Haber and Menaldo 2011a). There is strong, *prima facie* evidence that natural resources, especially oil, do not harm countries' ability to generate revenues, grow their economies, or become and stay democratic.

The first puzzle is the salutary role that natural resources have played throughout European and North American history. Mineral wealth helped secure the consolidation of powerful empires and states with impressive territorial reach in both European countries and their colonial offshoots. The industrial revolutions that were unleashed during the nineteenth and twentieth centuries, and which lifted millions from penury into plentitude, were fueled by coal, hard rock minerals, and eventually oil (see, e.g., David and Wright 1997).

The second is that the first global oil shock, which occurred in 1973, provides a quasi-natural experiment that roundly rejects the resource curse thesis. After Arab oil producers imposed an embargo on the Western allies of Israel during the Yom Kippur War, this ushered in a huge increase in the oil price, amounting to an unprecedented structural break in the world oil market. Countries that were not significant oil-exporting countries before 1973 became so after the shock; and on the back of their newfound bounty they improved their state capacity, level of democracy, and economic development (see, e.g., Heilbrunn 2014).

The third puzzle is about the Middle East and North Africa (MENA), a region of the world that is often held up as the poster child of the resource curse. There, countries were underdeveloped well before oil was discovered. Moreover, oil-rich countries such as Iran and Saudi Arabia are not radically different today than oil-poor Morocco and Jordan (see, e.g., Kuran 2008).

In Chapter 3, I provide a broad review of the literature on the political economy of the resource curse. There, I begin by outlining and critiquing three main views about the consequences of oil. The first is the resource curse theory. The second is a more sophisticated vein of literature that argues that the negative effect of natural resources on a nation's development is conditional on other factors. The third, a much smaller literature than the first two, maintains that resources are, quite simply, a blessing.

In the remainder of the chapter, I then do three additional things. I review recent contributions that argue that natural resources are endogenous to institutions and politics. I outline a political economy literature called neo-mercantilism. I then outline a literature on institutional origins called the factor endowment approach. The latter two tasks are critical because I draw on the insights provided by these literatures to construct the rest of the book.

In Chapter 4, I address why all societies don't simply adopt good institutions. Why are the rule of law and liberal democracy not universal? Why are corruption, cronyism, and despotism – and thus chronic underdevelopment – still so rampant? The institutions curse theory attempts to address these pressing questions, which paves the way for an endogenous explanation of resource reliance and crony capitalism. I explore the critical role played by commitment problems and transaction costs in conditioning elites' strategies of power acquisition and maintenance. In turn, these strategies deeply affect present investments that culminate in future fiscal transaction costs and levels of state capacity. When commitment problems are particularly thorny and fiscal transaction costs too high, incumbents turn to strategies that can generate rents in ways that procure political loyalty and generate easy-to-tax revenues. This comes at a steep, long-run cost, however; it further promotes the cartelization of property rights at the expense of the majority, enervates state capacity, and fuels underdevelopment.

In the latter part of the chapter, I also tackle what explains the origin and stability of the world's contemporary institutions by zeroing in on factor endowments. I evaluate the political history of Western Europe and the Middle East in particular.

In Chapter 5, I directly challenge the view that there is a causal relationship running from oil to political and economic underdevelopment. The chapter seeks to empirically identify what determines a hydrocarbons sector in the first place. I argue and find that revenue starved states with low capacity are more likely to launch oil exploration efforts, goose the production of extant wells, export oil to a higher degree, tax it more heavily, and attract higher levels of capital in hydrocarbons. While NOCs have increasingly shouldered more of the heavy lifting to make this happen, private investors also continue to play a prominent role. They exploit huge advantages in power, money, and information to protect their property rights in host countries across the developing world; IOCs increasingly engage in regulatory arbitrage to sidestep stringent environmental regulations in their home countries, as well as higher taxes.

As a first step in corroborating these claims, I undertake a case study of Azerbaijan. I highlight the state's deliberate attempts to revive the country's oil industry after its independence from the Soviet Union, primarily because it was bereft of regular tax sources. It therefore both looked for oil and drilled it at the highest rates in its history to generate easier-to-collect revenues. In the Azerbaijani case, we can identify a strong shock to state capacity that occurred unexpectedly and swiftly, making it, for all intents and purposes, exogenous. Its independence from the Soviet Union threw a relatively strong state into a perilous situation. Finding itself in a fragile and desperate situation after a war against Armenia, a huge banking crisis, and an economic collapse, the government was left with no other option than to rev up oil exploration and hasten the depletion of extant wells, despite the fact that oil discoveries had peaked. These claims are corroborated by oil exploration and production contracts penned between the state-run oil company (SOCAR) and IOCs under the auspices of Production Sharing Agreements (PSAs); these contracts are particularly helpful because they reveal the preexploration fees and predrilling bonuses collected by the Azerbaijani state.

A series of statistical analyses then yield results that support the theoretical claims advanced in this chapter across countries. Crucially, this is the case after controlling for geological endowments, oil prices, and production costs. Weak states are more likely to court capital in the oil sector, explore for oil, extract it at high rates, export it, and tax it, no matter how I operationalize oil, or state capacity, and across a host of specifications that address endogeneity bias.

In Chapter 6, I systematically explore if there is actually a resource blessing instead of a curse. The chapter reevaluates the relationship between oil and a host of political and economic outcomes across the globe since 1930 after isolating the exogenous variation in fuel income as instrumented by geological endowments, and after controlling for exploratory efforts. These outcomes include non-resource public revenues; regime type; the quality of a country's institutions; the government's ability to credibly commit to its promises; and the size and sophistication of the market economy. Across the board, I find evidence for a resource blessing. This is even after exploring the effects of oil on democracy in the post-1980 period, in the wake of a wave of oil firm nationalizations. I also adduce considerable evidence for the mechanisms that explain a positive association between resources and a country's political economy in Latin America over the long run. Chapter 6 therefore shatters the consensus that oil is a curse, including recent claims that it is conditional on the time period.

In Chapter 7, I attempt to gain purchase on the political instability that buffeted the MENA during the Arab Spring. The region's monarchies have largely elided turmoil and violence. The "republics" have not. I show that this has also been the case historically. The association between political stability and monarchy is not driven by oil wealth. Nor does oil explain why monarchies have better institutions, provide more public goods, and have higher levels of educational attainment and faster economic growth.

To help understand why there is a correlation between monarchy and these outcomes in the MENA, the chapter explores a theory about how an invented, yet historically rooted, political culture can solve a ruler's credible commitment problem. By securing elites' rights and interests, it bolsters their support of the regime. This chapter also illustrates the evolution of monarchic political cultures over the history of the MENA. I document the geographic and biogeographic underpinnings of monarchy, arguing that extreme aridity and pastoral nomadism centered on camel herding sustained a tribal social structure. This unique equilibrium held despite millennia of imperialism, Islam, and European colonialism.

In Chapter 8, I conclude the book by raising and broaching two puzzles. First, do those countries cursed by their institutions, but subsequently blessed by the resources they elicit, eventually graduate beyond their reliance on an oil and mineral intensive economy? Second, how do we make sense of the fiscal contract view of the world – where democracy, the rule of law, and public goods are thought to be exchanged by rulers for tax revenues – in light of the institutions curse and resource blessing?

2 | *Three puzzles and some building blocks*

After outlining three important puzzles that challenge the resource curse, this chapter provides other essential building blocks that put these puzzles in perspective and previews some of the important themes that recur across the book. This chapter's second section suggests an alternative way to make sense of the so-called resource curse. It provides other examples of the institutions curse that are not related to natural resources. This serves to show that the pathologies that have been causally attributed to natural resources, and especially oil, are actually symptoms of an underlying syndrome, as are other maladies such as crony capitalism and corruption. The third section identifies important conceptual and methodological themes that will be pursued in the remainder of the book.

The first of three puzzles

The ascendance of the resource curse theory sharply clashes with the fact that natural resources have been a key engine of political and economic development throughout history. This is particularly the case for Europe and North America. While mineral wealth has repeatedly bankrolled imperial expansion in the former, it also buoyed fledgling nations founded by European settlers in the latter. Industrial revolutions were fueled by coal, precious metals, and oil. Today, countries as diverse as Canada, Australia, and Norway have thriving economies centered on mining and hydrocarbons.

Over the ages, the ability to control gold mines and, by extension, mint gold coins has been the fulcrum to imperial conquest and control. Consider various European and Middle Eastern kingdoms that rose and fell in concert with their dominion over the much vaunted Nubian gold mines in southern Egypt and northern Sudan. This was as true of the Egyptian pharaohs, beginning as early as 3100 B.C., as it was of their latter day successors, the Roman emperors.

The post-Roman examples are the most instructive.[1] The Byzantine kings inherited control of these inimitable North African mines from the Romans and exploited them to coin gold specie. This allowed Byzantine rulers to finance numerous wars and pay hefty bribes to potential invaders, such as the Lombards, therefore dissuading them from crashing Constantinople's gates. When control of the Nubian mines was transferred to the Rashidun Caliphate in 641, after Arab Armies wrested control of Egypt from the Byzantines, the Muslim empire quickened the pace of gold extraction, while reopening abandoned mines in Ethiopia. The upshot is that Rashidun rulers quickly came to dominate long-distance trade inside the Byzantine's sphere of influence; they instaurated commercial links with the Mediterranean, Russia, and Scandinavia; and they greatly expanded their territorial ambit – reaching as far West as Tunisia, as far East as Central Asia, and as far North as the Caucuses.

The historical connection between copper mining and Swedish political and economic power tells a similar story.[2] In the 1520s, a Swedish nobleman, Gustav Vasa, launched a successful bid to break away from the Kalmar Union, a merger of the Swedish, Danish, and Norwegian kingdoms that had been in place since 1397, but that was dominated by Denmark. After crowning himself king, Vasa enhanced Sweden's military and political power by investing heavily in the extraction and smelting of copper. Having fought against Ivan the Great between 1495 and 1497 to retain control of Viborg, Sweden continued to fear Russia's imperial ambitions. Therefore, between 1611 and 1632, Vasa's grandson, King Gustavus Adolphus, marshaled vast copper revenues to create an empire that incorporated a disparate set of Germanic, Scandinavian, and Baltic lands.

By 1650, at the height of Sweden's power, the country's Great Copper Mountain produced 3,000 tons of raw copper. This occurred under the auspices of one of the most storied mining companies of all time, Stora Kopparberg. While Stora is the world's oldest corporation, it still ranks among the wealthiest. Meanwhile, mining continues to play a vital role in Sweden's economy.

The history of European coal tells a similar story. There is a growing consensus that this fuel was pivotal to that continent's industrial

---

[1] This paragraph draws extensively from Bernstein (2000).
[2] This paragraph draws on Lynch (2002) and Rothkopf (2012).

revolution.[3] Researchers such as Wrigley (1988) and Pomeranz (2009) point to several reasons why. First, coal was very abundant in England, the revolution's birthplace.[4] Second, it was portable. Third, unlike firewood/charcoal, it was available all year round. Fourth, it strongly increased the efficiency of combustion across all manner of physical and chemical processes, especially iron and steelmaking. Eventually, it replaced water as the primary method used to power machinery. Fifth, and most importantly, it accelerated the transportation revolution. As in the case of water, it gradually displaced wood as the chief fuel source for steam engines. This underwrote a newly specialized division of labor and trade that translated into increased economic growth.[5]

Coal had many indirect benefits as well. It was converted to gas to provide artificial light. This conversion also yielded coal tar, from which chemicals used for industrial and commercial applications were derived. And coal-powered steam engines could be used as water pumps to facilitate the extraction of ores, for example. This allowed miners to bore into much deeper shafts than before. This not only increased the amount of coal that was available but also significantly bolstered the production of bauxite, copper, zinc, nickel, and especially iron – metals that served as key components of plants, machinery, and finished products. As the yields of coal and these minerals increased exponentially across Europe, their prices plummeted, further fueling industrialization.

Moreover, coal underwrote the British Empire. While coal allowed the British to conquer the Chinese Empire and become the world's preeminent naval power during the nineteenth century (see Morris 2010), it also helped export the industrial revolution abroad. Coal not only served as the primary source of fuel for the British Navy until the end of World War I but was the island's biggest generator of foreign exchange and revenues. It constituted almost 10 percent of the value of British exports at the turn of the nineteenth century (see Goldberg n.d.b).

---

[3] For a skeptical view, see Acemoglu, Johnson, and Robinson (2002).

[4] Cities such as Yorkshire, Durham, and South Wales were dotted with several deep mines. They employed millions.

[5] See Pomeranz (2009, pp. 60–67), who argues that, beyond ample stocks of ore, the deep and pedigreed stock of knowledge around coal mining and smelting was also critical – for example, the body of skills centered on precision boring and calibration.

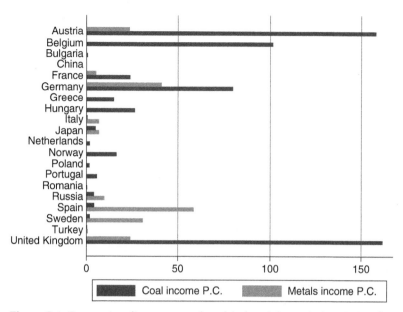

Figure 2.1 Economic reliance on coal and industrial metals in 1900, select countries.

Figure 2.1 puts some numbers on this phenomenon. It graphs the income from coal (per capita, in 2007 dollars) as well as from industrial metals (per capita, in 2007 dollars) in 1900 for European countries and a few non-European countries.[6] Two facts are readily apparent: the production of both coal and metals in Western Europe far outpaced its production in other places, and the continent's industrial powerhouses – England, Belgium, Germany, and Sweden – had the greatest overall production.

While mineral wealth and abundant and cheap coal contributed to industrialization in Western Europe, natural resources did not hinder state capacity, democracy, and development in Britain's settler colonies. Indeed, Canada, the United States, and Australia thrived as they harvested their frontiers' copious mineral and hydrocarbon wealth. Figure 2.2 graphs the total income from natural resources (per capita,

---

[6] The data are from Haber and Menaldo (2011a). The values for industrial metals include all income from antimony, bauxite (from which aluminum is produced), chromium, copper, gold, iron ore, lead, manganese, mercury molybdenum, nickel, silver, tin, tungsten, and zinc.

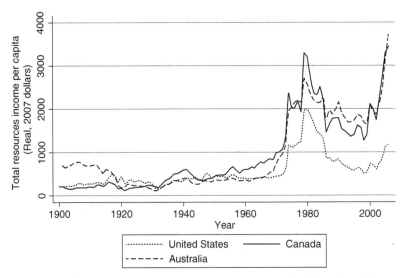

Figure 2.2 Economic reliance on natural resource income for the settler colonies.

in 2007 dollars) between 1900 and 2006 for the United States, Canada, and Australia.[7] The trajectory is one of steadily increasing resource rents, culminating in the hydrocarbon and mining powerhouses we know today. While in 2006 Canada's proven oil reserves were 178.8 billion barrels, second only to Saudi Arabia, Australia's highly productive economy is centered on gold, iron, and coal mining.

The United States is perhaps the most revealing case. Gold and silver were discovered on federal lands during the middle of the nineteenth century, unleashing an unprecedented rush of mineral prospecting across the Western territories. By 1900, the United States was the largest producer of industrial and precious metals in the world, generating US$87.52 (in 2007 dollars) per capita (or US$ 6.7 billion raw dollars) in income from gold, copper, silver, copper, and nickel mines. Indeed, the United States was the top producer of virtually all of the world's industrial metals by 1920, especially copper. It took until 1954 for it to fall to second place in total mineral production, behind Russia.

---

[7] This data, which reflect totals for metals, oil, natural gas, and coal, and all other data on natural resource stocks, flows, and revenues that follow in this section, are from Haber and Menaldo (2011a).

In 2006, it was the fourth-largest mineral producer, behind China, Chile, and Australia.

Similarly, the United States experienced separate oil booms in California, Oklahoma, and Texas throughout the twentieth century. As early as 1892, drilling began in earnest in the Los Angeles area and continued in Beaumont, in 1901, when a huge oil strike ushered in Texas' so-called Gusher Age. Indeed, this pattern continues today, with an unprecedented boom underway in North Dakota, as oil producers have flocked there to extract the state's abundant shale oil and gas using sophisticated techniques such as horizontal drilling and hydraulic fracturing.

It is therefore no surprise that while in 1900 the United States was the largest producer of petroleum in the world, generating US$24.87 (in 2007 dollars) in oil income per capita, it continues to rank as one of the largest producers today – if not the largest, according to some estimates. Although Mexico surpassed it in per capita terms in 1917, in absolute terms the United States was still the world's top producer until 1973, when it produced US$51.8 billion (in 2007 dollars) of oil income.[8]

What consequences have these mining and oil booms had? Here in Washington, where I reside and wrote this book, the timber, gold, and coal industries literally built the state. Waves of resource speculation and production motivated the construction of the territory's first railroads, as well as its ports. This was also true of California, Montana, Nevada, Idaho, Wyoming, and Colorado. Similarly, Wright and Czelusta (2007) argue that the United States' abundant natural resources were a critical driver of manufacturing across the entire country.

This was through three channels. First, natural resources were key components in the manufacturing process itself. Second, their exploration and extraction incentivized the creation of important backward and forward linkages. Third, their exploration and production engendered technological innovations that complemented the industrialization process.

Furthermore, natural resource wealth and its associated rents do not seem to have had a deleterious impact on taxation and democracy in the United States. Figure 2.3 traces the trajectory of U.S. federal revenues

---

[8] However, the United States lost its top position in the oil reserves category in 1955 to Saudi Arabia, which registered 36.2 billion barrels of proven reserves that year, versus the United States' 29.56 billion.

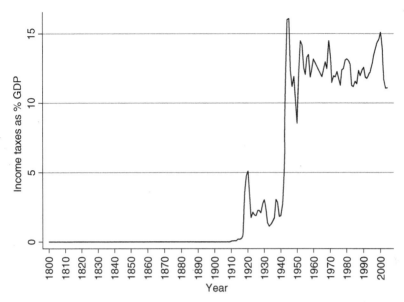

Figure 2.3 United States' income taxation.
Notes: Includes only income tax receipts at the federal government level.
Sources: National Bureau of Economic Research; OECD Fiscal Statistics.

from personal income taxation (as %GDP) over the twentieth century. After the end of World War II, as the United States reached the pinnacle of its status as the world's most important oil producer, reliance on income taxes also skyrocketed. In so far as taxing income calls on a competent and professional bureaucracy and an educated citizenry that must voluntarily comply with self-assessed tax returns, this strongly gainsays the resource curse. Similarly, it was also during this era that the civil rights revolution ended racial segregation in the South and razed barriers to black enfranchisement.

But could it be that resource blessings of this sort have been confined to settler colonies founded on huge landmasses with expanding frontiers, with the United States as the paradigmatic example? This does not appear to be the case. Take Norway, for example. It is one of the world's largest oil producers and exporters – it ranked sixth in 2006, ahead of Mexico, Venezuela, and several Middle Eastern producers, after generating US$74 billion (in 2007 dollars) in oil income. In 2006, an incredible 37 percent of government revenues were generated by petroleum. More incredibly, that year 20.6 percent of Norwegian GDP was invested in publicly provided education, health, and housing, as well as allocated to social insurance, and welfare spending.[9]

Moreover, while Norway's Central Bank has taken an extremely hawkish stance against inflation, the country's sovereign wealth fund, *Government Pension Fund-Global*, has fastidiously saved and invested the country's oil rents. It has aimed for a 4 percent rate of return over the long run to effectively husband oil income for future generations. This has obligated the state to undertake a countercyclical fiscal policy in which deficits above this rate of return are only allowed during economic recessions and must be offset during non-recessionary periods. And it has allowed the fund to become one of the largest sovereign wealth vehicles in the world, accumulating total assets of close to US$400 billion in 2009, or 111 percent of Norway's GDP (see Lücke 2010).

Although a skeptical reader might acknowledge that Britain, Sweden, the United States, Canada, Australia, and Norway thrived while under the influence of copious natural resource wealth, she might argue that their experiences are exceptional. These nations' resource blessings were only possible because their institutions immunized them from oil and minerals' pernicious effects. Had these countries been characterized by insecure property rights and authoritarianism on the eve of their mineral and oil discoveries, their natural resources would have cursed them.[10]

There are several counterexamples that suggest this objection is wrongheaded. Australia was set up as a penal colony, and it only became a rich, liberal democracy after subsequent waves of settlers flocked there to exploit its vast gold and copper stocks. In the case of the United States, the federal government deployed very few troops beyond the frontier. In turn, this negligible military presence in the periphery undermined the state's political and legal authority, so that claims to subsoil riches made by mineral prospectors and petroleum wildcatters extended as far as they could personally defend them. In Nevada and California, formal titles were only codified and enforced after mining booms helped defray the costs of state building (La Croix 1992). Canada's western expansion evinced a similar dynamic.

---

[9] This data and all ensuring data on public expenditures are from Albertus and Menaldo (2014).

[10] Several researchers have argued that the political and economic effects of natural resources are conditioned by the quality of a country's institutions on the eve of discovery. The next chapter will identify some of the entries in this camp.

The second puzzle that motivated this book offers yet more evidence that the beneficial impacts of natural resources are not aberrations. Resource blessings have materialized not only in places with good initial institutions but also in places beset with serious institutional handicaps. Indeed, one of this book's key contributions is to argue that the effect of oil and minerals is not a conditional one.

Second puzzle

In 1973, Arab oil producers colluded to embargo Israel's Western allies during the Yom Kippur War. This ushered in a huge, immediate increase in the global oil price labeled the first oil shock. Gelb (1988), Haber and Menaldo (2011a), and Liou and Musgrave (2014) argue that this constituted an unparalleled structural break in the world oil market: there was an 800 percent increase in the price of oil between this shock and the second one in 1979, which was catalyzed by the Iranian Revolution. Several countries that were marginal oil producers before 1973 became major exporters after the shock, raking in billions of dollars in unexpected oil receipts and revenues. These include, among others, Trinidad and Tobago, Nigeria, Indonesia, Gabon, Ecuador, and Algeria.

This event represents a quasi-natural experiment. Did these countries' newfound bounty curse them, make no difference whatsoever, or help them? Below I consider two illustrative cases, Trinidad and Tobago and Indonesia, and refer readers to Haber and Menaldo (2011a) and Liou and Musgrave (2014) for similar evidence from several other developing countries.

Between 1973 and 2006, Trinidad's average income per capita from oil and natural gas (in 2007 dollars) was US$3,392; and the government's average revenues from these hydrocarbons were 42 percent (as a share of total revenues). This bankrolled the growth of the country's middle class and helped consolidate democracy. While the Trinidadian government provided ample public goods – average public spending on education, health, and housing, as well as social insurance and welfare spending, was almost 11 percent of GDP during this period – the island nation also diversified its economy. Indeed, its aluminum industry is a direct offshoot of the post-1973 oil boom. The state cultivated Trinidad's aluminum sector to exploit the fact that its oil fields produce natural gas as a by-product of oil production, and the marginal cost of firing blast furnaces with this gas are essentially zero.[11]

In the case of Indonesia, between 1973 and 2006, its average income per capita from oil and natural gas (in 2007 dollars) was US$159; and the government's average revenues from these hydrocarbons were 38 percent (as a share of total revenues). This helped fuel rapid economic growth during the 1970s and 1980s. Annual real economic growth was in the 6–10 percent range during the 1970s, remained strong in the 1980s, despite a collapse in oil prices in 1985, and continued into the 1990s, when Indonesian development was hailed as miraculous (see Rosser 2007). Moreover, while Indonesia transitioned to democracy in 1999, after Suharto stepped down, it has since embraced a battery of reforms that have strengthened the rule of law and reduced ethnic tensions.

Most importantly, neither Trinidad and Tobago nor Indonesia had what one would label "good institutions" on the eve of Israel's war against its Arab neighbors in 1973. Trinidad was populated in the nineteenth century by indentured Indian and Chinese laborers who toiled in a kind of quasi-slavery on the islands' sugar plantations and were subject to apartheid-like laws. Indonesia's colonial history was similar to Trinidad's, in that the Dutch imposed racial segregation there and ruled with an iron fist. On the eve of the 1973 oil crisis, it was governed by a brutal dictator, Suharto. It had no industrial base to speak of.

Third puzzle

The final puzzle that motivated this book is the political history of the MENA. Its oil-rich and oil-poor countries both share a history of unbroken authoritarianism and illiberalism. While Jordan, Egypt, Yemen, Syria, and Tunisia are relatively oil scarce, Saudi Arabia, Libya, Kuwait, Qatar, and the United Arab Emirates are relatively oil abundant. During the modern era, electoral turnout in the MENA has been much lower than the average registered in the world's other "electoral" autocracies. Moreover, the margin of victory has been substantially higher (see Brownlee 2011). Neither of these patterns is driven by oil. Finally, in countries where oil was discovered, it did not make much of a subsequent difference.

---

[11] I thank Steve Haber for bringing this example to my attention.

Since the first pharaoh in 3150 B.C., oil-poor Egypt has never once experienced anything approaching democracy. The overthrow of the Alawiyya Dynasty in 1952 engendered the dictatorship of General Gamal Abdel Nasser. Hosni Mubarak, who ruled Egypt with an iron fist from 1981 to 2011, was one of a long list of repressive dictators. He was summarily ousted during the Arab Spring protests. In June 2012, the Muslim Brotherhood's presidential candidate, Muhammad Morsi, won Egypt's first free and fair elections; yet he proceeded to impose an illiberal constitution and unleashed a wave of repression against religious minorities and dissidents. Morsi was soon ousted in a coup and jailed after failing to comply with an ultimatum issued by the military. The army then brutally cracked down on his supporters, killing hundreds. A former general, Abdel Sisi, is now Egypt's president, after having received 97 percent of the vote in a heavily restricted election. He has presided over massive repression.

Similarly, the territories that now make up oil-rich Iraq constituted a recognizable political entity since Sargon of Akkad conquered the city-states of Mesopotamia in the twenty-third century B.C., and ever since then it has witnessed despot upon despot. Saddam Hussein's repressive regime was only the latest incarnation until the U.S.-led invasion in 2003. After the invasion, Nouri al-Maliki consolidated power at the expense of democracy, unleashing a vicious insurgency led by Sunni militants and Islamic extremists.

Oil-rich Iran, a recognizable political entity since the emergence of the Persian Empire in the sixth century B.C., has also witnessed a parade of tyrants over its history. Its last monarch, Reza Pahlavi, was overthrown in 1979 and replaced by another autocrat, the Ayatollah Khomeini. He founded a theocracy that is still ruled without any tolerance for dissent, despite the trappings of political representation.

Or, consider Yemen. Prior to the discovery of oil in 1980, Yemen was a long-lived autocracy. And, if anything, Yemen has experienced a modicum of political liberalization during the oil era, including greater competitiveness between political parties after the unification of South and North Yemen in 1990. Today, Yemeni oil wells are close to being exhausted – current projections forecast total depletion by 2017. This has not pushed Yemen anywhere closer to democracy, however. Civil liberties are at a greater risk than they have been in the past. Repression has escalated after the Arab Spring.

Syria tells a similar story. Damascus is one of the oldest continually inhabited cities on the planet, yet its people have never tasted democracy. Massive repression ensued in the aftermath of three coups in 1949, and another in 1951. While oil was discovered in Syria in 1956, the country only became a consequential producer in the late 1980s, when petroleum rents began to account for between 40 and 95 percent of government revenues. Yet, before this occurred, it had already been ruled by the *Baath* Party for more than twenty years. Syrian oil fields are now in a state of sharp decline and are forecast to be exhausted by the end of the decade. This has not augured greater political liberalization. Since 2011, President Bashar al Assad – the son of the previous dictator, Hafez al Assad – has orchestrated a bloody crackdown against protestors that is still ongoing and has resulted in almost 500,000 deaths.

This book is the outgrowth of my attempt to grapple with the three puzzles outlined above. They encouraged me to develop a theory to make sense of the contemporary correlation between natural resources and underdevelopment, while refraining from imputing a causal arrow that runs from the former to the latter. The theory accepts many of the stylized facts in the literature, but departs from consensus in a fundamental way. Drawing on a rich literature on the outsized effect of institutions on political and economic development, I suggest that countries may be cursed by their institutions curse, not their natural resources.

The institutions curse in light of these puzzles

Governments are more aggressive at launching oil exploration efforts and converting oil plays into active wells exploited at high rates when they rule weak states and are desperate for revenues and foreign exchange. Resource production can be dialed up or down through policies that either encourage or discourage the heavy capital investments required to identify and extract reserves. Yet rent-seeking, corruption, and illiberalism associated with oil and minerals is only one of several possible manifestations of rent-seeking, corruption, and illiberalism. Other industries and economic practices can be dialed up or down by the state to produce tax revenues and foreign exchange when it cannot lean on deep financial markets and vibrant and diversified economies with low fiscal transaction costs and a stream of export revenues.

In countries cursed by their institutions, if it were not oil that appeared to wreak havoc on the political system and economy, it would be another economic activity. The appropriate counterfactual of a country without oil is not a better run country without oil. The institutions curse will equally manifest itself as the industrialization curse, the hospitality curse, the fisheries curse, or the construction curse.

For example, states that are cursed by their institutions but cannot cultivate natural resource industries may instead cultivate fiscal monopolies centered on goods with relatively inelastic demand, neo-feudalistic land tenure regimes that squeeze farmers, or crony capitalism fueled by politicized finance.

Gehlbach (2008) masterfully describes the creation out of whole cloth of a vodka industry in northwestern Russia's Pskov oblast after the fall of the Soviet Union. While the potential for this industry was always present, it was only when a relatively weak state faced empty coffers that the regional government encouraged local officials to develop an industry that they could tax at low cost.[12]

In England, during the fourteenth and fifteenth centuries, the state helped establish a commercial market for wool and grains to raise public revenues. Serfs were released from seigniorial duties after the end of feudalism, which ostensibly allowed them to make freehold claims to their dwellings. Landlords were nonetheless able to expand the size and scope of their estates through a series of land grabs under the auspices of new legal and commercial codes. Erstwhile manorial lords then pressganged peasants into copy holdings that could only be sold or inherited under the penalty of steep fines. They also rented land to tenant farmers at steep prices. The vast scale of the newly formed landholdings helped to create a new commercial market for wool and grains. While producing rents for newly anointed lords, it allowed the crown to swoop in and tax these products.

Bates (1981) speculates that in the post-colonial nation states of Sub-Saharan Africa, incumbents pandered to nascent – yet narrow – urban constituencies that could provide them with reliable political support and easy-to-extract revenues. This called on adopting industrialization policies that ran against these countries' comparative advantage and

---

[12] Schrad (2014) extrapolates this thesis spatially, arguing that it holds for the whole of Russia, and longitudinally, maintaining that Russian autocrats have promoted the Vodka industry throughout history to generate revenues and consolidate their rule.

were subsidized by indirect taxes on the countryside imposed via marketing boards. It also called on erecting protectionist barriers for infant industries rooted in overvalued exchange rates and the politicized distribution of credit.

Other illustrative examples are more recent. In China, an increasingly totalitarian regime monopolizes the banking sector and maintains key fiscal monopolies in telecommunications and salt to generate revenues at the expense of productivity and consumer surplus. In India, the government owns the major banks and directs credit, opaquely and inefficiently, to its friends and state-owned enterprises. In Cuba, the communist regime has fully embraced crony capitalism when it suits its interests. Both the state-run monopsony that imports – and rations – food and monopolies across the tourist sector have been strengthened, not undermined, by foreign investment.

The above examples are of oil-importing countries but are never lumped together and labeled as a curse. Yet they perhaps should. Oil is a silhouette that renders the same institutional contours observed in these cases more visible in countries such as Nigeria, Russia, and Venezuela. It simply makes a country's dysfunctions, such as cronyism and corruption, more translucent.

Recasting the resource curse

So what should we make of the resource curse in light of these puzzles and attendant insights? One way to re-conceptualize it is as a particularly strong symptom of the institutions curse.

Several aspects that are unique to natural resources shine a spotlight on underlying dysfunctions that are part of a larger syndrome. First, oil exports can yield very high profits, which can bring institutional rot and endemic corruption to the surface faster and more clearly than other industries.[13] Second, the prices for raw commodities, especially

---

[13] This is due to the industry's unique economics. Oil rents, which are the returns above the minimum required to attract the labor, capital, and expertise necessary to extract oil, are a function of the fact that oil fields' total extraction costs usually lie below the costs of the marginal producing field in the oil market (see Manzano and Monaldi 2008, p. 62). One should note, however, that average marginal costs have been rising steadily over time as supergiant oil fields have become exhausted and fewer of them have been discovered. Instead, new oil reserves are increasingly found in deeper waters offshore or are from unconventional sources such as shale rock that have much higher marginal costs.

for oil, are highly volatile, contributing to dramatic booms and busts. Third, the extraction of natural resources tends to produce notable and visible negative spillovers in weak states that do not have the political will or wherewithal to mitigate environmental damage, or which precipitate environmental degradation themselves by indulging in accelerated extraction that is tantamount to plunder. Finally, countries characterized by weak states and low-quality institutions are not able to handle volatile prices well. They are not equipped to engage in the smoothing out of expenditures, and therefore they tend to indulge in pro-cyclical public spending that grows too fast during a boom and either contracts too much during a bust or is financed at similarly high levels by inflation and foreign debt.

This does not imply that natural resources are to blame for these problems, however. Strong and competent states such as Norway and Chile, where the rule of law is consolidated, have had great success mitigating these problems through prudent monetary and fiscal policies.

The important thing to note is that strong states with good institutions are able to address issues just like these across economic sectors. Even resource-poor countries that are blessed by their institutions adopt countercyclical fiscal policies and prudent monetary and labor policies that ensure that their economy will not overheat and that allow them to smooth investment and consumption. And resource-rich countries can also crack down on any corruption that crops up in the bureaucracy or national oil companies over how oil drilling licenses and contracts are allocated, investment decisions are made, and oil money is spent. Even in developing countries this has become quite common. For example, in Mexico and Brazil, independent watchdogs have recently been empowered to do just that.

Consider Brazil's so-called petrolão, or the "big oily." This corruption scandal has engulfed the country and outraged its citizenry since 2013, when federal prosecutors accused a higher up in PETROBRAS, Brazil's publicly controlled oil industry, of money laundering. Soon after, they stumbled upon evidence that the company had deliberately overcharged contractors for goods and services that then kicked back a portion of these inflated margins with politicians. And soon after that officials learned that oil was just the tip of the iceberg: this type of graft cuts across Brazil's entire public sector and economy.

But this is not tantamount to causation that runs from natural resources to these pathologies. Whether it manifests itself as a corrupt natural resource sector, a bloated public sector, or a gaggle of uncompetitive firms sheltered by tariffs or subsidies, institutions are ultimately to blame. Countries cursed by their institutions are populated by rulers who are largely unaccountable, public officials who are on the take, and citizens who do not trust each other and are often engaged in a war of all against all, albeit one moderated by a weak state that takes sides.

The implications of the findings presented in this book are therefore profound and wide ranging. Perhaps most importantly, they call into question the paternalistic admonishments about the evils of natural resource riches that are reflexively belched out by pundits in the Global North. Instead, they suggest that a certain failed vice-presidential candidate from Alaska might have gotten her populist chant right, even if her rallying cry to drill for oil was not intended to apply to the Global South. The problem for the world as a whole, of course, is that this call to just "drill, baby, drill" violently conflicts with the imperative to wean ourselves from fossil fuels to curb climate change. If there is a resource blessing, it is only in the narrowest sense if it ultimately comes at the expense of our survival as a species.

Some important conceptual and methodological themes

In exploring the causes and consequences of natural resources, rather than the causes and consequences of just precious metals, or just oil, the rest of this book is of two minds. On the one hand, it takes the most inclusive view possible and attempts to make sense of the common causes and consequences of oil, natural gas, minerals, and, in some cases, exportable cash crops. For this reason, at times it simplifies matters and assumes that the only salient variation between these natural resources is that they differ in degree, not kind. Everything else equal, oil generates the largest quantity of rents. Natural gas comes in second. Most precious metals come in third. On the other hand, this book also gives pride of place to oil, acknowledging that hard rock minerals and natural gas do differ from oil in some important respects.

How does oil differ from minerals that are mined, exactly? First, it is usually easier to ascertain the quantity and quality of oil stocks. Second, the extraction of non-hydrocarbon minerals is usually more technically complex and calls upon higher initial investments, especially in regard to refining and transportation infrastructure. Third, oil tends to have a higher rent share by gross value and can be taxed more easily, which helps explain why oil-exporting countries tend to exhibit higher fiscal reliance than mineral-exporting ones.[14]

Oil differs from natural gas in important respects as well. It is traded on global markets and thus has a global price. It can be divided physically and thus is subject to being taxed via royalties. The financing and planning for oil discovery can be separated from its processing, transportation, and distribution. Finally, there is no need to guarantee a final market for oil beforehand, implying that a final market for it does not have to be developed in advance.[15]

For all these differences between oil and other natural resources, however, I primarily focus on oil going forward for practical reasons. First, doing so sets a higher bar: there are some researchers who claim that the resource curse should only hold for oil, most prominently Michael Ross (for example, Ross 2012). That means that if I am going to trumpet that there is a resource blessing instead of a curse, this has to hold true for oil first and foremost. Second, because for most of the key variables implicated in the political economy of natural resources, the only viable way of constructing valid and reliable measures across time and space is to focus on oil. While it is impossible to reliably measure the exploration efforts for metals and tally up the cumulative public revenues across all mines, it is viable to do both of these things for oil. Third, and similarly, while it is not feasible to capture exogenous variation in mineral income, it is feasible to do so for oil. In Chapter 6, I perform statistical analyses where oil income is instrumented with information about giant oil fields.

However, when I believe that the theoretical framework and its assumptions are applicable to minerals other than oil, I accommodate this possibility. This is especially the case in Chapter 6.

Distinguishing between institutions and their outcomes

Although this book makes sharp analytic distinctions between institutions and their outcomes, in some cases I follow conventions in the empirical literature in political economy and measure institutions with proxies that capture their purported outcomes. For example, in Chapter 5, I measure state capacity as total tax revenues as a share of

---

[14] See Barma, Kaiser, and Minh Le (2012, p. 18) on all of these points.
[15] See Greenwald (1988) on all of these points.

GDP. Yet, this is ultimately a pragmatic decision, not a theoretical concession or, worse, a submission to tautology. I sidestep the pitfalls of availing this strategy by instrumenting the exogenous variation in state capacity and retrieving the signal from the noise.

This brings me to the unique research strategy I avail throughout this book. Because my overarching methodological goal is to mitigate the serious endogeneity problem that has bedeviled the resource curse literature, I always opt for an approach to gaining purchase on the direction of causality connecting natural resources and underdevelopment. Because I finger institutions as a fundamental driver of natural resource wealth, income, and reliance, this means that I repeatedly seek to exploit exogenous variation in institutions throughout this manuscript when my objective is to explain variation in natural resource exploration, extraction, production, exports, and taxation. I sometimes opt for using factor endowments: climate and soil types; other times I exploit shocks such as the fall of the Soviet Union.

Similarly, I seek to exploit exogenous variation in natural resources when my objective is to look at the impact made by oil and minerals on political and economic outcomes of interest. This calls on exploiting unusually large oil deposits that are largely explained by geology. Or, it calls on exploiting unexpected shocks to commodity prices or commodity stocks.

3 | Intellectual heritage of the institutions curse view

This chapter traces the intellectual pedigree of the key ideas that animate this book. Its purpose is to give readers a fuller sense of where the book's innovations begin and where its lack of originality ends. In doing so, this chapter clarifies my debts to earlier contributions and pays homage to a gaggle of intellectual forbearers.

I have benefited from others' research in two main ways. The first is in regards to my desire to undertake a critical reanalysis of the resource curse theory and the larger fiscal contract paradigm that spawned it. The second is in regards to my attempt to construct an alternative theory that can make better sense of the patterns and stylized facts that these approaches grapple with. Therefore, this chapter provides a panoramic view of the literature on the political economy of natural resources that is informed by criticisms of the resource curse theory and several responses to those criticisms.

This chapter also reconsiders the fiscal contract approach to political and economic development by leaning on several previous works that call into question its main premises and conclusions. This includes an eclectic literature on neo-mercantilism. It also includes the factor endowment approach to explaining institutional origins.

The neo-mercantilist approach to political economy is centered on the idea that some states face difficulties generating public revenues through regular taxation sources. It suggests that fiscal monopolies, crony capitalism, and politicized finance help to kill two birds with one stone. They provide an incumbent's political allies with valuable rent-seeking opportunities while simultaneously generating easy-to-collect revenues for the state.

Exposure to this body of work has been helpful to me because it is compatible with the idea that natural resources are endogenous. It suggests a strong motive for why governments would seek to cultivate hydrocarbon sectors and mining even if knowledge of geological potential remains shaky and the international price of commodities is in the dumps, namely, to quickly generate as many revenues as possible. And it suggests a context under which this gamble would make sense – when it is hard for the state to tax other stuff. The neo-mercantilist literature helped me conclude that natural resource laws and policies are, to put it simply, one of several possible policy instruments that can raise revenues in the face of high fiscal transaction costs. In this way, they are similar to a bevy of regulations that govern trade, agriculture, industry, and finance; many do not appear, on the surface, to raise revenues that can be appropriated by the state, but in fact create quick and often opaque rents that can be shared between governments and interest groups.

The factor endowment approach to institutional origins has also proven inordinately helpful to me when writing this book. This approach evolved largely as the result of a pragmatic consideration: to improve causal inference when studying the impact made by institutions on development. This happens to be one of the chief reasons I draw on this approach myself.

Although several political economy theories have posited that institutional differences explain variation in political and economic development, issues of causal identification have plagued these claims. Do institutions explain development, or does development explain institutions? Specifically, it has been difficult to establish that the causal arrow runs from differences in institutions to financial development, economic development, and a more egalitarian distribution of income. That is, until several intrepid researchers began to explore how deep-seated factor endowments represent exogenous sources of institutional variation.

It has been argued that differences in climate, soil quality, the size of the native population, and disease propensity across former European colonies gave rise to vast differences in important outcomes. These include the distribution of physical and human capital, property rights institutions, tax structures, migration policies, and public goods. In turn, these differences explain contemporary variation in political and economic institutions and, running through these modern institutions, in political and economic development today. This has helped researchers gain purchase on the direction of the causal arrow. In so far as contemporary institutions can be proxied for with exogenous variation in geography, climate, soils, native population densities, and diseases, then differences in these institutions are the cause of differences in political and economic development, not the other way around.

The factor endowment approach to political economy provides me with two important tools, one theoretical and the other methodological. First, it helps this book proffer an answer to the question about where institutions come from in the first place – given that I aver that both natural resources and development are ultimately a product of institutions, this seemed like a good idea. Second, variation in factor endowments, which include differences in the propensity for different crop types, agricultural practices, and patterns of animal husbandry, allow me to exploit an exogenous source of variation in state capacity and institutional quality.

In turn, this allows me to do the three big things that set my manuscript apart. First, establish a causal link that runs from weak state capacity to the creation of natural resource sectors. Second, to show that once you properly neutralize state capacity/institutional quality, the effect of natural resources on political and economic development is actually positive. Third, to explain variation in development outcomes within the MENA while abstaining from fingering oil as the driving factor.

The rest of this chapter continues as follows. I first provide a broad review of the literature on the political economy of natural resources. I outline and critique three main views about the consequences of oil and minerals. The first is the resource curse theory, which I conceptualize broadly to also include the so-called fiscal contract paradigm. The second is a more sophisticated vein of literature that argues that the negative effect of natural resources on a nation's politics, economics, and society is conditional on other factors. The third is a much smaller literature than the first two that maintains that resources are actually a blessing.

The remainder of the chapter is then dedicated to providing three building blocks that are crucial for the rest of the manuscript. I review recent contributions that argue that natural resources are endogenous to institutions and politics. I next outline the political economy literature on neo-mercantilism. I finish by summarizing the literature that explains modern institutions as originating as a result of deep-seated factor endowments.

The political economy of natural resources

The resource curse view has come to dominate thinking about the political economy of natural resources. The rentier state theory evolved from the study of state building and democratization in Western Europe. It holds that if a ruler wishes to collect revenues by taxing her citizens, she must make concessions in exchange for their compliance. That is, she must grant them political representation and provide public goods.

Why *this* intellectual etiology? The initial research on the question of the relationship between natural resources and political and economic development emerged from the field of Middle Eastern Studies. Researchers were trying to make sense of the despotism and corruption that they saw all around them. In blaming oil for the region's pathologies, Middle Eastern specialists took their cue from political sociologists such as Charles Tilly (1975), who put the so-called fiscal contract between rulers and the ruled at the heart of state building and democracy in Western Europe. Most simply, these continents' political evolution was widely different.

The argument runs as follows. The kings and princes who lorded over Europe after Charlemagne had an imperative to wage war, either to acquire valuable territory or to defend themselves against interlopers. They therefore had strong incentives to tax their populations. In turn, sovereigns reciprocated tax revenues with public goods and political representation, helping to improve fiscal compliance, if not persuade citizens to enlist in their nation's armed forces. Patriotism simply did not suffice, and suffrage was eventually extended for similar reasons.

This story has become the prevailing wisdom about Europe's political history. While the menace of a land-hungry France helped to build the country we now know as Spain, the Russian threat helped build modern Germany – and for that matter Finland, Sweden, and Austria. Meanwhile, the Soviet Empire itself came into being as a reaction to its enduring rivalry with the Ottomans, if not the British.

By the same token, the reverse image is often summoned as the reason behind the chronic weakness and underdevelopment that characterizes many non-European states. Centeno (2002) pins Latin America's exceptional underdevelopment on the paucity of mass mobilizing wars waged between its nations. Herbst (2000) applies the same logic to Africa, arguing that, due to the lucrative slave trade, what was historically valued on that continent was control over peoples' bodies, not necessarily territory. Similarly, in the case of the Middle Eastern and Central Asian states that emerged after the collapse of the Ottoman

Empire, state building was adventitiously stifled. External forces led by Great Britain and the Soviet Union artificially redrew boundaries and kept the peace, precluding an otherwise organic state-building process from emerging (Jackson 1990).

What do natural resources have to do with any of this? Think of the endemic state of bellicosity that prevailed between European nations for much of recent history as one end of the spectrum. In the middle is a relatively pacific international system that does not incentivize state building through mass taxation. While there is no pressing, obvious need for a fiscal contract between a ruler and the ruled in this context, it might nonetheless develop if, for example, capitalists can exercise an exit option and must be rewarded to stay put by a ruler who is wont to raise revenues for reasons besides conquest or defense, such as lining his own pockets. The extractive sector lies at the other end of the spectrum.

A fiscal bargain between the ruler and the ruled that is more favorable to the ruled is particularly likely to occur when capital is hard-to-tax because it is liquid and mobile (Bates 1991). The more elastic the tax base, the harder it is for a ruler to raise taxes without the consent of citizens, whether the revenues are used to finance wars or not. It therefore follows that the taxation of modern, formal sectors, composed of investors, salaried white-collar workers, and wage laborers, is more likely in the absence of natural resources (Ross 1999).

Hydrocarbons and mining are largely fixed assets that putatively yield unearned revenues. Therefore, they do not require any sort of fiscal contract. They can be taxed without much bargaining. According to this logic, natural resource rents displace regular revenues – especially taxes levied on citizens (e.g., Chaudhry 1994). Once they become adept at capturing "easy to collect" rents from minerals, oil, and gas, the fiscal authorities in resource-producing countries stop exerting the efforts needed to tax the larger economy; they simply cease investing in the tools needed to do so (Karl 1997). Eventually, the state's administrative apparatus atrophies, until it is unable to collect regular taxes and becomes totally dependent on unearned rents (see Ross 1999).

By extension, democracy suffers (Ross 2001). Resource-rich countries acquire "an independence from people seldom found in other countries [...] In political terms, the power of the government to bribe pressure groups or to coerce dissidents may be greater than otherwise" (Mahdavy 1970, pp. 466–467). Luciani (1987, p. 74) similarly declares that "[t]here is 'no representation without taxation' and there are no exceptions to this version of the rule."

The broader political and economic effects wrought by rentierism are tragic. As the state becomes a shell of its former self, the fiscal link between taxation and democracy is destroyed. If political institutions such as an elected parliament, an independent judiciary, and ombudsmen already exist, they are sidelined or eliminated (Eifert, Gelb, and Tallroth 2002). If they do not yet exist, then they never see the light of day. Rulers instead shower citizens with clientilistic transfers to procure legitimacy (Anderson 1987; Crystal 1990). This depoliticizes organized groups and erodes social capital (Soares de Oliviera 2007). In this way, oil rents usher in a repressive and unaccountable dictatorship (Ross 2001, 2012).

Eventually, capitalism is also undermined. The accumulation of capital hinges on secure property rights (North 1981). Moreover, the provision of public goods reduces the transaction costs of exchange and promotes trade between strangers at long distances and over longer time horizons. Yet, when they have vast oil rents at their disposal, rulers may fail to provide property registrars and courts, let alone infrastructure and education. Or, they may indulge in opportunistic behavior themselves. The cumulative effect of these dysfunctions is that big, capital-intensive investments in activities other than oil production fail to materialize (Jensen and Johnston 2011).

Empirical applications

The sweeping nature of these claims is matched by their popularity. This story has become a favored explanation for chronic underdevelopment beyond the Middle East.[1] For example, many researchers even blame Spain's prolonged economic decline, which began in the seventeenth century, as well as its inveterate despotism, on natural resources. Specifically, they finger its sequestration of Latin America's precious metals, especially silver, after Columbus (e.g., Drelichman and Voth 2008). Access to Latin America's bountiful natural resources doomed Spain to backward institutions and fostered complacency. Spain's concerted "rentierism" is unfavorably contrasted to

---

[1] For example, on Venezuela see Karl (1997). On Indonesia, see Smith (2007).

England's commercial and industrial development – even though the British Crown continued to earn rents from land and wool well after the Glorious Revolution waged in 1688.

For all of these colorful anecdotes, it is a host of large N, quantitative studies that have really put the resource curse on the map, however. In the late 1990s and early 2000s, researchers such as Jeffrey Sachs and Andrew Warner, Michael Ross, and Jim Fearon and David Laitin began to subject the hypotheses that oil and mineral reliance is associated with economic stagnation, authoritarianism, and civil war to statistical tests using cross-national and panel datasets (see, respectively, Sachs and Warner 2001; Ross 2001; and Fearon and Laitin 2003).

Several researchers also seem to adduce evidence for a rentier effect: that increases in resource rents displace non-resource government revenues. Cheibub (1998) finds a negative relationship between "mining" as a share of GDP and taxes as a share of GDP. Kenny and Winer (2006) find that crude oil production is negatively correlated with the share of total revenues from income taxation, property taxation, and social security taxation. Bornhorst et al. (2009) investigate whether government revenues from hydrocarbons offset revenues from non-hydrocarbon domestic sources in a panel of 30 hydrocarbon-producing countries and find that increases in oil reliance lead to a decrease in overall domestic taxes as a share of GDP.

In terms of distinct nodes in the resource curse view's causal mechanism, the greatest empirical support seems to be centered on the claim that natural resources undermine political accountability. Ross (2001) was one of the first researchers to uncover cross-country evidence that oil, gas, and minerals are correlated with authoritarianism. Others corroborate this finding using similar large N approaches. They include Jensen and Wantchekon (2004); Smith (2007); Papaioannou and Siourounis (2008); Aslaksen (2010); Ramsay (2011); Ross (2012); and Andersen and Ross (2014).

Drawing on the same fiscal contract logic outlined above, researchers also seem to have demonstrated that democracy is undermined in cases in which the state has access to other sources of non-tax revenue. This includes foreign aid, non-tax revenues such as the sale of goods and services by state-owned monopolies, and fiscal transfers from the center, if the governments in question are subnational (see Smith 2008; Morrison 2009; and Gervasoni 2010, respectively).

Theoretical and empirical flaws

Perhaps you are convinced by this line of reasoning and evidence. It is definitely appealing on many grounds. But there are many reasons to remain skeptical about the logic and evidence outlined above. There are several theoretical problems that beset the claims that natural resource rents displace non-resource government revenues and undermine democracy. Some of these flaws are quite deep, and also call into doubt the entire fiscal contract paradigm that underpins the resource curse. Moreover, several methodological issues afflict the resource curse view's empirical findings.

Challenges to the fiscal contract approach

It is helpful to start at the beginning and explore the problems that bedevil the fiscal contract paradigm. In this school of thought, the idea that citizens are a force to be reckoned with and must be bargained with by rulers is axiomatic. A constant, in other words. From this premise flows the assertion that the "discovery" of natural resources and their associated windfalls frees incumbents from the onerous burden of having to negotiate with citizens over the tax bill. The default scenario, in other words, is that rulers are forced to give up concessions in the face of this constraint – unless some extenuating factor impinges upon this natural course of affairs.

The idea that politics is centered on bargaining between rulers and citizens about taxation is wanting in several ways, however. This approach treats the ruling group as a unitary actor. No informational asymmetries are believed to afflict rulers and their core supporters; nor are there problems of opportunism within this group. Also, citizens do not suffer from collective action problems.

In the real world, none of these assumptions holds. The ruling group is often far from cohesive – and, if it is, it is because politics has evolved to solve the problems that threaten this cohesion. Also, citizens will matter politically for similar reasons. Politicians might strategically mobilize citizens and make appeals and concessions to them, but this is the exception, not the rule, as the latter tend to lack leverage ex ante. Instead, they rely on politicians to organize and empower them. A more realistic theory of political and economic development should therefore relax many of these heroic, ultimately untenable, assumptions.

In the next chapter, I flesh out just such a theory. I maintain that it is not usually bargaining between a ruler and citizens that matters for political stability and political and economic development, but negotiations between factions within a ruling coalition. If any concessions are made by the state, therefore, they are usually made to a small cadre of insiders, not to citizens who can threaten to withdraw their consent to taxation if they are not placated with representation and public goods. This dynamic is most apposite in developing countries, which tend to be the main focus of the resource curse view. In the rest of this section, I outline the intellectual foundation behind these alternative assumptions and claims.

The idea that citizens typically command much less leverage and influence when it comes to fiscal matters than the fiscal contract paradigm assumes seems to be corroborated by *prima facie* evidence. This evidence concerns both the history of what are now developed liberal democracies in which citizens eventually – but only recently – secured political power and influence and the contemporary politics of developing countries that are either authoritarian or formally democratic but, for all-intents-and-purposes, are devoid of genuine voice for citizens or accountability for elites.

First, consider that, historically, most tax revolts did not culminate in representative government or even in an immediate reduction in the tax burden for the rebelling party. For every successful case in which a tax revolt engendered fiscal relief, there are countless examples of debacles. Refreshingly, the successful campaigns that we lionize today seem to over-represent women. Two examples stand out. First, the Queen of Anglia led a successful tax revolt against the Roman authorities in the British Isles in 60 AD. Second, Lady Godiva famously rode naked on a horse through Coventry, England, during the eleventh century, and her exhibitionism secured tax relief for commoners (see Abba and Wälde 2008, p. 316).

Yet, successes such as these are far outnumbered by spectacular failures, even in cases in which the nobility were the tax authorities' prime targets. For example, Magna Carta, codified in 1215, was originally an attempt to try to stop King John from imposing a tax on all British landowners. It ultimately proved to be a failed bid by a few disgruntled English nobles at acquiring political representation – that victory would have to wait until the Glorious Revolution of 1688 – and did not secure them any tax relief (see Menaldo and Webb-Williams 2015).

More recent examples of citizens that successfully toppled repressive regimes to try to lower crushing tax bills have proved pyrrhic victories. Succeeding rulers eventually embraced the same fiscal regime as their predecessors, or raised taxes even more upon coming to power, in bids to consolidate their authority. Examples of this phenomenon include the aftermath of colonial rule in Indonesia, Ghana, and India. Peasants were integral parts of the independence movements in these nations and were keen on ousting their colonial overlords to reduce onerous fiscal burdens; alas, however, their foreign masters were soon replaced with native ones who were more brutal and taxed them at even higher levels (see Cohen, Brown, and Organski 1981).

Similarly, across most developing countries today, average citizens increasingly face more regressive tax structures centered on Value Added Taxes (VAT). This is even the case in democracies (Kato and Tanaka 2014). Moreover, spending on public goods has generally decreased across the developing world, including in democracies (see Cai and Treisman 2005). Of course, this could be the case because although average citizens are blessed with enviable bargaining power, they consistently find a way to squander it, and thus end up conceding to a burdensome tax bill and fewer benefits in return. The more likely explanation is that they never had the bargaining power to begin with because democracy in the developing world is often an elite-based affair (see Albertus and Menaldo 2014).[2]

How could this be? There are two types of reasons. The first is sociological and organizational. The second is economic.

The first big reason for average citizens' relative political weakness – if not increasing irrelevance across the developing world – is collective action problems. Radnitz (2012, p. 71) avers that ordinary citizens face considerable collective action costs in their attempts to wring concessions from rulers, especially when resources are unequally distributed. Weingast (1997) countenances this precept. He stresses that collective action is made more difficult by the presence of ethnic, linguistic, and

---

[2] An alternative explanation is that average citizens support VATs because they are less distortive and conducive to trade liberalization, and both features are better for economic growth. The evidence does not seem to bear this contention out, however (see Kato and Tanaka 2014).

religious heterogeneity, the default scenario in most of the developing world.

The second big reason is more recent, and centered on the nature of capital. On the one hand, under a truly global financial system in which assets flow freely between countries, investors have exit options if they are taxed heavily, which therefore drives taxes on capital gains and other forms of liquid wealth down (see Freeman and Quinn 2012). On the other hand, in most countries only a minority of citizens possess significant amounts of this type of capital (Bucks, Kennickell, and Moore 2009; Guiso, Sapienza, and Zingales 2008). Across most of the world, the majority of the population's assets are physical; they are held in the form of real estate in higher-income and middle-income countries and livestock in poorer countries.[3] This means that, especially in the developing world, average citizens really have no "exit option" to speak of when it comes to their wealth and are thus at the mercy of rulers.

Indeed, as this book makes clear in Chapter 5, it is multinational companies, including foreign oil companies, which have enviable amounts of leverage across the developing world today. Thus, it is *their* power and influence that is a force to be reckoned with by rulers in host countries, not unorganized and vulnerable citizens. Therefore, we should expect the former and not the latter to be able to wring generous concessions from the state. Similarly, whether allied with multinationals or pitted against them, it is domestic regime insiders – the elite – who tend to prevail in the developing world today.

This is most obviously the case in authoritarian regimes and quasi-democratic regimes. Consider accounts by Philip Roeder and Scott Radnitz about how the military and bureaucracy operate in the former Soviet republics and neighboring states. Roeder (1993) argues that the politics that govern relations between executives and their "administrative agents" are characterized by "reciprocal accountability," not accountability between government officials and the people. While incumbents work hard to cultivate the support of their bureaucratic and military constituents, the latter need to win the sustained confidence of the former to keep their offices.

---

[3] For the former claim see, for example, Tracy, Schneider, and Chan (1999). For the latter claim see, for example, Dercon (1998), who offers an explanation based on credit market imperfections.

Radnitz (2012) focuses on the informal means by which this occurs. Official posts are distributed based on intra-elite bargaining, and members of the reigning coalition are entitled to use their official positions within the state to pursue their own interests. Moreover, this phenomenon is not relegated to Eastern Europe and Central Asia. Albertus and Menaldo (2012a, 2012b), building on Haber (2006), extend this logic to Latin America.

It is important to note that this type of elite-centered politics is not limited to non-democratic regimes. Especially in the still consolidating democracies located in the developing world, it is intra-elite conflict and negotiation that matters the most for trying to make sense of national political economies. Albertus and Menaldo (2014) have shown that, more often than not, elected officials are able to govern with the support of small, unrepresentative coalitions, and thus pander to narrow interests. This entails, moreover, that the biggest threat posed to rulers emanates from regime insiders, not outsiders (see Albertus and Menaldo 2012a; Haber 2007; Radnitz 2012).

Of course, that does not mean that citizens are never important and that rulers never negotiate with them and confer them with valuable concessions. It is only under a set of limited circumstances that a larger and more diverse set of private actors become important political players, however. As I will make clear in the next chapter, when politicians inherit low fiscal transaction costs and technologies that allow them to make more reliable promises, then they will find it propitious to recruit citizens into the political game, not just rely on insiders. In turn, they will adopt policies that have a hand in cultivating a more diversified economic and fiscal system. Yet, historically, this occurred in a subset of countries that tend to be geographically clustered in Western Europe, North America, and Oceania. More often than not, politics is a game dominated by elites, for the benefit of elites.

As I will make clear in Chapter 7, when discussing the Arab Spring, citizens can and do matter sometimes in the developing world, and even in autocratic regimes. Indeed, as attested to by events since February of 2011, ordinary citizens can help take down unpopular regimes. However, I will argue that this is a rare circumstance and tends to happen fleetingly. It is a symptom of unresolvable conflicts within the ranks of regime insiders and attendant uncertainty. Specifically, when successions are mishandled, or crises management bungled, average citizens have an opportunity to seize the initiative. These constitute windows of opportunity in which they can substantially reduce their collective action problems (see Radnitz 2012, p. 71; Menaldo 2012). Once they smell blood in the water and are galvanized, it is hard to demobilize citizens without unleashing civil wars or instigating palace coups.

Problems with the resource–taxation link

It can be argued that the resource curse theory's most problematic assumptions undergird the rentier effect mechanism, which directly flows from the fiscal contract paradigm. This is the idea that natural resources enervate non-resource taxation. There are many problems with it. First, the resource curse assumes that resource wealth will invariably translate into fiscal reliance by the government on the rents produced by natural resources. Second, it also assumes that said fiscal reliance will displace non-resource revenues.

These contentions are flawed in several ways. A country that experiences an influx of rents from natural resource production may not necessarily tax these sectors all that much. Moreover, natural resource discovery and production may have several salutary knock-on effects on state capacity and fiscal capacity, therefore boosting overall revenues net of any displacement effects experienced in the short run. Ultimately, the rentier state view assumes that although governments are revenue-maximizers when it comes to taxing natural resource rents, they are revenue-satisficers when it comes to taxing non-resource sources of revenues.

This is logically inconsistent (see Ross 1999, p. 313). On the one hand, the state adopts the optimal tax rate in the resource sector. In other words, the tax rate on mineral and hydrocarbon production stops just short of inducing resource-producing firms to reduce production – so that the state would not receive a higher yield if it lowered the tax rate. On the other hand, the state fails to apply the optimal tax rate to non-resource products, services, and sources of income. In other words, by allowing these sources of revenues to atrophy, it chooses to leave large bills on the sidewalk. It is not clear *a priori* why governments would act in such a fiscally schizophrenic way.

Moreover, even if governments are willing to levy high taxes on resource extraction, production, and exports, it is often hard for them to actually enforce such taxes, making it difficult for them to arrive at the point where they entirely "depend" on these revenues. This is especially the case if the firms operating in the extractive sector are large foreign corporations. Multinational corporations are wealthy and sophisticated – especially those operating in the international hydrocarbon market. They therefore hire skilled tax attorneys and accountants with the express purpose of reducing their tax bill. One tried-and-true method is to engage in transfer pricing, in which one of the firm's subsidiaries "sells" goods or services to the others at a steep markup that helps lower its taxable income. Plus, while multinationals repatriate much of the profits they earn abroad instead of reinvesting them in host countries, they also shelter a sizable amount of taxable income in tax havens.

But even when they can tax the resource sector effectively, there are many reasons why governments may choose not to substitute ordinary taxation with revenues from resources.[4] Chief among these is the urge to hedge against price risk. The price of primary commodities, especially oil, is highly volatile and unpredictable. When the world oil price falls dramatically, governments may face incredibly difficult, if not course-altering, budgetary decisions.

Governments in oil-exporting countries that suddenly face large budget deficits after unexpected collapses in the oil price may have to adjust their taxing and spending policies away from commodity exports. They may be forced to do so in short order. A crash in the international price of a major commodity may induce its major producers to devalue their currency and turn to the inflation tax. This is the case in 2016 Venezuela, for example. Sometimes this is coupled with the sudden removal of fuel subsidies; an anti-populist decision that can catalyze fierce resistance.[5]

In oil-exporting countries, economic crises often serve as leading indicators of big, sometimes permanent, increases in non-oil revenues.

---

[4] For example, although in the Philippines commodity exports have traditionally constituted from 15 to 25 percent of GDP, the government has received only between 1 and 3 percent of its revenues from these exports. In fact, the Philippines did not tax exports for most of its history and has often shown restraint *vis-à-vis* commodity taxation during price booms.

[5] For example, in Bolivia fuel subsidies were removed in 2010. This precipitated a fierce backlash. Labor unions spearheaded a wave of strikes and demonstrations that swept across, and paralyzed, Santa Cruz, La Paz, and other major cities. The government capitulated, and reinstated the subsidies with celerity.

In the case of important oil producers, including Mexico, Venezuela, Ecuador, Nigeria, Angola, and Russia, the International Monetary Fund (IMF) has in the recent past negotiated standby agreements in the wake of economic crises stoked by sharp declines in the oil price. Under said agreements, the IMF provided these countries with credit in exchange for tax reforms aimed at broadening the tax base and increasing revenue yields. Many of these efforts proved successful.

Similar to countries that are resource poor, incumbents' fiscal and budgetary decisions in resource-rich countries help determine whether they will survive in office. In the wake of a collapse in the price of commodities, will incumbents be forced to cut capital investments? Public goods and services? Clientilistic transfers to key political supporters? When an incumbent's fiscal portfolio is undiversified, these tough choices are made even tougher. They may threaten a regime's very survival.

The implications are straightforward. First, forward looking governments may not abandon non-resource taxation, even in the wake of sizable fiscal windfalls associated with high commodity prices. At minimum, they may continue to invest in overall state capacity. At maximum, they may strategically cultivate countercyclical sources of non-rent revenues to compensate for future, and perhaps unforeseen, reductions in oil rents. This may help explain why Tijerina-Guajardo and Pagan (2003) find that, in the case of Mexico, although oil duties respond negatively to tax revenues, ordinary tax revenues do not respond to changes in oil duties. By extension, they do not crater when the oil price is high.

Problems with the taxation democracy link

There are serious problems with the claim that there is no representation without taxation. The gist of the problem is that it is not axiomatic that the key to democratic government is actually a fiscal compact forged between the ruler and the ruled.

The fiscal contract view of democracy is flawed in three important ways. First, autocrats can tax both elites and the masses at high rates without succumbing to democratization if they can put together the right political coalition and deploy the right survival strategy. Indeed, dictators may explicitly seek to divide and conquer the opposition and tax them into poverty and political fecklessness. Examples of this strategy include, among many others, Nicholas II, Bismarck, Mussolini, Franco,

Chang Kai-shek, Stroessner, Somoza, and the Duvaliers. Second, irrespective of how good the regime is at neutralizing its challengers, the
theory assumes that groups who are taxed can solve their collective
action problem to force the government to grant them representation.
Third, it assumes that what the citizenry desires in exchange for taxation
is representation, when in fact democracy may not represent the most
effective way for citizens to obtain their ultimate goals, whether these are
increased spending on public goods or net redistributive transfers (see
Albertus and Menaldo 2012a).

Yet, perhaps the most elegant critique of the resource curse is not
really a coherent critique at all; it is, instead, the disparate cases in
which countries democratized through mechanisms other than the
taxation–representation nexus. Indeed, that many resource-rich countries are paragons of these alternative democratization routes means
that resources cannot be dispositive barriers against regime transitions.
One path is when rivalry between enfranchised and disenfranchised
groups induces democratization from below (Conley and Temimi
2001). This is what ultimately occurred to bring democracy about in
oil-rich Mexico. Another is when economic elites are split, and the
ruling elite extends suffrage strategically to advance its interest against
rival elites (Llavador and Oxoby 2005), as occurred in nitrate-rich
Chile in the nineteenth century. A third path is when political elites
split and agree to democratize in order to avoid violence (Bardhan
1993). Oil- and coffee-rich Colombia evidences this scenario, embodied in the National Front pact hatched between conservatives and
liberals in 1958. A final path is democratization as a vehicle by elites to
procure public goods when they become more highly valued than pork
(Lizzeri and Persico 2004) – a transition path exemplified by oil- and
gas-rich Trinidad and Tobago.

The conditional effect of natural resources

A newer literature that claims that the effect of natural resources is
conditioned by preexisting institutions shares many of the concerns
about the resource curse reviewed above. Many researchers have therefore offered a more nuanced view about the potential effects of natural
resources on politics and economics. The main thrust of this conditionalist literature is that while "bad" institutions in some countries indeed
allow oil and minerals to produce deleterious economic, political, and

social outcomes, "good" institutions actually allow natural resources to register salutary outcomes.[6]

Mehlum, Moene, and Torvik (2006) try to make sense of the fact that, although on average the cross-sectional correlation between natural resource reliance and economic development is negative, there are several oil- and mineral-reliant countries that are very high performers. They argue that this variance is explained by the incentive structure represented by countries' institutions. While greater natural resources push aggregate income down if institutions encourage rent-seeking and corruption, they bolster GDP when they reward production and innovation.

Dunning (2008) argues that, although on average there is a negative association between natural resources and democracy, there is a resource blessing in Latin America. He bases this conclusion on a panel dataset that observes Latin America since 1960. His explanation for the region's exceptionalism is that Latin American countries' notoriously high levels of income inequality reverse the typical effect of natural resources on politics. When a society has a highly unequal distribution of income, natural resource wealth permits democratization; elites do not fear redistribution by the enfranchisement of the poor because they can deploy resource rents to placate demands for transfers. Conversely, if the distribution of income is more equal, natural resource wealth reinforces authoritarian regimes; leaders do not face demands for redistribution and can therefore deploy resource rents to weaken or co-opt the opposition.

Jones-Luong and Weinthal (2010) put forth a similar story as Dunning's. In trying to make sense of the different outcomes observed in the former Soviet republics after the fall of the Berlin Wall, they posit that variation in the ownership structure of the hydrocarbon sector impacts fiscal regimes and political outcomes. This is because ownership structures constitute a set of social relations. They therefore assign what actors are the direct or indirect claimants to mineral wealth.

Moreover, fiscal institutions are products of supply and demand. On the supply side, different ownership structures engender different levels of transaction costs, therefore conditioning states' ability to tax mining activities. On the demand side, the identity of the claimants to

---

[6] See Waldner and Smith (2014) for several examples, as well as how the evidence they adduce sizes up against the resource curse and resource blessing camps.

this wealth and attendant differences in societal expectations around how it will be spent constrain the state's ability to tax and spend these rents.

Clear predictions flow from this framework. Ownership structures with stronger international components will be more vibrant and efficient. Specifically, the quality of fiscal institutions will be greatest when private ownership is in domestic hands, will suffer slightly when private ownership is in foreign hands, and will deteriorate when ownership is public. While state ownership without control is the best possibility within this latter set, state ownership without control is the worst.

Jones-Luong and Weinthal (2010) find that reality conforms to their theoretical priors. During the period in which they conduct their empirical analysis, Azerbaijan exhibits state ownership without control and suffers from poor fiscal institutions and rampant corruption; Uzbekistan and Turkmenistan exhibit state ownership with control, and fare a bit better; Kazakhstan exhibits private foreign ownership and does even better, but not as well as Russia, which witnesses private, domestic ownership.

Michael Ross's *The Oil Curse* (2012) seems to follow in Jones-Luong and Weinthall's footsteps, in several respects. In this new – and improved – approach to the resource curse, Ross argues that even oil states must negotiate with citizens who care deeply about their country's subsoil riches and their natural patrimony. In other words, the logic of the contractarian approach to state building and democratization does not stop at the water's edge in places where natural resources are abundant. Indeed, Ross shows that even the rulers of very oil-rich states have to resort to bargaining with, taxing, and providing services to everyday citizens. The key difference between themselves and the rulers of poorly endowed nations is that they can successfully *hide* the lion's share of the state's revenues, granting them more latitude and breathing space – but never freeing them from the quotidian exigencies of politics.

Ross tenders several novel predictions and adduces evidence that generally supports them. For example, while oil rents should fuel secessionist wars because independence in oil-producing regions is lucrative, they should not make civil war and authoritarianism more likely in general. Increases in oil rents should make democratization less likely after 1980, however, because of the proliferation of National

Oil Companies (NOCs). Also, increases in oil rents should translate into greater social spending.

The resource blessing

As of late, some researchers have gone even further than this "conditionalist school" in casting doubt on the resource curse view. They have pointed out that natural resources have an unequivocally positive effect.

Let's start with state building. Snyder and Bhavnani (2005, p. 571) claim that resource-rich states may use rents to improve their tax capacity and coercive capacity, thus boosting revenues across both natural resource and non-resource sectors. La Croix (1992) shows that such a dynamic played itself out in Australia during the gold rush of the 1850s. Similarly, while Canada's western provinces focused exclusively on taxing timber and minerals during the nineteenth century, a portion of these revenues was allocated to improving tax administration. This helped provincial governments collect property and income taxes (see Sokoloff and Zolt 2007).

Others find similar patterns. Bräutigam (2008a, p. 136) writes that primary commodities "have the potential to play a wide variety of positive state-building roles [...] to build productive capacity, or as a way to direct scarce private capital into specific activities ... [and] can serve as the arena for bargains that give shape to constructive 'embedded' relations between the state and producers." She finds evidence that this has been the case in Mauritius, as well as in other Sub Saharan African countries (Bräutigam 2008b). Similarly, Khoury and Kostiner (1990) argue that oil fueled the consolidation of the state and national identity in Iran and Saudi Arabia by financing transportation and communication networks.

The salutary role of natural resources goes beyond state building. Haber (2014) argues that Latin America's industrialization was catalyzed by resource booms. Other research finds that oil boosts public goods (Stijns 2006), bolsters economic development (Alexeev and Conrad 2009; Brunnschweiler 2008; Brunnschweiler and Bulte 2008; Lederman and Maloney 2008; Smith 2015), does not cause civil wars (Brunnschweiler and Bulte 2009; Cotet and Tsui 2010), and improves governance (Heilbrunn 2014; Kennedy and Tiede 2013).

Perhaps the most promising variety of the resource blessing view is the recent literature on the positive relationship between oil and democracy. The first is Herb (2005). He reasons that resource-reliant countries would have been substantially poorer had they not found oil, gas, or minerals, and that their lower GDPs would have caused them to be less democratic. He therefore estimates what their GDP would have been in the absence of these resources, and then estimates their level of democracy at those lower, counterfactual levels of GDP. Once Herb does this, the evidence for a resource curse weakens considerably. Bruckner, Ciccone, and Tesei (2012), Wacziarg (2012), Wright, Frantz, and Geddes (2015), and Liou and Musgrave (2014) conclude that oil actually bolsters democracy instead of undermining it.

Haber and Menaldo (2011a) find the most robust evidence of a resource blessing across time and place. To arrive at these conclusions they employ state-of-the-art econometric methods to identify the long-run effect of resource reliance on regime types on an original panel dataset that observes 168 countries since 1800. They opt for this research strategy to address the possibility that numerous sources of bias may drive the results obtained thus far in the resource curse literature. Haber and Menaldo are especially concerned about omitted variable bias induced by unobserved, country-specific, and time-invariant heterogeneity.

In the quest to address this possibility, they make several novel contributions. These include putting together new data series on all possible sources of rents from natural resources and constructing innovative instrumental variables that can capture the resource data's exogenous variation. They also focus on the data's within variation, evaluate a bevy of conditional effects, and estimate difference-in-differences models based on the operationalization of explicitly specified counterfactuals.

Haber and Menaldo evaluate if there is a long-run relationship between resource reliance and regime type within countries over time, both on a country-by-country basis and across several different panel datasets. They consistently uncover evidence for a resource blessing. This is even when they use split-sample techniques to try to detect a resource curse among poor countries, countries with relatively equal distributions of income (as hypothesized by Dunning 2008), and countries that are extremely large oil producers. A positive relationship between resources and democracy is observed on a region-by-region basis and across different time periods. The results also hold after Haber and Menaldo conduct their analyses on a country-by-country basis.

Finally, the resource blessing is ratified after the authors look for a possible divergence between actual and counterfactual paths of political change. These counterfactual paths are posited on the basis of the paths followed by resource-reliant countries' resource-deprived neighbors. After constructing what these counterfactual paths might look like, Haber and Menaldo then determine whether any divergence between the actual and counterfactual paths of political development correlates with increases in resource reliance. Using a similar approach based on the construction of synthetic counterfactuals, Liou and Musgrave (2014) ratify these results for a smaller set of countries.

A reaction against the resource blessing

Recently, there has been a counter response to the iconoclastic findings adduced by Herb, Dunning, Haber and Menaldo, and Liou and Musgrave. Some researchers have taken these authors' theoretical and empirical critiques to heart. And, after upgrading their research designs, they have attempted to reanimate the resource curse view.

Ramsay (2011) addresses endogeneity bias by instrumenting oil income with out-of-region natural disasters to proxy for price increases. He reasons that if a tsunami hits Indonesia, for example, it increases oil income in the rest of the world's producers without affecting their regime types through any other channel. Estimating two-stage least squares regressions, Ramsay confirms the resource curse.

Meanwhile, Andersen and Ross (2014) draw on Haber and Menaldo's (2011) regression models to reassess the relationship between oil and democracy. They aver that, since 1980, there has been a resource curse. Andersen and Ross argue that oil wealth began to hamstring democratic transitions only after the oil nationalizations of the 1970s, since these allowed developing country governments to capture previously unavailable oil rents that they could then deploy to block political liberalization.

Where we now stand

While these neoresource curse contributions represent a significant step forward, they are not without considerable fault. Ramsay (2012) assumes that his instrumental variable satisfies the exclusion restriction on its own, and therefore does not introduce country-fixed effects into his regressions. This assumption is problematic, however, since short-term shocks to oil prices are likely to be offset by the immediate increases in oil production undertaken by a few big producers with substantial excess capacity. Saudi Arabia, the world's largest oil producer, expressly seeks to create a stable world oil market through its production policy and ramps up output to counter shocks associated with natural disasters. Therefore, Ramsay's instrument may be picking up a "big producer" fixed effect, an intuition that is corroborated by the fact that his instrument is rendered weak if the Middle East is excluded from the regressions.

Andersen and Ross's (2014) paper is beset by similar problems. Their regressions do not control for country-specific time trends, and they do not address endogeneity bias via an instrumental variables approach. Moreover, the substantive effect implied by their results is trivial. When estimated from a dynamic fixed effects model with a five-year lag (represented by Table 5, Column 3 of their paper), "a one standard deviation rise in total oil income (US$2,618) leads to a one point reduction in the Polity score (using Haber and Menaldo's 0–100 scale) over a 5-year period, and a 0.6-point reduction over the long run" (p. 19). Furthermore, as stated above, this effect only applies in the post-1980 era.

This implies, however, that oil has no material effect on the level of democracy in any actual country during this time period. For example, if Kuwait, currently one of the world's biggest oil producers, and a country that earned over US$60,000 from oil and gas exports in 1980 (in 2007 money) had never discovered oil, it would instead have the Polity Score of Egypt under Mubarak. For all intents and purposes, an oil-poor Kuwait would be as equally authoritarian as its oil-rich doppelganger.[7]

What to make of all this

The debate between the resource curse literature, the conditionalist view, and the resource blessing has been vibrant and interesting. It has left us at sort of an impasse, however. I have come to the

---

[7] Although Andersen and Ross claim that the substantive effect of oil is strengthened if it is evaluated after 1984, they do not actually report any regression results where they interact oil income and a post-1983 dummy variable. So it is hard to know what the confidence intervals around these bigger point estimates are. Nor is it possible to evaluate the statistical significance of any of the long-run effects they report in their paper, because they never employ the Delta Method or Bewley Transformation to estimate the standard errors of their long run multipliers (LRM), despite the fact that these LRMs are ratios in which the lagged dependent variable is included in the denominator (see Haber and Menaldo 2011a).

conclusion that there is a way around this problem. We should think more carefully about where natural resources ultimately come from. We should consider the important role of institutions and deliberate decision making in bringing hunches about underground pools of dinosaur bones and seismographic tests with wide margins of error into the reality that is the diesel fuel sitting in your gas tank. Fortunately, there is an emerging literature that can help us accomplish this task.

The causes of natural resources

What are the causes of natural resources beyond geology and luck? A first generation of work on the endogeneity of natural resources takes an orthodox approach and gives pride of place to private property rights and the rule of law. Bohn and Deacon (2000) and David and Wright (1997) argue that secure property rights incentivize resource exploration and production. Bohn and Deacon predict that hydrocarbon firms will underinvest in the capital-intensive operations that characterize the upstream oil industry – extraction, transportation, and the exportation of crude oil – in weak states due to insecure property rights. David and Wright argue that one of the chief reasons the United States came to dominate the production of most minerals after the Civil War was due to mining laws that granted open access and private property rights for prospectors.

These predictions draw on a time-inconsistency dilemma coined the "obsolescing bargain" (Vernon 1971). When oil exploration and production contracts are signed and financing is committed, investors have substantial power to extract concessions and promises from host governments: they are, after all, the ones with the technology, capital, and expertise necessary to extract the oil. Over time, however, this power shifts to the hosts. Plants, machinery, and storage facilities associated with oil exploration, drilling, and transportation can be confiscated quite easily. Investors must make expensive investments in these assets several years before the oil starts flowing, and several years before they can realize a return on their investment.

While these costs are sunk at the beginning of a project, it can remain profitable for oil companies to continue to produce oil even if the terms of the initial deal worsen significantly. Host governments can therefore exploit this fact and pounce when the time is right. Especially when the oil price rises, governments face incentives to increase royalties and introduce windfall taxes, if not expropriate foreign oil firms altogether. And the host's commitment problem is exacerbated by the fact that it can renege on a contract while a private oil firm cannot appeal to a higher authority to remedy this violation.

But natural resources may be endogenous to low-quality institutions
A newer literature takes a contrarian position and arrives at opposite conclusions. Some works show that low state capacity and institutional quality are not a hindrance to oil exploration or production. Broadman (1985) demonstrates that high levels of political risk are not a deterrent to oil exploration. Focusing attention on the post-World War II era, Smith (2015) finds no evidence that institutional quality or regime type is systematically associated with oil discoveries.

In fact, autocracies are more likely to develop oil sectors. Haber (2006) argues that resource dependence may be endogenous to authoritarianism, along the lines articulated by Brunnschweiler and Bulte (2009). Dunning (2010) posits that democracies might be more likely to develop their natural resource sectors at a slower pace than autocracies – if incumbents do not expect to internalize the future benefits of increased oil production because of future electoral turnover.

Other researchers similarly argue that, ironically, weak states may be more likely to cultivate oil sectors. Fearon (2005) maintains that oil exports proxy for weak state capacity, which entails that weak states are more likely to export their oil instead of consuming it domestically. Brunnschweiler and Bulte (2009) aver that while civil wars incentivize the faster extraction of oil and minerals, they destroy other economic sectors, making them a default sector. Haber and Menaldo (2011a) speculate that the correlation between resources and authoritarianism may be driven by poor state capacity.

Some political ecologists advance similar arguments, positing that when states in the developing world are desperate, they are more likely to turn to cultivating their natural resource sectors. According to Bury and Bebbington (2013), "[w]ithin Latin America, the extractive sector was seen as a critically important driver of economic growth by policy-makers seeking to overcome the economic and political crises spurred by successive oil price shocks and massive national debt burdens" (p. 38). Latin American governments therefore courted FDI into their mining and hydrocarbon sectors after the economic crises of the 1980s, often with reckless abandon. This was part and parcel of trade and financial liberalization, and meant

reorganizing and clarification of mining and hydrocarbons concessions, removal of local hiring and sourcing requirements, limitations on expropriation rights, ratification of international arbitration accords, and the creation of investment protections [...] natural resource extraction legislation was either abolished or amended to limit public interest and eminent domain, reform environmental protection, establish minimal taxation regimes, formalize mineral and hydrocarbons concession taxation and leasing, and create investment incentives." (Ibid., pp. 44–45)

Furthermore, Latin American countries "developed infrastructure to provide access to remote areas where new hydrocarbons and mineral deposits were being discovered" [and] "provided the necessary military and police support to ensure the safety of new extractive operations and their foreign personnel" (ibid., p. 45).

Moreover, Bury and Bebbington (2013) point to the possibility that the myriad problems faced by the citizens of weak states in the Latin American periphery are ultimately due to the state's neglect or incompetence, and not natural resources per se. They argue "that, at their core, most struggles over extraction reflect demands for a stronger state – for stronger regulatory presence, for planning, for protection of human rights and environmental assets, and for predictability in the lived environment of rural populations" (p. 24).

The iconoclastic claims that weak and corrupt states are more likely to attract investment from abroad in hydrocarbon and mining sectors fly in the face of the so-called obsolescing bargain. Why, exactly, do foreign investors trust governments in the developing world to keep their word? Do they really expect these sometimes struggling and unpredictable states to honor subsoil rights that favor FDI, respect mining legislation, and uphold contracts?

Maurer (2013; see also 2011) provides a way to reconcile this issue. His book does not view the absence of the rule of law in developing countries that host foreign investors operating in extractive industries as a major roadblock. This contrasts with sectors such as manufacturing or software. He shows that American government interventions on behalf of U.S. foreign investors in the developing world have been astoundingly successful at extracting compensation, often above market value, after expropriations.

Maurer demonstrates how, over time, and through learning-by-doing, the U.S. government found innovative and crafty ways to protect investors' property rights abroad. This included bribes, threats, and outright changes in foreign governments. Unlike the explicit pursuit of imperial conquest undertaken by other Great Powers, however, the United States failed in efforts aimed at outright annexation and, with a few notable exceptions such as Iran and Chile, largely eschewed covert action. Instead, "by the 1990s, American investors had access to an array of mechanisms to protect their property rights that did *not* depend on executive action" (Maurer 2013, p. 389).

International arbitration gradually allowed for the depoliticization of the enforcement of multinationals' property rights in the developing world. Maurer shows how this freed the U.S. government from having to intervene on behalf of American investors who faced expropriation.[8] He also outlines the growing role of investor insurance in allowing foreign investors to hedge against sundry risks, including contractual violations and exchange rate risk.

This review of the literature on the endogeneity of natural resources suggests that although the rule of law and high state capacity might matter for stimulating the first big exploration push for "new" industrial metals and hydrocarbon stocks in developed countries, it is less important for latter generations of exploration and production in developing countries. While initial exploration and production forays may be technologically advanced, and centered on innovation and even entrepreneurship – as argued by David and Wright (1997) – later forays benefit from the diffusion of technology, best practices, and investments in, and even transfers of, human capital.

In fact, developing countries can leapfrog many of the problems that eventually offset early successes in the developed world. Take the United States. Despite the fact that it was the site of the first modern example of oil drilling, and the scene of innovative wildcatting, drilling, and unitization techniques, oil exploration became increasingly

---

[8] Maurer argues that American governments once used threats and coercion to ensure adequate and swift compensation after expropriations of American companies. This was sometimes accomplished under the aegis of the Hickenlooper Amendment, a statute that called on the U.S. government to suspend foreign assistance to countries that expropriated U.S. property without adequate compensation. Similar provisions called on the United States to vote against loans from the World Bank and Inter-American Bank to these countries and suspend tariff preferences.

difficult to conduct in the United States over time. Disparate private prospectors had to negotiate unitization agreements with each other to distribute the income generated from common pools, thus incentivizing wars of attrition and holdup problems. The same goes for obstacles to the coordination of exploration efforts on federal lands. Prospectors have faced perverse incentives to keep information from each other about the commercial potential and value of prospects and free ride on the exploratory efforts of others, therefore engendering a Tragedy of the Commons: an industry best by under-exploration (see Hendricks and Porter 1996).

That is, until very recently, due to the fracking revolution. Consistent with the logic outlined above, this is a high technology sector in which innovation, smallness, and nimbleness rule. Fracking is characterized by cutting-edge hydrocarbon recovery techniques and horizontal drilling, giving the United States, in particular, a distinct competitive advantage. There are hundreds of versatile firms operating across the country; they are very good at increasing productivity and slashing costs and tend to have a very high rate of profit reinvestment. Fracking has therefore attracted a huge influx of physical and human capital to North American producers.

Yet, also consistent with the logic outlined above: although the fracking revolution began in the United States, it has quickly spread to other developed countries, and eventually developing ones as well. Hydraulic fracturing is now ubiquitous. It has made headway in several countries with seemingly high levels of political risk.[9]

Similarly, innovative secondary recovery techniques that use cutting-edge technology often spread quickly throughout the developing world, if not begin there, as countries that depend heavily on oil may throw everything but the kitchen sink at their declining industries in order to stay afloat. For example, in Oman, IOCs, sometimes working in concert with the Omani government, have experimented with an eclectic array of enhanced oil recovery strategies. Earlier versions are based on steam, natural gas, and polymers. Most recently, they are centered on solar thermal energy (see Kantchev 2015, p. B5).

---

[9] Take Argentina, for example. Chevron has partnered with newly nationalized YPF to extract huge deposits of shale oil and gas from the Vaca Muerta field. This requires the use of expensive horizontal drilling and hydraulic fracturing technology; it is expected to cost over US$100 billion.

Why this literature matters

What if natural resources are indeed a reflection of the political institutions and political will of host countries that attract foreign investment into these sectors, if not the imperialistic might of hegemonic powers that stand up for their nationals' economic interests overseas? If so, this raises serious doubts about most of the political economy literature on the effects of oil and minerals.

This is for two reasons. First, it debunks the naïve belief that natural resources, most particularly oil, are an exogenous, randomly assigned variable. That is, that natural resource rents fall like manna from heaven. Second, if natural resource rents are not exogenous, then it could very well be the case that an omitted factor both increases the propensity that hydrocarbon and mining sectors will reach fruition and also makes it more likely that countries in the developing world will experience authoritarianism, economic stagnation, civil wars, and corruption. In short, if the assumption that natural resources are exogenous is mistaken, then it very well could be the case that the impact of minerals and oil on political and economic development has been centered on spurious inferences.

Neo-mercantilism

The eclectic, fascinating literature on neo-mercantilism suggests a possible candidate for what said omitted variable might be. Relatively weak and desperate states in search of easy-to-collect revenues cultivate their natural resource sectors in order to generate rents. This would not be a significant departure from the past. Throughout history governments have been in the business of creating sectors from scratch for the express purpose of taxing them. Nor would it be a significant departure from the present, either. Governments continue to do this across the world, usually under the guise of development strategies that funnel subsidized credit to bloated and inefficient monopolists.

Why would this be the case? Levi (1988) theorizes that fiscal transaction costs influence governments' revenue generation strategy and, when these are high, incumbents may adjust not just their fiscal strategy, but their political one as well. Low tax collection costs made possible by modern bureaucracies, the spread of elementary education and literacy, and modern record keeping may constitute a luxury that only a few countries can afford (see Aidt and Jensen 2009; Kenny and

Winer 2006). That the introduction of and reliance upon income taxa-tion, the consolidation of democracy, the widespread provision of public goods, and the development of a generous welfare state all occurred jointly in a handful of countries in the Western world might not be all that coincidental.[10]

When these collection – or, better put, fiscal transaction – costs are prohibitive, states might turn to protectionism or erect barriers to entry. Ultimately, the costs of using coercion to curtail market entry are lower than those associated with raising revenues directly. The rents that are created can be confiscated and distributed through obscure and relatively easy to enforce government regulations. The cheapest revenue genera-tion option may be for the state to step up its presence along ports and borders to collect tariffs, which are much easier to collect than income and consumption taxes (see also Reizman and Slemrod 1987). Similarly, the strategic creation of any cartel, monopsony, or monopoly provider represents a method of virtually frictionless taxation.

History is replete with examples. For example, Anderson and Boettke (1997, p. 39) write that "[i]n 17th century England and France, the government employed the sale of various monopoly rights as a means of raising revenue. That is, the monarch sold monopoly privileges for cash or other consideration (often loans on preferred terms)." These authors also argue (on p. 38) that communism in the Soviet Union was a cognate system; it was not actually organized around central planning but instead, it was "really a market economy heavily encrusted with central government regulation and restrictions [. . .] to extract revenue from the economy, as an alternative to collecting revenue via the use of taxation."

Why do states erect such inefficient and patently venal systems? Monopoly rents are easy to tax because profits are voluntarily revealed by firms in exchange for their monopoly rights. As Ekelund and Tollison (1981, p. 85) write:

Monopoly creation was [. . .] a more reliable source of state revenue than taxation, in which the state has to bear the costs of discovering taxable values

---

[10] Along these lines, Kau and Rubin (2002) conclude that the single most important determinant of the growth in the size of the U.S. government over time is the increase in female labor force participation because it reduced the costs of taxation by creating a larger formal labor force and promoted increased bookkeeping.

and policing corruption among tax collectors, because aspiring monopolists will reveal the present value of monopolies to the authorities in their efforts to secure such grants from the state. State officials thus do not have to seek out estimates of the value of their enforcement services in the case of monopoly grants.

Virtually any market can be distorted in this way. The state can, quite shockingly, use ordinary policy instruments to ration and subsidize foreign exchange, capital, intermediate inputs, products, labor, and land. The rents that can be generated are potentially large and usually considerably opaque.[11]

Consider import substitution industrialization. This calls on sheltering so-called infant manufacturing firms. Politicians do so by erecting import tariffs and quotas, requiring permits for intermediate goods, and overvaluing exchange rates. Towards the same end, they subsidize credit and foreign exchange, and restrict foreign ownership. In a sense, this is a system of both revenue generation and stealth redistribution, as assets and income are taken from unorganized consumers, commodity exporters, petty capitalists, and non-unionized labors and given to politically favored industries, banks, and unions.

A vast literature on politicized finance and financial repression is also, at its core, about neo-mercantilism. Several researchers have shown that governments can generate revenues by exchanging the right to operate a bank (a charter) and enforce stringent branching restrictions for revenues – usually in the form of monopoly rents – that are then shared with the state.

There are several possibilities. Banks can earn income by discounting bills of exchange generated through trade, and loans are then made to the state at favorable interest rates. Or, banks can allow states to obtain an equity stake in the bank and allow the state to purchase its shares with a favorable loan that is subsequently repaid with the state's portion of the profits. High reserve requirements imposed on banks, in exchange for scarce charters, can be a vehicle for the state to monetize public debt (see Barth, Caprio, and Levine 2006; Becerra, Cavallo, and

---

[11] The works that have most influenced my thinking about neo-mercantilism include: Anderson and Boettke (1997); Auriol and Warlters (2005); Bates (1981); Ekelund and Tollison (1981); Krueger (1974); Haber, Razo, and Maurer (2003); North, Summerhill, and Weingast (2000); North, Wallis, and Weingast (2009). The ensuing passages draw almost entirely from this literature.

Scartascini 2012; Calomiris and Haber 2014, especially p. 74; and Haber, North, and Weingast 2008). Directed credit to large conglomerates that can be taxed at low cost can serve a similar end (Menaldo 2016). Governments can also tax financial transactions and levy similar fees and "fines" to raise revenues.

Finally, another strand of literature that also roughly falls under the neo-mercantile label, and that has influenced this book, is work by Phil Keefer and collaborators on how policymakers in developing countries are forced to compensate for "credibility deficits" when it comes to pursuing political and economic objectives (see Keefer 2004; 2008; Keefer and Vlaicu 2007; Keefer and Vlaicu 2008). When politicians inherit political parties that lack reputations for providing programmatic policies centered on the provision of public goods, they are instead relegated to a default, ultimately unwanted, position. To survive politically and raise revenues, they must promote clientelism and indulge in corruption. Although patronage is not governments' first preference, in most cases in the developing world, it may be their only resort. If they are starved for credibility, it is their remaining comparative advantage in the political marketplace.

The consequences are grave. This strategy may make it more likely for nascent democracies to backslide into autocracy instead of consolidate, for civil wars to break out instead of conflict be reconciled via institutionalized political competition, and for countries to fall prey to an underdevelopment trap.

The factor endowment approach

This book has also been strongly influenced by the factor endowment approach to institutional origins. This literature is exceedingly creative and quite fertile, if readers will forgive the pun!

Acemoglu, Johnson, and Robinson (2001) argue that differences in disease environments due to climate in former European colonies explain contemporary differences in the property rights institutions. In turn, these institutional differences explain economic development today. Their practical aim is to use initial settler mortality rates to instrument for these institutions, to establish a causal relationship running from institutional quality to per capita income.

Engerman and Sokoloff (1997) spell out a similar path-dependent mechanism to explain contemporary institutional differences between countries. In Brazil, the West Indies, and several Latin American countries, soils and climates are ideally suited for growing cash crops with economies of scale such as sugar. After Columbus's arrival, the Portuguese, Dutch, and Spaniards set up large plantations and imported West African slaves to work on them. Similarly, in most of Spanish America, large-scale estates and mines were granted to a privileged few European explorers. These "conquistadores" then settled in the urban areas inhabited by Amerindians and exploited large pools of native labor. Spanish elites replicated the tribute system used by the Aztec and Incan Empires, forcing indigenous men, women, and children into indentured servitude.

Extreme disparities in wealth and human capital between white landowners and slaves and servants then took hold as colonists set up institutions to protect their privileges and repress the mass of the population. And, after independence, elites refrained from extending anything beyond token political or economic rights to the mestizos, Native Americans, and black slaves who inhabited Portuguese America, the Caribbean, and Spanish America. Indeed, caste systems relegated these peoples to the bottom of the social pyramid and elevated whites to the top of it. Social stratification was reproduced through restrictions on the franchise, repeated land grabs by the rich, and the total absence of public education (see Mariscal and Sokoloff 2000; Sokoloff and Zolt 2007).

Things were quite different in Canada and the United States. There, climates and soils were not conducive to cultivating sugar and other cash crops at large scales; moreover, indigenous populations were sparse. The resulting societies were composed of mostly white settlers who usually immigrated as families and were evenly matched in terms of educational attainment and political sophistication. These families secured titles to small and medium-sized farms dedicated to growing wheat and similar cereals.

After independence, elites in Canada and the United States were forced to bargain with educated citizen-farmers. The latter became increasingly adept at securing a larger share of political power and policies that promoted a more level economic playing field. While the federalization of fiscal authority and local provision of public education and infrastructure broadened the distribution of human and physical capital, an expanding franchise and open access land regimes ensured that equality would also prevail in the Western states and provinces. Incentives for entrepreneurship, such as a patent system that rewarded innovation, also helped to underwrite upward mobility. So too did the fact that the frontier was opened up to migrants who moved to the United States and Canada in droves in exchange for secure titles.

Many of these claims have been ratified empirically. Easterly (2007) shows that countries where land is more suitable for wheat tend to have smaller parcels of agricultural property run as family farms. More importantly, they are less unequal, more democratic, more liberal, more educated, and more economically developed today (see also Haber 2011; 2012a; 2012b).

In the next chapter, I will seek to broaden the geographical coverage of this approach to account for the political and economic history of Europe and the Middle East.[12] The most prominent generation of factor endowment theories outlined above attempt to explain variation among ex-European colonies; the most promising focus on the suitability of the soil for growing wheat versus sugar. However, these approaches also suffer from an important shortcoming. They ignore the types and role of factor endowments in places where the climate is unsuitable for either crop – a shortcoming I seek to overcome in the coming chapters.

Conclusion

In writing this book, I have benefited tremendously from several, seemingly disparate, literatures. My debts to works that fall under the neo-mercantile approach to political economy and the factor endowment explanation for institutional origins and survival are particularly big.

How does this matter going forward? Insights from neo-mercantilism will help anchor Chapter 4, which fleshes out the book's theoretical framework, and Chapter 5, which lays out how natural resource sectors may reflect a revenue-generation strategy in the race of high fiscal transaction costs. Indeed, it may not be an exaggeration to say that this book's key theoretical contribution can

---

[12] This book is not the first place where this extrapolation has been attempted. As I will discuss in the next chapter, other attempts include Easterly (2007); Haber (2011; 2012a; 2012b); Haber and Menaldo (2011b); Menaldo (2012); and Midlarsky (1998).

be restated as the effort to identify natural resource sectors as yet another example of neo-mercantilism.

But this is only possible if I can credibly establish a causal link that runs from weak state capacity to the creation of a natural resource sector. I do that by exploiting insights from the factor endowment literature in Chapter 5. I then show that once one properly neutralizes state capacity/institutional quality, the effect of natural resources on political and economic development is actually positive (Chapter 6). I also offer a twist on the factor endowment approach that helps me explain variation in development outcomes within the MENA while abstaining from fingering oil as the driving factor (Chapter 7).

In Chapter 4, I argue that *within* the Middle East, the driest countries are among the most developed today because of a history of tribalism tied to camel herding and involvement in long-distance trade. This is ironic. These places once lagged countries in which there were pockets of irrigated, settled agriculture and earlier state building. Therefore, the pattern observed in the Middle East is a departure from the general rule. While moderate rainfall is typically good for development because it is associated with wheat grown on small family farms and thus a more egalitarian social and political structure, pockets of agriculture in very dry regions rely on irrigation and thus do not give rise to these same outcomes. Meanwhile, and quite surprisingly, a history of pastoral nomadism has been generally good for liberalism – narrowly understood – although not democracy. It has proven supportive to the relatively benevolent monarchs who currently rule countries such as Jordan, Kuwait, Dubai, and Morocco.

Chapter 7 provides empirical evidence to support these claims about the Middle East.

4 | *The institutions curse theory*

Good institutions provide the means by which individuals can achieve personal security, improve their material welfare, and reach their potentials. Countries blessed by their institutions experience consistent economic growth and, in some cases, egalitarianism. The result is development in every sense of the word: liberal democracy, prosperity, and social flourishing.

Several channels help to link good institutions to these outcomes. They include the rule of law and checks and balances; honest and professional bureaucracies; economic policies that reduce transaction costs and foster competition; and the widespread provision of public goods. If these things are present, citizens tend to feel good about their personal safety and the safety of their investments, and enjoy greater economic opportunities. They will tend to trust each other and their governments, cooperate, and make continued investments in physical and human capital. The collective result is enduring political and economic development.[1]

We can use logical inference to deduce the vicissitudes of the institutions curse. Countries are cursed by their institutions when the rules of the game, and the shared beliefs and expectations that underpin those rules, produce outcomes that harm the majority of the population, if

---

[1] This does not imply that there are not groups excluded from these bounties in liberal democracies. Consider, for example, the continued marginalization of, and discrimination against, blacks in the United States, which has its origins in slavery. Nowadays, this takes the form of, *inter alia*, repeated attempts by some factions to curtail the franchise and rollback similar civil rights; still pervasive residential and institutional segregation; and aggressive policing practices and harsh correctional policies that disproportionately impact blacks. This goes on despite the Civil Rights Act of 1964, which officially ended segregation in the South and the horrors of Jim Crow, and subsequent attempts to dismantle lingering barriers to political participation and provide greater economic opportunities for blacks and other minorities. Similar examples are the Maoris in New Zealand, the Aboriginals in Australia, and marginalized immigrant groups from the developing world who live in Britain, France, Spain, the Netherlands, and Germany.

not portions of the ruling class. Citizens are forced to navigate between the Scylla of government predation and repression and the Charybdis of citizen-on-citizen predation and crime. Elites face a different, if not deadlier, set of challenges: coups, purges, show trials, and revolutions. The upshot is political and economic underdevelopment as trust, cooperation, and investments that promote productivity remain stillborn.

These insights, all inspired by neo-institutionalist political economy, suggest an important puzzle.[2] If institutions are the key to development broadly understood, then why don't all societies simply adopt good institutions? Why are the rule of law and liberal democracy not universal? Why are corruption, cronyism, and despotism – and thus underdevelopment – still so pervasive?

They also raise some tangible questions. Why did the initial emergence of private property rights, liberalism, and democracy take place in Western Europe – not in Central Asia or Sub-Saharan Africa? Why did these countries become more inclusive and egalitarian over time? Why was it possible to recreate Western Europe's institutions in some places and not others? Why did liberalism and democracy flourish in Canada, the United States, and Australia, for example, but failed to emerge in Tanzania and Jordan? Finally, why is there so much variation in the political strategies and institutions selected by leaders in the developing world? What explains why, in the MENA, a terrible tyrant like Saddam Hussein existed alongside a benign monarch like Morocco's Hassan II for the better part of three decades?

To address these questions and provide a foundation for endogenous natural resources, this chapter fleshes out the institutions curse theory. It is rooted in the fundamental premise that politicians do not pursue economic strategies for the sake of development. Rather, regulatory, tax, and trade policies are the handmaidens of *political* strategies. Elites' ultimate aim is to secure power, generate revenues, and lock in advantages that give them access to flows of income or rents. Political and economic development is sometimes the result of these efforts, but development is rarely explicitly intended.

---

[2] The literature on this topic is huge. A few noteworthy entries include: Acemoglu, Johnson, and Robinson (2005); Bueno de Mesquita et al. (2003); Calomiris and Haber (2014); Clague, Keefer, and Olson (1996); Lake and Baum (2001); North (1990); North and Weingast (1989); Olson (1993); and Weingast (1997). See Levi and Menaldo (2015) for the intellectual genealogy behind these contributions.

Why do political strategies systematically differ in ways that matter for development outcomes? Politicians face serious constraints. These vary systematically from society to society. Not every strategy is equally viable across all societies, as politicians inherit a chessboard in which the pieces are already arrayed in a particular way. Thus, they face a restricted set of possible moves consigned by preexisting moves they may not have made themselves.

The rules of the game, and attendant expectations about the future, are themselves byproducts of the political strategies adopted by past rulers. To be sure, politicians can sometimes modify the chessboard, rearranging the pieces as it suits them (see Haber 2007 for a similar analogy). But, even though elites constantly strive to modify the rules of the game to guarantee a more favorable distribution of resources and opportunities, the relative stickiness of institutions across time seriously impinges upon their ability to do so.

Institutions are sticky because they are characterized by "increasing returns." The structure of incentives faced by both elites and citizens favors a set of policies and behavioral strategies that then make status quo institutions more valuable. To elucidate: the incentive structure gives birth to regularized behavior, and regularized behavior, in turn, rewards the original incentives that gave rise to that behavior in the first place. It also forecloses alternative choices by raising the costs of doing things differently. This is the gist of a self-reinforcing equilibrium (see Pierson 2000; Greif and Laitin 2004).

This is especially – and ironically – the case when society's incentive structure is centered on economic distortions that create suboptimal outcomes.

On the one hand, actors embedded in cursed institutions develop a stake in perpetuating pathologies if they receive selective rewards – even if institutional reform would be better for the entire society. The winners from dysfunctional institutions are not usually able to engineer a way to internalize the future, lagged benefits of reforms undertaken in the present. They can definitely use their political power to secure the rents associated with today's suboptimal policies, however. The key point is that even if their rents are meager compared to the potential income they *could* earn in an alternative future, it is very difficult for elites to devise a novel, lasting way to capture these imagined benefits. Generating a larger share of the pie for themselves means creating a larger pie overall, which paradoxically requires elites to limit their own power and discretion. And a bird in hand is better than two in the bush.

On the other hand, even the losers from the status quo may unwittingly recreate those rules of the game, therefore perpetuating an institutions curse. Actors who lack political power may hedge against the worst consequences of the economic distortions engendered by those who wield power, and, in so doing, create new and worse distortions that only reinforce unfavorable institutions.

Take the following example. If financial repression is rampant because it creates rents for government officials and crony capitalists, thus reducing the rate of return on bank deposits and cash holdings, citizens may decide to hold their meager savings as gold. This will not only serve to crowd out investment, as gold is illiquid and usually not accepted as collateral, but if the gold is imported from abroad, this may aggravate a current account deficit. In turn, this will induce incumbents to ration foreign exchange, fueling smuggling and corruption. And this might make it even more enticing for governments to perpetuate financial repression in order to finance their operations.

Where does the institutions curse originate in the first place? This chapter argues that the proximate cause of the institutions curse is credibility problems and fiscal transaction costs. When incumbents find it difficult to consolidate power because they cannot make credible commitments, and because they face high transaction costs that make it next-to-impossible to raise regular taxes, they resort to a series of perverse policies. Although these policies introduce serious distortions and are economically inefficient, they make it much easier to consolidate power and raise revenues.[3]

This chapter also argues that the ultimate cause of the institutions curse is factor endowments. Historically, in places where a majority of the population was able to farm grains at a small scale, secure property rights emerged and were broadly distributed. Political rights soon followed. Both encouraged widespread investments in physical and educational capital to take place, and eventually fostered sophisticated legal and financial systems. In turn, this fueled economic growth and reinforced liberal democracy.[4]

---

[3] This notion builds on the neo-mercantilist literature outlined in the previous chapter.

[4] As outlined in the previous chapter, this follows a huge literature. It is worth recapitulating a few, key entries here, however: Acemoglu, Johnson, and

The theoretical framework fleshed out in this chapter also helps to explain why the rule of law, democracy, and economic development tend to go together. These things tend to be provided as a package of policies because they complement each other as political and fiscal strategies. But this is only under certain conditions. They are compatible in some societies, and in some circumstances, because they are the best way for political incumbents to make credible promises to their supporters and generate revenues. These circumstances are historically contingent, relatively rare, and rooted in geography and climate.

This chapter continues as follows. The first section introduces a few building blocks. I flesh out concepts such as institutions, property rights, and state capacity; I also explore how these variables interact. I then review the critical role that commitment problems and transaction costs play in conditioning politicians' strategies of power acquisition and the state's capacity to raise taxes and govern. The next section describes the elements that compose the institutions blessing and the institutions curse. The latter half of the chapter addresses the question of institutional origins and persistence. Drawing on previous research, I apply the factor endowments approach to Western Europe and the Middle East.

Conceptual building blocks

This section discusses institutions, property rights, transaction costs, the state, and the importance of credible commitments. These are building blocks that can help explain why some countries are cursed by their institutions while others are blessed by them. In other words, why there is so much cross-national variation in state capacity, the rule of law, and development.

Institutions 101

Institutions are the matrix of incentives, constraints, opportunities, and beliefs that represent the formal and informal rules of the game. Different rules of the game may regulate the behavior and expectations of individuals embedded across different families, organizations, firms, and societies.

Robinson (2001); Calomiris and Haber (2014); Easterly (2007); Easterly and Levine (2003); Engerman and Sokoloff (1997); Haber (2011; 2012a; 2012b).

Institutions structure individual choice by providing collective protocols, constraints, and expectations. In a quest to advance their objectives, individuals and organizations with different endowments and opportunity costs respond to the incentives, constraints, opportunities and beliefs imposed by an institutional structure. In this way, institutions condition individuals' strategies.

What is common among social groupings, both small and large, is politics; all institutions are therefore imbricated in political relationships where power is the coin of the realm. Institutions allocate power. The powerful actors who control institutions get to make collective decisions that affect both themselves and those with less power. That they distribute power in ways that are enduring makes them valuable and contestable.

Institutions tend to have sharp distributional consequences. Sometimes an institutional matrix is set up in a way in which the behaviors of those who govern are aligned with the best interests of the majority of those who are governed, so that distributional asymmetries are ameliorated. Other times, these actors' incentives are not aligned, and those in power rule in ways that maximize their power and advance their interests even if it seriously harms those who lack power.

What institutions are the most important?

There are two institutions that are particularly critical to understanding economic and political development at the national level. These are the market and the state.

Property rights are foundational. While the state plays a crucial role in sustaining property rights, preexisting property rights regimes also have wide-ranging effects on state capabilities. This is because property rights determine the size and sophistication of previous investments by creating markets for land, resources, labor, capital, goods, and services. By affecting the size, sophistication, and value of markets, these investments determine the transaction costs faced by politicians when they attempt to extract revenues from the economy.[5]

---

[5] This section draws heavily on Acemoglu, Johnson, and Robinson (2005); Calomiris and Haber (2014); North (1981; 1990); and Haber, Maurer, and Razo (2003).

Property rights are the laws, regulations, and norms that govern the ownership, use, and exchange of assets. Assets range from tangible property to abstract ideas. A property rights regime is the chorus of institutions and policies that (1) assigns and enforces titles to these assets and control over them, (2) governs their inheritance, and (3) codifies and regulates contracts.

While a property rights regime spells out rights, it also includes a body of property registers, bankruptcy law, and contracts. And it also encompasses the regulation of capital and labor markets, monetary policy, fiscal policy, and trade policy.

The reason all of this matters is because the ownership, control, transformation, and exchange of assets generates value – in the form of discrete income streams and rents. Property rights entitle agents to channel savings into investments and transform maturities: deploying liquid liabilities to finance illiquid and risky assets with longer horizons.[6] Those powerful enough to design and control the property rights regime also control the allocation of society's profits, power, and opportunities.

Transaction costs, property rights, and the state

In modern times, the state defines and enforces property rights, and thus creates (or ultimately destroys) markets. This is because an organization that enjoys a comparative advantage in coercion, if not an absolute monopoly, is best positioned to specify and enforce property rights. This is embodied in the Northian definition of the state (North 1981, p. 21): an organization with a comparative advantage in violence that extends over a geographic area with boundaries determined by its power to tax constituents and demand their obedience.

The state's power and authority also reflects the property rights regime – and thus markets – it inherits. This is because the transaction costs of exchange and taxation determine the size, shape, and complexity of both the actors and exchanges that make up an economy.[7] Laws,

---

[6] In this way finance is tantamount to declaring claims over the ownership of real resources and to securitizing against risk (Haber, Maurer, and Razo 2003; Haber, North, and Weingast 2008; Demirgüç-Kunt and Levine 2009).

[7] This claim derives from Coase's (1937) theory of the firm. His intuition is that firms with complex production chains have to decide whether to produce an intermediate good or service in house or buy it from the open market. When

regulations, and fiscal policies impact the liquidity, size, sophistication, and value of the markets where goods, services, and ideas are produced and traded.

What is state capacity?

It follows from this discussion that state capacity includes the writing of legislation, the administration of law, the monitoring of economic activity to secure compliance with regulations and taxes, and the judicial and policing power needed to enforce laws.[8] A state's fiscal and legal capacity also implies that credibility is an aspect of state capacity. Political actors who are strong enough to obtain power, codify rights, and enforce laws are also strong enough to withdraw these rights and abrogate the law.[9] Therefore, how a state convinces others that it will exercise restraint in these matters is critical.

Widespread political representation and an independent judiciary is one way to do this. These institutions allow a broader group of citizens to translate their preferences into policy and they moderate the political influence of the wealthiest and most powerful. However, this is far from the only way to accomplish this task. More typically, only a smaller subset of the population enjoys true rights.

Variation in state capacity is sizable

The bottom line is that there is wide variation in state capacity across each of the dimensions articulated above – a claim that I will empirically corroborate in later chapters. Many states still find it exceedingly

---

making this decision they face a trade-off. On the one hand are the advantages of specialization along the lines of comparative advantage, which militate against in house production. On the other hand are the transaction costs it faces when exchanging with other firms. If the latter are high, this militates in favor of keeping production within the firm.

[8] This notion therefore hues closely to Besley and Persson (2009). These researchers argue that there are two primary dimensions of state capacity. Fiscal capacity is (ibid., p. 6) "the necessary infrastructure – in terms of administration, monitoring, and enforcement – to raise revenue from broad tax bases such as income and consumption." Legal capacity is "the necessary infrastructure – in terms of administration, monitoring, and enforcement – to raise private incomes by providing regulation and legal services such as the protection of property rights or the enforcement of contract rights."

[9] This is known as the Weingast paradox after Weingast's seminal articulation of the puzzle. See Weingast (1995).

hard to penetrate the hinterlands, establish a monopoly on the use of force, and govern and tax effectively. Most states are unable to make credible commitments to a majority of their citizens, and thus cannot protect property rights inclusively. They are unable or unwilling to erect professional bureaucracies and impartial judiciaries. For this reason, state capacity is intimately linked to institutional quality.

To be sure, most every state today has a judicial system, as well as regulatory and tax bureaucracies. Yet professional jurists who make impartial decisions based on preestablished rules are the Weberian exception that proves the Huntingtonian rule. Courts and bureaucracies across the developing world remain patrimonial and incompetent. Law enforcement is politicized for the benefit of the few.

A theory of property rights regimes and state capacity

What explains variation in state capacity? Why do so few states embody the Weberian ideal? Commitment problems and transaction costs impinge upon property rights and contract enforcement; they also condition the state's ability to tax the economy. Laws, regulations, and public investments are attempts by politicians to figure out how to enhance their credibility and raise revenues in the face of thorny commitment problems and fiscal transaction costs.

The importance of the early stages of rule

All politicians who seek power face a set of problems that complicate their ability to consolidate that power. Each must assemble a coalition that can both launch them into power and staff their regimes (Albertus and Menaldo 2012a; Haber 2007). Because the members of these launching organizations (LOs) are strong enough to catapult a politician into power – whether it is because of their wealth, weapons, ability to mobilize co-ethnics, or association with a compelling ideology – they are also strong enough to oust her from office. This makes it difficult for a ruler to fully trust her LO.

The opposite is also true. The ruler is the chief threat to the members of the LO. She can withdraw their property rights. She can convene a kangaroo trial to rubberstamp trumped up charges against them. She can purge them from her cabinet or the military. She can order that they be killed.

The fear and uncertainty felt by members of the LO is compounded by the fact that there are a number of things that a ruler knows that her LO is not privy to. She has a better grasp of the costs of honoring her promises; by dint of controlling the security apparatus, she has knowledge about the true likelihood of resistance to her policies. Similarly, only she truly knows her level of risk acceptance, and she may have secret plans to throw caution to the wind and chart a new course that cuts the LO out of the deal.

Therefore, it is during the dawn of a new regime that LO members most fear that their rights and interests will be transgressed by the ruler. This is also a time when the LO is still powerful enough to reverse course, and withdraw their support from a new ruler. The early moves after a ruler is launched into power are therefore critical: the information they reveal about a ruler's intentions can make or break the new regime. The ruler's inability to quickly mitigate uncertainty may sow the seeds of distrust among members of her coalition and lead to her ouster – whether it take the form of a coup, vote of no confidence, impeachment, or a lost reelection bid.

Problems of credible commitment and fiscal transaction costs

After ascending to power, rulers must credibly commit to their LOs and members of the LO must credibly commit to the new ruler. Establishing trust in such a short order is difficult, however.[10] Institutions may still be inchoate, and neither party has an incentive to extend the benefit of the doubt to the other. A key to surviving in power therefore is for rulers to institutionalize commitments to members of their coalition.

There are many ways to do this. A common way for incumbents to do this across regimes is to regulate the economy for political gain. The manner in which incumbents regulate the economy differs, however, according to the distinct political and fiscal strategy they pursue. On the one hand, incumbents can design stable arrangements that create income flows through competitive markets underpinned by the broad distribution of property rights and perhaps also redistribute some of the growing surplus catalyzed by a productive economy. On the other hand, incumbents can design a stable rent-sharing

---

[10] See Albertus and Menaldo (2014) and Cox, North, and Weingast (2013) for evidence of how tenuous it is for executives to survive in office; average durations after 1950 are less than one year.

arrangement and engage in aggressive redistribution, albeit a variety usually not linked to improvements in economic productivity.

What is the role of fiscal transaction costs? No matter which of the above described arrangements they choose, new incumbents must quickly find a way to tax their economies to generate revenues. It is expensive to consolidate authority, run the country, and line their supporters' pockets. Moreover, rulers face costs to taxing their economies. These costs deeply affect their survival strategies and the economic policies they deploy to reach their objectives.

The fiscal transaction costs faced by rulers are heterogeneous.[11] One set is forensic. It includes the costs of identifying taxpayers' wealth, income, and salaries; of verifying tax obligations; and of conducting audits on tax returns. Another is related to projecting a credible threat of sanctions in retaliation for tax evasion. Yet another is administering tax laws.[12]

The most important fiscal transaction costs, however, are those that are inherited: they are the fruits borne by previous investments made by previous incumbents in sustaining markets and bolstering state capacity. When property rights have been secure for a larger number of citizens and for longer time periods, a more valuable and diversified economy will develop. It will be characterized by more intensive, sophisticated, and valuable economic activities. It will house a greater number of firms that conduct exchanges with other firms in open markets.

For tax agents, this is great news. Networks of horizontally organized firms and individuals participating in the formal economy are like bulging green veins that are easy to spot and easy to tax. The income, profits, and capital gains they produce generate a paper trail recorded through transactions in domestic banks. Modern firms operating in the formal sector produce salaried jobs, regular payrolls, and tax withholding. They regularly process accounts receivables and accounts payable. All of these features make individuals and firms' taxable obligations much easier to monitor, making it much less likely that

---

[11] See Levi (1988) for the seminal treatment of this concept and its importance to consolidating power.

[12] Of course, taxpayers also bear costs when satisfying the demands of the tax authorities. These include expenses related to record keeping and accounting; costs of acquainting themselves with their fiscal obligations and the penalties involved; and fees paid to professional tax advisors.

they will fail to submit self-assessed tax returns. Similarly, they should be less likely to claim fraudulent exemptions and deductions.

Conversely, when property rights have historically been specified and enforced for only a privileged few, then a more rudimentary economy evolves – one with anemic, barely visible, veins that are much harder to tax. This means a less sophisticated economy with a dearth of formal economic activities. If populations are poorly educated, rural, and are remunerated by in-kind payments, then this exacerbates the already high fiscal transaction costs endemic to these economies. The invasive, costly procedures that would be required to successfully conduct progressive, direct taxation, or even indirect taxation through value added taxes, are foreclosed.

What is the institutions blessing?

The purpose of the preceding discussion is to contextualize the twin dilemmas that all incumbents face. They must credibly commit to their supporters while also finding a way to tax their economies. Yet, while all rulers must consolidate political power and raise revenues, some have the luxury of doing so in a liberal order characterized by widespread investments and firms conducting exchanges on horizontal markets.

In a society blessed by its institutions, property rights and civil liberties are secure for a relatively large number of citizens. The broad provision of public goods reduces transaction costs. This means that the commitment problems and fiscal transaction costs that politicians inherit are relatively manageable. This allows politicians to peacefully assemble large coalitions on the basis of cross-cutting cleavages.

On the back of these inclusive coalitions, politicians double down on policies that promote public investments and minimize economic distortions. If there are elections and checks and balances, this ensures that incumbents develop a self-enforcing commitment to welfare enhancing policies (see Olson 1993; McGuire and Olson 1996; Acemoglu and Robinson 2006). These democratic institutions punish clientilism, cronyism, and corruption.[13] They reward governments for delivering

---

[13] Although see Albertus and Menaldo (2014), Keefer and Vlaciu (2008), and Calomiris and Haber (2014) for why democracy is not sufficient for bringing about outcomes desired by the median voter.

public goods and other programmatic policies.[14] They favor the provision of inclusive property rights by the state. They also motivate it to solve market failures, both mitigating negative spillovers and encouraging positive ones. This includes reducing pollution, ameliorating credit market imperfections, and providing intellectual property rights that incentivize research and development in light of the free rider problem that afflicts the production of new ideas, inventions, and innovation when fixed costs are high but marginal costs are negligible.

Taken together, these incentives encourage citizens to exchange goods and services on open markets, as well as make investments that bolster productivity. Widespread gains from trade and specialization along the lines of comparative advantage blossom. A plethora of specialized firms emerge and are organized horizontally. Individuals and firms make physical and human capital investments that augur payoffs over long horizons.

Lending and borrowing money also predominates, as does securitizing against risk on highly liquid markets governed by prices, not politics.[15] Depositors, savers, investors, and bankers are placated by the fact that other interested parties and the government will not confiscate or devalue their holdings. Majority shareholders refrain from exploiting information asymmetries and other advantages that allow them to tunnel the assets of minority shareholders. The government likewise refrains from expropriating deposits, savings, and investments (see Keefer 2008, p. 126). Bankers are able to repossess the collateral posted by debtors if they fail to pay back their loans.

The upshot is a sizable, liquid, and sophisticated financial system. A ready supply of retail banking and capital matches the demand for credit. Capital is priced by market mechanisms and flows to its most productive use. Bankers lend more readily because they have confidence that they will be repaid and investors invest because they trust that future profits will be forthcoming. Financial intermediaries compete to underwrite a healthy public bond market.

---

[14] To be sure, there are alternative ways of accomplishing these outcomes besides liberal democracy. Prominent example are autocratic city states such Singapore and Hong Kong. These alternatives are less reliable, however, because they are less effective at offsetting concentrations of power and underwriting credible commitments to inclusive coalitions. Nor are they very effective at protecting the rights of minorities. See Haber, Razo, and Maurer (2003) and Olson (1993).

[15] This section draws closely on Haber, Razo, and Maurer (2003) and Haber, North, and Weingast (2008).

Reduction in fiscal transaction costs

The bottom line is that financial development of this sort reduces the costs of taxing the economy.[16] It allows the tax base to deepen and reduces the marginal costs of tax administration. Broad participation by citizens and firms in the financial sector makes it easier for the government to tax income, payrolls, profits, and capital.

When citizens and businesses conduct their transactions in the formal economy and rely on the banking system to save and transact, they generate a record of transactions that the tax authorities can use to secure compliance with taxes, especially if they are self-assessed – income and property taxes, for example (Gordon and Li 2005; Reizman and Slemrod 1987). The existence of a financial paper trail allows the tax authorities to identify wealth, income, and salaries. It also allows them to verify tax obligations and conduct audits on tax returns. The upshot is that they are able to develop a credible threat of sanctions that deters tax evasion.

Finally, public goods such as reliable transport and power, and adequate telecommunications networks, also make it easier for the state to identify and collect taxes in this context. Their widespread provision also produces compliance spillovers. Citizens are motivated to contribute to the treasury because tax compliance is rewarded with tangible benefits: roads, schools, and public safety (see Levi 1988; Alm, Martinez-Vazquez, and Schneider 2004).

What is the institutions curse?

The institutions curse refers to a scenario in which politicians' commitment problems are thorny and the fiscal transaction costs they face are serious. This is usually because of a set of interconnected pathologies. Countries cursed by their institutions suffer from revenue shortages and macroeconomic crises associated with balance of payments problems and chronic budget deficits. These problems are exacerbated by the fact that governments face onerous costs of borrowing. Executives' inability to credibly commit to repaying their debts increases the risk premiums demanded by investors.

---

[16] A country's financial sector has been found to be a critical driver of long run economic growth (see Beck et al. 2000; Fisman and Love 2003; Levine et al. 2000; Rajan and Zingales 1998).

What are governments to do when they are faced with this predicament? On the one hand, they may try to extend a credible commitment to insiders by engineering a process that makes it difficult – if not suicidal – for them to betray their small but dangerous launching organizations. On the other hand, they may turn to several creative ways of regulating the economy to generate easy-to-collect revenues.

One predictable response by politicians who aim to consolidate power and raise revenues in difficult ecosystems is to enshrine laws and practices that distribute political power narrowly and make it easier to create big firms and similar organizations that can be more easily taxed. The politicized generation and distribution of rents is one way to kill two birds with one stone. On the one hand, it may create a revenue base where one is entirely absent. On the other hand, it may cultivate loyal political supporters who come to rely on politicians for their livelihood.

The strategic cultivation of a natural resource sector represents one of several options available to politicians seeking to survive when fiscal transaction costs are high and it is hard to credibly commit to a large group of supporters. The state can, alternatively, operate "fiscal monopolies" dedicated to the production of inelastic goods and services such as salt or spirits. Or it can impose steep tariffs on trade and step up its presence in the country's ports and borders to collect them.

In modern times, besides deliberately creating natural resource industries from scratch by exploring for, producing, and taxing minerals, oil, and natural gas, states have also sought to industrialize their economies via crony capitalism. I describe that model below, and return to natural resources later, in the following chapter.

Industrialization via crony capitalism

Industrialization is not necessarily launched to engender economic development via a big push, as argued by scholars such as Gerschenkron (see Haber 2006). Rather, this is an excellent strategy for consolidating power and raising revenues when incumbents find it hard to credibly commit to a large set of private actors and fiscal transaction costs are high. In ministration of this political-fiscal strategy, the state also tends to engage in politicized finance and raise revenues via seignorage and similar techniques.

Politicians may erect barriers to entry in the supply of capital, goods, and services, with the express intent of rationing their supply and generating monopoly profits. This can be paired with protectionist policies and macroeconomic policies that favor manufacturing over agriculture.[17] Incumbents may then seize a portion of those profits via entry fees/charters/licenses, taxes, and reserve requirements.

Because these represent methods of virtually frictionless taxation and are often opaque, they are particularly attractive to politicians who face the institutions curse. Monopoly rents are easy to tax because profits are voluntarily revealed by firms in exchange for monopoly rights. Depending on the demand for the products they affect, they are potentially large. They can also be redistributed quite easily – from unorganized consumers and farmers, for example – to secure political loyalty among those who are organized and have large stocks of weapons or other politically valuable assets.

This strategy is usually paired with the creation of a purposely small and politicized financial sector. Incumbents achieve this state-of-affairs by restricting the supply of capital. For example, policymakers may curtail bank charters and award them to political insiders who then artificially ration credit to widen the spread between the interest rates they pay on savings deposits and what they charge for business and consumer loans.[18] The government can then extract a share of these rents for itself via a variety of eminently creative methods (see Calomiris and Haber 2014).

How do rulers make these rent-generating and rent-sharing arrangements credible? One way is to construct interlocking directorates. On the one hand, politically privileged firms are staffed with government officials who have special access to the executive branch and regulatory bureaucracies. On the other hand, the heads of politically privileged firms run key government agencies (see Haber, Maurer, and Razo 2003; Razo 2008). This scenario can help enforce an "exchange of hostages." Government protected monopolists can threaten to withhold taxes and credit from the government if it ever attempted to dismantle barriers to entry that curb competition and

---

[17] The previous chapter identified various works that describe this phenomenon.
[18] The barriers to entry in the supply of credit widen the spread on interest rates, the primary source of profits for financial institutions. They also allow elites to enjoy human capital premiums.

produce rents. For its part, the government can threaten to withdraw abnormal rates of return if monopolists attempt to pilfer the government's rent share.

How crony capitalism becomes a self-reinforcing equilibrium

While the system of crony capitalism outlined above can stoke inflation, macroeconomic imbalances, and the underutilization of labor, its ultimate result is much worse. Ironically, and perversely, while it is usually a response to high fiscal transaction costs and credibility problems, it raises fiscal transaction costs and foments chronic underdevelopment. This often makes it even harder for incumbents to credibly commit to a larger share of the population and incentivizes them to double down on a game of narrowly distributing the benefits of a shrinking pie to loyal supporters who will kick back revenue to them. In other words, this is a self-reinforcing equilibrium.

Without the security of property rights to their savings and capital, most households and firms eschew productivity-enhancing investments centered on education and technological diffusion. The fear of government intervention, coupled with the absence of secure property rights to collateral, makes arms-length loans risky (see Hoffman et al. 2007, pp. 39–41). Therefore, the firms that do participate in the formal sector are too few in number, too large in size, and painfully inefficient.

Moreover, rulers who manage to survive in countries cursed by their institutions are usually too distracted by more immediate concerns to indulge in investments that will enhance state capacity. For this reason, governments will find it increasingly difficult to penetrate the hinterlands, establish a monopoly on the use of force, and govern effectively. The consequence is that the tax base remains perpetually small and hard to tax. Trust in the government erodes further, making it even harder for the tax authorities to elicit compliance with taxes.

Clearly, bad institutions tend to recreate themselves over time. Incumbents who find themselves encircled by both their inability to make credible promises beyond a small launching organization and the ever escalating costs of taxing the economy can only respond as they know best: they will continue to make targeted promises to a narrow coalition and to double down on crony capitalism to finance the government.

How this theory differs from the fiscal contract paradigm

Before exploring where institutions come from, it behooves me to restate how the institutions curse theory differs from the theory that undergirds the resource curse, the so-called fiscal contract paradigm. To be sure, my theoretical framework and the latter share a few similarities; both attempt to make sense of the fact that state capacity, democracy, the provision of public goods, and economic development often go together. Yet, this book ultimately does not accept most of the premises or conclusions of the fiscal contract paradigm.

Several of the key points advanced in this chapter contrast sharply with the fiscal contract approach that undergirds the resource curse view of development. The ruling group is not a unitary actor. Elites are riven by conflicts of interest and informational asymmetries. These are decisive in driving fiscal and economic strategies and, ultimately, differences in political and economic development. Citizens suffer from collective action problems and usually need to be mobilized from above. Above all, and unlike the fiscal contract paradigm, this chapter has advanced an elite-centered framework.

What is the upshot of these differences? This book avers that the interests of, and incentives faced by, elites, and not citizens, is what usually matters most for explaining the causes and consequences of natural resources. More broadly, how conflicts between elites are resolved and how their solutions interact with fiscal transaction costs are the key to what types of industries will materialize and how efficiently they will be run, in particular, and whether development is promoted or not, in general. The fiscal contract paradigm, by contrast, puts bargaining between rulers and citizens at the heart of political and economic development, and thus predicts that natural resources interrupt an otherwise "frictionless" process in which democracy and public goods that promote a diversified and valuable economy are exchanged for tax revenues.

A theory of institutional origins and persistence

Where do bad institutions come from in the first place? Why do incumbents in some countries always seem to inherit a chessboard in which the pieces are set up for them to struggle because they make it very hard for them to credibly commit to supporters and raise revenues, while others never seem to lose their Queen in a gambit, or even a Horse, let alone allow themselves to be checkmated?

To arrive at answers to these questions, it is helpful to first consider an important set of stylized facts. The early adopters of representative government and liberalism have tended to be literate family farmers who practiced self-government at the local level. While colonial New England is certainly the paragon, there is a plethora of other examples that also fit this model. They include Ancient Athens, seventeenth-century Holland, England and Switzerland after Charlemagne, and nineteenth-century Sweden, Canada, Australia, New Zealand, and South Africa. They even include France before the 1789 Revolution. Conversely, in places like the Middle East, where there were no family farmers to speak of, tribalism, hereditary demarcations in status and wealth, and illiberal authoritarianism predominated.

Writing about the connection between rainfall and democracy, Midlarsky (1998) provides a clue that can help us make sense of these examples (p. 496):

A third reason for identifying rainfall or precipitation as a basis for democracy is the ability of individuals to escape from a despotic authority and establish a more egalitarian and democratic society. Without the necessity for a central distribution network either of food or water, communities can be established independent of any central authority. As a consequence, norms of egalitarianism and democracy can develop that would be difficult to assimilate into an authoritarian system. Local precipitation becomes the basis for community agriculture and establishing [...] "open" communities in England as an "egalitarian structure" and a "worrying degree of independence" from the perspective of the prevailing political authorities.

I draw inspiration from this passage, as well as the factor endowment approach to institutional development. The latter argues that differences in climate, soil quality, and the size of native population across the Americas during European colonization gave rise to vast differences in the distribution of physical and human capital. In turn, these differences explain contemporary variation in institutions.

Before going forward, let me make clear that I do not mean to assert that all good institutions and outcomes always go together. Instead, my goal in this section is to attempt to shine light on why they are highly correlated in practice, while also accounting for important exceptions. In fact, in this chapter and in Chapter 7, I will argue that in the Middle

East there are many places that have experienced salutary developments despite lacking endowments that have generally been associated
with "good institutions."

Extending the factor endowment approach

As it is usually constituted, the factor endowment approach focuses on
a narrow set of former colonies – most typically, the countries that
make up the Americas. It therefore excludes Europe and the MENA.
Does the factor endowment approach hold beyond the Americas? Does
it apply to the European colonists themselves? What about places that
were ignored – or only lightly colonized – by European powers? Does it
hold for places that were inhospitable (e.g., the Arabian Peninsula)?
Conquered by hegemonic neighbors (e.g., Turkistan, which was
absorbed by Russia)? Remained outside of the colonial system because
they served as buffer states (e.g., Thailand)? And how about those
places that remained sovereign because they successfully resisted colonization (e.g., Japan)?

In this section, I build on recent research to argue that the factor
endowment framework can indeed be extended to the European
colonial powers themselves and places in which European influence
was much less pronounced and belated.[19] I focus particular attention
on European state development and the political and economic history of the MENA and bring both of these regions back in to the study
of the deep geographic determinants of development. In this way,
my approach echoes not only a select few recent works but also
Montesquieu's Spirit of the Laws, Wittfogel (1957) and Midlarsky
(1998).

Like previous authors who have embraced the factor endowment
framework, I assume that climates, levels of precipitation, and soils
have a big impact on institutions. The sequence is as follows. First,
climate determines what types of crops can be cultivated, and at what
cost. Second, the features and economics of different crop types affect
the organization of agriculture. In turn, this strongly conditions the
distribution of assets, power, and income, which then maps onto

---

[19]   These include, but are not restricted to, Easterly (2007); Easterly and Levine
(2003); Haber (2011; 2012a; 2012b); Haber and Menaldo (2011b) and
Menaldo (2012).

institutions. A broader distribution of political power and economic opportunities provides incentives to a majority of individuals to specialize along the lines of their comparative advantage and engage in trade. The acquisition of specialized skills reflects secure property rights to physical and human capital. As a final step, the initial distribution of power and resources is reinforced by the policies that flow from distinct institutional constellations.

I also introduce some modest innovations to the factor endowment approach. First, I argue that, like in the United States and Canada, European state development was also driven by the political and economic legacy of cereals produced on moderately sized family farms. Second, I theorize that extreme aridity, animal husbandry, and incentives and opportunities to broker long distance trade are just as important as crop types and the size of agricultural plots in explaining development patterns. These variables influenced levels of political centralization, strategies of rule, and political cultures in the MENA. Either irrigation-based agriculture favored a feudal state building system that culminated in today's repressive republics, or the lack of settled agriculture favored nomadic pastoralism and monarchy.

Moreover, unlike the previous generation of factor endowment theorists, my approach to institutional origins is less deterministic and non-linear. It allows for intervening factors to condition the relationship between climate and development. Most particularly, my spin on the factor endowment approach gives political culture a big, mediating role within the transmission channel that links geography and climate to political and economic institutions. On the one hand, the social structures from which political cultures emerge are themselves a product of the economic structures favored by distinct factor endowments. On the other hand, these political cultures can take on a life of their own and rely on certain ideational contexts and peculiar social networks even after the salience of geography and climate has long receded into the background. These ideas are shared by elites, who inhabit social networks that spread and reinforce these ideas. In this way, the elite-centric nature of the theoretical framework advanced in this book helps breathe new life into the factor endowment approach.

The MENA is the best example of this. There, tribalism had a big role in driving surprising connections between levels of rainfall and political and economic development. Unlike the vast differences in precipitation between Western Europe and the Middle East, differences within the MENA do not follow a neat, linear script from agriculture to modernity to liberalism. In other words, at very high levels of aridity, increases in precipitation do not tend to map onto better institutions and thus better outcomes. This is because, in the MENA, the islands of settled agriculture that cropped up in the region's vast deserts did not give birth to a political culture that could harness farming towards the precursors of liberalism and democracy. This differed from what happened in Western Europe.

Another way to put this is that there is a threshold effect and it operates through political culture. To be sure, and true to the general pattern, the places that developed state capacity and modern institutions more quickly within relatively arid regions such as the MENA did so because they were the site of pockets of settled agriculture. This mirrors what occurred in Europe. However, ironically, these islands of precociousness were also more likely to fall prey to authoritarianism and underdevelopment during the post-World War II era due to polarization and zero sum politics. In the case of Middle Eastern countries that are now republics, such as Egypt, a feudal system based on irrigation was erected and endured as an oligarchy, similar to some Eastern European countries.

The opposite was true of the monarchies. Yes, they developed state capacity much later due to aridity. Yet, rulers ultimately harnessed tribalism to create a more stable and, surprisingly, more liberal political and economic order. There, a history of tribalism – connected to extreme aridity and pastoral nomadism – has helped elites coordinate to discipline incumbents, contributing to relatively better outcomes today. A monarchic political culture evolved and now carries substantial bite. This aspect of the theory will be more fully fleshed out in Chapter 7.

The theoretical mechanism

Historically, in zones of moderate rainfall it was possible to grow cereals that are storable and that favor a modest scale of production. This fostered specialization and trade. It also represented low costs to assigning and enforcing property rights broadly, as a public good, instead of selectively, for privileged insiders. Zones of moderate rainfall therefore proved to be fertile ground for the growth of centralized states that standardized property rights, promoted liberalism, and practiced representative government. For these reasons, these zones have also stimulated economic development.

High aridity zones, by contrast, have favored a different state building model. It was not centered on public goods or private property rights for the many. State building was instead based on elitism, repression, and authoritarianism. These zones therefore failed to take off economically.

Why are specialization, trade, and the advent of inclusive property rights likely when rain-fed grain agriculture is preponderant? There are four reasons. First, small farmers can usually protect the claims to their moderately sized plots. Second, nobody owns the rain; thus, nobody has the ability to monopolize the water supply. Third, surpluses associated with grain agriculture can be captured, stored, and traded by individuals working alone or in small families. Fourth, political entrepreneurs have strong incentives to try to centralize political authority and heed the demand by farmers and merchants to extend standardized property rights over larger territorial domains, as well as extend other public goods.

Wheat, sorghum, barley, oats, and most legumes are storable and favor modest economies of scale in production. Indeed, both grains and legumes can be stored almost indefinitely because they have very low moisture contents and lie dormant after harvest. Farmers' ability to accumulate surpluses creates incentives to save, specialize, and trade.

The fact that cereals are suited to a moderate scale of production also matters. While it is certainly possible to produce these grains on a large scale, it has not been economically efficient to do so until the late twentieth century. This is for several reasons. It is impossible for a powerful actor to monopolize the property rights to water that is rain fed and it is therefore very difficult for a single actor to monopolize the property rights over land in this context. Moreover, since they are not harvested year round, but are instead subject to a discrete harvest season that requires the coordination of farm labor, cereals have not historically been characterized by economies of scale.

Before the twentieth century, family farms were operated with relatively low levels of physical and human capital. They required, on the one hand, access to a small plot of land, plows, and mules; access to multiple children who could help harvest in the summertime was also helpful. Beyond this scale, grain cultivation proved inefficient because labor monitoring costs did not obey decreasing returns to scale.

Historical experiments in which the production of cereals was attempted at a larger scale therefore only succeeded when those farms were geographically isolated or employed very costly systems of labor repression. For example, grains were grown in Rome by slaves working on latifundia (Haber and Menaldo 2011b, p. 25). When forced to compete against smaller and more efficient farms, those experiments usually failed.[20] As I will explain shortly, and as has been recognized by other scholars, this was the case in Germany, for example.

In the twentieth century, things changed. Technological advances in agricultural equipment and artificial fertilizers now promote economies of scale, but only *when high levels of physical capital are present.* If a farmer possesses tractors and combines, she can now farm much larger quantities of land at decreasing marginal cost.

By contrast, at low levels of precipitation, agriculture at any scale is next-to-impossible. Prolonged aridity damages the soil's fertility due to both chemical and biological processes. While most seeds do not germinate when planted in arid soils, those that do tend to wilt before they can reach maturity. In arid climates there is also an underlying dearth of cereals and animals, therefore reducing the odds of agricultural experimentation and domestication (see Hibbs and Olsson 2004, p. 3716).

In some arid contexts there is nonetheless the possibility of exploiting the moisture associated with fertile river valleys. This often calls for building and maintaining elaborate irrigation systems, which contrasts with rain-fed grain production in important ways. It adds a high degree of fixed costs: the canals and trenches needed to harness a river are quite expensive. This makes smaller farms economically infeasible. And while the control of water can offset these costs by serving as a barrier to entry in production, this favors solutions based on the use of coercive authority: ultimately, a powerful organization must find a way to physically control the banks of a river to block competitors from entering the market (see Haber and Menaldo 2011b; Haber 2012b).

The organization of agriculture has important effects on political institutions. The rain-fed production of cereals tends to culminate in

---

[20] Engerman and Sokoloff (1997) aver that experiments with large estates farmed by indentured servants in North America failed. These include attempts by William Penn in the United States and the Seigniorial System in Canada. The reason is that any settler could exit and set up her own farm. There was plenty of fertile land available for all to enjoy and economies of scale were not required to succeed.

state building centered on the provision of public goods and more pluralistic strategies of consolidating authority. Reliance on irrigation to produce crops tends to culminate in state building centered on patrimonialism and authoritarianism. Extreme aridity promotes nomadic pastoralism and the brokering of long-distance trade.

Political entrepreneurs have strong incentives to heed the demands for standardized property rights made by small grain farmers and the merchants who trade these agricultural surpluses as finished goods. Voluntary property rights enforced in a decentralized fashion are inherently unstable. In a self-enforcing property rights environment bereft of a strong central state, individuals are forced to defend their own, self-assigned property rights via the threat of violence.

This is not only inefficient but also ineffective and temporary (see Bates et al. 2002). According to Benson (1994, p. 146), centralized order and standardized property rights emerge when a political entrepreneur finds a way to credibly transfer wealth to his potential competitors. Subsequently, an "authoritarian protection racket" emerges and turns its attention to redistributing wealth to itself by extorting weaker citizens (see Bates et al. 2002; Benson 1990; Carneiro 1970; Tilly 1992). Eventually, however, wealth and power become distributed more evenly on the back of standardized property rights – codified, at first, for elites, but eventually extended to others.

Below, to set the stage for a comparison between Europe and the Middle East, I document the correlations between precipitation, grain agriculture, family farms, and contemporary political and economic development. These are logically implied by the theoretical mechanism outlined above.

Prima facie evidence

First, consider the global distribution of rainfall, as well as the relationship between rainfall and agriculture. The amount of precipitation that is most propitious for growing grains ranges from 540 millimeters of annual rainfall, the upper bound of a semi-arid climate following the Holdridge Life Zones classification system, to 1,200 mm, the lower bound of a rainforest climate, following the same system.

Map 4.1 showcases the average annual level of precipitation in a 50-mile radius around countries' largest cities between 1980

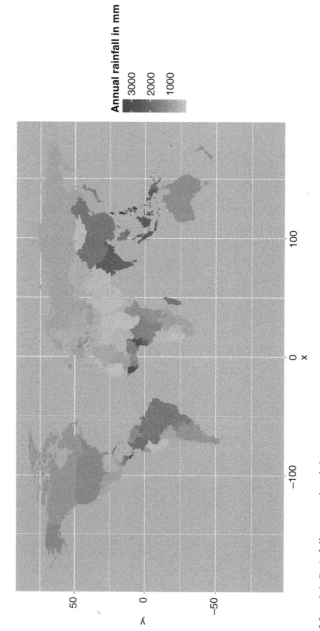

Map 4.1 Rainfall across the globe.

and 1989.[21] By focusing on the factor endowments of every country's largest cities, I can circumvent many of the problems that beset cross-national geographic measures for larger countries that have mixed climates, such as the United States. This is because, historically, the economic, political, and social developments that have shaped countries have occurred in or in the vicinity of countries' largest cities (see Haber and Menaldo 2011b). Institutions and policies have then radiated outward, eventually spreading out to cover the entire territory via state-building projects (see Herbst 2000).

The patterns revealed by this figure are striking. Most Western European countries and the black earth region stretching from Bulgaria through Romania and Ukraine into southwest Russia lie in the moderate rainfall band. The MENA looks like a veritable desert, albeit one interspersed with a few oases.

Map 4.2 graphs the ratio of land suitable for growing wheat to sugar, with higher values capturing the type of soils that are more propitious to growing grains.[22] There is an almost exact match between Map 4.1 and

[21] This is from the Global Historical Climatology Network Database version 2.0, available from the National Oceanic and Atmospheric Administration, National Climatic Data Center Accessible at: www.ncdc.noaa.gov/ghcnm/. The NOAA data include monthly readings from up to 14,907 weather stations across the planet. Rainfall is estimated by triangulation (weighting by distance) for any location in the world if that location does not have a weather station. Although the 1980–89 decade has the most weather station observations (> 10,000 weather stations around the globe), time-series graphs of the data for weather stations that have existed since the early eighteenth century do not evidence a significant trend. Time series regressions on the data for all weather stations reveal a trend rate of growth that is only 0.2 mm per year. Therefore, it would take 500 years for average rainfall to increase by just 100 mm. The fact that the basic distribution of precipitation across world regions has held since at least 800 BC (some climate scientists would say 5600 BC) means that we can reasonably extrapolate modern measurements back into the historical past. The results are not sensitive to the decade chosen. Similar results are obtained when using the NOAA precipitation data from the 1860s. Similar results are also obtained if 100-mile, 200-mile, and 500-mile radii are generated around countries' largest cities, as well as the entire country's territory.

[22] I follow Easterly (2007) and measure this variable as log((1+% land suitable for wheat)/(1+% land suitable for sugar)) because the land suitable for either or both of these crops is zero in some countries. I measure the arable land suitable for these crops within 50 miles of the country's largest city. Data on the arable land suitable for each crop come from the Food and Agriculture Organization (FAO) GAEZ (2002) dataset that considers measures of soil characteristics, such as moisture, temperature, chemical composition, depth, texture, and organic matter, a suitability index for a large number of crops. That suitability index (SI)

Map 4.2. This is partially because most of the countries that lie in the moderate rainfall band also exhibit moderate temperatures – summers are not too hot; winters are not too cold – and, on average, more than one-third, but less than 70 percent, of yearly rainfall falls in the hottest months.

There is also a high correlation between moderate rainfall, grains, and family farms. Figure 4.1 is a scatterplot that adduces a positive relationship between the ratio of land suitable for growing wheat to sugar and the percentage of agricultural land used as family farms in 1888.[23] In other words, more cereals means greater asset equality during the nineteenth century – a pattern that is also replicated in the twentieth century (no figure shown).

Additionally, consider that places where these attributes co-occur tend to exhibit liberal democracy. This includes most of Western Europe, as well as the United States, Canada, New Zealand, Japan, and South Africa. Across all of these places, and up until the nineteenth century, family farms tended to be the modal production unit for the vast majority of the population. Conversely, the world's persistently authoritarian regimes tend to lie in both of the rainfall extremes. They either inhabit the 0 to 540 mm precipitation band or the 1200 mm and above band. In either of these zones, settled agriculture has tended to take place on large holdings (e.g., Brazil) or feudalistic communes watered by irrigation (e.g., Iran).

Finally, and most importantly, factor endowments, working through the distribution of agricultural assets as instantiated by the proportion of family farms, explain variation in contemporary political and economic development. First, there is a strong, positive relationship between the ratio of land suitable for growing wheat to sugar and financial development, as proxied for by Private Credit by Deposit Money Banks as

is scaled from 0 (completely unsuitable for that crop) to 100 (the highest possible yield for that crop under rainfed conditions). This is done crop by crop, by parcel, on a global scale. Each parcel roughly corresponds to 36-mile by 36-mile squares. The parcel SIs are then used to compute, via triangulation, the average SI for each crop 100 miles in radius from the largest city.

23 I use Vanhanen's (2000) measure of 'Family Farms' computed as (area of family farms)/(total cultivated area or total area of holdings)*100%. A family farm employs no more than four people and the family owns and cultivates the land. The regression used to estimate the predicted line, along with those in the ensuing figures, is estimated via Ordinary Least Squares (OLS).

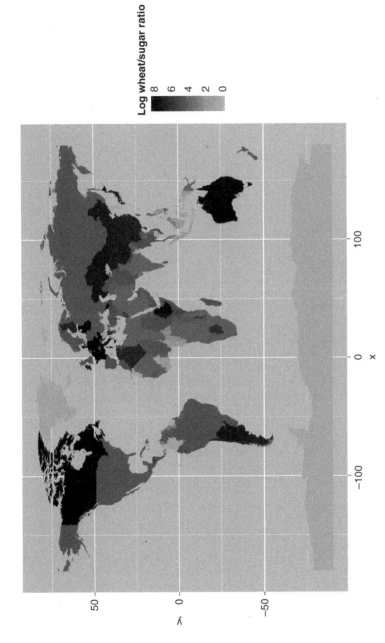

Map 4.2 Wheat-growing vs. sugar-growing regions of the world.

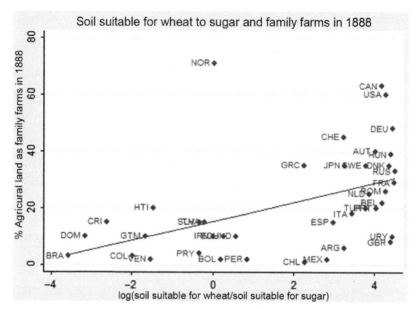

Figure 4.1 The relationship between wheat and moderately sized farms.

a percent of GDP (no figure shown).[24] An almost identical relationship exists between the agricultural land used as family farms in 1888 and financial development (no figure shown). Second, there is a negative relationship between the percentage of agricultural land used as family farms in 1888 and income inequality in 2005 (Figure 4.2).[25] Third, there is a positive relationship between the percentage of agricultural land used as family farms in 1888 and the quality of institutions in 2007 (Figure 4.3).[26]

[24] Private Credit by Deposit Money Banks as a percent of GDP, from the *Financial Development and Structure Database* is commonly used as an indicator of financial development (e.g., Rajan and Zingales 1998). The dependent variable is averaged between 2000 and 2006. The r-squared of the regression used to estimate the predicted line is 0.17; an increase of 1 percent in the ratio of land suitable for wheat to sugar is associated with an increase of about a 6.5 percentage point in private credit (% GDP).

[25] I measure inequality from the Standardized Income Distribution Database (SIDD). This Gini coefficient adjusts the raw UN WIID by standardizing differences in scope of coverage, income definition, and reference unit across countries.

[26] The Indicator of Quality of Government (IQOG) from the International Country Risk Guide is the average of the ICRG "Corruption," "Law and

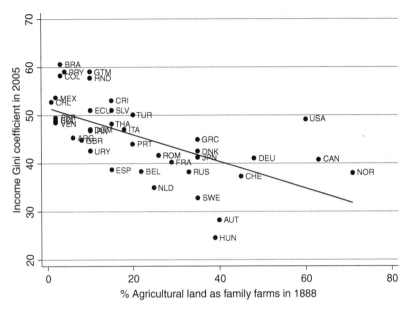

Figure 4.2 The relationship between moderately sized farms and income equality.

Western Europe's development

The story of how secure property rights for a majority of citizens and liberal democracy eventually spread across Western Europe is about political centralization. The first step in this process was the transition from tribalism to feudalism: increasingly specialized societies began to trade on a larger scale and at longer distances, therefore echoing the glory days of the Roman Empire. The second step was the transition from long-distance trade that depended on a voluntary system of property rights enforced in a decentralized manner to the centralized regulation and taxation of national economies. The final steps were the transition from absolutism to liberalism and, eventually, democracy.

Order," and "Bureaucracy" indexes, which are each based on investors' perceptions about the prevalence of corruption in the public sector, how professional the bureaucracy is, and respect for the rule of law. While each of these components is measured on a 6-point scale, the IQOG is normalized to run from 0 to 1, with 1 denoting the best institutions.

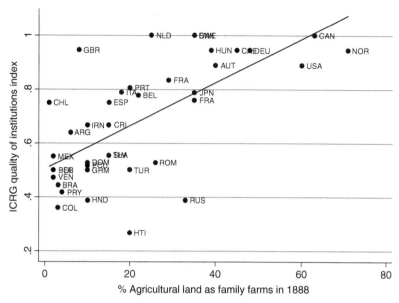

Figure 4.3 The relationship between moderately sized farms and institutional quality.

Agricultural booms and a European revival

After centuries of decline in aftermath of the Roman Empire's demise, in the twelfth century European agricultural production experienced a strong revival. This catalyzed increased trade at longer distances. This was, in a sense, a return to form, as grain surpluses had bankrolled empires and city states along the Eastern Mediterranean for millennia. Gradually, grain surpluses fostered increased specialization in what were once the western and northern peripheries of the Roman Empire.

What accounts for this agricultural and commercial revival? It was made possible by the fact that cereals such as barley, millet, and wheat were being produced at a modest scale, were highly storable, and were relatively broadly distributed. Soon, the continent was suffused with handicrafts, machinery, and weapons – developments that reflected a series of interlocking investments in physical and human capital.

Although these investments were awkwardly grafted upon a rapidly decaying feudal system, they also served to supplant it. In a relatively short order, the Balkanization of power that was ubiquitous during the

Middle Ages was replaced by centralized order imposed by some of the most effective specialists in violence to ever inhabit the earth. These experts at violence were skilled in the use of horses and armor and exchanged protection from marauding hordes for taxes. It is worth quoting Jacoby (1973, pp. 12–13) at length here:

> The fundamental reason for the existence of the feudal vassalic system was the defense of the established agrarian society [...] But it was precisely in the pursuit of its military tasks that the feudal system destroyed itself. An offensive weaponry improved with the use of armed cavalry and armor, and with the establishment of castles which aided defense, higher revenues were required. However, medieval agriculture was unable to increase production. The power and income of a seigneur could only be enlarged by the acquisition of new territory and demesnes. This led to constant struggles and feuds [...] At the same time, the development of an economy based on commodities began to displace the feudal nobility's authority. As soon as wealth ceased to consist only of landed property, but included money and goods, the nobility no longer had a monopoly of wealth. With the increase in the barter of goods and resultant demand, self-supporting agricultural economy no longer sufficed [...] The new principle of social survival and the new type of wealth developed along with towns. As their economic power grew, medieval cities tried to become independent of the feudal lords, to the point where they formed their own spheres of influence. The town became an independent municipal authority [...] In these medieval towns it was the business of the burgesses to concern themselves with the administration of finance, law, trade and crafts; they constituted that group of people from which government officials were later to evolve [...] The coexistence and conflicts of the feudal system's numerous small entities, and the social and economic contrasts which arose, promoted the growth of a third force, namely, the centralized authority of the state in the form of the monarchy.

Excursus on European land inequality

I have so far maintained that a relatively egalitarian, quasi-autonomous agricultural system spanned across Western Europe before 1500 AD – a contention that seems at odds with received wisdom about the distribution of assets, income, and consumption in this region of the world before the twentieth century. Indeed, many have argued that the kingdoms and principalities that populated the region after Charlemagne – who ruled between 768 and 814, and controlled territories in what is now France, Italy, Germany, Britain, and Spain – were characterized by a highly stratified society. This implies that an impoverished peasantry languished at the bottom of the social pyramid.

There is indeed some truth to the claim that land, income, and consumption opportunities were unequally distributed in Western Europe – but inequality only set in *after* 1500 AD. In fact, anthropological evidence adduces that European farmers across Northwest Europe were relatively well nourished and tall at the onset of the state building that redrew the continent's political map. While a majority of citizens had access to land, which mitigated poverty and promoted dietary diversity, low population densities helped to reduce disease.

This all changed at around 1600 AD, however. Steckel (2004, pp. 214–215) writes that:

It is noteworthy that average heights during the early and late Middle Ages exceeded by several centimeters those prevailing on the eve of the Industrial Revolution [...] Taking the evidence at face value indicates that average heights fell from about 173.4 centimeters in the early Middle Ages to a low of about 167 centimeters during the seventeenth and eighteenth centuries. This decline of 6.4 centimeters substantially exceeds any fluctuations observed during the various industrial revolutions of the nineteenth century. Recovery to levels achieved a millennium ago was not attained until the early twentieth century.

O'Rourke and Williamson (2002) corroborate this basic pattern and provide a mechanism. They show that land rents increased pronouncedly in Northwestern Europe between the sixteenth and nineteenth centuries. Specifically, rents per acre increased as population growth led to increasing population densities and decreasing land to labor ratios. Hoffman et al. (2002) help bring the same picture into sharper focus, arguing that consumption inequality increased in Western Europe during this same period; the purchasing power of the poor diminished as they faced higher relative prices for staple fuels and food while the wealthiest paid lower prices for luxury goods and services. Part of the reason for this change was an increased concentration of land in the hands of the rich, coupled with higher population densities.

I hasten to emphasize, however, that deepening population densities were in fact spurred by population growth, and the latter was made possible by the broad distribution of farmland and agricultural production surpluses.[27] Indeed, growing urbanization also reflected the advent of centralized states and the spread of capitalism. Furthermore, greater concentrations of land ownership were political innovations that required massively expensive systems of repression and labor control. They were never natural, economically efficient production modes.

Consider the large landholdings that emerged in Prussia and Eastern Europe after feudalism had run its course. Most of these estates arose during the so-called second serfdom. Pockets of feudalism did not reemerge because there were large economies of scale in growing grains. As the first feudal era came to a close, a free peasantry arose throughout Europe and worked quasi-collective landholdings. However, in the wake of the Black Death, which killed over 35 million people throughout Europe between the 1330s and 1600s, labor became scarcer. Consequently, serfdom made a comeback in Germany and Eastern Europe, where huge landlords introduced infamously repressive labor practices.

According to Moore (1966), the result was a political economy based on grain exports that bankrolled a militarized aristocracy. These landlords suppressed small farmers[28] and constituted the social force that drove fascism in the twentieth century. Moore, however, quite explicitly states that this quasi-feudalistic system was economically inefficient compared to the family farms that it replaced. It was precisely for this reason that repression was a necessary ingredient to make it work (see ibid., p. 437). It is also noteworthy that once Argentina and the American breadbasket became powerhouse exporters of grains, large European landholdings could no longer compete on the global market. They therefore went bankrupt in large numbers.

And perhaps most damning to Moore's view of the world, an emerging literature has actually shown that even at the height of rural inequality in Germany, during the twentieth century, the distribution of land was not as unequal as previously thought. Compared to other countries, it was indeed not that unequal after all. Following Grant

---

[27] This was made possible, in part, to several technological innovations that were introduced in the open field systems that typified the feudalistic method of political and agricultural organization. This included the wheeled plough, better field drainage, the modern harness, the triennial rotation of crops, the use of the horse, and the planting of legumes, which improved soil fertility. See Hechter and Brustein (1980).

[28] This was accomplished under a nominally representative government, however.

(2005), Mares (2015) shows that the level of landholding inequality is very sensitive to different indicators; that most indicators fail to actually capture this concept; and that when measured correctly, inequality was quite low. Moreover, she argues that Germany's rural inequality was concentered in only a handful of Eastern districts. Whether land inequality has also been exaggerated in the case of other European countries during this time period remains to be seen.

This view complements, and geographically expands, an earlier claim by Skopcol (1979), who drew on work by Landes (1969). She argues that, by the middle of the nineteenth century, the distribution of land was relatively egalitarian in Western Germany and across France. Peasants had been freed and possessed secure property rights to their land, including the right to transfer their deeds. Importantly, these lands were assigned and enforced by central governments that were in the throes of elbowing out nobles. Indeed, by that point the latter were living on fumes. In comparison to freeholders, who increasingly paid much more in taxes, erstwhile feudal landlords did not merit favorable treatment from the state any longer.

Finally, whatever the case, the degree – or, perhaps surprisingly, relative lack – of asset inequality in European nation states between 1500 and 1900 is a moot point. Even if it is the case that the carriages of European peasants were at some point turned into pumpkins, and their dresses into rags, our focus should be on the period before the clock struck midnight. The key issue is how relative equality spurred state building and economic development that may or may not have subsequently fueled new inequalities in land ownership, income, and consumption.

Standardized property rights and state building

The story is as follows. Factor endowments that favored grain agriculture at a moderate scale before 1600 AD led to the advent and consolidation of Western Europe's modern states. Centralized political authority arose through a process in which property rights became standardized as both rulers and the ruled sought to capitalize on increased trade and specialization bankrolled by grain surpluses. This then ushered in liberal democracy, which, ironically, helped to reverse many of the inequalities generated by increased urbanization (see Acemoglu and Robinson 2006).

The broader the distribution of a tradable surplus, the stronger is the incentive for farmers and merchants to demand institutions that protect property rights (Cox, North, and Weingast 2013; Vardy 2010). In the case of Western Europe, a broad swath of citizens sought to maximize, save, and trade agricultural surpluses. In turn, these surpluses underwrote investments in specialized skills. This phenomenon increased the stock and broadened the distribution of both human and physical capital writ large. It also intensified demands by farmers and merchants for both credit and insurance markets; both required reliable and standardized property rights.

Farmers demand credit as agricultural production becomes more capital intensive and also to hedge against risk. Consider that agricultural revenues only materialize several months after a farmer plants his crops, after grain has been harvested and sold on markets. This means that a considerable lag separates production and profit. Therefore, a farmer may have to borrow money to invest in seeds, fertilizer, oxen, and machinery.

Farmers also have a natural demand for insurance, of which access to credit to smooth consumption can form an integral part. This is because agriculture is inherently risky. It is usually subject to two serious threats: drought and pest infestations. If a farmer does not trust that she will be reimbursed for the losses she may incur due to the vagaries of the weather and disease, she will not plant the amount of seeds required to reach her potential yield. Indeed, a cottage industry in microeconomics has materialized around the idea that in the presence of steep transaction costs and market failures, farmers will engage in a high degree of precautionary savings.[29] What this means is that they will "overinvest" in assets in order to hedge against future income risks, allowing them to draw down those assets if a shock, such as a drought, occurs. Moreover, they will also hold an "inefficiently" large share of this wealth in the form of assets that can be converted to food with minimal transaction costs; in other words, in animals such as livestock.

A liquid and reliable insurance and credit market can, however, allow farmers to hedge against unforeseen crop failures without requiring them to hold "unnecessary wealth" or distort the form that these

---

[29] The literature on this topic is huge. As just one example, see Jalan and Ravallion (2001).

assets take. It will therefore underpin higher levels of consumption, more efficient investments that promote productivity, greater agricultural production and, indirectly, greater specialization and trade.

By the same token, merchants have a demand for credit and insurance too. They basically specialize in intermediating farmers' agricultural surpluses. If they are engaged in long-distance trade, they must pay for the merchandise that they are purchasing before they are themselves paid. To take the simplest example, suppose merchants serve as brokers between farmers' grain surpluses and a final customer. These merchants might only receive cash for these grains at the very end of a transaction, once the wheat and barley are already consumed. Yet the merchants must pay the farmers for their cereals upfront, perhaps months before they are actually sold. This means that they will require the services of a discount facility that can grant them an advance payment – after interest has been deducted (discounted) – so that they can make their grain purchases. Similarly, merchants will also want to insure against unforeseen problems associated with storing and transporting their products; these include fire, floods, and bandits.

Calomiris and Haber (2014) have shown how the demand for these services by merchants engaged in long-distance trade gave rise to the supply of financial institutions in Western Europe. They also argue that these were increasingly regulated, if not initially founded, by nascent states. Calomiris and Haber aver that over the course of the latter part of the second millennia A.D., larger and more centralized states in Western Europe took an active part in stimulating modern banking institutions in order to stimulate trade, finance their own fiscal operations, manage their finances, and underwrite imperial conquest. They trace the evolution of chartered banks in key European kingdoms as joint stock companies that introduced financial technologies such as debt annuities, bills of exchange, and the securitization of debt. In their story, chartered banks were the culmination of variegated efforts during the Renaissance by merchants to create and enforce debt contracts – usually through coordinated actions under the aegis of creditor cartels – made with sovereigns.

The supply of credit and insurance does not always automatically match its demand, however. Private providers of credit and insurance will only emerge to satisfy demands by farmers and merchants for these services when they themselves can count on their property rights being protected and on reliable contract enforcement. Both bankers and insurers are in the business of making very detailed and precise agreements that are characterized by significant time lags and involve the coordination of strangers at long distances.

Secure property rights were a prerequisite for the advent of modern credit and insurance markets for several reasons. As a start, farmers and merchants who wanted to borrow money to undertake costly investments and smooth consumption had to possess stable property rights to their land, machinery, storage facilities, livestock, and vessels. Only then could they collateralize their loans. Moreover, as Calomiris and Haber (2014) point out, bankers require steadfast contract enforcement and secure property rights. In order to invest in the pooling and deploying of capital, they had to have faith that sovereigns would repay their debts – since rulers were among their biggest customers – and not forgive the debts of politically influential private actors. They also had to have faith that rulers would enforce sophisticated contracts penned between merchants that underpinned markets for bills of exchange, which gradually supplanted specie as mediums of exchange.

The key question, therefore, is whether key parties have incentives to provide the secure property rights and enforce the contracts that are required to bring financial and insurance markets to life. Calomiris and Haber spell out *how* this occurred in Western Europe over the sixteenth, seventeenth, and eighteenth centuries, especially in Venice, the Netherlands, England, and Scotland.[30] Below I evaluate *why* this may have been the case.

The supply side logic of credit and insurance
Standardized property rights are a public good that is non-rival and non-excludable. Where do they come from? There are two possibilities. First, a stable property rights regime *can* emerge voluntarily and be enforced in a decentralized manner when there are repeated interactions between

---

[30] In the case of Scotland, they show how crucial financial innovations that blossomed in the middle of the eighteenth century were connected to a regulatory system that sought to stimulate competition in the banking sector – a deliberate political act. These innovations included interest bearing deposits, small denomination banknotes that circulated as mediums of exchange, jointly managed clearinghouses to exchange notes issued by different banks, lines of credit available to borrowers, and branch banking (see Calomiris and Haber 2014, p. 75).

private actors concerned about their reputations.[31] Acording to Greif, Milgrom, and Weingast (1994), this is precisely what occurred in Europe during the middle ages, before the advent of modern nation states.[32] Second, powerful actors may attempt to centralize political power and provide these public goods in exchange for tax revenues.

In the European case, political entrepreneurs had strong incentives to provide and enforce standardized property rights for farmers and merchants around 1500 AD. Specifically, the kings who had risen to the top of the social pyramid during feudalism faced relatively low transaction costs to taxing farmlands and the merchandise associated with their surpluses. Indeed, this was precisely because of the abundance of moderately sized farms distributed broadly among the general population.[33] Monarchs therefore began to offer clearer delineations of private property. While they undertook cadastral surveys and erected title registries, they also invested in the coercive tools needed to enforce claims and contracts. Tilly's (1992, p. 27) description of Sweden's state formation embodies this process.[34]

[T]he overwhelming presence of a peasantry that held plenty of land well into the eighteenth century [...] [coupled with] the relative inability of landlords either to form great estates or to coerce peasant labor on their lands. That exceptional rural class structure prevented the royal strategy of granting nobles fiscal and judicial privileges and assistance in bending peasants to their will in return for collaboration in extracting revenues and military service from the peasantry [...] It also helps explain the survival of a separate peasant Estate which actually had some power over governmental action, and the fact that in its period of imperial expansion Sweden turned

---

[31] This phenomenon has therefore been modeled as a repeated Prisoner's Dilemma; the so-called Folk Theorem proves that several cooperative equilibriums are possible. See Weingast (1997).

[32] However, and as these authors show, voluntary property rights arrangements based on repeated exchanges always rest on the existence of meta-institutions – in this case trade guilds and world trade centers – that are enforced through coercion (see, also, Skaperdas 1992, p. 732).

[33] Compare this to the high fiscal transaction costs faced by the Kingdom of the Kongo during the same period. It was characterized by a low population density and lacked widely distributed grain agriculture. In order to generate revenues, the political elites were relegated to capturing their own citizens and selling them to Portuguese traders as slaves (Haber and Menaldo 2011b, p. 23, citing Broadhead 1979 and Thornton 2001).

[34] The Swedish model was far more typical than exceptional, despite Tilly's use of the term.

rapidly from the hiring of mercenaries on the European market to the creation of militias whose members received land, or the income from land, in return for their service. In Sweden as elsewhere, the ambient class structure constrained rulers' attempts to create armed force, and therefore left its impact on the very organization of the state.

These activities incentivized kings to assess tax revenues in a more systematic manner. Previously, kings had relied on ad hoc tolls, custom duties, tax farming, and the sale of land and offices. Monarchs gradually replaced these scattershot tactics with a permanent and professional fiscal system. At first, kings relied on parliaments to extract revenues (Herb 2003, p. 2053). Eventually, a professional tax bureaucracy was erected to collect taxes permanently. Kings soon found themselves caught up in the mundane tasks of operating chanceries and training professional corps of tax assessors who needed to learn how to read and do math, and also expected taxpayers to be literate and numerate. Before long, therefore, monarchs also provided public education.[35]

Kings also began to provide additional public goods to farmers and merchants. As with permanent taxation, this reinforced property rights. These included a permanent police force, uniform weights and measures, a reliable currency, and a uniform legal code (North's 1981; 1990; Spruyt 1994).

As kings sought to standardize the metal content of coins and units of exchange – and monopolized coin minting – a rationalized monetary system also emerged. The advent of modern banking was concurrent with this phenomenon. Calomiris and Haber (2014) argue that as the scale of the state and its financing needs grew, European sovereigns also gained a strong incentive to enforce sets of contracts underpinned by novel legal principles such as limited liability and corporate governance. These fueled sophisticated financial exchanges that generated greater revenues by stimulating trade – increasingly across borders and oceans. They also held the promise of allowing rulers to better organize and collect public finances, secure new lines of credit, industrialize, and engage in economic engineering to advance different political, strategic, and economic objectives.[36]

[35] There was wide variation in the timing of tax professionalization, however. For example, in France monarchs continued to sell titles to nobles in exchange for revenues well into the seventeenth and late eighteenth centuries.

[36] This phenomenon was complemented by the wholesale reform of criminal law. Sovereigns standardized justice based on objective legal criteria, replacing

The advent of liberal democracy

How do farmers, merchants, and bankers ensure that their assets and incomes are not predated upon by a centralized state that grows to monopolize the business of standardizing property rights, security, and justice? In medieval Europe, merchants sought to preserve their independence and protect their property rights by creating walled towns that paid a local noble, or the king, for the right to autonomy. Eventually such physical barriers ran their course, however. They were replaced by self-enforcing restraints on government opportunism.

Many researchers have written about this phenomenon. North and Weingast (1989) argue that, similar to farmers and merchants, European states also sought to smooth consumption by securing access to cheap and reliable credit. Monarchs sought to inoculate economic growth from surprise increases in tax rates during wars or emergencies (see Schultz and Weingast 2003, p. 8; Root 1989, p. 241). To gain access to cheap and reliable credit, many rulers eagerly adopted limits on their authority and ceded power over the purse to elected assemblies (Herb 2003). And even before doing that, to gain continued access to credit, states faced incentives to sustain a healthy economy and nourish an effective tax bureaucracy in order to be able to raise the taxes needed to service their ongoing debt (see Calomiris and Haber 2014).

But the bigger story is that centralized power was tamed by liberalism across Europe gradually and fittingly. Many European kingdoms took one step forward and two steps back. After all, the Magna Carta, which King John signed at Runnymede in 1215 in the face of a revolt by English barons, was pretty much ignored until the Glorious Revolution in 1688, when William of Orange finally accepted parliamentary supremacy. Similarly, the ideology of individualism and rights, another chief precipitant of Europe's "exit from kinship," preceded the Enlightenment by centuries. But it only really took off after the Reformation spread the gospel of religious liberty from Saxony to Brittany (Fukuyama 2011).

At the end of the day, absolutism was defeated by the passage of a series of modest, cumulative reforms. In writing about the Spanish case, Tortella and Comin (2001, p. 161) remark that:

> arbitrary and capricious practices such as "trial by ordeal" or "trial by combat." Kings began to directly administer justice in capital cases, or delegated it to royal officials (provosts) and parliaments (Strayer 2005). They also created permanent courts.

It was during the Carlist War (a civil war between liberals and absolutists between 1833–39) and the next decade (i.e., the period roughly from 1833 to 1850) that the so-called liberal revolution established a series of modernizing measures: a set of medieval institutions (the guilds, the tithe, the Mesta, feudal landownership, and internal customs) was [sic] abolished and a commerce code, disentailment, free trade, and a liberal tax system were put into place. With these measures, private property rights were established and public intervention in the market was reduced [. . .] There were also changes in the monetary and banking systems, although the most durable of these changes, the establishment of the Bank of Spain as a central bank and monopolist of issue and of the decimal system in money, and introduction of the peseta as the monetary unit, were the result of protracted processes that lasted well into the twentieth century.

A self-reinforcing equilibrium

Over time, an increasingly broader swath of European citizens gained the ability to enforce their rights and hold politicians accountable. This is because politicians developed a comparative advantage in reaching political office via elections. A diversified and productive economy meant that politicians could deliver public goods at a decreasing marginal cost to expanding constituents. This gave incumbents an incentive to create broader coalitions. They thus extended the franchise (see Lizzeri and Persico 2004).

Increasingly educated, urbanized, and middle-class citizens responded in kind. They rewarded politicians for the provision of public goods, rather than for constructing clientilistic networks and indulging in patronage politics (see Keefer and Vlaciu 2008). This further incentivized rulers to bolster the efficiency of the tax system and to improve the quality of the public goods demanded by citizens.

In turn, the increasingly sophisticated public goods provided by centralized states promoted the practices needed to make democracy work among strangers across relatively large territorial expanses. On the one hand, physical and communications infrastructure sustained civic engagement and widespread voluntary association (Stasavage 2011). On the other hand, a legal system based on the rule of law promoted the impersonal, impartial enforcement of contracts and administration of justice. This increased citizens' trust in their governments (see Levi 2002, p. 45).

Explaining the Middle East and North Africa

Further above we discussed how European colonial powers reacted to the factor endowments they encountered upon arriving in the New World. Where Europeans encountered climates and soils conducive to settling these new lands as family farmers, they dedicated themselves to grain agriculture and liberal democracy followed. Where they encountered endowments that favored large plantations, oligarchies instead ensued. Generally speaking, however, the Europeans largely ignored areas that were too dry to support agriculture.

To the degree that they showed any interest at all, it was because these areas had strategic importance. For example, Great Britain created protectorates over the tribal monarchies of the Persian Gulf because those areas were on the way to India: had another power controlled them, Britain's trade to its most valuable colony could have been interdicted. Similarly, Great Britain and Russia divided up Afghanistan as part of "the Great Game" (the Anglo-Russian race for control of Asia).

Whatever the ultimate impetus, however, the British found themselves competing with the Ottoman Empire over control of the Middle East during the eighteenth and nineteenth centuries. After World War I, following the defeat of the Axis powers, the Europeans dismembered the Ottoman Empire. In 1916, Britain and France signed the Sykes-Picot Agreement, a pact in which they split the Fertile Crescent.

The map of the MENA was completely rearranged. While the northern slice running from the Mediterranean to the Tigris River was taken over by France, the southern slice running from Palestine to the Tigris was carved out for Britain.[37] The British created a national homeland for the Jews in Palestine in 1917; Jordan and Iraq were created in the 1920s. London then dispatched "political residents" throughout North Africa and the Persian Gulf – including agents who resided in Egypt, Somalia, Yemen, Bahrain, Kuwait, Oman, Qatar, and the U.A.E. Libya was ruled by the Italians; Spain held sway in most of Morocco. Iran, Saudi Arabia, and North Yemen remained sovereign.

---

[37] France exercised influence over Tunisia, Algeria, and Morocco. It sliced Lebanon out of Syria in a bid to create a Christian dominated republic and later carved out a Turkish speaking enclave in Syria and annexed it to Turkey.

The political economy of the desert

The rest of this chapter continues to draw on the factor endowment approach to institutions to explain why the map of the MENA looked the way it did when the British wrested control over it from the Ottomans. It also explains why the region is currently divided between unstable and repressive "republics" and more stable and increasingly liberalizing monarchies. Like the Ottomans before them, the Europeans encountered harsh environmental conditions. Scattered, nomadic tribes were diffused throughout the region. Agricultural enclaves ruled by oligarchs – Tunis, Cairo and Alexandria, Casa Blanca, and Damascus – occupied narrow strips of fertile land and river valleys.

The MENA's inveterate tribalism reflects the harsh geography faced by the ancestors of the populations that currently reside there. Tribalism remains important in the MENA monarchies. This is because they are located in extremely arid areas where settled agriculture failed to emerge, because of either a lack of sufficient rainfall or the inability to irrigate crops due to a lack of access to fertile river valleys. These areas favored nomadic pastoralism. Nomadic Bedouin and Berber tribes thrived in these ecosystems because they developed systems of clan-based solidarity that supported camel herding, raiding, and the provision of protection to agricultural oases and trade caravans.

While relatively arid places promoted nomadic tribalism, those with a modicum of rainfall, or fertile river valleys, yielded settled communities centered on agriculture, commercialism, and a stratified social system. This ecosystem favored state building and the weakening of tribal identities. There, monarchic experiments eventually failed. Iran, Iraq, Yemen, and Egypt are now home to a variety of non-monarchical regimes that supplanted these failed experiments. To be sure, today's "republics" are not necessarily strong states; yet they are certainly more state-like than their monarchic counterparts.[38] Chapter 7 will provide statistical support for these claims.

Historically, economic activities in the MENA's desertic and semi-arid environments have centered on nomadic pastoralism, raiding, or

---

[38] Moreover, state weakness in many of the "republics" is a relatively contemporary development; As Anderson (1987) reminds us, in the case of Lebanon, Libya, and Yemen, the state has been largely gutted by personalistic dictators or civil wars. In the case of today's Syria, the ongoing civil war has rented the state asunder.

the provision of long-distance transport for the goods produced by neighboring, settled societies. In extremely dry places, such as Morocco, Qatar, or Bahrain, the transition to settled agriculture was considerably delayed or never occurred.

While extreme aridity caused by low levels of annual rainfall posed serious challenges to the desert-dwelling peoples of the MENA, climate variability was also a veritable concern. In the Arabian Peninsula, the highly arid period begins in late June and lasts through September.[39] The incidence of droughts is frequent. The rainy season occurs during autumn and spring. However, the rainy season is characterized by precipitation with a high variance and violent storms of very short duration.

In the MENA's deserts, camels evolved to survive these inordinately harsh conditions and were also bred for this purpose. They became the dominant form of economic organization. Across the Maghreb, Sahara, and the Arabian Peninsula, nomadic herders who dwelled in large tents were in constant search for grazing areas. Chasing down scarce water and food provided by occasional rainfalls or oases, nomads moved their animals and possessions across large distances. This forced nomadic tribes to store any surpluses as animal protein that was harvested by milking or slaughtering herds.[40]

This economic organization favored a tribal social structure. While each nomadic family lived in a tent, an encampment of tents forms a *hayy*. In turn, compilations of *hayys* composed a clan (*qawm*), and a number of kindred clans organized formally according to genealogical principles constituted a tribe (*qabilah*).[41] Tribal affiliation conferred land tenure rights in the desert. This allowed Bedouin camps to move freely within large tracts of land (*dirah*). It was typical for these routes to extend hundreds of miles and across several tribal boundaries.

The harsh geographic conditions that favored nomadic pastoralism, and the social structure this spawned, created a culture of absolute loyalty to one's kin, and indifference or outright hostility to competing groups.[42] Other unique cultural characteristics also followed in a logical

---

[39] These facts about rainfall and drought build on Bell (2004), p. 36.

[40] Interestingly, it has been speculated that the heavy reliance on camels for transportation throughout important corridors linking Anatolia to the Arabian Peninsula and Nile Valley helps explain the low provision of paved roads by the Ottoman Empire – another channel by which the emergence of centralized states was retarded among tribal peoples.

[41] On these classifications, see Zeitlin (2007, p. 34); Fandy (1994, pp. 48–49).

[42] This section draws from Zeitlin (2007); Bell (2004); and Kressel (1996).

manner. The seclusion of women and a concern over their safety was borne by the outsized value of female fertility and, concomitantly, their ability to bear numerous sons who could be employed in both herding and camel raiding.[43] The concern for the family's honor and reputation, and an ethical code of manliness (*muruwwa*) that valorizes strength, bravery, and fierceness, was also connected to raiding and the defense against raiding. Grand gestures of generosity were deployed as expressions of family honor and to solidify alliances.

Tribalism in the MENA helped foster communication and cooperation. Clear and recognized tribal identities promoted valuable communication links between nomadic families. Specifically, knowledge of rainfall and pasturage conditions was exchanged both within and between tribes. When rain was abundant in one area, resident tribes would host tribes from rain deprived areas. Access to these lands and reciprocal grazing rights were secured via alliances based on intermarriage (Bell 2004, p. 35).[44]

Yet grazing opportunities were not always secured peacefully. Intertribal warfare was common during prolonged droughts in concert with competition over water and grazing lands as well as camel raiding (Bell 2004, p. 37).

Since time immemorial, the MENA's nomadic groups have also relied on long-distance trade. Bedouin tribes dominated several Eurasian trade routes – characterized by the flow of luxury goods from India – as well as trade between Arabia and Mesopotamia. For example, they monopolized the flow of goods that transited across Mecca, which was located at the crossroads of trade between Yemen and Syria, Egypt and Iran, and Ethiopia and Iraq. Tribes such as the Himyarites, Ghassanids, and Lakhmids provided security and protection (*khafara*) to trade caravans traversing trade routes throughout the Arabian Peninsula and headed to markets and fairs (*ilaf*) in the Hijaz located in Medina, Khaybar, and Taif (Michalopolous, Alireza, and Prarolo 2012, p. 5; Zeitlin 2007, pp. 157–159). Meanwhile, Berber

---

[43] Similarly, it has also been argued that the so-called parallel cousin marriage practiced among nomadic tribes in the MENA reflected the incentive to produce – and hoard – as many male children as possible to conduct, and protect against, raids (see Bell 2004).

[44] Big tribal confederacies across Iran, Arabia, and Transjordan were centered on political alliances and conflict resolution, control over land and water for cultivation and grazing, seasonal migration, the provision of personal security, conflict resolution, and marriage (see Alon 2005, p. 216).

tribes controlled the trans-Saharan trade between the Magreb and the Sahel in what is modern-day Morocco.

But nomadic tribes also had a parasitic relationship to trade. They orchestrated periodic raids on commercial caravans (*ghazw*). Captured booty usually included local produce, spices, gold, ivory, pearls, precious stones, as well as textiles imported from Africa, India, and the Far East (Michalopolous, Naghavi, and Prarolo. 2012, p. 5, citing Berkey 2003).[45]

The political economy of MENA's settled agriculture

In some places, it was possible to practice settled agriculture. Usually, it was clustered in the vicinity of river valleys. This promoted specialization and trade. It also favored a more stratified social structure.[46] This was especially the case in Egypt, where crops were fed by irrigation. It was also the case in Iraq, where both the first Islamic caliphates and Ottomans helped create an oligarchy based on a quasi-feudal structure. According to Migdal (1988, pp. 61–65), the Ottomans, in particular, orchestrated land transfers and incentivized land grabs under the guise of land reform and modernization. This exacerbated land inequality. It also weakened tribal relations by eliminating communal landholdings and by eroding the legitimacy of *shaykhs* who enriched themselves at the expense of fellow tribespeople by literally taking over their land.

Like in Europe, settled agriculture was conducive to state building in the MENA.[47] The chiefdoms that established themselves in cities drew on urban financial and human resources. They were able to assimilate

---

[45] Of course, this does not mean that nomadic pastoralism has remained as strong as it was in the past. Over time, nomadism has inexorably weakened. Alon (2005, p. 230) helps explain why. Many tribal members became sedentary and cultivated land as governments financed projects to provide irrigation. Moreover, as states became more involved in providing law and order in the desert, they displaced tribal chiefs' provision of personal security. This was coupled with a decline in the value of camels and, accordingly, nomadic herding. As migrations became less frequent and shorter, herders were consigned to traveling within the frontiers of MENA nation states. As the threat of camel raids diminished, it became less important for herders to camp in large groups, therefore weakening tribal linkages. New sources of public sector employment, as well as the advent of more secure property rights over land, also favored a settled, urban lifestyle.

[46] Limited agricultural production did occur in the heart of the MENA's vast deserts. Tribes living in and around oases (*Sha'b*) were able to cultivate some crops – most famously, date trees.

[47] The information contained here draws on Khoury and Kostiner (1990, p. 11).

new populations, territories, and sources of economic activity. Local landowning elites and a military-administrative class (*mamluks*) became unbound by kinship or blood ties and provided the manpower and expertise needed to promote state building. Unlike Europe, however, feudalism was a more natural, if not permanent, fit.

The role of different waves of imperialism, Islam, and colonialism

Far from attenuating tribalism, several waves of imperialism, Islam, and European colonialism have at times reinforced nomadic pastoralism and tribalism. The Romans and their latter day inheritors, the Byzantines, were among the first empires to exercise control over large swaths of territory in the MENA.[48] The Byzantines were soon challenged by the Sassanid Empire. In 570 CE, they moved southward, invading Yemen and displacing the Ethiopian Empire, which had been allied with the Byzantines and occupied the bottom tip of the Arabian Peninsula since 525 CE. And the Sassanids were themselves succeeded by several centuries of Islamic rule. The Ottomans, ruling indirectly from Istanbul, were but the final caliphate in a long parade; they ceded control to the British beginning in the nineteenth century. Despite these variegated influences, nomadic pastoralism and tribalism endured. Khoury and Kostiner (1990, p. 13) write that:

[i]n the regions over which the imperial state had exercised effective rule (Turkey, Syria, Palestine, and to some extent, Iraq and Libya) or where European colonization replaced that rule (Algeria, Tunisia, and Egypt), the foundations of the modern states were built on the old imperial framework of institutions or on the new colonial order [. . .] tribal formations still persisted as chiefdoms, particularly in the desert and mountain peripheries where they remained beyond the reach of the Ottoman and Iranian governments and where they continued to thrive and to maintain the traditional cultural basis for their group identity.

The so-called Pax Islamica ushered in a community that aimed to moderate tribal strife (*Ummah*) during the Muslim caliphates but did

---

[48] Several Jewish tribes settled in the Arabian Peninsula (primarily in Yathrib, Khaybar, Wadi al-Qura, and Medina) and included the Qurayza, Nadir, and Quaynuqa. These tribes fled from Palestine due to Roman persecution, shortly after the advent of Christianity.

not dissolve tribal identity. To be sure, the Islamic caliphates were able to conquer huge swaths of territory and effectuate mass conversions to Islam (Newby 1988, p. 53). In short order, Muslims moved eastward from Medina into Anatolia and the Indus Valley. They moved westward and conquered communities of Christians from Europe dwelling in North Africa and Berbers in the Maghreb. They forged northward, extending into the steppes and towns of Iraq and Syria (and eventually reaching as far north as Sicily and Spain). They also reached as far south as Yemen, and later encroached into the southern fringes of the Sahel in Africa.[49] Yet, the Islamists did not force conversions upon the conquered, nor impose Arabic. They also respected tribal structures, if not strengthened them.

Indeed, provincial governors often discouraged conversion to Islam because non-Muslims contributed substantial revenues – although this practice was reformed during Umar ibn Abd al-Aziz's rule (717–20 CE) when the poll tax was made universal. MENA communities of Jews and Christians eventually capitulated to invading Muslim armies and received protection in exchange for taxation (*jizyah*). In Egypt, Coptic Christians accepted Muslim rule and many remained in positions of political authority (Kennedy 1998, p. 72).

While the Islamic faith was never able to supplant tribal solidarity, Muslim leaders co-opted several aspects of tribalism, including sundry polytheistic practices. Islamic enclaves in Persia, North Africa, and the Southern Arab Peninsula tended to mirror pastoral economic structures and tribal social structures when these were already in place (see Chaney 2012; Michalopoulous, Naghavi, and Prarolo 2012). Tribes continued to dominate areas that never came under control of the Islamic caliphates: the Iranian Turkish plateaus, the Syrian Desert, much of the Arabian Peninsula outside of Mecca, Medina, and the

---

[49] Imperial conquest proceeded in haste. By 640, Muslims controlled Mesopotamia, invaded Armenia and had ousted the Byzantines from Syria. A year later, they took Egypt and, a year after that they had conquered the Persian Empire. In 647, the Islamic Empire invaded North Africa and conquered it by 709. While in 652 they conquered Sicily, Spain was occupied in 711. In 664, Kabul fell to Muslim armies and, in 1453, Constantinople did, putting an end to the Byzantine Empire. Timbuktu was converted to Islam in 1591. And starting in the thirteenth century, Arab traders ventured into Southwest Asia and spread Islam to Malaysia and Indonesia (see Michalapoulos et al. 2012, p. 28).

larger urban centers, the Upper Nile, and the deserts, mountains, and plateaus of North Africa (see Khoury and Kostiner 1990, pp. 2–12).

There were several reasons for this turn of events. Each of the original Muslim caliphates – spanning from the Rashiduns, who ruled from Medina since 632 CE, after the death of the Prophet Muhammad, to the Fatimeds, who ruled until 1171 CE from Egypt – was headed by a distinct tribe and dependent on alliances with other tribes. Islamic leaders forged many alliances with non-believing tribes when convenient (Zeitlin 2007, p. 122). In Morocco and Algeria, Islamic armies forged an alliance with the desert-based Mauretanian tribes and in Tunisia with the Massylii and Masaesyli. Moreover, the tribes that first converted to Islam in the MENA did so in part to gain access to booty associated with caravan raiding and imperialistic conquest (*ghanima*).

The Bedouin armies that help to spread Islam also tended to migrate to areas that were similar to their ancestral homelands. Islam's first foot soldiers were nomadic pastoralists with context specific economic and military skills. Sometimes, entire tribes were relocated. This includes the Northern Arabs (*Qaysi*) who colonized Syria, Egypt, and, eventually, Spain, the Southern Arabs in Yemen, and untold Bedouin tribes that immigrated to North Africa over centuries, often displacing autochthonous Berber tribes. Arabization of North Africa proceeded along these lines until the eighteenth century.

The result was clear. Tribal members continued to identify with their clans, not with other Arabs. Expounding upon a thesis first voiced by the philosopher Ibn Khaldun in the fourteenth century, Zeitlin (2007, p. 28) remarks that:

[T]he particularistic, centrifugal forces of the desert-Arabian tribes had never ceased to operate in spite of Islam, which proved to be only a temporarily unifying ideology. For the Arabs neglected their religion, and eventually lost the central political leadership or common power that is the *sine qua non* of inter-tribal solidarity. They thus returned to their desert, and to domination by the adjacent, neighboring populations.

Because of this, customary, tribal law (*'ada*) has typically superseded *Shari'a* law across the MENA. Indeed, Shari'a was only formally codified in the late nineteenth century under the aegis of the Ottoman Civil Code. And it is only relatively recently that tribal groups have assimilated Islamic legal practices in connection with increased sedentarization, the spread of religious education, modern communication, and tribes' exposure to urban and administrative centers (Layish 2004, pp. 85–88). Indeed, this process has been amplified by MENA nation states' deliberate efforts to impose Shari'a on nomadic groups in a bid to consolidate their political, administrative, and legal control.[50]

The perpetuation of tribalism and its relevance continued under the Ottoman Empire.[51] The Ottomans used the official recognition of chiefdoms to strengthen some tribal *shaykhs* and undermine others. In Transjordan, for example, the Ottomans doled out subsidies and honorary titles to secure the allegiance of some chiefs (Khoury and Kostiner 1990, p. 9). After the Ottomans' withdrawal from the region in 1918, strong clans headed by historically important families reasserted their authority.

Great Britain capitalized on this development during her colonial efforts, establishing protectorates over several tribes in the Persian Gulf and beyond. Britain's colonial administrators exploited the MENA's tribal system to help them control and rule these protectorates.[52] Shaykhs and other notables were summarily coopted. Tribal leaders (*mukhtars*) then helped exercise control over local populations. In Jordan, for example, the British empowered tribal courts that used customary law. One of the pillars of this system was the principle of collective responsibility, where an entire village or tribe was held responsible if a crime was committed.

This colonial strategy set the stage for modern monarchical rule. London recognized the sovereignty of tribal chiefs within certain borders and land ownership was transferred to one tribe or ruling family. London propped up dominant tribes and the dominant families within those tribes, providing them with political, economic, and military support. Cooptation was codified in a series of treaties between the British and "ruling" families between 1820 and 1916, beginning with

---

[50] This is not to downplay the revolutionary and wide-ranging role of Islam in the MENA. For example, Islamic theology helped to reduce inequality and alleviate poverty via obligatory charity (*zakat*), in which a fraction of accumulated income is used to finance alms, and egalitarian inheritance laws that favor wealth redistribution across distant family members and discourage capital accumulation (Kuran 2008).

[51] The Ottomans conquered Egypt in 1517 (Napoleon arrived in 1798).

[52] These insights draw directly from Alon (2005, pp. 214–222).

families in what is today the U.A.E. In the *Hijaz*, the *Anza* tribe, represented by the *Sabahs* of Kuwait and the *Sauds* of Saudi Arabia, was favored. This allowed Abdul Aziz ibn Saud to subjugate several tribes in the Arabian Peninsula (Fandy 1994, p. 44). In Transjordan, it was the Hashamite tribe. Although London never entered into any official treaties with Oman, they had a strong presence there since the mid-nineteenth century. Similarly, Britain maintained a strong political and military presence in Bahrain.

Powerful families soon rose to political hegemony and, gradually, obtained royal status. In Bahrain, it was the AlKhalifa; in the U.A.E. it was the AlNuhayyan in Abu Dhabi, the AlNuaimi in Ajman, the AlSharqi in Al Fujayrah, the AlMaktum in Dubayy, the AlQasimi in Ras AlKhaymah and Sharjah, and the AlMualla in Umm AlQaywayn; in Kuwait it was the AlSabah; in Qatar it was the AlThani; and in Oman it was the AlSaid. While these families adopted the titles and trappings of monarchical rule, the British continued to police their country's borders well after independence.[53] Monarchism then survived in places with "weak pre-oil state structures in which bedouin have a relatively greater demographic weight" (Herb 1999, p. 246).

Conclusion

In this chapter, I introduced the institutions curse theory to explain why some countries are developed and others underdeveloped. I defined and fleshed out institutions, property rights, and the state, and explored how these variables interact. I explored the critical role played by commitment problems and transaction costs in conditioning the strategies of power acquisition and maintenance practiced by political actors and, in turn, in affecting state capacity. I introduced a theory of property rights regimes and state capacity, arguing that both are jointly determined by the strategies selected by politicians seeking to gain and consolidate power and tax the economy.

I also described the elements of the institutions blessing and institutions curse, considering each as a distinct equilibrium. I identified the political, policy, and economic effects of institutions in each scenario, and the channels by which they impact development. The latter part of

[53] For example, the British sent troops to Kuwait in 1961 to deter an invasion by Iraq.

the chapter addressed the question of institutional origins and institutional stability by availing and expanding upon the factor endowments approach to explaining institutions. I evaluated the political and economic history of Western Europe and the Middle East using this lens.

In the next chapter, I elaborate upon a key empirical implication generated by the institutions curse theory: that the creation of a natural resource sector, which often becomes the only game in town, is a product of the same dynamic that drives industrialization via crony capitalism. Namely, when they face thorny commitment problems and high fiscal transaction costs, politicians often seek to survive and generate revenues by investing in oil exploration and production. If possible, they seek to export that black gold to earn coveted foreign exchange.

5 | Not manna from heaven after all
The endogeneity of oil

Why have some countries discovered bountiful amounts of oil? Why are many of these countries also willing and able to export it, thus allowing them to finance the consumption of goods and services produced elsewhere? Why do their governments rely on these exports for the lion's share of their revenues? Conversely, why do other countries instead import petroleum in equally large quantities to fuel the assembly of products consumed at home, if not exported abroad?

The most popular answer to these questions is geology. The presence of large, shallow, and easy-to-access sedimentary basins is crucial to extracting high-quality oil, at low costs, and in large volumes. In other words, a natural lottery plays an outsized role in determining where oil exploration, oil production, and oil exports occur. You've either got oil or you don't.

Consider Saudi Arabia. The areal extent of the Arabian plate's northeast margin shelf endows it with ideal conditions for plentiful, easy-to-extract oil. It has superior carbonate and sandstone reservoirs in good juxtaposition. It also possesses top-notch regional seals and expansive anticlinal traps due to repeated and extensive source rock beds over geological time (see Beydoun 1998). These are ideal conditions for easy to extract, high-quality oil. It is no wonder, therefore, that Saudi Arabia has the world's largest conventional reserves of petroleum.

Yet, as this chapter will make clear, geology is not the whole, nor even the most important, story. Once we hold oil endowments constant, oil producers generate wildly differing degrees of oil extraction. Figure 5.1 adduces this fact by graphing the residuals calculated from an Ordinary Least Squares estimation where countries' rate of oil extraction, proxied for by Fuel Depletion percent GNP, is regressed against their underlying oil wealth.[1] Countries with a positive value

---

[1] This sample contains 57 countries that evince positive values for data on oil endowments. Fuel Depletion is the value of oil, gas, and coal, minus the costs of

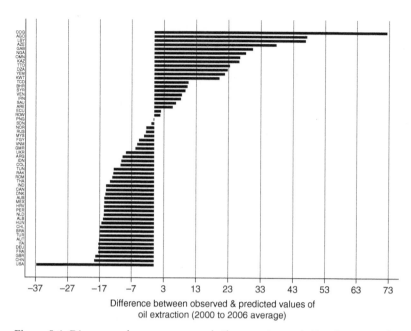

Figure 5.1 Divergence between expected oil extraction and oil endowments for oil producers.

exhibit a level of oil rents that is higher than would be expected from their underlying endowments; a negative value means countries exhibit lower oil rents than predicted by nature alone.

Simply put, geology does not explain that much of the variation. The r-squared from the underlying regression is a paltry 0.06; the standard deviation of the residuals is 20.9 percentage points; and the most oil-extractive quartile of countries evinces about 26 percentage points more extractiveness than the least oil-extractive quartile. While the rate of fuel extraction is higher than what one might expect on the basis of endowments in 37 percent of the cases, it is lower than what one might expect in 63 percent of the cases. With a residual of 72.4 percentage points, Congo is the country with the most pronounced positive difference between its observed value of oil reliance and its

production and the opportunity cost of capital; it is from the World Development Indicators. The values that this variable takes on are averages calculated between 2000 and 2006. Oil endowments are measured as ultimately recoverable reserves, and are from Tsui (2011); these estimates do not rely on countries self-reporting their proven oil reserves.

expected value – Angola, at 47.24, is not far behind. Conversely, the United States is the most "underperforming" country – its level of Fuel Depletion is 36.7 percentage points lower than what is predicted from its 222 billion barrels of reserves.[2]

What explains why countries at the same level of oil endowment vary so much in the magnitude of the rents they extract from their oil sectors? If not geological potential alone, what determines differences in the rate of oil exploration? Oil extraction? Oil Exports? Levels of oil taxation?

Figure 5.1 helps reveal a puzzling fact. It is developing countries that tend to be highly economically and fiscally reliant on minerals and oil, despite, in many cases, possessing relatively modest geological endowments. Meanwhile, the United Kingdom, the United States, Canada, Australia, South Africa, Norway, and the Netherlands are not, despite an abundance of minerals and hydrocarbons, overly reliant on their natural resources. Quite the opposite, in fact.

The chief objective of this chapter is to explain both why and how developing countries disproportionately generate and extract oil rents despite middling or even low levels of oil endowments. It locates the cause of this phenomenon in the institutions curse theory introduced in the previous chapter. This is not to say, of course, that developed countries with good institutions were not once very important producers of oil and natural gas; some of them, such as the United States and Canada, remain in this category. It is to say, however, that most developed countries, such as the Netherlands and Australia, are quite mature producers that have depleted easy-to-extract stocks and focus on exploiting marginal fields that are costly to operate. These stocks are quite hard to tap – often located offshore, in deep waters – and require expensive surveying procedures and extractive technology. The latter include techniques such as horizontal drilling and hydraulic fracturing.

Most importantly, most developed countries have left the dirty, difficult, reviled task of exploring for and extracting new oil and natural gas to the developing world. There, both foreign National Oil Companies (NOCs) and International Oil Companies (IOCs) exploit

---

[2] The average value for Oil Endowment is 30 billion barrels, the standard deviation 55.7 billion, and the maximum value is 260 billion barrels. The United States' observed value of Fuel Depletion is 37.92 (% GNP).

laxer environmental and labor regulations. They also take advantage of more propitious fiscal conditions, including tax breaks and weak and corrupt tax bureaucracies that cannot fully enforce the formers' fiscal obligations. In the hydrocarbon sector, regulatory arbitrage of this sort is often the key to big profits for Western companies.

Therefore, since the end of World War II, the oil and gas game has been played primarily in the playgrounds of the developing world. It is in the Middle East, Latin America, and Africa where the lion's share of exploratory drilling and extraction has taken place. This has been no accident: it is by design. Because of oil's potential to attract huge inflows of capital, generate sizable revenues, and earn hard currency, its exploration is never left to nature or the market alone. If discovered and produced at commercial quantities, the sale of oil generates attractive profits that can help politicians raise public revenues and line their own pockets.

Part of this is due to the industry's unique economics and low fiscal transaction costs, at least relative to other economic sectors. Oil rents, which are the returns above the minimum required to attract the labor, capital, and expertise necessary to extract oil, are the result of the fact that oil fields' total extraction costs usually lie below the costs of the marginal producing field in the oil market (Manzano and Monaldi 2008, p. 62). And, once oil is extracted, states can capture revenues via fees, drilling leases, royalties, production taxes, refinement taxes, export taxes, corporate taxes on oil firms' profits, and dividends distributed by NOCs. Often times, these payments are made upfront, years before any oil is actually drilled – sometimes before it is even discovered.

This chapter therefore outlines a theory of oil exploration and extraction in countries cursed by their institutions. It explicates how the rulers of weak states that attempt to consolidate power when commitment problems are thorny and transaction costs high turn to the deliberate construction of an oil sector to accomplish both tasks simultaneously. States are more aggressive at launching discovery efforts and converting oil plays into active wells exploited at high rates when they are strapped for cash or face current account deficits. That is, if they are desperate for revenues. This is usually the case when governments do not have much else to tax, face high costs to taxing it, and find it difficult to credibly commit to a broad section of the population. Provided that there is an inkling of geological potential, low capacity states will therefore do their best to conjure an oil sector.

This chapter also adduces evidence for several empirical implications generated by this theory. Revenue-starved states explore for oil more intensively. They court larger volumes of capital in the oil sector. They produce oil rents at greater rates by goosing the production of extant wells. They also export and tax it at higher rates.

These findings were produced by two distinct "laboratories." First, they correspond to the political-economic history of Azerbaijan, a historically important oil producer and, increasingly, a force to be reckoned with in the natural gas sector. Second, they correspond to a global panel dataset to which I apply advanced econometric techniques to reliably identify the causal effect made by state capacity on the oil industry.

This chapter focuses on Azerbaijan for several reasons. It adduces considerable variation over time in the key independent and dependent variables and across several units of analysis. Moreover, I can identify a strong shock to the state's capacity that occurred unexpectedly and swiftly, making it, for all intents and purposes, exogenous. Its sudden independence from the Soviet Union in 1992 threw a seemingly strong state into a perilous situation. Also, I was able to identify the number and magnitude of pre-drilling fees and bonuses received by the Azerbaijani state from IOCs as part of its effort to generate revenues before oil was even extracted from several offshore fields. In short, the Azerbaijani case study demonstrates that, upon finding itself in a fragile and desperate situation after a war against Armenia, a huge banking crisis, and an economic collapse, the government was left with no other option than to rev up oil exploration and hasten the depletion of extant wells, despite the fact that oil discovery had peaked.

This chapter also tests its hypotheses on a panel dataset using state-of-the art techniques. I find that state capacity is negatively associated with oil exploration, extraction, exports, taxation, and capital. The results hold after controlling for geological endowments, oil prices, and oil production costs, as well as measuring state capacity in different ways: as total taxation as percent GDP, private credit, foreign reserve holdings, military size, or the state's antiquity. They also hold after isolating the exogenous variation in state capacity. In short, I empirically corroborate the claim that countries cursed by their institutions are more likely to invest in oil and reap its benefits.

Yet, these findings suggest a paradox. Large and constant flows of capital are required to transform fossil fuels into gasoline. It is much more complicated than just drilling a bunch of holes in the ground. Investors are required to deploy intrinsically valuable fixed assets with sunk costs across an exploration and production phase, a petrochemical separation process, and a transportation phase, which hopefully culminates in the safe, uninterrupted departure of oil from export terminals. A relatively long lag separates exploration from profits. Moreover, the oil price is very volatile.

Given these complicated, capital-intensive phases, it would seem that capital would be attracted to the natural resource sectors of strong states with secure property rights; conversely, although desperate for revenues, weak states should be unable to erect oil sectors from scratch (see Bohn and Deacon 2000). Indeed, the oil industry is bedeviled by frequent increases in taxation and expropriations (Kobrin 1984). Yet, renegotiation events reflect the necessarily imperfect contracts endemic to a commodity with volatile prices, and investors anticipate these events and price them into their calculations (Hogan, Sturzenegger, and Tai 2010). Moreover, weak states with insecure property rights have happened upon creative ways of honoring the core of their oil contracts to avoid signaling *unexpected* renegotiations.

Several strategies have evolved to selectively protect property rights in the oil sector. Older methods were colonialism, Gunboat Diplomacy, and the oligopolistic structure of the market. Contemporary methods are centered on vast asymmetries in information and power between foreign investors and host governments. They include NOCs partnering with investors through Production Sharing Agreements (PSAs) enforced by Bilateral Investment Treaties (BITs).

This chapter continues as follows. I first review how countries can bring an oil sector into fruition where one does not yet exist. This is followed by an analysis of the growing importance of NOCs. I then explore the critical role still played by private capital in a world where most oil reserves are ostensibly under the custody of the state. This is followed by an explanation of how weak states beset with insecure property rights nonetheless manage to curry significant hydrocarbon investments, despite these handicaps. I then outline the reasons why rich countries with secure property rights have tended to eschew the creation of large oil sectors. This is followed by the empirical section of the chapter, which begins with a case study of Azerbaijan and ends with a panel data analysis that finds that state capacity is negatively associated with oil exploration, extraction, exports, taxation, and capital.

The endogeneity of oil

Many developing countries are low capacity states with pressing fiscal needs. To boot, their rulers face prohibitive fiscal transaction costs when trying to tax their economies; moreover, they cannot credibly commit to protecting property rights broadly. Sometimes, they simply lack the institutional wherewithal to do so. As we saw in the previous chapter, in this context it is simply not feasible for incumbents to cultivate a diversified economy that can be taxed at scale. Indeed, they are usually too busy just trying to hang on to power, if not avoid a bullet to the head.

Therefore, states with weak state capacity are characterized by large informal sectors and a dearth of modern firms with readily taxable assets and income. Even if they possess a broad revenue base that might be taxed at scale, they usually lack the administrative infrastructure required to levy regular income and domestic consumption taxes. And because they have trouble exporting high value added products and courting foreign investment in modern sectors, they often suffer from a scarcity of foreign exchange.

These challenges motivate low capacity, revenue-starved countries to promote oil exploration. This is often the case even if their geological potential seems wanting, the oil price is low, or their production costs are high. While politicians operating in weak states can usually find a way to credibly commit to a coalition that includes investors in hydrocarbons and mining, they can also find ways to tax natural resource rents despite steep fiscal transaction costs. Although this is not always done in the most effective manner, it usually produces the revenues needed to help incumbents survive in office.

Conversely, states with secure property rights face high opportunity costs to pell-mell drilling. This makes it unlikely that they will match the efforts and capital allocated towards hydrocarbons by their cousins in the developing world at all but the highest levels of geological endowment.

The implications of this phenomenon are profound. The construction of a natural resource sector is often an endogenous response by politicians who rule over weak states. They are, more often than not, a last recourse. Indeed, natural resources are the default economic sector in most developing countries (see Brunnschweiler and Bulte 2008). What this means for the study of the effects of natural resources is that the observed levels of hydrocarbons and mineral stocks and flows across countries are not randomly assigned and exogenous and should therefore not be treated as such.

Some representative examples

Consider Saudi Arabia. The impetus behind the Saudi oil industry's takeoff was a fiscal crisis. The Great Depression indelibly shaped the sector's genesis and subsequent evolution. After the Saudi economy cratered in 1933 due to a contraction of over 50 percent in the number of pilgrims visiting Mecca, a severe fiscal shortfall informed King Ibn Saud's energy strategy and determined the timing of the kingdom's first oil discoveries.

Or take Mexico at the turn of the nineteenth century. Haber, Razo, and Maurer (2003) find that during the Mexican Revolution (1911 – 1929), oil output was several orders of magnitude greater than before the revolution, between 1901 and 1910. This was the case despite the fact that the railways were destroyed; there were several coups, political assassinations, and rebellions; and a socialist constitution announced the nationalization of hydrocarbons. None of this mattered. In this case oil production thrived under conditions that destroyed other sectors; in part because foreign investors had found a way to outfox the Mexican state – or, rather, what remained of it – and hold it hostage to the few oil revenues it depended on to survive (see also Maurer 2013).

Some readers may be left scratching their heads, and wonder if a fiscal strategy marked by a considerable lag between initial investments and the flow of revenues does not apply to rulers with short time horizons struggling to hang on to power. No. Even in said scenario, a desperate bid to nurture an oil industry is the best bet given a bad hand. Although the attempt to develop manufacturing industries through protectionism that can generate monopoly profits is another possibility, as was discussed in the previous chapter, these firms cannot simply be willed into existence at the stroke of a pen. More importantly, the lag between oil exploration and production does not deter the rulers of weak states from pursuing a fiscal strategy centered on oil because revenues can often be produced from oil before it is ever extracted.

There are a variety of fiscal instruments that governments can avail to generate revenues during the oil exploration phase and similar, pre-commercial production phases. These include requiring prospecting and exploration licenses. They also include collecting fees associated with signing oil contracts and undertaking initial drilling activities. Similarly, governments can conduct auctions to sell exploration and exploitation rights. Investors can make their bids in cash, or provide work programs, or finance and construct infrastructure (see Sunnevåg 2002). States may also demand that private oil firms pay discounted royalties before oil is sold. Or, states can sell equity in projects that augur future profits.

Consider Saudi Arabia again. Because King Saud sought to generate revenues as quickly as possible in the wake of the Great Depression, he made a series of attractive overtures to the Aramco coalition of multinational oil companies to induce them to provide large amounts of capital to oil exploration. Before oil was even discovered, Aramco furnished the Saudi Treasury with a lump sum advance payment in exchange for a favorable oil development concession. While the concession obligated foreign firms to produce a minimum amount of crude petroleum, the state's fiscal take took the form of fixed royalty payments to guarantee a constant revenue flow and minimize price risk.[3]

Another, similar reason why the rulers of weak states often center their fiscal strategies on oil is because, unlike other sources of public revenues, oil rents can be produced in short order once oil wells are operational. Incumbents in countries with mature oil sectors can therefore ramp up production in times of fiscal need, especially when balance of payments crises loom. Drilling contracts can be drawn with alacrity to expedite the production of known fields. Governments can offer to pay a fixed amount for every meter drilled and the time allocated to oil well services.

This was the strategy pursued by Argentina and countries like it during the 1960s. In just four years, Argentina obtained the third most active drilling rigs in the world. This constituted a threefold increase in oil production and allowed Argentina to obtain oil self-sufficiency (see

---

[3] This section draws from Goldberg (n.d.a, p. 7).

Gadano 2010). Haber (2006) identifies a similar phenomenon across Latin America during the height of industrialization efforts; many countries in the region primed the oil pump to finance current account deficits produced by their desire to accelerate industrialization through the substitution of manufactured imports.

Yet oil is difficult to produce and tax consistently

Notwithstanding these upfront revenue schemes and incumbents' ability to prime the oil pump in times of fiscal need, erecting an oil sector from scratch is never easy; nor is maintaining one. Oil does not flow like water from a river. Bringing it to life is a very capital-intensive endeavor. Investors must have relatively long time horizons and engage in intricate planning. Capital-intensive activities cut across a very sophisticated value chain. Its nodes include oil exploration, extraction, distribution, and export.

Moreover, taxing multinational corporations, especially oil companies, is an incredibly difficult task. They are very wealthy and sophisticated. They employ accountants and attorneys whose sole job is to help them evade taxes. Their budget is larger than the GDP of many oil-producing countries.

How hunches about dead dinosaurs are converted into rents

The identification of oil prospects first involves core sampling and seismic testing to discern whether there are subsurface rock formations that can trap crude petroleum. Yet, if explorers seek to assess whether there is actually oil under the ground or water, wildcat wells must be drilled. This is time- and capital-intensive. It can also create costly environmental damage.

It is also not inevitable that the next step in the process, oil production, will follow. Suppose that an untapped stock of oil is suspected to exist underground, and preliminary seismic analyses bear this suspicion out, albeit with considerable uncertainty. Even if this stock is believed to be big and valuable, it might lie dormant for generations. If the world price is too low or, more importantly, if the politics are just not right, further drilling to divine its true magnitude might not be immediately undertaken. As we shall see shortly, this is a quite typical occurrence nowadays in advanced, Western democracies: concerns about land use and environmental degradation, or the high opportunity costs of capital, often deter the full exploitation of mineral and hydrocarbon endowments there.

If oil-producing wells are actually drilled and extraction is attempted at commercial quantities, the marginal costs of producing the oil are, at first, flat. This is because an oil well produces its own pressure and this naturally releases the liquid at rates that allow it to be captured and possibly stored and transported. Yet, even at this early stage of production, costs associated with environmental damage and cleanup arise, because oil extraction calls for the dumping of the residues produced by drilling into standing pools. Therefore, infrastructure is needed to avoid soil and water contamination.

Eventually, an oil well's intrinsic pressure is not enough to release the liquid. And the processes and equipment necessary for secondary recovery are quite costly and complicated. After initial pressure falls off, there are several methods intended to produce continuous pressure to maintain oil flow. Those that are ultimately employed depend on the type of rock underground and how the oil is produced. Water, gas injection, or steam injection is necessary if the oil contains high levels of tar.

Water injection, in particular, can be a huge headache. Water might be scarce in agricultural areas, or during droughts. It may also be difficult to recruit this method in areas where salt water, fresh water, and oil are all involved in pressure communication underground. Moreover, potentially millions of barrels of water are needed to accomplish this task. Extracting it and distributing it is no small task.

Furthermore, states or private actors also face the need to finance and organize transportation as well as separation and processing. Engineers must first construct and maintain pipelines running from the oil wellhead to a storage terminal. This calls on a huge amount of pressure that must be provided by pumps; and because these pumps themselves require fuel, a parallel gas line must be placed next to the petroleum pipeline. In turn, geologists must identify the optimal location of pipeline corridors, which calls on conducting sophisticated analyses that involve expensive cadastral surveying.

Finally, a separation and processing facility must be built and operated in order to remove associated gas from the crude oil, which is either flared off or itself processed and distributed elsewhere. Sometimes, sulfur compounds – that are highly toxic – sand, salt, and water must also be separated. Finally, the oil must be deposited to a collection point, where it is stored in huge and expensive tanks and then taken to an export terminal which, if optimally designed, will avoid bottlenecks as a massive and continuous flow of oil is shipped off to be refined abroad.

The refinement of crude may also occur in a producing country before oil is exported. Basically, the goal is to boil the crude until it separates into different fractions. Refineries vary greatly, however. Each is designed to handle a blend of oil endemic to a specific place and therefore entails specialized chemical processes. These processes differ according to, for example, the unique blend of light and heavy hydrocarbon molecules, and the level of sulfur and heavy metals.[4]

In short, states that hope to produce and tax oil must court big investments in capital-intensive infrastructure and knowledge or do it themselves. This includes drilling exploratory and production wells, undertaking secondary recovery, and building pipelines, gas–oil separation plants, collection points, and export terminals. Yet, since the late nineteenth century, this has happened on separate occasions and repeatedly – and often in the unlikeliest of places. Costly, uncertain investments have been made and oil eventually produced across developing countries, if not exported in large quantities.

Mapping the historical and cross-national variation

Table 5.1 displays the first date of oil production across countries. The world's first oil producer, Romania, began commercial production in 1857. This set off a production wave that continued in North America – the United States (1859) and Canada (1862) – and across several European countries, for example, Russia, in 1863. It culminated in the advent of important Latin American producers: Mexico (1901), Venezuela (1917), and Colombia (1921) were among the world's largest oil producers before 1940.

Three big waves of oil production soon followed. The first of these rippled across the Middle East. While It began in Iran (1913) and was followed by Iraq (1927), and then Saudi Arabia (1936), it really only took off after World War II. The next big wave of oil producers includes several West African countries, foremost among them Nigeria (1958),

---

[4] Had Chris Perry not shared his expertise and time with me, this section would not have been possible. It draws strongly on insights he shared with me, both in person and over electronic correspondence.

Table 5.1 *First year of commercial oil production for all countries in the world*

Romania	1857	Angola	1958
USA	1859	Israel	1958
Canada	1862	New Zealand	1958
Russia	1863	Congo Brazzaville	1960
Italy	1865	Libya	1961
Azerbaijan*	1872	United Arab Emirates	1962
Poland	1874	Thailand	1964
Japan	1875	Malaysia	1964
Germany	1880	Belarus	1965
India	1889	Spain	1966
Indonesia	1893	Tunisia	1966
Peru	1896	Oman	1967
Mexico	1901	Syria	1968
Tajikistan	1907	Norway	1971
Argentina	1908	Kazakhstan	1972
Trinidad and Tobago	1909	Denmark	1972
Turkmenistan	1909	Barbados	1974
Egypt	1911	Congo Kinshasha (Zaire)	1975
Iran	1913	Sweden	1976
Brunei	1913	Cameroon	1978
Venezuela	1917	Guatemala	1979
Ecuador	1917	Ghana	1979
Ukraine	1917	Ivory Coast	1980
France	1918	Greece	1981
Czechoslovakia	1919	Suriname	1984
Colombia	1921	Benin	1984
Iraq	1927	Uzbekistan	1985
Bolivia	1930	Jordan	1986
Bahrain	1932	Yemen	1986
Austria	1933	Senegal	1987
Albania	1933	Bangladesh	1987
Australia	1933	Vietnam	1990
Burma/Myanmar	1934	Philippines	1990
Saudi Arabia	1936	Papua New Guinea	1991
Hungary	1937	Croatia	1992
China	1939	Serbia	1992
Brazil	1940	Slovenia	1992
Great Britain	1940	Lithuania	1992

Table 5.1 (*cont.*)

Taiwan	1941	Georgia	1992
Cuba	1942	Equatorial Guinea	1992
Netherlands	1943	South Africa	1992
Yugoslavia	1943	Sudan	1992
Morocco	1943	Kyrgzstan	1992
Algeria	1944	Czech Republic	1993
Kuwait	1946	Slovak Republic	1993
Pakistan	1947	Chad	2003
Turkey	1948	Mongolia	2003
Qatar	1949	East Timor	2004
Chile	1950	Moldova	2004
Bulgaria	1955	Belize	2006
Nigeria	1958	Mauritania	2006
Gabon	1958		

Notes:

* Some production as far back as 1846, with primitive production methods (wells of 21 meters depth), but first derricks erected 1872. Data for Uzbekistan, Georgia, Kyrgzstan, and Lithuania: the first year of commercial production may actually be earlier than indicated.

Source: Haber and Menaldo (2011a)

Gabon (1958), and Angola (1958). Finally, late bloomers include Malaysia (1964), Indonesia (whose first commercial wells produced oil in the nineteenth century but only began exporting in the 1970s), Norway (1971), Kazakhstan (1972), and Equatorial Guinea (1992).

The ultimate result of these waves is evidenced by Maps 5.1 through 5.8. These maps depict the spatial variation in (logged) fuel production per capita at different cross-sections, as well as in proven petroleum reserves in 2006. Map 5.1 depicts the variation in 1900; Map 5.2 in 1920; Map 5.3 in 1940; Map 5.4 in 1960; Map 5.5 in 1980; Map 5.6 in 2000. Finally, while Map 5.7 showcases the cross-national variation in fuel production per capita in the year 2006, Map 5.8 exhibits the variation in proven oil reserves that same year.[5]

---

[5] These data on fuel income include oil and natural gas. It, along with the data on proven oil reserves, is from Haber and Menaldo (2011a). Materially similar patterns are obtained if only oil income is graphed instead of total fuel income, or if oil, natural gas, and coal income is graphed.

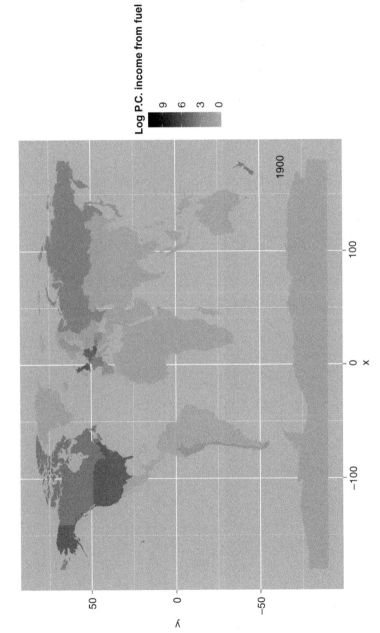

Map 5.1 Total fuel production per capita in 1900.

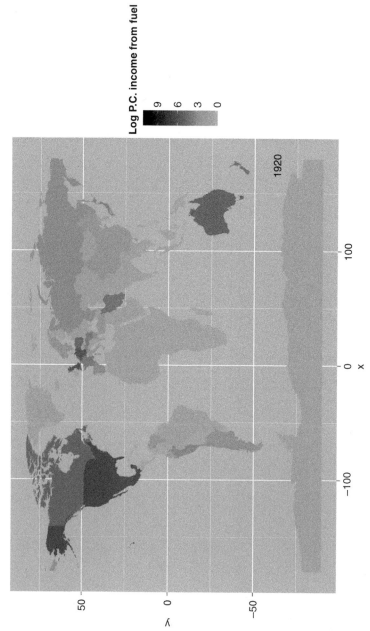

Map 5.2 Total fuel production per capita in 1920.

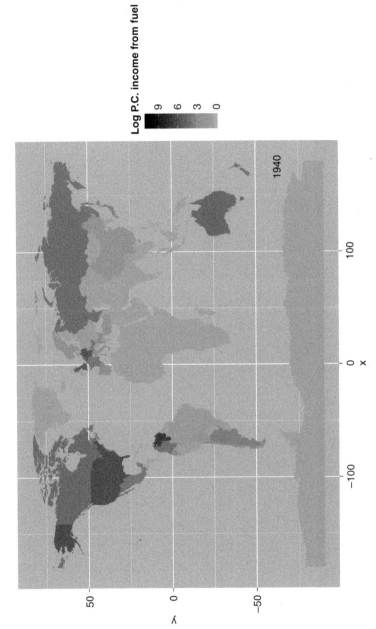

Map 5.3 Total fuel production per capita in 1940.

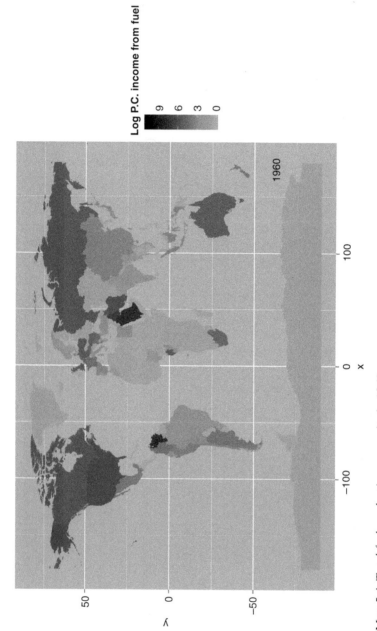

Map 5.4 Total fuel production per capita in 1960.

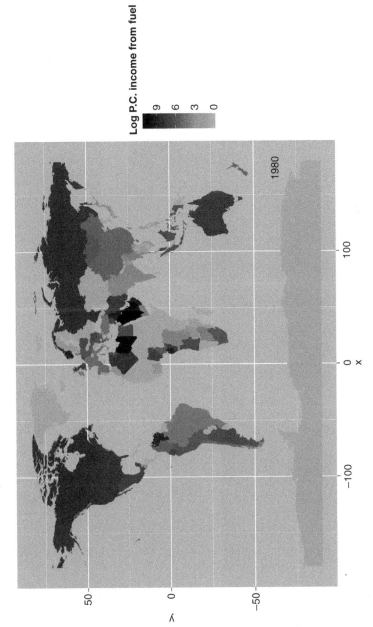

Map 5.5 Total fuel production per capita in 1980.

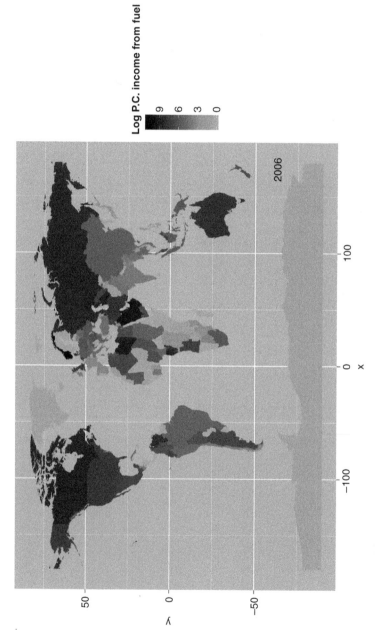

Log P.C. income from fuel

9
6
3
0

x

Map 5.6 Total fuel production per capita in 2000.

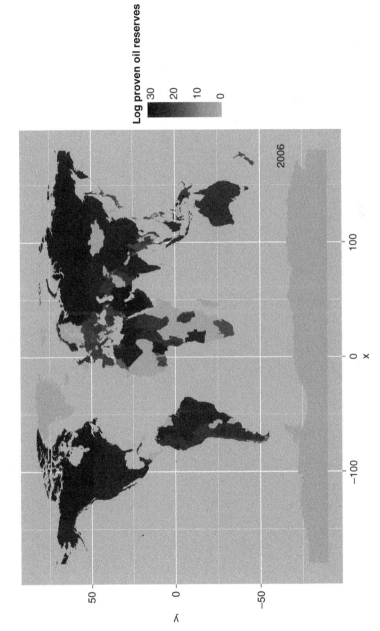

Map 5.7 Total fuel production per capita in 2006.

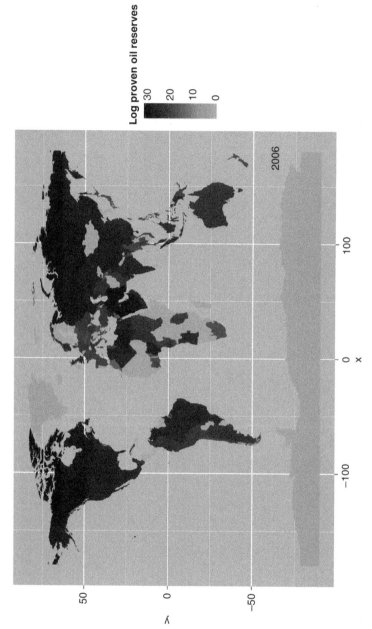

Map 5.8 Total proven reserves in 2006.

These maps help tell the story of how, over time, a larger and larger portion of the globe became populated with oil producers. More importantly, the trend depicted across these figures is of developing countries increasingly joining the family of established oil and gas producers from the developed world.

We now move to exploring how oil production evolved in this way, despite the formidable challenges and complexities outlined above. How does one breathe life into an oil sector when one does not already exist? How does this happen in a country bedeviled by weak state capacity and low-quality institutions? The answers to these questions call on us to take stock of the role of the state, NOCs, and private investors. This will set the stage for us to then statistically examine the relationship between state capacity and oil exploration, oil extraction, oil export, oil taxation, and oil capital.

How to construct an oil sector from scratch

How do governments go about constructing and generating revenues from an oil sector?[6] The first step is to set up a legal and regulatory framework. The second is to set up an ownership model for subsoil wealth. The third is to construct agencies and staff them in order to regulate hydrocarbons and possibly have a direct role in producing and exporting them. The fourth is to allocate exploration and production licenses. The last is to devise methods to tax oil rents.

While a country's constitution usually spells out who owns and has rights over subsoil wealth, petroleum and mining statutes and executive orders may also have a hand in delineating important decisions about the extraction, production, and export of natural resources. Property rights to oil, gas, and minerals encompass titles to subsoil wealth. Rights of access to these resources, known as allocation rights, are similar. They govern rights to exploration, extraction, and production of subsoil wealth through licensing and contracting. In most countries, an all-encompassing oil contract provides a single legal title, obviating the need to specify separate rights to oil prospection, exploration, drilling, and extraction (Waelde 1988, p.11).

---

[6] This section builds on Haber, Razo, and Maurer (2003); Jones-Luong and Weinthal (2010); and Barma, Kaiser, and Minh Le (2012).

In terms of awarding exploration licenses and production contracts, there is wide variation in how stringent the screening of applicants and bidders is, as well as how competitive the process of allocating permits. While so-called open door systems allow for the direct negotiation between the state and interested producers through solicited or unsolicited channels, criteria-based licensing involves open bidding rounds (Barma, Kaiser, and Minh Le 2012, p. 95).

Moreover, the state's regulation of oil and gas does not stop there. Laws and regulations both govern how exploration and production auctions are conducted and the monitoring of ongoing operations. They may also promote efficiency-promoting policies, such as unitization (Waelde 1996, p. 197), and policies intended to mitigate the environmental and health and safety impact of oil and gas. Finally, states indirectly regulate the oil industry by affecting access to labor, influencing management practices, and through trade and exchange rate policies.

Taxation

The state derives revenues from hydrocarbons through myriad fiscal instruments. Beyond the upfront payments outlined above, these include drilling leases, royalties, production taxes, refinement taxes, export taxes, corporate taxes on oil firms' profits, and dividends distributed by NOCs. Taxes on windfall profits are also common.[7] Other fiscal instruments that are less prevalent include property taxes and value added taxes.

In terms of ease and immediacy of collection, while royalties are the easiest oil revenues to collect and most immediate, income taxes are the hardest and least immediate, as a project typically becomes more profitable over time (Baunsgaard 2001, p. 20). Royalties can be imposed on either the physical output of resources or their value and apply to either a particular well or the total quantity of commodity produced. Income taxes are more difficult to levy, as they are self-reported and apply to a share of the value of production after a proportion of operating and investment costs are deducted.

---

[7] This tax is imposed only at the threshold at which accrued cash flows become positive; that is, after netting out the investor's cost of capital.

Ownership structure

There is also wide variation in the ownership structure of hydrocarbons. According to Jones Luong and Weinthal (2010), there are four main ownership options available to oil producers. These run the gamut, and include state ownership with control, state ownership without control, private domestic ownership, and private foreign ownership. Empirically, there are examples of each model and several combinations and permutations in between.

Table 5.2 identifies several countries with NOCs, as well as the year they were established. The first NOC was established in Austria-Hungary in 1908, when the government took a stake in the storing and processing of crude oil (Tordo, Tracy, and Arfaa 2011, p. 30). During the 1920s, Britain and France took an ownership stake in their nation's premiere oil companies – Anglo-Persian Oil Company and the French Petroleum Company, respectively. In Latin America, Argentina established an NOC in 1922, Peru in 1934, Bolivia in 1936, and Mexico in 1938.

The 1970s witnessed a rash of nationalizations in the wake of a transition away from concession-based contracts. Under auspices of the latter, International Oil Companies (IOCs) received titles to subsoil wealth across large swaths of land over several decades in exchange for signing bonuses and royalties. This system was upended after a rash of renegotiations of long-standing concession agreements by host countries, as well as the wholesale expropriations of major IOCs. In the Middle East, Saudi Arabia established an NOC in 1973, Qatar in 1974, the UAE in 1971, and Oman in 1974. In Africa, Nigeria established an NOC in 1971, Angola in 1976, and Gabon in 1979.[8]

The upshot is that fully private ownership is now very rare. Examples include the United States, Canada since 2004, the United Kingdom, and Australia. Indeed, in 2011 NOCs controlled 90 percent of the world's oil reserves (Tordo, Tracy, and Arfaa 2011, p. ix). However, partnerships between NOCs and IOCs are quite common

---

[8] These include several OPEC members (OPEC was founded in 1960). The five founding members are Iran, Iraq, Kuwait, Saudi Arabia, and Venezuela. They were later joined by Qatar (1961), Indonesia (1962), which left in 2008, Libya (1962), the United Arab Emirates (1967), Nigeria (1971), Ecuador (1973), which left in 1992, and rejoined in 2007, Gabon (1975), which left in 1995, and Angola (2007).

Table 5.2 *National oil companies around the world and dates created*

Afghanistan	1972	Japan	1955
Algeria	1966	Kazakhstan	1991
Angola	1976	Kuwait	1946
Argentina*	1922	Libya	1970
Azerbaijan	1945	Malaysia	1974
Bangladesh	1972	Mexico	1938
Belarus	2005	Nigeria	1971
Brazil	1954	Norway	1972
Cameroon	1960	Oman	1974
Canada**	1975	Peru	1968
China	1988	Qatar	1974
Colombia	1951	Romania	1945
Congo	1957	Russia	1917
Denmark	1972	Saudi Arabia	1973
Ecuador	1972	Syria	1974
Egypt	1964	Thailand	1978
Gabon	1979	Trinidad and Tobago	1969
India	1956	Tunisia	1966
Indonesia	1957	U.A.E.	1971
Iran	1951	United Kingdom	1976
Iraq	1967	Venezuela	1976
Ivory Coast	1975	Vietnam	1977

* NOC privatized in 1991; new NOC established in 2004. ** NOC privatized fully in 2004.

Notes: excludes countries with trivial oil production due to unpropitious geological features.

Sources: country-specific sources (source worksheet available upon request).

and critical to oil exploration and development. I explore how these work later.

National oil companies

State ownership with control encompasses several possibilities. States may own 100 percent of the shares of National Oil Companies (NOCs), with Mexico's Petróleos Mexicanos (PEMEX) as the quintessential example. Alternatively, the state may be a majority shareholder even though the NOC is partially privatized. Indeed, the state may exercise control even in situations where it has minority ownership and exercises veto power over important decisions made by the NOC's management and board of directors.

There is also wide variation on how active a role the NOC plays in producing oil versus regulating the oil sector.[9] There are NOCs that produce oil, but do not regulate it. There are NOCs that regulate it, but do not produce it. There are NOCs that do both. Finally, there are NOCs that do not do much of anything.

Norway's Statoil is perhaps the paragon of an NOC that produces oil but does not regulate it. Statoil is involved in production, but constrained by a separate regulator. On the one hand, a government ministry sets policy. On the other hand, there is a regulatory body that provides oversight and technical assistance (see Barma, Kaiser, and Minh Le 2012, p. 92). Another example is Brazil's Petrobras.

While producing NOCs are involved in upstream production and operations, managing NOCs only regulate the oil sector while private firms handle operations, extraction, production, distribution, and possibly refining. NOCs with the exclusive right to exploit petroleum within their territory are usually found among OPEC nations and Latin America. Managing NOCs are involved in running the licensing process, ensuring compliance with hydrocarbon laws by private investors and actors, and monitoring the collection of revenues and adherence to other regulations, such as environmental cleanup. And some NOCs both produce oil and regulate the sector. Examples of the latter include Malaysia's Petronas and Venezuela's PDVSA.

Finally, some NOCs are merely vehicles for the state to take an equity share in oil projects and not an active role in management and day-to-day operations. In these cases, the NOC serves as a financial intermediary between the state and private actors. The state oil company may collect royalties and taxes. Or it may even be tasked with selling oil produced by private firms. Two examples include Ghana (GNPC) and Chad (SHT).

Whatever their ultimate configuration, governments often maintain NOCs as quasi-independent enterprises that pay profit taxes and maintain royalty schedules. The same is true for major mineral exporters

---

[9] This section benefited greatly from various insights from Paasha Mahdavi.

that have nationalized production. This often influences how NOCs finance their operations.

NOCs rely on different mixes of reinvested profits, state capital, and private sources to undertake exploration and production. These include self-generated cash flows, loans and subsidies from the national treasury, loans from international commercial banks and non-governmental organizations, and the sale of equity.

Some examples are instructive. In the case of Abu Dhabi, ADNOC retains a share of its profits to cover current and capital expenditures, while seeking state approval for this expenditure via its budgeting process. Saudi Aramco and Algeria's Sonatrach are able to retain after tax and dividend profits and do not need to seek approval for royalties, taxes, and dividends (see Marcel 2005). And while some NOCs, such as PEMEX, are barred from incurring debt outside of the state, others often turn to the international bond market or commercial banks.

There are several ways in which this is done. Loans are extended by international commercial banks in exchange for oil production posted as collateral, or in exchange for a share of equity, in addition to regular interest payments. Multilateral institutions, such as the World Bank and its sister organization, the *International Finance Corporation*, co-finance loans or repurchase commercial loans, and usually provide long maturities and low interest rates (Waelde 1988, p. 19). Another financing instrument available to NOCs is the sale of petrobonds, in which interest rates are tied to oil prices. Lenders have also been known to arrange co-financing schemes with a cross-default clause to deter delinquency.[10]

Alternatively, NOCs have increasingly sought equity capital. These firms are often listed on American capital markets. For example, PetroChina, China's NOC, has sold shares not only on the Chinese stock exchange, but also in Hong Kong and on Wall Street.

Why do countries nationalize oil?

Consistent with the logic of the institutions curse theory, countries usually nationalize natural resources to improve the government's take of oil revenues (see Kemp 1992, p. 105). First, many host governments have nationalized their oil industries to bolster their foreign

---

[10] That is, if the NOC defaults on one creditor it triggers a default on all creditors, therefore putting all future credit at risk. See Mikdashi (1985, p. 290).

exchange reserves.[11] Second, lower exploration and production might be traded off for greater knowledge of reserves and costs and, thus, an enhanced ability to tax oil production and profits.

While simple service contracts and conventional tax-and-royalty arrangements are characterized by the fact that the state accepts zero exploratory risk, the tradeoff is a loss of control and inability to have access to geological and technical information. By bringing exploration and production within the four corners of the state, governments can bolster their knowledge of the true quantity of oil stocks, the true amount extracted, and the true costs of extraction and transportation.

This matters because IOCs are extremely good at reducing their tax liabilities. This is especially the case when they incur income taxation on the profits earned from resource extraction and exports. It is quite typical for IOCs to expense fraudulent deductions and engage in transfer pricing, for example. Transfer pricing may include (1) the buying of materials or leasing of capital goods and equipment from the parent company at above-market prices, (2) borrowing from the parent company at excessive interest rates that are tax deductible in the host country, and (3) the charging of excessive management or consultancy fees and overhead costs (see Gillis 1982, p. 623).

An inherently political strategy

Once the oil sector is nationalized, the goal of maximizing revenues, which would be achieved by optimizing not only the taxation of natural resources but also their production, often runs against political goals. NOCs are usually driven by considerations beyond the maximization of profits and shareholder return. Incumbents' quest to consolidate power and authority often trumps concerns about efficiency.[12] Indeed, the

---

[11] Foreign-owned companies earn profits in their host country currency. These must be converted into dollars before they are repatriated. Dollars sent back to U.S. stockholders as profits reduce the foreign exchange holdings that host governments earn by exporting goods abroad, however. This deprives host governments from the opportunity to spend those dollars on capital goods and other imports (see Allen 2005, p. 67; Mares 2011, p. 12; UNCRET 1980).

[12] A vast literature documents how inefficient NOCs are (see Jones-Luong and Weinthal 2010). Several reasons have been put forth to make sense of this phenomenon. The government's fiscal take is higher under NOC control, even though oil production levels may be higher under private hands. Another is that it is often the case that IOCs are not interested in making investments in risky and untested projects due to high opportunity costs of capital. This leaves less capable NOCs as the default investor and operator in many fledgling oil producers.

politicization of the oil sector is also consistent with the institutions curse theory. Incumbents' fiscal strategies are but one symptom of a larger political strategy predicated on the consolidation of power. Revenues are a means towards this greater end, and the maximization of revenues is often constrained by the other requirements of political survival. This may include using the oil sector to strategically cultivate a racket that is based on corruption, wasteful spending, and rent-seeking.

To achieve these objectives governments may often compromise the independence of NOCs, if not directly micromanage all of their decisions. This is through the politicization of appointments to their boards and managerial positions, and interfering in day-to-day management decisions (Webb 2010). Prominent examples of this phenomenon include Mexico and Nigeria.

Of course, this is not to say that these machinations might not produce some positive spillovers along the line. They include the state's ability to gain expertise and experience in both the upstream (exploration and production) and downstream game (petroleum refining and marketing). They also include the cultivation of backward linkages, such as the development of an indigenous source of oil technology and geologic, engineering, and managerial expertise, and forward linkages, such as manufacturing (see McPherson 2003). It is to say, however, that these are often the byproducts of the politics of consolidating power and generating revenues in weak states in which politicians face thorny commitment problems and high fiscal transaction costs to raising regular revenues.

Yet, the fact that NOCs are motivated as much by political objectives as economic ones does not gainsay the fact that they have often served as hubs of innovation. This is often precisely because states have sought to maximize oil exploration, as well as production and exports, at the expense of profits. They have therefore ploughed huge amounts of resources into investments that have more than paid off over the long run.

The Soviet Union during the heyday of its oil industry is perhaps the best example. In the aftermath of World War II, the country's oil industry grew exponentially, catapulting the communist state into becoming the world's top oil producer. This was partially the result of the fact that the ministries in charge of oil exploration and production did not face serious commercial constraints and were encouraged by Moscow to experiment with new technological and organizational approaches with reckless abandon. Novel approaches to exploration that were innovated across the Soviet Union during the Cold War include turbine powered directional-inclined and cluster drilling. Novel approaches to production included water flooding and infill drilling informed by specialized geological information. These innovations allowed the Soviets to double their oil recovery rate and more than double the level of oil production (see Krylov, Boksernan, and Stavrovsky 1998).

This brings into high relief the major point about oil and other natural resources that has been advanced in this book. Natural resources are ultimately endogenous and the byproduct of manmade institutions and processes. Their existence is as much the result of political decisions based on fiscal needs and the quest to survive in office as much as geological fact and economic reality.

The role of private companies

Even after oil nationalizations, NOCs rarely go it alone. After the heyday of contract renegotiations and expropriations in the early 1970s, which was followed by the establishment of many new NOCs across the world (see Table 5.2), NOCs cooperated closely with IOCs. Even in the largest oil-producing states, NOCs quickly encountered several problems after nationalization. They had trouble financing new projects, maintaining extant operations, expanding facilities, and marketing their oil. During the 1980s, in particular, established NOCs seeking to replenish exhausted reserves and develop marginal fields were forced to court Foreign Direct Investment (FDI) in light of low oil prices.

Today, NOCs continue to turn to private firms to finance most or all of the exploration and production activity in risky Greenfield developments. IOCs also provide NOCs with expertise, technology, and international experience across the hydrocarbon value chain. Generally, IOCs contribute process and management skills to NOCs, as well as distribution channels into key global markets.

Consider the case of Venezuela's state oil company. Shortly after the state raided its coffers in the 1980s to address a fiscal crisis, PDVSA lost its ability to self-finance projects (Mares 2011, pp. 38–39). This induced it to seek foreign investment to finance upstream operations in the Orinoco Belt and to seek partnerships with foreign refiners located in its major import markets.

The most typical way in which NOCs and IOCs partner up is through PSAs. The NOC retains the title to any oil fields that are discovered and is a mandatory partner throughout the process. While the state oversees environmental and safety issues, it is entitled to receive geological information and technology from its IOC partners (Waelde 1996, pp. 193–194). In cases where the NOC is not the regulatory body, these roles are played by the independent regulatory agency.

Meanwhile, the IOC conducts exploration and development as a service contractor and is usually remunerated in kind. During the cost-recovery phase, the NOC and IOC split the oil according to a predetermined agreement. Freed from paying any taxes at this stage, the IOC is able to recover costs associated with exploration, drilling, and production through the sale of its share of the oil. In lieu of collecting royalties and income taxes from the IOC, the NOC receives a share of the oil produced and is itself responsible for paying any taxes owed to its national treasury. After costs are recovered, the remaining oil is shared between the NOC and IOC, and the latter pays taxes on its share of "profit oil."

Through these arrangements, IOCs continue to play an outsized part in financing and organizing oil exploration, production, and transportation throughout the world – even in countries in which NOCs have ostensibly taken the lead. Notable examples of NOCs and IOCs collaborating under the PSA framework include Iran (NIOC), Saudi Arabia (Petromin), Indonesia (Pertamina), and Kuwait (KPC); see Bentham (1988, pp. 257–261).

Given the important role that IOCs still play in the global oil market, it behooves us to examine their perspective. This will help us to understand how, when, and why investments by private actors in oil exploration and production are made. Therefore, it will also help us address the paradoxical hypothesis at the heart of this chapter. Namely, that after controlling for oil endowments, prices, and costs, it is in the countries with the weakest states that oil exploration and oil rents are greatest.

Private oil firms and what matters to them

Private firms' primary objective is to maximize profits according to an optimization principle that calls for maximizing the net present value of their investments. Because there is a finite stock of oil, marginal revenue equals marginal costs and rents in the oil sector, where the rent equals the difference between the market price and the costs of extraction. Although marginal costs have increased gradually over time as the easiest-to-deplete oil stocks have already been discovered, if not depleted, and although there have been numerous price collapses over the years, profits have usually remained high enough to reward oil exploration and production despite formidable risks. For example, during the late 1980s, when global oil prices were relatively depressed, oil firms could expect to make, on average, a 15 percent return on their capital in real terms (Waeld 1988, p. 15).

The costs faced by oil firms can be broken down into exploration costs, development costs, and operating costs. To sustain a healthy return on their capital investments, firms must adjust to changes in the costs of inputs and the price of oil and its derivatives over the short run; and to changes in tax rates and other regulations over the longer run.[13]

However, there is high variance around the estimated rates of return to these investments owing to a variety of unknown parameters. These include geological and technical risk, commercial risk, and political risk (Van Meurs 1988).

Let us consider geological and technical risk first. Exploration often occurs in countries that have recently undertaken seismic studies that hint at stocks of oil, but where the oil may be located in hard-to-reach places served by inadequate infrastructure and reserves are not yet proven.

Commercial risk mostly revolves around price uncertainty, since commercial production occurs with a considerable lag and future prices are hard to predict. They are based on future demand and supply, both of which are subject to shocks and a host of parameters that interact in unforeseen ways. Ultimately, the global oil price is volatile and experiences sharp swings, despite – or sometimes because of – the fact that Saudi Arabia acts as a swing producer and can move the price either up or down by withholding oil from the market or increasing its production rate, respectively.

Political risk also matters greatly to IOCs. Oil investments are susceptible to expropriation for three structural reasons. First, they are fixed assets with high sunk costs that include seismic studies, exploration and production wells, and pipelines. Indeed, oil has the highest ratio of fixed

---

[13] This rate of return also depends on global interest rates and technology that influences costs.

capital to total assets of any industry. Second, the exploration, drilling, and transportation of oil is remarkably capital intensive. The required investments are very technologically complex and demand high levels of human capital and training. These plants, machinery, and storage facilities are quite valuable in their own right. Third, there is a considerable lag between exploration and development. Investors must conduct exploration several years before oil starts flowing; before they realize a return on their investment.[14]

These unique features of the oil industry create a time-inconsistency dilemma coined the "obsolescing bargain" (Vernon 1971). When oil exploration and production contracts are signed and financing is committed, investors have substantial power to extract concessions and promises from host governments: they are the ones providing the technology, capital, and expertise necessary to extract the oil. Over time, however, this power shifts to the hosts. It is relatively easy to confiscate the plants, machinery, and storage facilities involved in oil exploration, drilling, and transportation as investors wait to make a return on their investment.

While the aforementioned costs are sunk at the beginning of a project, it can remain profitable for oil companies to continue to produce oil even if the terms of the initial deal worsen significantly. Therefore, especially when the oil price rises, governments face incentives to increase royalties and introduce windfall taxes, renegotiate long-standing oil concessions, impose exchange controls, or expropriate IOCs outright.[15]

Hedging against risk

To understand how private firms hedge against these risks, it is imperative to appreciate the crucial role played by portfolio diversification across several parameters. According to Broadman (1985, p. 229), oil firms make investment decisions by exploration project, not necessarily by country. This means that each project is governed by its own risk adjusted net present value. Risk is operationalized as the variance of the project's profits. While some risks are ecumenical, such as the global oil price, others are idiosyncratic: driven by the unique geological features

---

[14] It takes from six to ten years for an oil discovery to come online (Waelde 1988, p. 12).

[15] Other forms of creeping expropriation involve the rejection of access to labor or raw materials; interference in the right of management; and revocation of licenses and permits.

of the area under exploration. The upshot is that a project-specific risk can be offset by another project that is less risky on the same dimension.

This allows IOCs to construct sophisticated global portfolios to hedge against risk. For example, if intangible exploration expenses can be deducted by an oil firm from its income across oil fields, this will incentivize firms to reinvest in places in which oil has already been discovered, take greater risks and, on average, explore for new oil in new places (Van Meurs 1988). However, project diversification cannot eliminate all risks, as there is always a portion of risk that is completely unique and cannot be offset by another project. Managing this "residual" risk is important to IOCs.

Cycles of expropriation as a natural consequence of imperfect contracting

Oil exploration and development contracts are often designed to compensate IOCs for the risk of *foreseen* renegotiations and expropriations *ex ante*.[16] That is to say, renegotiations and expropriations are often anticipated by foreign investors. Indeed, the terms of the intrinsically incomplete contracts that are endemic to the oil industry actually contribute to triggering opportunism by host governments in the first place. Because the original terms are very favorable to investors *by design*, host governments may be unable to resist "renegotiating" the contract once oil price rises generate politically intolerable windfalls for IOCs. Once prices fall, a new cycle begins: generous concessions for IOCs are again baked into contracts with the expectation they will be renegotiated later.[17] Therefore, contract renegotiations are an endemic feature of the oil sector. In fact, contractual renegotiations have occurred after pronounced price rises in several developed countries as well, usually in the form of windfall taxes.

Yet, even if investors anticipate some degree of renegotiation if oil prices increase, especially when taxation regimes are regressive and inflexible, they usually do not anticipate or tolerate egregious violations of property rights – for example, expropriation with

---

[16] This section draws heavily from Hogan, Sturzenegger, and Tai (2010).

[17] In 1985, oil prices plummeted, ushering in a new round of concessions to IOCs to entice investment. In 2000, the oil price again began a sustained ascent. Predictably, there have been many high-profile oil contract renegotiations and IOC takings since then. This pattern has recently been reversed yet again: the price of oil has fallen precipitously from recent highs, starting in June of 2014.

compensation below book value. Indeed, *because* oil contracts are incomplete, and tend to bake in the possibility of future renegotiations, it is imperative for governments to credibly commit to the core of the contract. If not, an expected renegotiation may inadvertently signal an unexpected one. This may lead host governments to incur serious costs and risks, as will be discussed further below.

How do weak states that have a hard time making their promises credible to general audiences curry the capital needed to finance oil exploration and development in light of the equilibrium outlined above? One answer is that they do not do a good job at it. While Saudi Arabia, Libya, Algeria, Iran, and Kuwait all produced fewer than 2,000 wells in 2007, for example, some developed countries were among the world's top capital spenders on mineral and oil exploration that year. The United States produced 500,000 oil wells and Canada 60,000. And with the fracking revolution underway, they continue to drill new wells and build more rigs.

This is a wrongheaded view, however. Consider that in 2007 Russia also drilled 100,000 wells and China 70,000. The reason is that the United States, Canada, Russia, and China are all mature producers that have depleted their easiest-to-extract and cheapest stocks. Much extraction therefore involves infill drilling which means that new wells are drilled in preexisting fields or are drilled for purposes of secondary recovery. Conversely, Saudi Arabia, Libya, Algeria, Iran, and Kuwait have massive fields that have not yet matured. They therefore do not need to drill new wells.[18] But, as we shall explore further ahead, they did at various points in the recent past. And new producers such as Ghana and Uganda are currently doing so today.

Therefore, IOCs and other foreign investors have historically devised creative ways to protect their rights and interests in developing countries, despite the fact that property rights are insecure generally. And they continue to do so today.

How private oil investors protect their rights

First and foremost, to protect their rights to oil profits, private investors have invariably concocted ways to exploit their asymmetric information and power to bolster their negotiating leverage, extract

---

[18] I thank Paasha Mahdavi for bringing this to my attention.

concessions, and evade taxes. Key aspects of oil exploration and extraction are characterized by significant information asymmetries between foreign investors and host governments. IOCs tend to have much better information than host nations about geology, the best oil production schedules, and production costs. One reason is that extraction often occurs in remote areas. And IOCs often misrepresent this knowledge to obtain stronger negotiation leverage and extract higher profits. The state therefore usually has only a shady sense of the volume and quality of hydrocarbons at most exploration sites.[19]

In addition, it is often IOCs that alone possess the skilled personnel – such as engineers and managers – and technology needed to explore for, extract, transport, export, and market crude oil. This is because there are high start-up costs to acquiring and using sophisticated equipment. Even host governments that pony up much of the capital for oil exploration and production often rely on IOC expertise and, thus, on their information about the size, quality, and costs of new discoveries.

IOCs: Extracting concessions

Historically, and partially because of the asymmetries outlined above, IOCs have been very good at wringing concessions from host countries in the developing world; these have allowed them to earn high rates of return. They have included low tax rates. They have also included government commitments to build needed infrastructure, such as pipelines, bridges, and ports. Finally, they have included guarantees to supply a cheap and steady labor force and look the other way when pollution occurs.

Generous fiscal incentives are perhaps the most popular and effective strategy that has been deployed by host governments. While some countries have offered tax holidays for limited periods of time, others have enticed IOCs with a reduced rate on corporate income taxes for an oil project's entire lifespan. Moreover, host countries have usually exempted imported machinery, equipment, and materials used in the exploration and extraction of hydrocarbons from duties and domestic taxes.

---

[19] For example, the quantity and quality of hydrocarbon stocks in areas that abut those where resources were initially discovered are more uncertain than the stocks in adjoining blocks within the same area (Barma, Kaiser, and Minh Le, p. 97; see also Haber, Razo, and Maurer 2003, chapter 6).

Income tax credits have also predominated. This has allowed companies to incur liabilities for one project yet receive a credit for investment costs made in another. For example, exploration costs or expenses related to new oil fields can be credited against taxes owed on profitable oil fields where costs have already been recovered – provided that the IOC has enough taxable profits generated by oil production in the host country. The consequences should not be understated. "In those countries which provide generous incentives for exploration in calculations for corporate income tax [...] the tax credit can become so important that the explorer recovers 80% or more of his exploration investment in the year such an investment is made [...] oil companies are in a position to [...] undertake high-risk exploratory programs" (Van Meurs 1988, p. 60).

Similarly, IOCs often earn depreciation allowances, either on the quantity of oil produced or its market value, at exceedingly high rates. This allows them to reduce their fiscal liability during the initial years of a project, before it is profitable. Likewise, accelerated depreciation schemes have incentivized oil projects with relatively long lives. Finally, IOCs are often allowed to expense depreciation allowances all at once: to deduct the project's entire depreciation cost during its first year. This has often been a key to stimulating exploration and early development in green fields.

How have NOCs secured these benefits and their property?

Besides exploiting asymmetries in knowledge and power to obtain beneficial outcomes, IOCs and other private investors have also depended on either third parties or sophisticated methods tied to international law to enforce their rights. Before World War II, the oligopolistic structure of the international oil market allowed IOCs to extract a host of concessions. These were enforced via colonialism and neocolonialism, as well as Gunboat Diplomacy. Contemporary methods have included contracting with oil-producing states that bear a relatively large share of the risks. These contracts are often enforced via BITs.[20] They are also securitized through sophisticated insurance

---

[20] Foreign investors have also protected their rights in the oil sector by demanding that host governments offer a hostage that can be seized after expropriation (Monaldi 2002).

schemes, both private and public, and partially enforced through the financial participation of multilateral institutions.[21]

Erstwhile mechanisms to extract concessions

Consistent with the institutions curse theory, the administrative and political weakness of host governments has allowed IOCs to protect their property rights in developing countries. This helps explain why they have dominated the oil exploration and production landscape since the turn of the twentieth century.

Indeed, throughout most of that century, host governments' share of profits decreased as oil projects' profitability increased. Why was this possible?

For several reasons. First and foremost, private actors in Western nations have always played a prominent role in shaping international norms and international law to suit their commercial interests, especially in regard to their ability to secure access to raw materials in colonies and developing countries. This ranges from the doctrine of the freedom of the high seas espoused by Grotius in the service of the Dutch East India Company in 1609 to concepts of international law that standardized global business practices, and especially contracts signed between hosts and multinational firms, during the nineteenth century.[22] Second, and relatedly, IOCs have been able to drive hard bargains. The source of this leverage has invariably been the asymmetric knowledge and power exercised by IOCs.

Before 1970, it was the norm for IOCs to receive unqualified titles to subsoil wealth across large expanses of territory, sometimes over an entire country. These often lasted several decades (Erkan 2011, p. 43). Moreover, IOCs received generous signing bonuses to compensate for geological risk. If the oil field was productive, the government took an initial percentage of production as a royalty. However, IOCs had the exclusive power to determine the quantity of oil produced and the selling price. Usually, the IOCs then paid income taxes at the regular

---

[21] Rather than discuss those schemes in detail here, I refer the reader to Maurer (2013), and simply note that several organizations subsidized by the World Bank and other NGOs pay insured companies if they are expropriated by host governments and often undertake heroic efforts to recover expropriated funds from hosts with the backing of the United States and other Western governments.

[22] On this point and these examples, see Sornarajah (2010, p. 38).

corporate tax rate on the revenues generated by the sale of oil after taking allowable deductions of capital and operating costs. Simple, regressive taxes with low real rates were the norm.[23] More often than not, host governments were not made aware of the ultimate size of recoverable stocks or companies' exploration and production costs.

This was possible because only a handful of IOCs dominated the market and had dense and long-standing linkages. Especially before the 1960s, they interacted with each other repeatedly and these firms had strong incentives to organize and articulate collective demands (Woolcock, Pritchet, and Isan 2001). This allowed them to collude in ways that protected their property rights in the developing world (Frieden 1994, p. 583). The so-called Seven Sisters – the major oil firms operating before the advent of NOCs – jointly boycotted host countries that reneged on oil contracts. In turn, the threat that all foreign investors might jointly withhold much needed capital, know-how, and technology helped deter expropriations (see Manzano and Monaldi 2008, p. 80; Haber, Maurer, and Razo 2003, chapter 6).

Moreover, this could not have been possible without the military and political support of home governments provided to IOCs. Before World War II, a majority of host states were either colonies or recently independent states, making it easier for IOCs to uphold their rights and interests (Erkan 2011, p. 44). For obvious reasons, the political annexation of a host state by a capital exporter can obviate the interjurisdictional nature of property rights enforcement; accordingly, colonialism was once favored by great powers to secure access to oil and other site-specific raw materials (Frieden 1994, p. 560; Maurer 2013). British, French, and American IOCs, backed by their home governments' military and political power, had virtually free reign over the Persian Gulf.

Similarly, their home governments' willingness to engage in Gunboat Diplomacy was an effective way in which IOCs once defended their property rights to foreign oil in the developing world. Many researchers have documented how Western powers such as Britain, France, and the United States enforced contracts signed between ex-colonies/weak states and multinational companies during the nineteenth century and first half of the twentieth century (see Frieden 1989, p. 64; Haber,

---

[23] There were some notable exceptions to this rule. In 1943, Venezuela introduced a 50 percent tax rate; Saudi Arabia followed suit in 1950. However, the calculation of profit was based on posted prices instead of market prices (Tordo, Tracy, and Arfaa 2011, p. 30).

Razo, and Maurer 2003, chapter 6; Maurer 2013). For example, between 1895 and the 1920s, American and European governments intervened in Latin American oil producers, including Mexico, Venezuela, and Colombia, to protect IOC property rights and interests.

Finally, it was once quite typical for IOCs to completely capture weak governments. To protect their property rights and interests, they often repressed labor and commandeered the regulation of hydrocarbons. Or they teamed up with local firms with strong ties to host governments; and these local firms then acted as their surrogates and represented their interests in the domestic political arena (see Henisz and Williamson 1999). Today, investors continue to exchange bribes for favorable drilling rights, the relaxation of tax obligations, and favorable regulations (Cheung, Rau, and Stouraitis 2011, p. 7).

IOC property rights during the era of energy sovereignty

As NOCs have come to dominate the international oil market, it has become much less oligopolistic. Beginning in the 1960s, host governments provoked renegotiations of long-standing oil concessions and introduced regulations that amounted to "creeping expropriation," and even expropriated IOCs outright. These renegotiations and expropriations were fueled by increasing international prices – and thus profits – and countenanced by new concepts of international law under auspices of the United Nations' "Doctrine of Permanent Sovereignty over Natural Resources" (Vagts 1978).

Many of these takings occurred in South America and the Middle East and North Africa (MENA). In Saudi Arabia, there was a renegotiation of concessions and higher taxes. In Cuba, Peru, Bolivia, Libya, and Iraq, foreign firms were completely expropriated. While the seven largest IOCs controlled 90 percent of the world's crude oil in 1957, by 1970 this share was 78 percent. And, by 1979, it had dropped to just 24 percent (Gillis 1982, p. 626). In short order, bargaining power had shifted pronouncedly away from IOCs.[24] The era of NOC supremacy had arrived. Or had it?

---

[24] To be sure, this pattern has not been entirely unidirectional. In 1985, oil prices plummeted in the wake of a sustained global downturn and Saudi Arabia's introduction of "netback pricing" (Tordo, Tracy, and Arfaa 2011, p. 32). The price depression of the late 1980s and 1990s weakened oil-producing countries' hand, and ushered in generous concessions to IOCs – especially among marginal producers. This buyer's market did not last, however. In 2000,

Ordinarily, although multiple expropriation and nationalization events such as these would constitute a disaster for private property rights, this was not the case here. First, most of the compensations made by host governments in the wake of these takings were at, or above, book value (see Maurer 2013).[25] Second, IOCs often enjoyed better economic terms *after* nationalization. Freed from having to "retain enough profit to finance further exploration and development as well as pay dividends" upon paying royalties and other taxes to the state, multinationals were now able to focus on running oil installations and marketing with a guaranteed profit (Goldberg n.d.a, p. 40; see also Maurer 2013; Waelde 1978, pp. 274–275).

Indeed, many of the compensation agreements reached between oil-producing countries and the IOCs they expropriated included a service relationship. A notable example was in Venezuela, after major government takings in 1974 (see Maurer 2013, p. 383). For all intents and purposes, therefore, the symbiotic relationship between host countries and IOCs continued after the 1970s; the only real difference is that foreign companies' capital and expertise was now under the umbrella of host government control (see Gantz 1977, p. 489).

Production sharing agreements and concessions

Since the 1970s – and as already discussed above – PSAs have encouraged IOCs to partner with NOCs in weak states that generally suffer from high levels of political risk. This is primarily because PSA cost recovery mechanisms benefit IOCs in three ways. First, they increase the net present value of investors' cash flow calculations. Second, they accelerate loan repayment. Third, host governments internalize much of the exploration risk.

the oil price again began a sustained ascent due to successful output restrictions underwritten by OPEC and demand from emerging markets, only to be reversed again recently, beginning in 2014.

25 This is not to say that all such compensations were made willingly, without considerable pressure by the IOCs' home governments. Often, the United States used threats and coercion to ensure adequate and swift compensation after expropriations of American companies. This was sometimes accomplished under the aegis of The Hickenlooper Amendment, a statute that called on the U.S. government to suspend foreign assistance to countries that expropriated U.S. property without adequate compensation. Similar provisions called on the United States to vote against loans from the World Bank and InterAmerican Bank to these countries and suspend tariff preferences (see Gantz 1977; Maurer 2013).

PSAs encourage host governments to absorb risk in a variety of manners. They may allow IOCs to deduct the costs for exploration and development incurred in areas outside a contract area against the revenues generated within the contract area (Waelde 1996, p. 203). They may also permit accelerated capital cost allowances. Or NOCs may even assume the entire bill for high-risk exploration (Waelde 1988, p. 11). Oil contracts can also be written so that taxes are collected only if profits are generated.

The higher the percentage of cost oil, the faster the investor makes a return on her investment. Many PSAs also include accelerated recovery clauses that let the IOC write off expenditures much faster than normal, thus delaying payment of taxes on "profit oil." Indeed, some PSAs provide for complete cost recovery during the first year of production.

The role of bilateral investment treaties

IOCs have increasingly relied on BITs to enforce the contracts that govern these PSAs. BITs enshrined as international law include stabilization clauses that guarantee that the law in place when an IOC initially invests in the host state will not be invalidated by future legislation. Stability clauses may enjoin host governments to freeze tax rates, other fiscal details, and other major regulations over an agreed-upon time period. BITs may also outline the policies that govern currency conversion and profit repatriation. Many include provisions that safeguard investors' right to employ foreign nationals to operate exploration and drilling services, hire the domestic personnel of their choice, and subcontract as they see fit. Moreover, these international treaties usually complement indigenous stability guarantees inserted in host countries' domestic laws. Although these are most often found in mining and petroleum legislation, they sometimes appear at the constitutional level as well.

BITs also spell out the legality of, and remedies for, the expropriation of foreign investments, including compensation guidelines. BITs require host governments to only expropriate assets for a public purpose, in a nondiscriminatory fashion, upon the payment of prompt, adequate, and effective compensation – the so-called Hull Law – and in accordance with due process of law. BITs deputize international arbitration tribunals to settle conflicts between hosts and investors. Judiciaries in both the investors' home country and other countries are enjoined to enforce a damage award against a state that expropriates IOC assets.[26] Most importantly "foreign investors need not have exhausted domestic legal remedies and can thus bypass or avoid national legal systems, reaching straight for international arbitration, where they can freely choose one of the three panelists, where their consensus is needed for one other panelist" (Neumayer and Spess 2005, p. 1571).

There is vast empirical support for the efficacy of BITs in helping governments credibly commit to private investors. Neumayer and Spess (2005) find that in developing countries with weak property rights, BITs encourage FDI. Anecdotal evidence suggests that BITs have helped weak states mitigate political risk and credibly commit to foreign investors in the oil sector (Erkan 2011, ch. 4). And Kerner and Lawrence (2014) find that BITs are correlated with fixed capital allocation and fixed capital intensity. These are two patterns that strongly suggest the presence of a mature oil industry.

The role of multilateral financing

Many hydrocarbon investment projects in the developing world are characterized by the financial participation of multilateral institutions and investment agencies. Besides allowing for both the securitization of loans and the spreading risk across multiple parties, project financing of this ilk increases the credibility of the commitments made by host states to foreign investors. The high-profile participation of institutions such as the World Bank in the financing of big and promising projects means that if there is any abrogation of the contractual terms behind the project, a politically *prominent* victim will have been harmed and potentially draw in important third parties, such as the United States (see Moran 1998, p. 71).

---

[26] Maurer (2013) demonstrates how international arbitration of this sort has gradually allowed for the depoliticization of the enforcement of multinationals' property rights in the developing world, and freed the U.S. government from having to intervene on the behalf of American investors who faced expropriation. While Maurer argues that arbitration clauses that were unenforceable once served to create bright lines that the U.S. government could use to justify foreign interventions to defend FDI that was under threat, he shows that they gradually evolved into arbitration treaties that became self-enforcing. He identifies important milestones such as the *Foreign Sovereign Immunities Act of 1976*, which empowered U.S. investors to file lawsuits against foreign governments in U.S. courts.

This matters because, although, as mentioned above, the United States has ceased relying on the most obvious forms of coercive diplomacy to protect private interests operating abroad, it has not entirely stopped throwing its weight around in less visible ways. Neither have many of its European allies. This includes imposing economic sanctions or depriving host states of loans or financial aid or, more indirectly, by leaning on the World Bank and other multilateral lending agencies to stop the flow of funds to scofflaws. It also includes the widespread use of boycotts and embargoes.

Why is oil not as common in the developed world?

Unlike their counterparts in weak states, policymakers in states with high capacity do not tend to encourage pell-mell exploration or ramp up oil production above the optimal rate. Therefore, exploration in developed countries has been lackluster for decades and developed countries are less fiscally reliant on natural resources. Why is this the case?

There are several reasons. The first is regulatory arbitrage, which takes several forms. While IOCs look beyond their home countries to avoid strict environmental standards – and sometimes stringent labor laws and land use regulations as well – they also look to the developing world as attractive tax havens. Additionally, there are high opportunity costs of deploying capital towards the natural resource sector in most developed countries. Finally, in most developed countries the state has good reasons to eschew subsidizing hydrocarbons in favor of exploiting its competitive fiscal advantage in cultivating and taxing a diversified economy.

Regulatory arbitrage

The developing world is attractive to multinational corporations for several reasons. Besides the fact that locating in emerging markets might allow a company to gain entry into new markets and diversify its global portfolio, which helps it manage risk, these countries are capital scarce and labor abundant. They therefore represent cheaper labor costs than home countries. Similarly, building materials and other primary products might also be more cost effective in the developing world, and transportation costs sometimes lower.

However, perhaps the primary reason why IOCs are attracted to explore for oil and produce it in developing countries is because they can take advantage of regulatory arbitrage opportunities. Less-developed countries have laxer environmental, health, and safety regulations than developed ones. Moreover, as explored above, host governments often make huge fiscal and financial concessions to these multinational firms. Usually, it is because they have little choice.

Laxer environmental, health, and safety standards

Stricter environmental regulations in developed countries began as early as the Industrial Revolution. During the nineteenth century, pollutants emitted from manufacturing plants began to be declared public nuisances. Laws that sought to curb carbon, sulfur, and similar effluents included the British Smoke Nuisance Abatement Act (1853) and the Alkali Act (1863).[27] While such laws reduced emissions, they also had a hand in cutting into the profits of established industrial firms.

Vogel (2014) argues that, in the case of the United States, California was the precocious trailblazer. While the state adopted stringent air-quality standards as early as the 1950s, preceding the federal government by over a decade, as early as the 1860s the designation of the Yosemite Valley as a national park made it a pioneer in the conservation game. By the early 1900s, naturalist societies had sprung up across the state to protect forests from logging, coastal regions from oil drilling, and waterways from pollution.

As the pace of industrialization quickened across the Western World, along with the scale and rate of urbanization, increasingly prosperous and educated citizens demanded that governments improve public health and safety. They also called for greater attention to environmental sustainability as such. This phenomenon reached its heyday during the 1970s, as governments in several developed countries expanded and enhanced their regulatory wherewithal; the establishment of America's Environmental Protection Agency in 1970 – under Richard Nixon, no less! – is perhaps the quintessential example.

During this era, so-called command and control regulations prescribed tangible, enforceable reductions in pollutants and other negative spillovers. Over time, Western governments sought to limit or eliminate leaded gasoline, acid rain, ozone zone destroying aerosols,

---

[27] See Potoski and Prakash (2013, p. 400) for these examples and their policy implications.

and several other industrial and commercial practices that caused environmental harm and endangered citizens' health and safety.

Therefore, limits on oil drilling and mining have become commonplace across OECD countries, usually in the wake of protests organized by environmental groups. For example, both American and Canadian governments have curtailed mining and drilling activities in land reserved for Native Americans – or, as they are referred to in Canada, their "First Peoples" – across their Western states and provinces, respectively.[28] Outside of these reservations, opposition against oil drilling has intensified, even in states, such as Texas and Oklahoma, which are ostensible havens of deregulation.[29] And, to give just one recent example from Europe: in Spain's Balearic Islands, environmental activists, aligned with local politicians of all ideological stripes, have put up stiff resistance against plans by Madrid and Repsol to drill for oil offshore. A similar campaign has also spread to the country's Canary Islands.

One result of this phenomenon is that firms that can afford to exit Western jurisdictions with increasingly stringent and costly regulations have packed up and left. They have headed in droves to jurisdictions with lower levels of regulation in the developing world (Genschel and Plümper 1997, p. 2).

This is not to say that there has not been a pronounced backlash in the developed world to more stringent environmental regulations that cut into firm profits and that ostensibly reduced rates of economic growth. Such a backlash began in the early 1980s and continues today. Criticism against command and control regulation was centered on its high costs and rigidity (Potoski and Prakash 2013, p. 400); moreover, efforts to peel it back were centered on the recognition that it incentivized regulatory arbitrage and thus capital flight from developed countries and races to the bottom (ibid, p. 400).

It is to say, however, that this backlash and neoliberal policies that promoted deregulation and more market-friendly policies have not

---

[28] In Canada, several tribes have used the courts to flex their land rights, with the blessing of the Supreme Court, in bids to block pipelines seeking to transport oil to Western ports and, ultimately, Asian markets.

[29] In the United States, land with significant oil and gas drilling footprints are often rendered off limits by regulations that seek to protect endangered species. A recent example is curbs on extractive activities in federal lands in Western states populated by sage grouses, which have suffered huge reductions in their numbers due to habitat destruction.

really put a dent in the regulatory arbitrage phenomenon.[30] IOCs continue to prefer jurisdictions where governments do not have the political will or administrative capacity to make them internalize the costs associated with the upstream oil industry's negative spillovers. IOCs therefore maximize profits by performing these highly destructive and dangerous activities in polities with relatively weak contractual, fiscal, labor, and environmental regulations.

Across the developing world, the agencies in charge of regulating oil exploration, extraction, and its transformation and transportation are often beset by unqualified personnel who make low salaries. These agencies therefore experience high turnover rates (Barma, Kaiser, and Minh Le 2012, p. 99). Quite often, their personnel lack the vehicles, resources, or training to conduct the monitoring of hydrocarbon projects needed to enforce basic health, safety, and environmental regulations (Chevallier and Kaiser 2010). All too often, the result is the widespread flaring of natural gas, the accretion of huge deposits of toxic waste, and the chronic contamination of groundwater and forests.

Much of this phenomenon is due to weak state capacity, incompetent bureaucracies, and incoherent regulations. Regulatory agencies usually lack their own budgets. Or they are severely Balkanized. According to Barma, Kaiser, and Minh Le (2012, p. 98):

Institutional redundancy, or overlapping institutional mandates, and weak coordination among public agencies and officials constitute a major obstacle to the effective management and regulation of the natural resource sectors. Ghana, for example, has more than half a dozen institutions with jurisdiction over land ownership, while Niger has two environmental agencies. DRC is an example of little coordination even among members of the same agencies. In Lao PDR, the lead or coordinating agency for the minerals sector is the Ministry of Planning and Investment, instead of the Ministry of Energy and Mines, but it is the latter in which technical capacity and monitoring responsibilities are vested.

The result is that:

[P]rovisions penalizing companies for violating terms of the regulation and contracts were found to be seldom enforced. In Ghana, companies'

---

[30] Although see Potoski and Prakash (2004) for the conditions under which voluntary regulation that calls on voluntary compliance and self-policing can indeed reduce negative environmental spillovers.

uncertainty regarding environmental and community health and safety issues has led to contracts having to be treated on a case-by-case basis and has created considerable regulatory capture risks. Moreover, in spite of extensive evidence of health and safety problems, environmental damage, child labor, and other infringements, few companies [. . .] have been fined or have had their licenses revoked as a consequence. (Barma, Kaiser, and Minh Le 2012, p. 88)

The preeminence of a good tax deal

Throughout this chapter, I have identified several ways in which IOCs and foreign investors are offered attractive incentives by host governments to do business in the developing world. As recounted above, foreign hydrocarbon firms have been able to strike generous regulatory and fiscal deals both during the pre- and post-NOC era. Sometimes this has meant that IOCs have exploited weaker labor, safety, and environmental standards as well.[31]

I hasten to reemphasize the importance of the fiscal side of the equation, however. The developing world is replete with inefficient tax bureaucracies that are opaque and have trouble administering complex fiscal regimes. It is exceedingly difficult for developing countries to administer a progressive tax regime that is self-assessed, characterized by myriad brackets, and replete with deductions, exemptions, and tax credits (see Otto, et al. 2006). Quite often, these countries' internal revenue services simply cannot calculate the prices, quantities, and costs associated with the exploration and extraction of oil and natural gas. Moreover, they have difficulty auditing IOCs' complicated accounts. And even when weak states somehow manage to do this, IOCs often bribe tax officials to evade these taxes (Kolstad and Wiig 2009).

Moreover, there is also the other side of this story. Strong incentives emanating from the developed world push multinational firms to undertake their most profitable activities offshore. Indeed, many American multinationals stash their profits away in foreign subsidiaries to avoid U.S. corporate taxes. By some estimates, there are more than

---

[31] This is not to say that concerned publics in the West and Non-Governmental Organizations (NGOs) have not challenged this phenomenon. They have, and have called attention to the worst abuses. It is to say, however, that they have not been all too successful in fighting against the worst types of regulatory arbitrage, in particular in regards to hydrocarbons and mining. I take up this issue in Chapter 8.

1.7 trillion dollars in cash parked in these subsidiaries.[32] And this phenomenon is not limited to the United States. Oil firms doing business in developed countries with mature petroleum sectors are often leery of the costs imposed by taxation in their home countries.

The United Kingdom is an infamous example. High corporate taxes imposed on North Sea oil projects are legion. They have persisted well past the go-go years of the 1970s and early 80s, when oil prices were at their most frothy. Recent increases include 2001, 2002, and 2006. Nor are they solely the work of the Labor Party, as Conservative governments have also raised tax rates on oil firms. This phenomenon, coupled with regulatory uncertainties – such as revisions by the government of licensing agreements forged with private companies – and red tape have discouraged investment in extant North Sea projects and deterred further oil exploration (the Economist, March 1, 2014, p. 57).

Developed country governments lack incentives to promote oil

There is a final, and equally important, reason why the upstream petroleum industry is not thriving in most of the developed world. Because strong states with high-quality institutions can credibly commit to broad property rights, it makes more sense for them to encourage sources of high-value added capital and labor that they find relatively easy-to-tax. Though these are usually taxed at moderate rates, they yield significant revenues. Because advanced democracies can enforce compliance with regular taxation, they provide public goods in exchange for these tax revenues. This mirrors the fact that these regimes' inclusive coalitions demand public goods, not clientilistic transfers, further reducing oil's appeal.

Indeed, as outlined in the previous chapter, high-capacity states are usually involved in a positive feedback loop that reinforces incentives to nurture broad tax bases and raise consistent revenues in a smooth manner. The provision of reliable transport and power, and adequate telecommunications networks, make it easier for the state to identify and collect taxes. In turn, these public goods motivate citizens to contribute to the treasury because compliance is rewarded with tangible benefits.

---

[32] Moreover, the U.S. government actively supports this type of foreign exposure by subsidizing host government expropriations. According to U.S. tax law, a corporation is able to carry forward a foreign expropriation capital loss as a charge against tax liability for a ten-year period (see Gantz, 1977, p. 491).

This differs pronouncedly from a strategy in which the state offers investors in the oil industry generous fiscal incentives to engage in risky discovery projects that have uncertain prospects for success. For example, as discussed above, investors may be allowed to credit exploration costs against taxes owed on profitable oil fields where costs have already been recovered, or write off costs via accelerated recovery instead of over the asset's lifespan. While these policies might be justified *ex post* if high-quality oil is in fact discovered in commercial quantities, they are *ex ante* suboptimal if oil is not actually discovered. Thus, in light of their more attractive fiscal alternatives, high-capacity states tend to eschew such high-risk high-reward policies.

While high capacity states can afford to indulge in prudent regulation, low-capacity states are the accumulation of pathological policy choices made by generations of politicians responding to thorny commitment problems and high fiscal transaction costs. Most often, incumbents repeatedly opt for the same strategy. They provide selective commitments to a handful of elites, not average citizens, and raise revenues in ways that obviate the need for a modern and diversified economy. One of the most predominant political-cum-fiscal strategies availed by politicians in this predicament is to erect an oil sector that can be taxed with relative ease, at least at the beginning, and that can earn valuable foreign exchange. Provided that there is an inkling of geological potential, of course. I now move to reviewing some qualitative and quantitative evidence that bears these claims out.

Case evidence of oil in weak states: Azerbaijan

In this section, I flesh out a case study of Azerbaijan's oil industry. This serves to corroborate the theoretical framework outlined above. For several reasons, Azerbaijan is a great case.

First, it evinces considerable variation over time in both state capacity and the size and importance of its oil industry. As we shall see below, Azerbaijan went from being one of the most important oil producers in the world, and the linchpin of the Soviet Union's fossil fuel centered economy, to an afterthought in its energy strategy. And, as we shall also see below, Azerbaijan transitioned from experiencing the financial, administrative, military, and political security of being an integral part of the Soviet Union to suffering from extreme weakness on several fronts. Its independence from the Soviet Union after the end of the Cold War threw the new state into a perilous and unfamiliar situation. Azerbaijan was fragile, desperate, and nearly broke after experiencing a war against Armenia, a cycle of political instability, an unprecedented economic collapse, and a huge banking crisis.[33]

Second, in the Azerbaijani case, I can identify a strong shock to state capacity that occurred unexpectedly and swiftly, making the strength of the state, for all intents and purposes, an exogenous factor. This was precipitated by the rapid and surprising collapse of the Soviet Union.

Even Mikhail Gorbachev, the president at the helm of the regime at the time of its demise, who was ultimately responsible for setting in train the forces that felled the Soviet Empire, was caught off guard when the collapse happened. He had simply not seen it coming.[34] Although Gorbachev's much vaunted efforts at economic reform – *Perestroika* – were met with stubborn resistance from regime insiders and ushered in massive opportunism and rent-seeking from government bureaucrats, his political liberalization efforts (*Glasnost*) largely succeeded. They opened a gusher of political activity, criticism, and expression (see North 2005, pp. 151–153).

This had unforeseen consequences, however, in that the political reform process simply got away from Gorbachev. Ironically, once knowledge of the corruption and chicanery linked to attempts at economic reform became widespread, it quickly spiraled into a lack of confidence in the Soviet system as such and unleashed political disorder. Solnick (1998, p. 7) aptly describes the snowball effect that culminated in the rapid collapse of the Soviet Union as a "colossal 'bank run' in which local officials rushed to claim their assets before the bureaucratic doors shut for good. As in a bank run, the loss of confidence in the institutions makes its demise a self-fulfilling prophecy."

Consistent with the theoretical framework outlined above, the evidence suggests that in the aftermath of Azerbaijan's independence, a desperate state was left with no other option than to quickly bring offshore oil fields on line, hasten the depletion of extant fields, and explore for more oil and natural gas. This was despite the fact that oil

---

[33] Azerbaijan was conquered by the Russian Empire in the early 1800s. It was briefly independent between 1918 and 1920, the year in which it was officially absorbed into the Soviet Union after the Red Army took control from the British in the aftermath of World War I.

[34] According to an interview given in 2011 to Spiegel Online.

discoveries had already peaked and, by the late 1980s, Azerbaijan had been known more for its manufacturing prowess than its oil industry. For this reason, a state oil company was hastily erected and quickly forced to raise funds from abroad so it could venture further offshore, into deeper waters with more uncertain, and costlier to produce, hydrocarbon reserves.

The puzzle of Azerbaijan's recent oil boom

In retrospect, the fact that Azerbaijan is now so strongly associated with oil is quite puzzling. It would not have been odd to label Azerbaijan as a petro-state at certain points in its past history. Indeed, Azerbaijan experienced several spectacular oil booms – and busts – before its independence from the Soviet Union in 1992. Yet, its latest and still ongoing oil boom, which began in the late 1990s, is, in several senses, quite surprising and unique. One of the biggest reasons is because of the fact that it is its largest boom ever – greater than the previous ones by several orders of magnitude. Therefore, before going into all of the reasons why this phenomenon is such an interesting puzzle, it is helpful to get a sense of how the current boom sizes up to past ones.

Azerbaijan's first oil boom lasted, roughly, between 1870 and around 1916. For several reasons, the fact that this boom occurred in the city of Baku, during this time period, was not a big surprise. The Apsheron Peninsula was renowned for surface seepages going back millennia. During the late nineteenth century, modern methods of onshore oil exploration, production, and marketing were primarily undertaken by Sweden's Nobel Brothers and Paris's Rothschild Bank.[35]

The bulk of the boom occurred between 1872 and 1901, as capital, technology, and expertise poured in from all over the world. By 1888, there were 54 oil firms operating in Baku. By 1900, the city had become the world's number one oil producer – far surpassing the United States – and provided half of the world's supply, with a recently built Transcaucasian railroad serving to transport the oil to Western markets. The bust that followed the 1901 production apex – 70.6 million

---

[35] Baku was the site of a series of pioneering oil technologies. Many of the world's first oil wells were drilled there in the 1870s (previous to that they had been dug and extracted by hand; Drake drilled for oil in Pennsylvania in 1859). The first refineries were built there in 1859; the first kerosene plant in 1863.

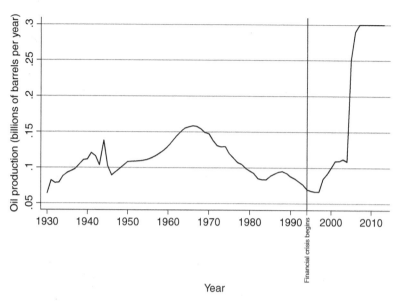

Figure 5.2 Azerbaijan's Historical Oil Production.
Source: Tsui (2011).

barrels of oil were produced that year (see Altstadt 1992, p. 22) – was just as precipitous as the boom that had brought it about; by 1918, oil production had declined by 69 percent (see Krylov, Boksernan, and Stavrovsky 1998, p. 71). This was due to a combination of factors, including the natural depletion of extant oil wells, World War I, and the Bolshevik Revolution (see Swietochowski 1995, pp. 19–20).

Another oil boom began in about 1920, when Azerbaijan officially joined the Soviet Union, only to implode during World War II (1940–45). This boom began after the re-commissioning of several abandoned wells, the drilling of new wells, and the introduction of new technologies (see Krylov, Boksernan, and Stavrovsky 1998, p. 72). In 1941, Azerbaijan accounted for 71 percent of the Soviet Union's oil production. Once World War II began, however, oil production plummeted in the wake of a shortage of supplies and equipment. Between 1944 and 1946 alone, a 36 percent decline had been registered. Figure 5.2 helps put this reversal in historical perspective; it graphs Azerbaijan's oil production in billions of barrels per year between 1930 and 2010.

Yet another boom was ignited at the end of World War II, but it proved to be short lived. In 1961, Azerbaijan's output of crude oil matched the 1944 peak level – it was just short of 0.15 billion barrels of annual oil pumped – and was surpassed in 1965, which, at 0.16 billion barrels produced that year, represents the country's pre-independence apex (see Figure 5.2). Immediately after reaching that milestone, however, oil production declined steadily. Figure 5.2 reveals that between the 1965 peak and 1990, the country's annual oil production fell by 44 percent (production was 0.09 billion barrels in 1990). Over the 1970s, 1980s, and 1990s, Azerbaijani oil production appeared to be on life support.

The most recent, and biggest, boom yet

The next phase of Azerbaijan's oil industry was not foreseen. This pronounced downward trajectory began to be reversed in 1997, when several new offshore oil fields were first brought online. This turn-of-events ultimately represented an unprecedented boom. Annual oil production growth rates averaged 15 percent between 1997 and 2007 (see Figure 5.2). It culminated in a historical record of 0.30 billion barrels of oil produced a year in the late 2000s – far more oil than was produced during the peak levels achieved under Soviet rule. This meant that while in 1992 Azerbaijan's oil income per capita was only US$302 (in 2007 dollars), by 2006 it had reached a record US$1,844 (in 2007 dollars).[36] By extension, the state went from receiving hardly any revenues from hydrocarbons in the late 1980s to relying heavily on them by the late 2000s.[37]

A boom against all odds

In light of the country's long-run economic history, it is not obvious that Azerbaijan's oil industry should have roared back to life as it did. First, there was the natural, inexorable depletion of Baku's onshore oil fields. On the one hand, the rate of drilling of new wells ground to a standstill. On the other hand, the average length of boreholes had

[36] The source is Haber and Menaldo (2011a).

[37] We can infer that revenues from oil were lower than 10 percent of GNP in the late 1980s, and perhaps much less than that; this can be gleaned from the average revenues obtained from indirect taxation during that time period. Along with sales taxes, excise taxes, and turnover taxes, this category includes revenues from oil exports (see UNESCAP, 2001, p. 21). The average level of indirect taxes between 1988 and 1991 was only 11.63 as a share of GNP (source: Suny 1995, pp. 245–246). Meanwhile, by 2008, revenues from oil were 38 percent of total revenues (source: Prichard, Cobham, and Goodall 2014).

been steadily declining over time (see Krylov, Boksernan, and Stavrovsky 1998, p. 72).

Second, there had been a marked shift in attention, capital, and expertise by the Soviet Union away from Baku's oil industry after World War II. The first shift was to the Volga Basin and the Ural Mountains, which augured huge volumes of untapped oil, and was soon followed by the ascendance of very productive oil plays in Kazakhstan, Turkmenistan, and Uzbekistan. Then, in the 1960s, Western Siberia quickly became the crown jewel of the Soviet Union's petroleum industry after various supergiant oil deposits were discovered there, including the famed Samotlor field – Russia's largest oil play and the sixth-largest field in the world.[38] By 1980, Western Siberia contributed over 50 percent of the Soviet's crude oil; by 1986, this had ballooned to nearly two-thirds of it.

While these changes in its energy strategy helped the Soviet Union become the world's number one oil producer by 1976, they further cemented Azerbaijan's position as a peripheral, if not forgotten, contributor to the country's petroleum output. By 1967, Azerbaijan was producing only 7.5 percent of the Soviet Union's total oil, down from 71 percent in 1940. By the 1980s, Azerbaijan accounted for less than 3 percent of the Soviet Union's oil production.

A third reason why Azerbaijan's post-independence oil boom is surprising is because it had reached its exploration and discovery peak during the Soviet era.[39] The zenith of exploratory activity – captured by the annual number of wildcat wells drilled – occurred in 1988 and marked the culmination of renewed efforts to search for oil off Azerbaijani shores, which were launched in the 1970s.[40] While its discovery peak was reached as far back as 1871, between the start of commercial oil production in the 1870s and 1991, on the eve of independence, a staggering 21.6 billion barrels of oil had been discovered in Baku and off its shores. This would prove to be the lion's share of Azerbaijan's proven reserves.

---

[38] Moreover, while the first generation of fields that were developed lay at relatively shallow depths, the rock they were ensconced within proved quite easy to penetrate. See Gustafson (1989, p. 99).

[39] The source for this and other figures on the number of wildcat wells drilled and the oil reserves associated with oil discoveries is from Tsui (2011).

[40] Between 1977 and 1988, a record 41 wildcat wells were drilled.

To be sure, Azerbaijan's latter day exploration efforts were not entirely for naught. While oil deposits were first discovered in the Caspian Sea, off the coast of Baku, in the late 1940s and early 1950s, about 8 billion barrels of oil were linked to the discoveries of bigger offshore fields, including Azeri, Chirag, Kapaz, and Gunashli, in the 1970s and 1980s.[41] Yet, the last giant oil field discovered in Azerbaijan occurred in 1987, and heralded only 0.9 billion barrels of oil.[42] Moreover, only 2.27 billion barrels were discovered subsequent to Azerbaijan's independence in 1992.

Finally, Baku was an unlikely place to witness a historically unprecedented oil boom during the 1990s and 2000s in light of its recent economic history. During the 1980s, Azerbaijan was known more as an industrial center than an oil producer. It had cultivated a host of mature manufacturing sectors over the twentieth century enabled by transportation networks built over land, primarily via rail, and by sea, including merchant fleets and tankers. This ushered in the fabrication of various products, including weapons, steel, aluminum, electric motors, canning, and textiles. Predictably, several of the country's largest plants produced products associated with oil, including the manufacturing of oil machinery, fuel, and petrochemicals, such as plastics and synthetic rubber tires. Moreover, despite its decline in the production of crude, Baku continued to refine oil that was primarily shipped in from Russia via pipeline.

Nevertheless, Azerbaijan's industrial sector was not dominated by these oil-based applications. The lion's share of its industrial base was instead composed of foodstuffs and light industry, including textiles and furniture (Suny 1996, p.119). This allowed Azerbaijan to register the highest industrial growth rate in the Soviet Union between 1976 and 1980 (See Cornell 2011, p. 43).

In short, Azerbaijan's most recent and biggest oil boom was, for several reasons, entirely unexpected. Two crucial questions remain to be answered about it, however. First, why did this boom happen despite the potential hindrances outlined above? What drove the nearly fivefold increase in oil production registered between 1997 and 2007 (see Figure 5.2), despite the fact that the Soviet Union had refocused

---

[41] This was coupled with the application of innovative offshore oil field development methods including water flooding and forced liquid withdrawal (see Krylov, Boksernan, and Stavrovsky 1998, p. 76).

[42] The last supergiant discovery was in 1985 and augured 5.3 billion barrels of oil.

attention to the huge volumes of untapped oil in Central Asia and the Russian interior during the Cold War and it had already reached its exploration and discovery peaks years, if not decades, earlier? Second, how did this oil boom happen? How was it planned, organized, and financed in light of the fact that Azerbaijan's oil sector had been largely left for dead on the eve of its independence? What explains the logistics behind how the production of crude managed to reach record levels despite the fact that the country's biggest discoveries were in the rear-view mirror?

Severe state weakness in the aftermath of independence

Some nations start their life as sovereign countries on third base – they are blessed with a slew of advantages. These include political stability and economic prosperity. They face few, if any, threats to their national security and territorial integrity. Then there is Azerbaijan.

The process by which Azerbaijan achieved independence was, at least on the surface, technical and bureaucratic. After the Soviet Congress of People's Deputies voted for the dissolution of the Soviet Union in September of 1991, the Supreme Soviet of Azerbaijan passed a constitutional act declaring independence the next month. This was followed by a national referendum on independence in December in which the "Yes Vote" achieved 95 percent support; international recognition followed later that month.

Yet, Azerbaijan's journey as an independent state began quite violently. Soviet troops had rolled into Baku in January of 1990 to try to quell a spasm of violence. Pogroms perpetrated by Azeri nationalists against Armenians in the capital city were catalyzed by the Supreme Soviet of Armenia's attempt to incorporate Azerbaijan's disputed Nagorno-Karabakh region, which is predominantly populated by ethnic Armenians.[43] Gorbachev then declared a state of emergency and the federal army violently suppressed the *Popular Front*, a militant Azerbaijani independence movement. Marked by hundreds of casualties, this infamous episode was labeled "Black January."

---

[43] Similar anti-Armenian riots had broken out in 1988 in the Azerbaijani city of Sumgait in reaction to secessionist agitation by Nagorno-Karabakh's Armenian ethnics and a resounding vote in favor of uniting with Armenia registered by the enclave's parliament.

But this moniker could have just as easily described January of 1992: shortly after gaining statehood, Azerbaijan was extremely vulnerable, politically unstable, and in economic and fiscal tatters. Immediately after independence, Azerbaijan was forced to address a set of problems that quickly mounted and fed on each other. These included the need to suddenly and quickly erect a national army and navy in the face of variegated threats to its security, if not survival. They also included the challenge of adapting to the shocks and surprises associated with liberalizing a command-and-control economy that had been heavily subsidized by the Soviet Union to that point. Unfortunately for Azerbaijan, the structural adjustments it attempted to hastily undertake coincided with the outbreak of several economic and fiscal crises. These not only set back economic progress, but almost rendered the state insolvent.

The start-up costs to sovereignty faced by Azerbaijan were compounded by the fact that it found itself trying to survive in a very dangerous geopolitical neighborhood. Russia, although also considerably weakened after the dissolution of the Soviet Union, continued to throw its weight around in the "near abroad." By supporting secessionist territories within Azerbaijan and other former Soviet republics – for example, in Georgia's troubled South Ossetia – it attempted to gain leverage over these nascent countries' foreign policies.

Basically, Moscow had three objectives.[44] First, it was to force its former republics into the Commonwealth of Independent States, the successor to the Soviet Union. Second, it was to gain basing rights within their borders. Third, to deter them from aligning with the West and the North Atlantic Treaty Organization.

Moreover, the troubled Middle East was only a stone's throw away. Indeed, the (first) Gulf War was raging during the flare-up in hostilities between Azerbaijan and Armenia surrounding Nagorno-Karabakh. Both conflicts were unsettling the wider region and threatening to draw in countries such as Turkey and Iran.

By far, the most important security threat that the new country faced was that disputed province. A costly and bloody war against Armenia and Armenian-backed rebels was ignited in the wake of the events of Black January. The decision by the Nagorno-Karabakh oblast to proclaim its independence from the Soviet Union in September of 1991, a month before Azerbaijan had declared its intention to do so, only

---

[44] This paragraph builds on Driscoll (2015).

added fuel to the fire. With Russian backing, Armenia attacked the city of Khojaly in Nagorno-Karabakh in early 1992. The death toll was over 600. Then, in May of that year, the city of Shusha fell to Armenia, unleashing political chaos throughout the province. By 1994, Armenia occupied all of Nagorno-Karabakh and almost 15 percent of Azerbaijan's territory outside of this province (see Radnitz 2012, p. 72, f.n. #6). That year, it had also inflicted heavy losses on Azerbaijan, capturing huge caches of military equipment and killing thousands. A cease-fire was finally declared in May, but not before hundreds of thousands had been displaced from Nagorno-Karabakh and Azerbaijan's political system had been left in disarray.

Indeed, perhaps the biggest victim of the war was the country's political stability and order. Ayaz Mutalibov was elected president of Azerbaijan in September of 1991 and resigned shortly after the country's independence, in March 1992, after a pogrom against ethnic Azerbaijanis by Armenians in Khojaly, Nagorno-Karabakh and a feckless response by his regime. This was followed by a short stint in power by Yaqub Mamedov, who was ousted by a coup in May of that year and replaced by Isa Gambar, who then handed over power to Ebülfez Elçibey after he won elections in June. Only a year after that, however, Elçibey himself was stripped of power by the Azerbaijani parliament after fleeing to Nakhichevan in the wake of huge military losses inflicted by Armenia in the Nagorno-Karabakh conflict and an insurrection led by a rogue militia leader (see Radnitz 2012, p. 62). In short, post-independence Azerbaijan was buffeted by a short-lived string of ineffective leaders.

Matters soon settled down some. Heydar Aliyev, who had spearheaded the soft coup against Elçibey from within parliament, took over the executive branch. A key member of the old guard, he was a political insider of the highest order: a former speaker of the Supreme Soviet of Azerbaijan, as well as a former leader of the Azerbaijan KGB and a former First Secretary of the Communist Party of Azerbaijan.[45] Moreover, several coup and assassination attempts were subsequently thwarted, including ones in 1994, 1995, 1996, and 1998 (see Radnitz 2012, p. 63).

---

[45] He was later elected president with 98.8 percent of the vote and 96 percent turnout.

An economic debacle

While the political front had stabilized, the Azerbaijani economy was in a tailspin, with seemingly no end in sight. In 1993, economic production was less than 40 percent of the level achieved in 1990 and public officials were not being paid in full (see Cornell 2011, p. 83). By 1995, production levels had barely recovered, standing at 40 percent of what they had been in 1989 (Cornell 2011, p. 98). The level of Per Capita Income achieved in 1992, US$4,907, was only reached again in 2004. This was reflected in a sharp reduction in real wages: by 59 percent in 1994 and a further 22 percent in 1995 (IMF 1997, p. 28).

Moreover, a prolonged period of hyperinflation further eroded salaries and purchasing power. The numbers are quite mindboggling. According to Siegelbaum et al. (2002, p. 87), inflation ran at 912 percent per year in 1992, 1,129 percent in 1993, and 1,665 percent in 1994. The inflation rate only fell below double digits in 1997, due to the adoption of a stringent stabilization program.

Economic crises and associated fallouts bedeviled the struggling country throughout the 1990s. In 1994, there was a currency crisis followed by a huge banking crisis. Three large state-owned banks were deemed insolvent and one large state-owned bank faced serious liquidity problems (see Laeven and Valencia 2008). Although the four largest banks were recapitalized, over 150 private banks eventually failed (Siegelbaum, et al. 2002, p. 41; 57). While the root causes of the crisis were insider lending, a proliferation of pyramid schemes, and overall bad management, the consequences continued to linger years later. For example, in 1999 non-performing loans (NPL) were 62 percent of the loan stock and, therefore, Azerbaijani banks posted only US$7 million in after-tax profits that year, which after adjusting provisions for the total quantity of NPLs, equated to a loss of US$266 million (Siegelbaum, et al. 2002, pp. 54–56).

These problems served to compound Azerbaijan's already low levels of monetization, a relic of the Soviet system of economic central planning.[46] After independence the economy was still characterized by high levels of barter, arrears, and netting – thus it relied heavily on non-cash settlements and was still largely informal. The upper bound estimate of the size of the shadow economy in the early 2000s is a stunning two-thirds of total economic activity. This meant that

---

[46] This paragraph draws heavily on Siegelbaum et al. (2002), especially, p. 37.

participation by Azerbaijanis in the banking system was quite low; moreover, a sharp reduction in the domestic deposit base *vis-à-vis* 1995 levels was registered.[47] The upshot is that systems of formal credit allocation and risk management that would otherwise be conducted through banks were inadequate. In the early 2000s, private sector credit as a share of GDP was only 2.5 percent; capital markets were virtually nonexistent.

By extension, regular taxation on citizens and businesses was very difficult for the Azerbaijani tax authorities to undertake during the 1990s, and investors tended to shy away from domestic, nontradables sectors (Siegelbaum, et al. 2002, p. 37). Between 1994 and 2000, the level of direct taxation excluding social contributions as well as rents from natural resources was stagnant (Prichard, Cobham, and Goodall 2014). Moreover, the weakness of the export sector during this period, which had been centered on the export of fuels, plastics, and machinery for use in the Siberian oil industry during the Soviet era, meant that large trade deficits were registered during this decade. Therefore, Azerbaijan suffered from a dearth of foreign exchange that could pay for basic imports; for example, in 1998, alone, the country's international reserves were reduced by 4 percent.[48]

An oil renaissance to fuel state-building

It is clear that something needed to be done to cauterize Azerbaijan's debacle. To address the arrant political instability that had beset the country in the had inherited from the disastrous aftermath of independence, and to try to stop the economic hemorrhaging described above, President Aliyev "[P]romoted stability over national assertion, and made state-building and regime consolidation the overriding objective of his remaining years in power" (Radnitz 2012, p. 62). On the military front, this meant cutting Azerbaijan's losses in Nagorno-Karabakh. On the political front, this meant focusing on rationalizing and streamlining the bureaucracy, and stacking it and the rest of the state

---

[47] While foreign currency deposits more than made up for this shortfall, this subjected banks to high levels of foreign exchange risk due to the risk that loans might not be repaid at full value (see ibid, p. 69).

[48] The definition of international reserves and its source are discussed further below, as I will use it as a measure of state capacity in the panel data analysis that follows the Azerbaijan case study.

apparatus with loyalists and pragmatists (see ibid). It also meant grooming his son, Ilham, to one day succeed him.[49] On the economic front, it meant finding a way to dig the country out of a huge hole.

What was Aliyev to do in the face of the formidable structural headwinds against an oil sector renaissance? As outlined above, there were many. First, the expected depletion of Baku's onshore oil fields; second, the pronounced refocus in attention, capital, and expertise to Western Siberia during the latter days of Soviet oil policy; third, the fact that Azerbaijan had reached its exploration and discovery peak during the Soviet era and production was at an all-time low (see Figure 5.2); fourth, on the eve of the collapse of the Soviet Union, Azerbaijan was known more as an industrial center than an oil producer.

Yet, for several reasons, the only real choice for Azerbaijan was the revival of its hydrocarbon sector. The country's manufacturing model was no longer viable under the strictures of a market economy. Although the industrial sector had risen to occupy the pinnacle of the economy by the twilight of the Soviet Union, this was the result of heavy subsidization by Moscow, which had come to rely on Baku's manufacturing of oil-related machinery such as drilling rigs, pipes, and oilfield equipment, as well as its large petroleum refineries.[50]

It is therefore not surprising that the basis for Azerbaijan's manufacturing prowess quickly dissolved as the Soviet system collapsed. On the one hand, industries located in Baku and Sumgayit dedicated to metallurgy, machine building, and chemicals lost the majority of their final market, forcing a contraction in production and the closing of several factories (see UN n.d., p. 90). On the other hand, the manufacturing plants left standing lost access to the cheap inputs – at prices subsidized by Moscow – that they had grown accustomed to, including steel and chemical products. Moreover, surviving firms in heavy industries relied on obsolete technologies and were beset with low rates of productivity (see IMF 1997, p. 21). Meanwhile, light

---

[49] In 1994, Ilham was appointed Vice President of SOCAR, and then became its president. He was later elected to parliament, headed Azerbaijan's Olympic Committee and, in the run-up to replacing his father as president in 2003, was elected prime minister.

[50] Although it should be noted that Azerbaijan had begun to become an unreliable supplier of equipment to the Western Siberian oil sector in the late 1980s as a result of the Nagorno-Karabakh conflict (see Gustafson 2012, p. 47).

industries such as textiles, clothing, furniture, and appliances found it increasingly difficult to gain access to markets and suppliers and could simply not compete with cheaper imports (Bell 2002, p. 112). And not even the petrochemical sector was spared, as several crude refineries shuttered their doors.

Therefore, by the mid-1990s, Azerbaijan's industrial sector was in shambles. In 1995, alone, manufacturing output had declined by 26 percent (IMF 1997, p. 21). Between 1992 and 2008, value added in manufacturing decreased by 63 percent. A comparison to neighboring Kazakhstan is telling. Like Azerbaijan, it is an ex-Soviet Republic best known for oil and natural gas – yet, it nonetheless managed to double the share of manufacturing in value added over the same period (Regine 2012, p. 258).

There were other, more positive, reasons that oil and gas was the only real alternative faced by the Aliyev regime in its attempts to revive the economy and fiscal base. First, given the country's shaky rule of law, declining domestic demand, and rising macroeconomic imbalances, hydrocarbons was the only sector of the economy that foreign investors were interested in. By the same token, it was crucial for the Aliyev government to court foreign direct investment (FDI) in order to finance trade deficits and obtain much needed capital in the aftermath of the devastating banking crisis outlined above. Also, the early 1990s were an era of recovering oil prices *vis-à-vis* the late 1980s, which witnessed a precipitous decline catalyzed in 1985 by the Saudi's decision to abstain from ratcheting down the rate at which its crude entered the market. Moreover, Azerbaijani oil is of very high quality – it is both light and sweet – and therefore does not have very high refining costs associated with it (see Ibrahimov n.d., p. 65). Finally, no matter how dilapidated and neglected, the country still possessed a formidable oil industry infrastructure, including both physical and human capital.

The revival of Azerbaijan's oil industry was the result of a series of shrewd decisions made by Aliyev, who from the start sought to maximize the inflow of foreign investment into the hydrocarbon sector. His regime pined for big oil and gas revenues, and in order to bring them about he transformed the country into a hydrocarbon juggernaut. By 2006, the oil sector as a share of GDP was 40 percent, the state's share of revenues from oil was over 50 percent, and the share of its exports consisting of oil was 85 percent (Bagirov 2006, p. 17).

Immediate challenges to reviving the oil sector

Yet, this does not mean that Azerbaijan did not face serious short-run challenges – aside from the structural ones outlined above – in its attempt to resurrect the country's hydrocarbon sector. Courting foreign investors was not without problems, especially in light of the fact that Azerbaijan had last relied on FDI in the early 1900s, before joining the Soviet Union. Also, there was the issue of a rather long time lag: oil was only projected to start flowing from a series of new offshore fields in the mid-2000s (see Ibrahimov n.d., p. 66). To make matters worse: Azerbaijan's oil-and-gas producing equipment and extraction processes were hopelessly outdated, scores of oil wells lie fallow, exploration had ground to a standstill, and oil workers faced sizable arrears (see Bagirov, 1996, p. 27).

But perhaps the biggest obstacle that the Aliyev regime encountered in its attempt to revive Azerbaijan's hydrocarbon sector was how to transport the country's crude and natural gas via pipeline, given the fact that the new nation was landlocked. For several reasons, this was a thorny dilemma. The worsening of the violence in Chechnya made it difficult to forge a northern route to a Russian terminal in Novorossiysk. And, even after the Nagorno-Karabakh's cease-fire in 1994, Azerbaijan continued to face Russian belligerence. Besides opposing Azerbaijan's attempts to court foreign oil companies to help SOCAR produce known hydrocarbons and explore for more of them, and its attempt to dictate the terms of how to divide Caspian seabed resources between the former Soviet Republics, Moscow also threatened to derail the construction of a new pipeline intended to bypass Russia and pass exclusively through Turkey (see Gustafson 2012; Ibrahimov 2010).

How Azerbaijan addressed these challenges and the consequences

In order to address both the structural and immediate challenges that the Azerbaijani oil industry faced, while also courting as much capital and generating as many revenues as possible in short order, the Aliyev regime adopted a multipronged strategy. First, it helped mold the state oil company into a Western-style, integrated oil company. Second, it pushed through a series of legal reforms intended to court FDI and sent strong signals about its desire to make foreign oil companies equal partners in the country's hydrocarbon future via PSAs. Third, it crafted a very aggressive depletion strategy for its offshore oil stocks that aimed to bring discontinued oil wells back into production and drill dozens of new wells to accelerate production to historical levels. Fourth, the Aliyev regime attempted to extract as much revenue upfront as possible. Fifth, it sought to build a series of new export pipelines that circumvented Russian territory. Sixth, it launched a renewed exploration campaign intended to unearth new oil and gas discoveries. Finally, it tended to the rehabilitation of several onshore fields.

The structure and size of SOCAR

Although it was his predecessor, Elçibey, who had decreed the creation of SOCAR in September of 1992, it was really Aliyev who brought Azerbaijan's national oil company to life. He was in favor of a vertical structure combining both upstream and downstream elements characterized by an ambitious scale and scope across onshore and offshore oil and gas. SOCAR was therefore designed to subsume exploration, production, refining, marketing, and transportation. The company accordingly encompasses geophysics and engineering geology, the construction of offshore, deep water platforms, machine building, oil pipeline construction, and crude refining. It also includes a huge oil fleet that runs the gamut from vessels for construction to oil exploration and transportation (Bagirov 1996, p. 26).

The numbers are staggering. SOCAR employs over 60,000 people, operates over 6,800 onshore oil wells and over 1,400 offshore oil wells, controls over 300 vessels, and operates six stationary offshore oil drilling platforms (Ibrahimov n.d., p. 69). It also produces and distributes natural gas in both Azerbaijan and Georgia, operates thousands and thousands of miles of oil pipelines, and runs two refineries in Baku that have a total processing capacity of over 20 million tons of crude a year.

A new legal regime and investment strategy

None of this could have been possible without massive amounts of capital to finance the exploration, production, refinement, marketing, and transportation of oil and natural gas. Aliyev therefore pushed through a series of legal reforms intended to court FDI. These reforms set the stage for foreign oil companies to become equal partners in Azerbaijan's revived hydrocarbon economy.

To do so, the Azerbaijani parliament began by passing the "Law on Protection of Foreign Investments."[51] This law is extremely favorable to foreign investors. It grants them complete and unreserved legal protection and puts them on equal footing as native born investors. It allows for the repatriation of profits, revenues, and other funds associated with their investments. It also provides for a ten-year grandfather clause that exempts foreign investors if new, non-fiscal legislation proves less favorable to them. Expropriation is only reserved in the case of natural disasters, epidemics, or extraordinary circumstances and, if it does occur, investors are entitled to prompt, effective, and adequate compensation.

Other measures have also helped the country signal a hospitable environment to foreign investors. The Azerbaijani government has, over the years, groomed itself to accede to the World Trade Organization (WTO). Specifically, it has adopted several reforms to achieve compliance with WTO standards – for example, by eliminating tariffs on cash currency exports – and has participated in several consultations with this organization throughout the years. It has also maintained a liberal, market-based exchange rate with zero restrictions on currency conversion or the entrance and exit of funds. This has meant that foreign exchange is freely and broadly available. Moreover, the Law on International Arbitration, passed in 2000, recognizes the validity of contracts involving foreign investors that call for international bodies to arbitrate disputes. Finally, Azerbaijan and the United States entered into a bilateral investment treaty in 2001, which provides American investors with recourse to the *International Center for the Settlement of Investment Disputes.*[52]

This basic legal, financial, and currency conversion infrastructure underpins the modal foreign investment arrangement in Azerbaijan's

---

[51] The information contained in this paragraph and the next one is from the Global Investment Center (2012, pp. 34–37).

[52] This complements the fact that Azerbaijan is a signatory to the *World Bank Convention on the Settlement of Investment Disputes between States and Nationals of Other States*, a party to the *New York Convention on the Recognition and Enforcement of Foreign Arbitral Awards*, and a member of the *Multilateral Investment Guarantee Agency*.

oil and gas sector, which is centered on PSAs between SOCAR and international oil companies. Once PSA contracts are signed, they are ratified by the country's parliament and become enshrined as law. These PSAs run the gamut and encompass hydrocarbon exploration, development, production, and the rehabbing of discontinued or idle oil fields. Currently, over 30 PSAs are codified, and the vast majority of Azerbaijan's oil blocks fall under the auspices of these agreements.

Several details stand out. The average year in which these contracts were penned was 2001. This supports the notion that the Aliyev regime was eager to generate investment flows as quickly as possible, as well as ratchet up hydrocarbon production in order to tax it.[53] While 56 percent of the blocks are located offshore, a whopping 41 percent are rehabilitation projects for onshore oil fields, which speaks to the fact that the Azerbaijani state sought to leave no stone unturned when it came to extracting as much oil as possible. The average projected initial (first year) investment across all blocks is US$3 billion dollars, denominated in 2011 values; while this number excludes money allocated in subsequent years, it was subsequently revised upward.[54] Finally, SOCAR's average percentage stake in these projects is somewhat low, at 32.3, which speaks to the fact that the company was reliant on the capital, technology, and expertise provided by its foreign partners.

The crown jewel in Azerbaijan's petroleum crest is the famed Azeri, Chirag-Gunashli oil block. In 1994, a group of companies led by BP signed a 30-year PSA to develop the copious oil stocks buried under the giant Apsheron Trend in the Caspian Sea, otherwise known as the string of pearls.[55] Ultimately, 11 major oil companies representing eight countries teamed up with SOCAR.[56] Estimated reserves were 5.4 billion barrels. Because of its scale and scope it was called the Contract of the Century. While it called for an initial investment of almost US$13 billion, close to US$4 billion was invested between 2002

---

[53] Indeed, it is not entirely surprising that many of these blocks would later yield inauspicious oil wells that turned out to be dry (for example, Oguz) or suffer from pressure related problems (for example, Inam).

[54] Some of these figures are estimates.

[55] The Azerbaijan International Oil Company was created by SOCAR and the IOCs to govern the terms of the contract and coordinate their activities.

[56] Russia's LUKoil was made a minority partner, with a 10 percent stake in the project.

and 2005 alone. Development began in 1997, and it currently represents 60 percent of Azerbaijan's oil production.[57]

This much-vaunted PSA stands out for several reasons. First, it entitled SOCAR to 80 percent of the profit oil; excluding value added taxes and royalties, this was projected to amount to over US$80 billion (see Bagirov 1996, p. 31).[58] Second, it prioritized the immediate stabilization of, and increases in, oil production from the Gunashli field, so that these revenues could enter the state's coffers as soon as possible. Similarly, even before this accelerated development timetable was intended to occur, the Contract of the Century prescribed that generous bonuses be paid by the IOCs, upfront, to the Azerbaijani state (see ibid., p. 29). Moreover, SOCAR was even exempted from having to immediately pony up its share of the financing, as it received a loan from other contract participants to do so (ibid., p. 32).

An aggressive extraction strategy

SOCAR engaged in a very aggressive depletion strategy for its offshore oil stocks that aimed to bring discontinued and abandoned oil wells back into production and drill dozens of new wells to accelerate crude production to historical levels. Figure 5.3 attempts to show how aggressive this strategy in fact was by plotting the annual change in the oil depletion rate (in percentage terms). As can be readily seen, this depletion rate begins to ascend steeply during the late 1990s, and really skyrockets after 2000.

Allow me to put this pattern in perspective. While between 1957 and 1979 the average depletion rate was 0.75 percent – and had only been above 0.60 percent once before that, in 1944 – it had fallen to 0.53 between 1980 and 1997, only to take a U-turn and increase sharply after that, reaching a high point of 2.54 in 2013. Projections are for even larger increases to continue, meaning that a greater and

---

[57] This process was not without false starts. Azerbaijan first put out bids from outside investors in January of 1991. And, in early 1992 the Elçibey administration had agreed to an operating concession with BP and Statoil to develop the Chirag field and signed a separate agreement with Pennzoil to develop the Gunashli field. These original contracts fell through due to the coup that felled his regime.

[58] Although SOCAR was originally endowed with a 20 percent ownership share, this share eventually fell to 10 percent (see Bagirov 1996, p. 32). Its share of profit oil assumes a 22.75 percent rate of return for the IOCs (see Bagirov 2006, p. 30).

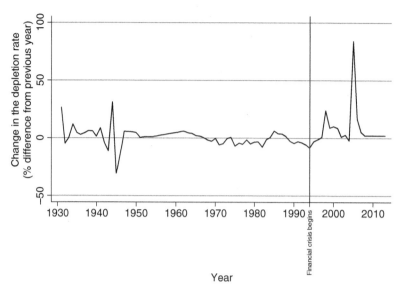

Figure 5.3 Azerbaijan's oil depletion rate.

Notes: This is measured as barrels of oil produced in year *t*/(ultimately recoverable reserves, in barrels – cumulative production in year t, in barrels).

Source: Tsui (2011).

greater share of oil will have to be produced in new fields just to offset yearly declines in older ones.[59] It is therefore not surprising that annual oil production growth rates averaged 15 percent between 1997 and 2007 (see Figure 5.3), culminating in a historical record of 0.30 billion barrels of oil produced a year in the late 2000s. In combination with relatively high oil prices during the 2000s, oil rents exploded. While in 1992 Azerbaijan's oil income per capita was only US$302 (in 2007 dollars), by 2006 it had reached a record US$1,844 (in 2007 dollars).[60]

---

[59] Some of the side effects of this strategy are that the volume of new oil wells that are drilled per field – so-called infill drilling – has increased steadily over time, as have the marginal costs per unit produced.

[60] The source is Haber and Menaldo (2011a). I should also note that there have been steady increases in the production of offshore natural gas. At first, most of the output was consumed domestically (see Petri, Taube, and Tsyvinski 2002). As of late, however, Azerbaijan has been exporting increasing levels of natural gas to Turkey and European markets (see Ciaretta and Nairov n.d., p. 14).

An aggressive revenue generation strategy

Luckily for the Azerbaijani state, it was well positioned to reap the lion's share of these rents. Indeed, the PSA contracts penned in Azerbaijan since its independence provide an excellent example of mechanisms used by weak states to generate revenues from oil and gas projects. As has been explained above, these revenues can accrue long before oil is pumped out of the ground, and they can accrue even when no commercial reserves are found.

Before launching into the details about how Azerbaijan extracts revenue from its hydrocarbon industry, it behooves us to review the magnitude of the capital flows that have been associated with oil exploration, production, refining, and transportation since 1992; after all, these flows carry benefits in their own right as well.[61] During the heyday of oil investments in the early 2000s, the stock of FDI was significantly bigger than Azerbaijan's GDP, reaching an apex of 132 percent in 2004 (UNCTAD 2012). Since then, things have predictably leveled off. Yet, the total FDI that flowed into the oil sector in 2010 was a very respectable US\$6.2 billion (out of US\$15.5 billion in FDI for the entire economy), which is 12 percent of GDP. Moreover, this constituted a doubling of the level observed the previous year (see Global Investment Center 2012, p. 33), and the numbers are expected to continue to grow as the Shah-Deniz block will receive close to US\$5 billion in capital to develop natural gas in the coming years after one of the biggest natural gas discoveries ever took place there.

There are several ways in which the Azerbaijani state has generated revenues from its hydrocarbons during the most recent oil boom. This includes the sale, mostly via export, of its share of profit oil. It also includes invoicing generous bonuses and acre payments made by the IOCs that SOCAR has partnered with in PSAs, the collection of various transit fees and rent, profit taxes paid by the IOCs once they have recovered their costs, income taxes paid by subcontractors that provide services to SOCAR and the IOCs, and income taxes paid by oil company employees (see Bagirov 2006, p. 5).

Most important for our purposes, through the way it has structured its numerous PSA agreements, the state has attempted to extract as

---

[61] Of course, they also carry risks. One big one is foreign exchange risk, which has increased profoundly in the shadow of increasing FDI. Indeed, the vast majority of bank deposits in Azerbaijan are in the form of hard, foreign currency (see Siegelbaum, et al. 2002, p. 69).

much revenue as possible from oil projects in the immediate term. First and foremost, this has taken the form of signing bonuses. These are lump sum payments made upfront by IOCs to Azerbaijan for the right to participate in PSA projects and are usually paid within 30 days of a PSA's effective date. In some cases, one-third of the bonus money had to be paid within ten days of the contract going into effect (Bagirov 1996, p. 29). And, in the case of the Azeri-Chirag-Gunashli PSA, Exxon and the Turkish Petroleum Corporation exchanged an immediate US$173 million cash payment to SOCAR to buy out 10 percent of its stake in the project (see ibid., p. 32).

The vast majority of Azerbaijan's PSA contracts prescribe these signing bonuses. The amount of money spans the gamut, starting as low as US$1 million and running as high as the US$228 million (2011 values) paid out by IOCs for the right to produce oil from the Azeri-Chirag-Gunashli oil block. A lower bound estimate of total bonus money associated with Azerbaijan's PSAs is US$785.3 million (2011 values). In 2007, US$72.4 million were paid out (Ciaretta and Nasirov n.d., p. 7).

Consistent with the theoretical framework spelled out in this book, the purpose of bonuses has been to help shore up a struggling state in need of immediate injections of revenues. According to Bagirov (2006, p. 11):

Bonuses were payable since 1992 and became a valuable response to the needs of the economy of Azerbaijan through 1999; in particular, these transfers were essential to fill in the budget gap, as well as solve emergency social projects, and afford monetary interventions in maintaining the exchange rate of the national currency.

Similarly, acreage fees are another early revenue-generating mechanism frequently used by the Azerbaijani government. These are typically paid during the exploration portion of a project. In the late 2000s, three PSAs had per square kilometer fees of US$1,200 annually. The remaining ones had acreage fees of US$2,000 per square kilometer annually (Bagirov 2006, p. 27; ABC Azerbaijan 2009). Between 2005 and 2009, an average of US$6.5 million was paid out in acreage fees per year (Ciaretta and Nasirov n.d., p. 7).

Finally, regular profit taxes levied on IOCs' share of the profit oil have also contributed vast amounts to the state's coffers. The tax rate varies according to these firms' ownership stake, and ranges from 20 to 32 percent.

Taken together, these revenue-garnering instruments have proven very successful. Between 1995 and 1999, the Azerbaijani government received about US$450 million in PSA payments (Siegelbaum, et al. 2002, p. 101). By the late 1990s, oil revenues were more than US$10 billion per year (Cornell 2011, p. 112). These numbers grew by several orders of magnitude during the 2000s on the back of relatively high oil prices. Therefore, the state became heavily reliant on oil revenues by the late 2000s. By 2008, revenues from oil were 38 percent of total revenues (Prichard, Cobham, and Goodall 2014).

A stealthy oil and gas pipeline strategy

Since independence, Azerbaijan has assiduously sought to build a series of new export pipelines to transport its newfound oil and gas to Western markets. Its top priority has been to circumvent Russian territory, as Russia has had a contentious relationship with Azerbaijan since the fall of the Soviet Union and has repeatedly challenged its sovereignty and hydrocarbon policies. Most practically, Moscow has attempted to charge SOCAR hefty transit fees when transporting its oil through Russian territory (see Ibrahimov 2010, p. 27).

With the help of the United States, other Western powers, and Turkey, Azerbaijan's pipeline strategy has wildly succeeded. On the one hand, it continues to operate an oil pipeline between Baku and Russia known as the Novorossiysk, which handled most of the "early oil" flowing from oil fields in the Azeri-Chirag-Gunashli block in the late 1990s. On the other hand, most of its oil and natural gas are now transported via pipelines that bypass Russia. These include the Baku-Supsa Pipeline, the Baku-Tbilisi-Ceyhan Pipeline, and the South Caucasus Pipeline. The latter three are operated by BP, total 3,571 km, and have necessitated US$5.46 billion in investment money (see Ciaretta and Nasirov n.d., p. 14). This double-pronged approach allowed Azerbaijan to avoid depending on Russia for access to Western markets for its oil while avoiding antagonizing Russia by shutting it out entirely – which was also reflected in the role given to LUKoil in the so-called Contract of the Century (see Babali 2005).

The unexpected fruits of Azerbaijan's institutions curse

Azerbaijan's GDP growth has been quite rapid during the 2000s, fueled by very high levels of FDI and oil rents. In order to blunt the inflationary effects associated with such a rapid influx of capital and revenues, in 2000 Azerbaijan created an oil savings fund, the State Oil Fund of Azerbaijan (SOFAZ), to help smooth oil revenues, and thus consumption and expenditures. As of October 1, 2010, SOFAZ's reserves were US$21.7 billion (additionally, the country's Central Bank had currency reserves totaling US$6.4 billion that year). While the norm has been for transfers of revenues from the fund to the state not to exceed 50 percent of its reserves any given year, public spending has nonetheless occurred at extraordinarily high levels (see Global Investment Center 2012, p. 33).

An aggressive exploration strategy

In order to compensate for its aggressive oil extraction policy, SOCAR also promoted an equally aggressive campaign for both oil and gas exploration in the Caspian Sea.[62] This is reflected in the record number of wildcat oil wells drilled between 1996 and 2013. During this time period, 74 of these exploratory wells were drilled, representing an average of 4.4 wells drilled per year. When compared to the six wildcat wells drilled between 1989 and 1992, the nadir of Azerbaijan's oil industry, this is a staggering turn around. It is impressive in comparison to other eras as well. For example, between the 1870s and 1929, during Azerbaijan's first and most impressive oil boom, 50 wildcat wells were drilled; between 1977 and 1988, the heyday of offshore exploration, only 41 wells were drilled.

No matter how aggressive this exploration push has been, however, it has not been as successful as past campaigns. Azerbaijan's oil discovery peak was reached in 1871. Yet even after that point, and before its independence, 21.6 billion barrels of oil were discovered. About 8 billion barrels of that oil are associated with offshore giant and supergiant fields, including those found in the Azeri-Chirag-Gunashli. It is these decades-ago discoveries that Azerbaijan has been living off since the 1990s despite its heroic efforts to unearth more oil. Only 2.27 billion barrels have been discovered since 1992. And because of the historically high depletion rates outlined above, Azerbaijan's proven reserves have decreased from 14.3 billion barrels in 1997 to 13.25 billion barrels in 2013.

---

[62] The source for the data on exploration and proven reserves in this section is from Tsui (2011).

Concluding thoughts about the Azerbaijani case

Clearly, the days in which the Azerbaijani state can offset its underlying weakness by drilling its way out of trouble are numbered. To be sure, relying on oil as a default political and economic strategy has allowed the state to maximize revenues and stoke economic growth in the immediate term on the back of the massive influx of foreign capital, technology, and expertise, and the rapid production and export of oil and gas. Whether Azerbaijan can now transition to a more diversified economy is an open question.

Cross-country evidence of oil in weak states

In this section, I statistically test five hypotheses implied by the theory that oil is ultimately endogenous to state weakness. First, *ceteris paribus*, states with lower capacity should exhibit greater oil exploration efforts. Second, they should exhibit higher oil extraction rates. As argued above, weaker states should offer incentives to both IOCs and NOCs to bring oil wells into production at a relatively expeditious rate; and they will not necessarily do so because the going price fetched by oil on international markets is attractive. Third, they should export oil in larger quantities. Fourth, they should tax it at higher rates. Last, they should attract higher levels of capital in the oil sector.

As outlined above, the latter is for two reasons. The first is that IOCs operating in developed countries would often rather do business in weaker developing countries where they can exploit regulatory arbitrage opportunities. Second, weak states have been surprisingly effective at making selective commitments to private investors' property rights, both foreign and domestic.

The dataset and research strategy

To test these hypotheses, I construct a time-series cross-section dataset of 62 countries (1930–2006) that possess the geological potential to discover and develop hydrocarbons. The dataset includes both developing and developed countries that, together, possess 99 percent of the world's proven reserves (calculated in 2006). These countries are Albania, Algeria, Angola, Argentina, Australia, Austria, Azerbaijan, Bahrain, Bolivia, Brazil, Cameroon, Canada, Chad, Chile, China,

Colombia, Congo, Croatia, Ecuador, Egypt, Denmark, France, Gabon, Germany, Hungary, India, Indonesia, Iran, Iraq, Italy, Kazakhstan, Kuwait, Libya, Malaysia, Mexico, the Netherlands, Nigeria, Norway, Oman, Pakistan, Papua New Guinea, Peru, Qatar, Romania, Russia, Saudi Arabia, Sudan, Syria, Thailand, Trinidad and Tobago, Tunisia, Turkey, Turkmenistan, Ukraine, the United Arab Emirates, the United Kingdom, the United States, Uzbekistan, Venezuela, Vietnam, Yemen, and Yugoslavia.[63]

Variable construction

To construct several of the oil-related variables, I rely on Tsui (2011). This includes the main dependent variable, which estimates oil exploration efforts, and important controls, such as countries' oil endowments and the date of peak oil production. By exploiting industrial scale information on oilfield geology and engineering, this source avoids the problems that beset data on proven reserves. Laherrère (2003), for example, demonstrates that the latter data are usually unreliable.

I also rely on a plethora of sources to construct other measures of oil intensity, as well as the key independent variable, state capacity, and several additional controls and instrumental variables. These are disclosed further below, in the detailed discussions of each variable.

Approach to causal inference

Endogeneity bias is a concern when estimating the effect of state capacity on oil exploration, oil extraction, oil exports, oil taxation, and oil capital. This is for two reasons. First, the causal arrow may also run from these outcomes to state capacity, whereby a government's access to oil rents disincentivizes it from investing in legal and bureaucratic capacity and taxing non-resource sectors (Ross 2001; Fearon 2005; Jensen, and Johnston 2011). Second, the regressions might omit variables that may be correlated with both state capacity and these outcomes, therefore confounding the results. To address these concerns, I avail a variety of econometric strategies.

In the regressions reported in Table 5.3, the models control for country-fixed effects, year-fixed effects, country-specific time trends, and several

---

[63] Only a few regressions are estimated on the entire sample of countries during the entire time period. Most are estimated on different subsets of countries during shorter periods; this is due to truncated coverage on the covariates. The results are nevertheless materially the same across each of these smaller samples.

time-varying controls. These techniques allow me to expunge multiple sources of both time-invariant and time-varying omitted variables from the panel regressions. They do so by exploiting the within-country variation in both state capacity and the outcomes of interest: oil exploration, oil extraction, oil exportation, oil taxation, and oil capital.

Furthermore, in a series of models that are discussed, but not reported, I estimate dynamic Structure Generalized Method of Moments (GMM) regressions that address both omitted variable bias and reverse causation. In these specifications, potentially endogenous variables are instrumented with appropriate lags in levels after differencing the variables to expunge country-specific, time-invariant heterogeneity. These models also confer a further advantage; they allow me to estimate the long-run, total effect of permanent changes in state capacity on the outcomes of interest.

I also estimate and report several Instrumental Variables Two Stage Least Squares (IV-2SLS) models in Table 5.4. In those regressions state capacity is instrumented with factor endowments and the country's age.

Finally, I should note that the first-stage regressions are over-identified in the GMM and IV-2SLS regressions. This allows me to estimate statistical tests of the over-identifying restrictions in both cases. These tests always suggest that the exclusion restriction is satisfied. Taken as a whole, these steps give me considerable confidence that there is in fact a causal relationship running from low state capacity to greater oil exploration, extraction, exports, taxation, and capital stocks.

Measuring the dependent variables

The first dependent variable, and the one that I will focus on the most, is *Oil Exploration*. The number of wildcat wells drilled is a good proxy for exploration efforts.[64] As explained above, oil exploration always requires drilling exploratory wells. This means that wildcat wells are drilled *outside of known oilfields* and are therefore located *outside of*

---

[64] While the average rate for discovering commercial oil is less than 50 percent (Tsui 2011, p. 112), there is wide variation in success rates between countries. Some examples are instructive. According to Tsui (2011, p. 112, f.n. 66), in 2003 the U.S. success rate was 46 percent; according to Flores-Macías (2010, p. 217), in 2005 Mexico had a success rate of 53 percent; Brazil of 57 percent; Colombia of 38 percent; and Malaysia of 29 percent.

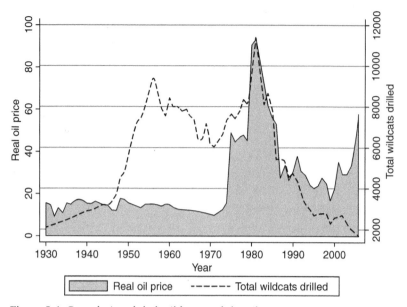

Figure 5.4 Cumulative global wildcats and the oil price.

the vicinity of known oil reserves. In other words, a wildcat well is drilled to find out if there is oil in the first place, even if seismic tests and other plausibility probes have already been conducted.

Descriptive statistics for Oil Exploration, calculated on the sample of country years with the most coverage for this variable, and represented by the regression in Table 5.4, Column 5 (N = 61; n = 2,862), follow. The mean number of wildcat wells drilled is 136; the standard deviation is 764; the minimum value is 0; and the maximum value is 9,151. Moreover, it appears that this variable is stationary in levels. Augmented Dickey-Fuller (Fisher) panel unit root tests reject the hypothesis that Oil Exploration is non-stationary, whether or not several lags or a trend are included.

Some plots of the data are helpful for understanding the variable's time-series variation. Figure 5.4 graphs the total wildcats drilled across the 62 countries in the dataset, by year, against the oil price in 2007 dollars. Figures 5.5–5.7 graph the wildcat wells drilled by 21 major oil producers since 1930. Together, these countries had 74 percent of the world's proven reserves in 2006.

To measure the intensity of *Oil Extraction*, I use Fuel Depletion. This is the value of oil, gas, and coal, minus the costs of production and the

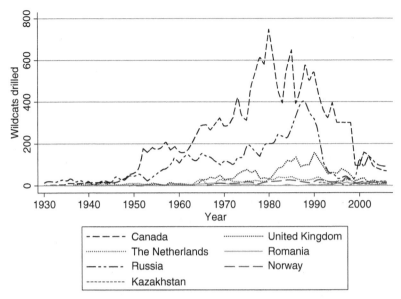

Figure 5.5 Wildcats in European countries (and Canada).

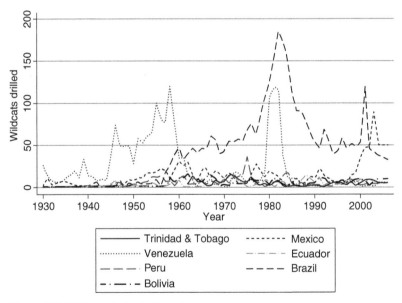

Figure 5.6 Wildcats in Latin America.

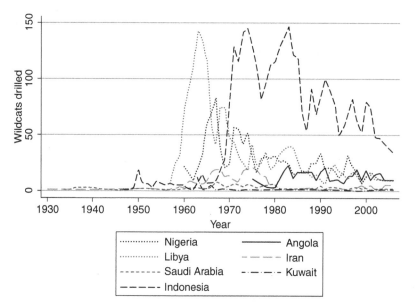

Figure 5.7 Wildcats in Africa, the Middle East, and Asia.

opportunity cost of capital, as a percentage of GNP.[65] This measure, originally developed by Hamilton and Clemens (1999), is from the World Bank Development Indicators (WBDI). While Augmented Dickey-Fuller (Fisher) panel unit root tests fail to reject the hypothesis that Oil Depletion is non-stationary when measured in levels, whether or not several lags or a trend are included, they reject the hypothesis that it is not stationary in first differences. Therefore, in all country fixed effects models this measure is included in first differences.

The other dependent variables are as follows. *Fuel Exports* is the value of exports of oil and natural gas as a percentage of GDP, from the WBDI. While Augmented Dickey-Fuller (Fisher) panel unit root tests fail to reject the hypothesis that Fuel Exports is non-stationary when measured in levels, whether or not several lags or a trend are included, they reject the hypothesis that it is not stationary in first differences. Therefore, in all country fixed effects models this measure is included in first differences.

---

[65] These costs vary greatly. For example, in the United States, the production cost of oil, including capital recovery, is US$15 per barrel. In the Middle East, it is only US$2 per barrel (Tsui 2011, p. 113).

Fiscal Reliance is the percentage of government revenues from oil, gas, or minerals. Unfortunately, it is only available for sixteen countries. They are Mexico, Venezuela, Ecuador, Chile, Trinidad and Tobago, Norway, Nigeria, Angola, Gabon, Indonesia, Iran, Algeria, Bahrain, Yemen, Oman, and Kuwait. This variable is from Haber and Menaldo (2011a). While Augmented Dickey-Fuller (Fisher) panel unit root tests fail to reject the hypothesis that Fiscal Reliance is non-stationary, whether or not several lags or a trend are included, they reject the hypothesis that Fiscal Reliance is non-stationary after first differencing. Therefore, this variable is included in first differences in the country fixed effects models.

Finally, *Oil Capital* is (log) real capital in the oil sector, per capita. It includes all sources of capital in the hydrocarbon sector, both foreign and domestic. The variable was constructed as follows. The real value added contributed by capital investments in the petroleum sector in 2000 dollars is divided by the population and logged, after adding 1 to deal with zero values. Petroleum-related sectors are identified at the three-digit industry level.[66] The main variables used to construct this measure are from the 2006 *UNIDO Industrial Statistics Database* (Version 2). Furthermore, Augmented Dickey-Fuller (Fisher) panel unit root tests reject the hypothesis that Oil Capital is non-stationary, whether or not several lags or a trend are included.

Measuring state capacity

As we saw in the previous chapter, state capacity is a sophisticated concept. It is multidimensional. It encompasses everything from the central government's grip over the nation's territory to the rule of law. It also connotes a sequence of events that unfold over relatively long stretches of time. While more capable states are those that can project power into the periphery and approximate a monopoly on the use of force, they are also able to administer censuses, collect taxes, and provide public goods. They tend to protect property rights, enforce contracts, and establish the rule of law. In turn, states that achieve these competencies are those that have made major investments in administration,

---

[66] In particular: ISIC 353 (Petroleum Refineries), ISIC 354 (Miscellaneous petroleum and coal products), and ISIC 369 (Other non-metallic mineral products). Any contribution made by the labor force to value added in these sectors is expunged.

compliance, and legal enforcement over sustained periods of time. Therefore, stronger states are characterized by a well-functioning legal system and a competent, professional, and honest bureaucracy.

One of the logical implications of this depiction of state capacity is that in low-capacity states it is quite difficult for the tax authorities to raise ordinary tax revenues. Assessing and collecting taxes on consumption, property, income, and investments calls on the fiscal authorities to identify potential tax bases, assess tax liabilities, collect taxes, and deter evasion. This meshes well with recent work on how to best operationalize state capacity. Hendrix (2010) urges researchers to focus on revenue-generating capacity measures. Besley and Persson also favor measures that tap into fiscal capacity: "the necessary infrastructure – in terms of administration, monitoring, and enforcement – to raise revenue from broad tax bases such as income and consumption" (Besley and Persson 2012, p. 6). Similar arguments are put forth by Lieberman (2002), and Hanson and Sigman (2011), as well as countless others. These researchers' prescriptions are consistent with the theoretical framework elucidated in the previous chapter.

Therefore, the primary measure of state capacity I employ is *Total Tax Revenues* (as a percentage of GDP). Yet, because any single measure of a multidimensional concept is bound to be incomplete, I also take a more conservative, multipronged approach to measuring state capacity and ensure that the results are robust to several other ways of operationalizing it. This reflects the fact that some researchers stress other aspects of state capacity besides fiscal capacity. For example, Kocher (2010) identifies four broad categories of state capacity: territorial and administrative capacity, a professionalized bureaucracy, institutional constraints, and military power.

Specifically, I develop and use four additional measures of state capacity. The first is *Private Credit*. The second is *Foreign Exchange Reserves*. The third is *Military Size*. The final one is *State Antiquity*. I explain the logic behind each of these below, after discussing my workhorse measure, Total Tax Revenues.

Total Tax Revenues is total domestic taxes as a percentage of GDP. These revenues include taxes from income, profits, and capital gains; property taxes; taxes on consumption, including sales and value added taxes; and import and export taxes. To code this variable I follow the guidelines set forth in the International Monetary Fund's *Government Finance Statistics Yearbook* (IMF-GFSY). I use both primary and secondary sources to maximize data coverage while adhering to the IMF-GFSY's coding rules. The major secondary sources I avail are the GSFY, the World Bank, the OECD, and various IMF country profiles. Albertus and Menaldo (2014) and Menaldo (2016) document the sources I employ on a country-by-country basis. This variable's coverage is between 1972 and 2006.

To acquire a sense of its variation, it might be helpful to consider some descriptive statistics. Using the sample of country years represented by the regression with the greatest coverage for Total Tax Revenues, reported in Table 5.3, Column 8 (N = 52; n = 1,356), the mean of this variable is 20.68; the standard deviation is 12.27; the minimum value is 0; and the maximum value is 54.26. In terms of the time-series variation, the within standard deviation is 4.24.

In terms of the spatial variation, OECD countries consistently display the highest values of tax revenues as percent GDP. In 2006, for example, total tax revenues in Denmark, Sweden, Belgium, France, and Finland exceeded 43 percent; in Austria, Germany, Italy, the Netherlands, Norway, and Germany, they exceeded 35 percent of GDP. Only Greece, Ireland, the United States, Japan, and the United Kingdom had values below 30 percent. By contrast, outside of the OECD during the same year there were only eight countries with over 30 percent of GDP. None of these countries are located in the MENA, East Asia, South-East Asia, South Asia, and the Pacific. For example, next to Israel, with 27.6, the country with the second greatest amount of tax revenues as percent GDP in the MENA is Jordan, with 23.6 in 2006. Countries with tax revenues that are fewer than 10 percent of GDP that year include Pakistan, China, Colombia, Nepal, Cambodia, Bangladesh, Iran, Afghanistan, Bahrain, Kuwait, and Liberia.

I also use Private Credit as a percentage of GDP to measure state capacity. This is motivated by both the institutions curse theory introduced in the previous chapter and by Besley and Persson (2012). The latter argue that this variable proxies for legal capacity because a vibrant market for credit requires the steadfast enforcement of contracts and an honest, effective bureaucracy capable of regulating the financial system prudentially. This variable is available from the *Financial Development and Structure Database* since 1960. The mean of Private Credit is 39.97 and its standard deviation is 36.13 (calculated on the country years represented by the Table 5.3, Column 5 regression; N = 54; n = 1,490).

State capacity is also measured as International Reserves. As outlined above, rulers who face balance-of-payments problems are usually found in weak states. They must seek creative ways to earn hard currency. Among other things, this may call upon bolstering oil exploration efforts. I follow Haggard and Maxfield (1996) and measure balance-of-payments difficulties as countries' international reserve position. Reserves are measured as total reserves: ((foreign exchange + Special Drawing Rights holdings + and the reserve position in the IMF) – gold holdings). This variable is available from the *External Wealth of Nations Database* since 1971.[67]

I also measure state capacity as the size of the armed forces. This variable is meant to capture the state's coercive capability. The size of the military reflects both the ability to mete out repression against citizens and the opposition and the culmination of complex efforts to undermine threats from within the regime. It therefore taps into the state's ability to marshal force and perform surveillance and intelligence gathering. I use Military Size per 100 inhabitants, taken from the *Correlates of War Project*.[68]

As a final measure of state capacity, I use state antiquity, a measure of the longevity of a state's infrastructure and bureaucracy. This variable is from Bockstette et al. (2002). They argue that countries with longer political legacies have had a greater chance to develop state capacity tied to the development of agriculture, urbanization, and the use of money. I follow the authors and use the normalized version (0 to 1) of this index while discounting the influence of the past for each half-century by 5 percent. I also follow Putterman and Weil (2010) and adjust the index by migration patterns because, during the colonization of America, Sub-Saharan Africa, and Asia, European settlers, non-European servants, and slaves migrated and imported their home institutions.[69]

---

[67] Employing raw reserves is not advisable; an identical reduction in reserves is expected to have different economic effects in different countries. Governments are likely to adapt policy responses to the country's average level of reserves and their variance. Therefore, to measure comparably the effect of changes in reserve position I standardize the country's yearly reserves by the country mean and standard deviation.

[68] Following Albertus and Menaldo (2012c), who also use this variable to measure coercive capacity, I take the natural log of Military Size (after adding .01 to address zero values).

[69] I adjust State Antiquity by these authors' *World Migration Matrix*. It contains the different shares of a country's population in 2000 that descended from

Instrumental variables for state capacity

In the IV 2SLS regressions depicted in Table 5.4, I instrument state capacity with factor endowments and the country's age. This strategy follows the theory of institutional origins and persistence outlined in the previous chapter. There I argued that, historically, places where the majority was able to farm grains at a small scale were able to secure broadly distributed property rights as well as political rights. The result was that a wide swath of society made physical and educational investments in response to policies that broadened access to markets and politics, such as those that fostered sophisticated legal and financial systems. The economy responded by growing consistently without fueling too much inequality. In turn, this reinforced liberal institutions and fortified state capacity by incentivizing rulers to make perennial investments in administrative bureaucracies, the rule of law, the military, and the prudential regulation of the economy.[70]

As in Chapter 4, to measure factor endowments I use the *Wheat to Sugar Ratio*. This is the ratio of land suitable for growing wheat versus sugar, with higher values bespeaking soils that are more propitious to growing grains. Using the arable land suitable for these crops within 50 miles of the country's largest city, I operationalize this variable as $\log((1+\%$ land suitable for wheat$)/(1+\%$ land suitable for sugar$))$ because the land suitable for either or both of these crops is zero in some countries. To address the fact that during the colonization of the Americas, Subsaharan Africa, and Asia, European settlers and non-European indentured servants and slaves migrated in different numbers, displaced indigenous populations to different degrees, and imported their home institutions with varying measures of success, I weight this ratio by the World Migration Matrix.

I measure a Country's Age as the natural log of the number of years a country has had sovereignty. The logic of using this as an instrument

people in different source countries in 1500. Consider Mexico. Its score is multiplied by Mexicans' share of ancestors of Aztec descent and adjusted by Spain's State Antiquity Score multiplied by Mexicans' share of ancestors of Spanish descent. This captures both the state capacity accumulated by Pre-Colombian Aztecs and the legacy of the Spanish state introduced by the Conquistadores.

[70] As discussed in the previous chapter, this theory follows Engerman and Sokoloff (1997), Easterly (2007), Haber and Menaldo (2011b), Haber (2011; 2012a; 2012b), and various other works mentioned there.

for state capacity is that, the longer a country has been independent, the greater its ability to penetrate the hinterlands, establish a monopoly on violence, and tax the economy. This variable is coded beginning the first year of independence for countries that were either colonized or seceded from another country. Those that became independent prior to 1800 are coded as sovereign since 1800.

Control variables

In the econometric analyses that follow I employ two types of control variables. The first set includes controls that vary over time and will be used across various FE estimations that exploit the data's within-variation. The second set of controls are time-invariant and will be used in the IV 2SLS regressions, which include both time-varying and time-invariant instruments, and the OLS regression in which state capacity is measured as State Antiquity. Both of these models exploit the data's within- and between-variation and include region fixed effects instead of country fixed effects.

Perhaps the biggest incentive to explore for and produce oil is a country's geological potential. Therefore, I operationalize a country's *Oil Endowment* as the cumulative total oil barrels (in billions) associated with giant oil fields, arguably the most exogenous, time-varying measure of a country's underlying geological potential.[71] A giant oil field has at least 500 million barrels of oil that can ultimately be recovered.[72] To put this in perspective, consider Russia, which has the greatest number of giant fields during the sample of country years represented by the regression reported in Table 5.3, Column 3. Namely, 33 giant wells were discovered by 1990, containing a total of 253.74 billion oil barrels. I take the natural log of this variable after adding 0.01 to address zero values. For robustness, I also reran all of the regressions substituting this measure with (i) the log of the running count of giant oil fields, and (ii) the log of cumulative total oil reserves, i.e., giant well oil + regular well oil.[73]

It is also important to control for the costs of oil recovery and address the fact that mature producers may be less likely to explore for oil.

---

[71] Its correlation with the Ultimately Recoverable Reserves, from Tsui (2011), is 0.80.
[72] A supergiant well contains at least 1 billion barrels of recoverable oil reserves.
[73] To operationalize these variables, I use information from Tsui (2011).

Therefore, I control for the *Years Since Peak Production*; using information from Tsui (2011), I calculate a running count that is negative until the peak year, 0 during the peak year, and positive thereafter. The logic behind this measure is that, as oilfields age, production costs rise since the recovery method needed to extract the oil becomes more sophisticated. Early on, oil is extracted by natural lift because the underground pressure is great enough to force it to the surface. Afterwards, when the pressure differential is insufficient for the oil to flow on its own, mechanical pumps are used to inject water into a neighboring well to force the oil out. At a final stage, pumps inject steam or chemicals to extract whatever oil remains.

Another important incentive to explore for and produce oil is its global price. I therefore control for the *Price of Oil* in 2007 dollars from Haber and Menaldo (2011a). To address the fact that there is a lag between oil price increases and oil exploration, as well as the decision to drill known wells, the regressions reported below employ a one-year lag; the results are also robust to introducing a five-year lag or a greater lag length. I also introduce the one-year lead of the oil price to capture oil price futures and, thus, long-run oil price expectations that affect current decisions to launch exploration efforts or drill. The results are also robust to higher order leads.

I also ensure that the regression results are robust to controlling for *Economic Development*. Wealthier countries are more likely to have a greater demand for energy and, therefore, are perhaps more likely to explore for oil. This variable is measured as the log of Per Capita Income in 2000 international dollars and is from Haber and Menaldo (2011a).

Finally, I add several time-invariant controls to the IV 2SLS regressions since these include region, instead of country, fixed effects. The log of *Elevation Difference* (between a country's highest and lowest points, in meters), from Fearon and Laitin (2003), addresses the fact that rougher surfaces make it harder to search for, and drill, oil. The log of *Surface Area* (in square meters), from the WBDI, addresses the fact that, due to the law of averages, larger countries are more likely to have oil. I control for OPEC *Membership* because this cartel imposes production quotas to bolster oil prices.[74]

---

[74] I also experimented with adding two additional controls across the regressions. The first is the income generated by alternate fuels, since these factors might affect oil investment and oil drilling decisions by energy firms and governments. The second variable is regime type, as democracies may limit exploration if

Excursus on validity of state capacity measures

In this section, I outline potential challenges to my measures of state capacity, as well as the strategies I use to mitigate them. I first take up the wisdom of using taxation to proxy for state capacity. I then turn to problems and solutions related to the secondary measures outlined above.

Perhaps there is an alternative explanation for why states with greater tax revenues may explore for oil less than those with fewer taxes. It could be the case that a common factor jointly determines both low levels of taxation and high levels of oil exploration. Large oil producers may simply have a reduced need to tax their economy – since they are generating sizable revenues from foreign consumption – and, quite naturally, also exhibit higher rates of exploration. If this is true, it challenges my purported mechanism, which is that weak states explore for oil because, while they find it hard to tax their economies, they find it relatively easy to tax oil.

Fortunately, the data analysis strategy I pursue below is designed to address this possibility. My econometric approach neutralizes the fact that larger oil producers may simultaneously drill a lot more oil wells than smaller ones for purely logistical reasons. The effect of state capacity on oil drilling that I report below is therefore the effect once a country's underlying potential for oil production is ruled out.

First, the regressions control for country-fixed effects. What this does, essentially, is relegate attention to the within country variation in the data. That means that I have already netted out the big differences in oil endowments – and thus production potential – between oil countries implicitly. To give an example, because I am focusing on the variation over time within countries, everything about, say, a country such as Saudi Arabia that is constant over time, such as its very large oil endowments, is held constant. The only contribution that Saudi Arabia will make to the regression results is therefore how the changes over time in its state capacity influence its changes over time in wildcat wells drilled. The same holds true for every other country. The coefficient on taxation in these regressions is the average impact that the variation

elected incumbents do not anticipate that they will capture future rents (Dunning 2010). While the results are robust to controlling for these variables, I have omitted reporting and discussing these results; both variables are possibly endogenous and neither of them is statistically significant once they are instrumented with spatial lags.

over time in this variable makes on oil exploration across countries in the dataset.

Second, in many of the regressions, I control for countries' time varying oil endowments. That is to say, I look at the relationship between taxation and oil well drilling after netting out how oil endowments influence oil well drilling. That means that even large changes in the potential for oil production within countries over time is not unduly driving the relationship between taxation and oil well drilling. The reason is that these changes are controlled for.

Third, I avail instrumental variables techniques to isolate the exogenous variation in taxation. Specifically, as I outlined above, I instrument taxation with the wheat to sugar ratio and the country's age. That means that any correlation between taxation and the potential for oil production has been stripped out so that I can identify the purely causal impact that taxation makes on oil exploration. I also report tests of the over-identifying restrictions to make sure that the exclusion restriction is satisfied. These strongly suggest that the effect of wheat to sugar and the country's age is working exclusively through taxation to affect oil exploration. In other words, taxation is not unduly picking up the effect of oil production or the potential for oil production on oil well drilling.

Robustness to other measures of state capacity

What about Private Credit as percent GDP, the size of Foreign Exchange Reserves, and the Size of the Military? Do these alternative measures of state capacity suffer from problems that threaten to confound causal inference?

While private credit may depend in part on legal capacity, it also depends on many other things that affect oil exploration, including the country's income level and prior structure of the economy. Moreover, high levels of private credit may sometimes be associated with a lack of effective regulation – for example, during the buildup of a credit bubble that mushrooms into a financial crisis.

As for international reserves, they have an entirely different role for countries with fixed exchange rates versus countries with floating exchange rates. While they are a necessity for the former, they are merely optional for the latter. Moreover, they might be much higher in oil exporters, which tend to accumulate sizable current account surpluses that are then converted into higher reserves.

Finally, it could be the case that very strong states have a reduced need for a large military and, thus, exhibit fewer military personnel.

These shortcomings represent a recurring issue. These variables are each noisy, imperfect measures of state capacity. They are characterized by important exceptions. Or they potentially suffer from endogeneity. Fortunately, across each measure, the noise and bias runs against my hypothesis. It makes it harder to find that weak states are more likely to explore for and rely on oil.

This is especially the case when state capacity is measured as international reserves. If oil-exporting countries tend to garner relatively high levels of foreign exchange, then this should make it *harder* to find that strong states are less likely to explore for, produce, tax, and export oil. After all, I predict that strong states should be less reliant on oil. Yet, in this case, the reverse causation potentially runs from high oil reliance to high levels of state strength – the opposite of what I predict.

Moreover, some states that are quite strong in reality score relatively low on these measures. Several strong states have relatively low levels of credit because their central banks are independent, empowering them to deflate impending financial bubbles before they mushroom. Similarly, because many strong states can credibly commit to sound money, they choose to let their exchange rate float, and thus maintain relatively low levels of international reserves. And several strong states choose to field relatively small armies, especially in Western Europe, even though they can afford larger ones. Therefore, when I measure state capacity as military size, countries such as Belgium are "miscoded" as weak states; and these states also have relatively low rates of oil exploration, low rates of oil production, low rates of oil exports, and low rates of taxation on oil.

In short, the coefficient on state capacity should be biased downward when these proxies are used. Many of the data points are being coded as "weak" when they should really be coded as "strong"; at the same time, they are coded as having low levels of oil exploration and reliance. This noise should thus make it harder to find a systematically negative relationship between state capacity and oil.

Econometric models and results

As a first step, I estimate a series of static FE models via OLS with Driscoll-Kraay standard errors, a technique that addresses heteroskedasticity, serially correlated errors, and spatial correlation.[75] These are followed by a series of autoregressive distributed lag models (ADL) performed via a Structure GMM approach. The final series of regressions consist of a set of region fixed effects models estimated via IV 2SLS in which state capacity is instrumented with factor endowments and the country's age.

The static FE (OLS) model has the following structure:

$$y_{it} = \alpha_i + \lambda_t + \beta X_{it-1} + (\phi \times \alpha_i)\xi + u_{it} \tag{1}$$

in which y_{it} is the estimated value of the outcome variable of interest for country i in year t; α_i addresses time-invariant country fixed effects and λ_t addresses country-invariant year fixed effects, both potentially correlated with X, a vector of k explanatory variables lagged by one year in most cases; β are estimated parameters; ξ are estimates of country-specific time trends produced by the interaction between ϕ, a linear time trend, and α_i; and u_{it} is an error term.

Static FE model results

As a first step, Table 5.3, Column 1 reports a basic regression where Oil Exploration is the dependent variable and state capacity, measured as Total Tax Revenues (t–1), is the sole variable in X.[76] This model also controls for country fixed effects, but nothing else. The results are in

---

[75] This called on making a Newey West adjustment to the error term, the lag length of which was determined by an Arellano Bond test of serial correlation.

[76] Technically, Oil Exploration is a count variable that is over-dispersed, in that its variance is greater than its mean value. Yet, there are good reasons to eschew estimating count models via maximum likelihood. First, these models do not return the average marginal effect when country-fixed effects are also estimated; they also suffer from the incidental parameter problem. Second, a histogram shows that the variation over time in the number of wildcat wells drilled appears to be normally distributed, which suggests that the residuals should also approach normality within an OLS approach. Nonetheless, for the sake of robustness, I also estimated a set of generalized Negative Binomial models in which I let the variance parameter vary by country. This yielded results that were materially identical to those reported in Table 5.3. Moreover, the Table 5.3 results are robust to measuring oil exploration as the number of wildcat wells drilled per capita; the variation over time in this variable also appears normally distributed. While I do not transform Oil Exploration in the Table 5.3 models by logging it, or taking its square root, because doing so introduces bias, inefficiency, and inconsistency (see King 1988, pp. 846–849), I do perform some robustness tests in the regressions in Table 5.4 where I apply a log based transformation to this variable.

Table 5.3 Static fixed effects regressions with different oil measures as the dependent variable

Autocorrelation and Heteroskedasticity Consistent Standard Errors in brackets

	1	2	3	4	5	6	7	8	9	10	11
Dependent variable	Oil exploration	Oil exploration	Oil exploration	Oil exploration	Oil exploration	Oil exploration	Oil exploration	Oil extraction	Oil exports	Oil taxation	Oil capital
State capacity measure	Total taxes	Total taxes	Total taxes	Total taxes	Private credit	Intl. reserves	Military size	Total taxes	Total taxes	Total taxes	Total taxes
State capacity	-2.520**	-1.996**	-2.027**	-1.776**	-1.118*	-38.85***	-25.88**	-0.120*	-0.143***	-0.510***	0.018
	[2.51]	[0.895]	[0.968]	[0.819]	[0.641]	[11.51]	[10.43]	[0.063]	[0.050]	[0.148]	[0.012]
Oil endowment			-3.045	-2.783	-22.67***	-5.779*	-6.743*	-0.413	-0.042	1.774	0.117
			[3.642]	[3.667]	[8.476]	[2.961]	[3.549]	[0.495]	[0.250]	[1.139]	[0.381]
Yrs. since peak production			-5.307***	-4.491***	-1.723	-1.547	-0.153	0.036	-0.015	-0.239***	0.150***
			[0.253]	[0.498]	[1.639]	[0.863]	[0.560]	[0.025]	[0.025]	[0.046]	[0.017]
Oil price t-1			2.589***	2.616***	3.455***	2.093***	2.178***	-0.098***	-0.036***	-0.075***	0.001**
			[0.126]	[0.130]	[0.178]	[0.027]	[0.061]	[0.003]	[0.004]	[0.004]	[0.001]
Oil price t+1			-0.421***	-0.364***	1.784***	0.360***	1.351***	0.109***	0.057***	0.166***	0.016***
			[0.087]	[0.070]	[0.371]	[0.036]	[0.192]	[0.005]	[0.004]	[0.016]	[0.002]
log(Per capita income)				-76.13***	-206.8***	-35.08**	-70.82***	0.588	4.080**	3.131	1.656
				[26.38]	[61.11]	[13.58]	[21.01]	[1.741]	[1.797]	[3.433]	[1.031]
Country-fixed effects	YES	YES	YES	YES	YES	YES	YES	YES	YES	YES	YES

Year-fixed effects	NO	YES	YES	YES	YES	YES	YES	YES	YES	YES
	NO	YES	YES	YES	YES	YES	YES	YES	YES	YES
Country-specific time trends	NO	YES	YES	YES	YES	YES	YES	YES	YES	YES
	NO	YES	YES	YES	YES	YES	YES	YES	YES	YES
Observations	1,318	1,318	1,278	1,277	1,490	1,691	2,274	1,356	1,215	433	833
Number of countries	52	52	52	52	54	59	61	52	53	16	44

Constant estimated across models but not reported; country-fixed effects expunged via within transformation; year intercepts estimated but not reported; country-specific trends estimated but not reported. Driscoll-Kraay Standard Errors estimated with Newey West adjustments reflecting Arellano Bond tests of serial correlation.

line with theoretical expectations. State capacity is negatively signed and statistically significant (p-value = 02).

A simulation based on the estimation performed in Column 1, and centered on Brazil, a fledgling oil producer, helps illustrate the magnitude of the results. Brazil has become the epicenter of oil exploration in South America, gaining that status in a relatively short time period by virtue of about three decades of fastidious exploration efforts off the shores of the Atlantic Ocean. Brazil's Total Tax Revenues in 1980 were 4.8 (% GDP), at around the time it began to really ramp up its drilling of wildcat wells. Had its tax revenues instead been 12 percent, closer to that of Turkey that year, it would have drilled 229 percent fewer exploratory wells (it drilled 126 wildcat wells in 1980). Furthermore, had Brazil evinced the tax revenues of Cyprus that year, 17 percent of GDP – the median of the variable's distribution – it would not have drilled any exploratory wells whatsoever. That is, given its geological endowments.

What is more: while this is a substantively important effect, it is actually a lower bound estimate. Later, when I discuss the Structure GMM models, I show that this is a considerable underestimate of the true causal effect of state capacity on exploratory effort. While those models allow me to calculate the total long-run impact of a permanent change in state capacity on exploratory drilling, they are also equipped to fully address endogeneity bias.

Columns 2 through 4 of Table 5.3 test the robustness of the results obtained from the simple regression represented by Column 1. In Column 2, I add both year-fixed effects and country-specific time trends. The statistical and substantive effect of Total Tax Revenues hardly changes. Column 3 then adds the basic suite of time-varying control variables outlined above. These variables operationalize geological potential, oil production costs, and oil prices. State Capacity remains negative, increases in size, and remains statistically significant (p-value = 0.04). As expected, Years Since Peak Production is negative and significant and Oil Price (t–1) is positive and significant.

Column 3 reports a couple of results that are surprising, however. First, Oil Endowment is negative, but not statistically significant. Second, Oil Price (t+1) is negative and significant.

What explains these counterintuitive results? These two variables are entered into a regression that does many other things simultaneously besides just controlling for the future price of oil and a country's oil endowments. It controls for other time-varying covariates, country-specific time-invariant heterogeneity, via country-fixed effects, time-varying heterogeneity that is invariant across years, and country-specific time trends. The latter means that any time trends that are unique to each country are expunged from the data.

This is a very exacting specification that makes it very difficult to find a substantively and statistically significant result for any variable whatsoever. The reason is that the country-fixed effects and country-specific time trends, in particular, are soaking up a lot of the variation that would otherwise be assigned to these variables. Consider a country's oil endowment. Controlling for country-fixed effects means that the largest share of a country's oil endowment has already been soaked up in the country-specific intercepts, and what is being captured in the coefficient that corresponds to this variable is isolated to the change in the level of oil endowment over time. Moreover, controlling for country-specific time trends means that any country-specific, idiosyncratic trend in the change in this variable over time has also been stripped out. That means that there is probably very little signal versus noise captured by this variable, making it more likely that the variance around the point estimates will increase beyond conventional levels of significance.

Thus, if I were to remove the country-specific time trends, in particular, we should be able to regain the fidelity of this signal; moreover, removing them would also recover the lion's share of the variation in the future price of oil, which otherwise is allowed to vary drastically by country depending on its age and, thus, when it enters the dataset. Indeed, if I remove, these trends – results not shown – I redeem orthodox expectations. The future price of oil and a country's oil endowment are, as expected, positive and significant predictors of its level of oil well drilling. Moreover, this modification does nothing to affect the main result of interest: state capacity remains negatively associated with oil exploration at the highest levels of statistical significance when I omit the country-specific time trends.

Except for the fact that Per Capita Income is added to the regression equation, Column 4 is identical to the specification reported in Column 3. While Per Capita Income enters the regression as negative and significant, state capacity is still negative and significant. This first result is not surprising. In so far as Per Capita Income captures elements of state capacity not measured by total tax revenues, this is consistent with the institutions curse theory. Yet, it is all the more remarkable that taxation remains such a strong predictor of oil exploration in such a conservative specification.

Robustness to other measures of state capacity

In Columns 5 through 7, I experiment with other measures of state capacity. Column 5 is identical to Column 4, save for the fact that I switch Total Tax Revenues out for Private Credit. Similarly, in Column 6 state capacity is measured as International Reserve Deviations. Finally, in Column 7 state capacity is measured as Military Size. The basic results hold across each of these models – except that in Column 5 Private Credit is only significant at the 0.09 level. For both International Reserve Deviations and Military Size, the substantive effect of state capacity on oil exploration is quite large.

Robustness to other oil-related outcomes

Columns 8 through 11 introduce alternative ways of measuring the dependent variable. In these regressions, I return to using Total Tax Revenues as state capacity, but the specifications are fundamentally the same – except for the fact that oil is no longer measured as wildcat wells. In Column 8, the extraction rate is the dependent variable; in Column 9, it is oil exports; in Column 10, oil taxation. Finally, in Column 11, it is oil capital.

Here, some of the results are a bit weaker than in the other models; yet they are generally supportive of the hypotheses outlined above. The statistical significance of state capacity is at the 0.06 level (Column 9), and oil capital has a positive – yet not statistically significant – sign (Column 11). Yet, these results are strengthened – if not reversed, in the case of oil capital – when further adjustments are made to address endogeneity and properly model dynamics. We now move to those regressions.

ADL models estimated via structure GMM

The regressions described above are predicated on two important assumptions. The first is that the effects on oil exploration made by increases in the covariates fully materialize in one year's time. The second is that the error term in equation (1) is uncorrelated with state capacity after expunging the country effects and controlling for both country time trends and the time-varying independent variables used above. Structure GMM Models, which are dynamic regressions that recruit instrumental variables, allow us to relax those assumptions. Moreover, they designed for "small T, large N" panel datasets.

It is important to get the dynamics right to avoid misspecifying the timing of the effect of state capacity on the dependent variables. I therefore take a very conservative approach and estimate ADL regressions within the GMM framework. These are infinitely distributed lag models that allow me to remain agnostic about the "correct" lag distribution. They also allow me to estimate Long-Run Propensities (LRPs): a point estimate of how a permanent change in the independent variable at some indefinite point in the past affects the long-run level of the dependent variable.[77]

To address different sources of endogeneity bias, the Structure GMM approach performs several operations. The first is first-differencing the equation to expunge the country-fixed effects. The second is instrumenting the lagged dependent variable, which is pre-determined, and thus correlated with the country-fixed effects and therefore the error term, with some of its lags in levels, which are uncorrelated with the error term. The third operation is instrumenting other potentially endogenous independent variables with some of their lags, also in levels. In this case, I treat total tax revenues as potentially endogenous.[78]

To conserve space, I only discuss, but do not report, the results of two of these regressions. The first is a model in which wildcats is the dependent variable. The second is one where oil capital is the dependent variable.[79] In both of these models, state capacity is again

---

[77] This requires that I include in the regression the one-year lag of the dependent variable (LDV) and the contemporaneous values and one year lags of the independent variables. The LRP is then calculated as follows: (Independent variable β + Independent Variable β_{t-1})/(1- ρ), where ρ is the coefficient on the LDV. Since the LRP is a nonlinear function of the estimated coefficients, its standard error is computed via the Delta Method. Wooldridge (2006, pp. 637–638) proves that the ADL has an infinite lag distribution.

[78] I employ the two-step estimator to ensure that the results are robust to autocorrelation and heteroskedasticity; year-fixed effects guard against cross-sectional dependence.

[79] Moreover, structure GMM is not designed for dependent variables that follow a Random Walk; therefore, system GMM, which calls on a bigger set of instruments, was employed when estimating the effects of state capacity on oil extraction, oil exports, and oil taxation.

measured as total tax revenues.[80] To simplify interpretation, I only discuss the calculated LRPs for total tax revenues.

The results are highly significant in both a substantive and statistical sense. A permanent increase of one percentage point in total tax revenues reduces the number of exploratory wells drilled by 213 over the long run (p-value = 0.001). A heteroskedasticity and autocorrelation consistent Hansen J test of the over-identifying restrictions returns a chi-square of 17.04 (p-value = 0.88). It thus fails to reject the hypothesis that the instrumental variables required by the GMM approach are exogenous. And an Arellano-Bond test of AR(2) returns a z-score of –1.00 (p-value = 0.32), satisfying the requirement that there be no autocorrelation in levels.

Similarly, permanently increasing tax revenues by 10 percentage point reduces oil capital per capita by 4 percent over the long run (p-value = 0.02). While a Hansen J test of the over-identifying restrictions again suggests that the instrumental variables used to isolate the exogenous variation in state capacity are valid, an Arellano-Bond test suggests that this model is also free of AR(2). Everything else held equal, and consistent with the institutions curse theory, weaker states are able to court more capital in the oil sector than stronger ones.

Exploiting additional state capacity instruments

I now take a slightly different approach to addressing causal identification. While the Structure GMM estimations reported above instrumented total tax revenues with appropriate lags, the regressions that follow instead use factor endowments and the country's age to capture state capacity's exogenous variation. This therefore calls on abandoning the Structure GMM framework to instead estimate static IV 2SLS models that can exploit both the data's within- and between-variation.[81]

These models are conducted in two stages. The first estimates the determinants of state capacity. The second estimates the determinants of either oil exploration, or oil extraction, or oil exportation, or oil

---

[80] The first-differenced LDV is instrumented with the LDV in levels in t–2; first-differenced state capacity in t is instrumented with state capacity in levels in t–2; and first-differenced state capacity in t–1 is instrumented with state capacity in levels in t–3. Results are also robust to experimenting with lower or higher order lags as instruments.

[81] To address heteroskedasticity and serial correlation, I estimate these models with Newey-West standard errors. This therefore requires a generic GMM, instead of OLS, approach to the estimation.

taxation, or oil capital. For our purposes, the most important thing to note is whether the predicted level of state capacity calculated from the first-stage regression explains the variation in these dependent variables in the second stage regressions.

The first stage regression is:

$$y_{it} = \alpha_j + \lambda_t + \beta X_{it-1} + (\phi \times \alpha_i)\xi + u_{it} \tag{2}$$

in which y_{it} is the estimated value of the outcome variable of interest for country i in year t; α_j addresses time-invariant region fixed effects and λ_t addresses country-invariant year fixed effects, both potentially correlated with X, a vector of k explanatory variables lagged by one year in most cases; β are estimated parameters; ξ are estimates of region-specific time trends produced by the interaction between ϕ, a linear time trend, and α_j; and u_{jt} is an error term.[82]

The second stage of the IV 2SLS model can be expressed as:

$$y_{it} = \alpha_j + \lambda_t + \beta X_{it-1} + (\phi \times \alpha_i)\xi + u_{jt} \tag{3}$$

in which y_{it} is the estimated value of the outcome variable of interest for country i in year t; α_j addresses time-invariant region fixed effects and λ_t addresses country-invariant year-fixed effects, both potentially correlated with X, a vector of k explanatory variables lagged by one year in most cases that includes the predicted values of state capacity produced by equation (2); β are estimated parameters; ξ are estimates of region-specific time trends produced by the interaction between ϕ, a linear time trend, and α_j; and u_{jt} is an error term.

Oil exploration

The results of these regressions are reported in Table 5.4. Each of the models, both first and second stage, includes the same set of control variables as before, plus Elevation Difference, Surface Area, and an OPEC dummy. This compensates for the fact that country-fixed effects are no longer estimated.[83]

---

[82] Countries are grouped by region following Haber and Menaldo (2011a).

[83] One might worry that over-dispersion may yield spurious results in this case, due to the fact that these specifications, unlike the previous ones, exploit both the data's between and within variation. Therefore, I reran those models after transforming the number of wildcat wells drilled in the following manner: ln (+/-exp − k), where both k and the sign of the exponent are chosen to create a new variable with zero skewness. Specifically, in this case the value of k is − 0.0175276. The results of these regressions are materially identical.

Table 5.4 Instrumental variables two state least squares regressions for various oil measures Autocorrelation and Heteroskedasticity Consistent Standard Errors in brackets

	1a	1b	2b	3b	4b	5b	6
Estimation Technique	IV 2SLS NWSE	IV 2SLS NWSE	IV 2SLS NWSE	IV 2SLS NWSE	V 2SLS NWSE	V 2SLS NWSE	OLS DKSE
DEPENDENT VARIABLE		Oil Exploration	Oil Extraction	Oil Exports	Oil Taxation	Oil Capital	Oil Exploration
	Total Taxes	Total Taxes	Total Taxes	Total Taxes	Total Taxes	Total Taxes	State Antiquity
STATE CAPACITY MEASURE							
State capacity		−72.86***	−0.409**	−0.294**	−0.641	−0.173**	−709.3***
		[18.81]	[0.194]	[0.137]	[0.466]	[0.072]	[136.4]
Oil endowment	−0.067	8.769	0.912***	0.451***	1.659*	−0.450***	39.90***
	[0.105]	[8.137]	[0.161]	[0.115]	[1.001]	[0.067]	[7.538]
Yrs. since peak production	0.084***	14.72***	−0.069*	−0.108***	−0.032	−0.007	9.881***
	[0.021]	[3.450]	[0.036]	[0.033]	[0.085]	[0.016]	[1.602]
Oil price t−1	0.13	8.399	0.283	0.201	0.114	−0.091	101.9***
	[0.161]	[13.70]	[0.257]	[0.222]	[0.565]	[0.259]	[14.00]
Oil price t+1	−0.075	−5.75	0.059	−0.004	0.046	0.034	0.183
	[0.073]	[6.367]	[0.104]	[0.094]	[0.307]	[0.144]	[0.482]
log(Per capita income)	−0.431***	−6.615	4.930***	4.486***	4.549**	1.189***	3.239
	[0.262]	[44.33]	[1.005]	[1.132]	[2.264]	[0.331]	[8.722]

Surface area	-0.431*	111.8***	-1.118***	-0.817***	1.805	-0.847***	-1.471*
	[0.262]	[31.34]	[0.312]	[0.265]	[2.806]	[0.106]	[0.784]
Elevation difference	-2.192***	-139.1***	-0.678	0.136	-6.13	1.882***	-347.3***
	[0.964]	[46.77]	[0.654]	[0.581]	[4.240]	[0.259]	[65.84]
OPEC membership	2.197***	-26.23	9.736***	14.23***	9.355***	2.520***	106.6***
	[0.963]	[77.95]	[1.442]	[1.437]	[3.396]	[0.396]	[18.16]
Wheat to sugar ratio	1.861***						
	[0.238]						
Country's age	0.497						
	[0.488]						
Region-fixed effects	YES	YES	YES	YES	YES	YES	YES
Region-specific time trends	YES	YES	YES	YES	YES	YES	YES
Year-fixed effects	YES	YES	YES	YES	YES	YES	YES
Observations	1,243	1,243	1,325	1,219	435	805	2,862

Constant estimated across models but not reported; region intercepts estimated but not reported; year intercepts estimated but not reported; region-specific trends estimated but not reported. NWSE = Newey West Standard Errors (estimated with 1 lag length)

IV 2SLS = Instrumental Variables Two Stage Least Squares (estimated via a Generalized Method of Moments approach).

DKSE = Driscoll Kraay Standard Errors estimated with a Newey West adjustment (lag length = 4).

a = First stage regression; these are estimated across all IV 2SLS models but only reported for Model 1 to conserve space. b = Second stage regression.

Column 1a reports coefficients from equation (2), the first stage regression. As expected: (i) countries with higher ratios of wheat to sugar have higher levels of state capacity and (ii) older countries do as well. While only the country's age is statistically significant at conventional levels on its own – owing to the fact that these instrumental variables are highly correlated with each other – the F-statistic of the excluded instruments is 30.60 (p-value < 0.001). This is well above the threshold separating weak from strong instruments.[84] Finally, the estimates also pass a suite of additional under-identification tests, weak identification tests, and weak instrument tests with flying colors.

Column 1b reports coefficients from equation (3) where the dependent variable is Oil Exploration. State capacity is, as expected, negative and highly statistically significant (p-value = 0.003). Moreover, its magnitude is quite large. Increasing total taxation by 1 percentage point reduces the number of wildcat wells drilled by 73.[85] This suggests that the results across Table 5.3 are possibly biased downward due to either omitted variables, reverse causation, or both.

Robustness to other oil measures

Columns 2–5 experiment with the different ways of operationalizing the dependent variable – in the second stage regression – while still measuring state capacity as total tax revenues, and thus continuing to instrument it with factor endowments and the country's age. Column 2 introduces Oil Extraction as the dependent variable; Column 3 Oil Exports; Column 4 Oil Taxation; and Column 5 Oil Capital. The results of the first stage regressions are excluded to conserve space. Except for Oil Taxation, which is shy of conventional levels of statistical significance (p-value = 0.17), these findings strengthen those associated with Table 5.3, in both a statistical and substantive sense. Holding all else equal, weaker states have higher extraction rates, export oil at higher rates, and attract higher levels of oil capital.

---

[84] Staiger and Stock (1997) argue that first-stage F-tests should be greater than 10.

[85] As mentioned above, I reran this regression with the number of wildcat wells drilled transformed to eliminate skewness via the following formula: ln (+/–exp +0.0175276). Therefore, that version of the model yielded a semi-elasticity, which also helps put the substantive effect into high relief. Specifically, for every 1 percentage increase in total tax revenues (% GDP) the number of wildcat wells drilled increases by 11 percent (p-value < 0.001).

Are the instruments valid?

Are a country's factor endowments or its age really valid instruments for state capacity? For these instruments to satisfy the exclusion restriction they must affect oil exclusively through state capacity. I allay this concern in three ways. First, I have controlled for oil endowments, region-fixed effects, region-specific time trends, and geographic factors such as surface roughness that might signal the presence of sedimentary basins blessed with oil deposits.

Second, since I have over-identified equation (2), by including two instruments for state capacity, I can perform statistical tests of the hypothesis that state capacity is orthogonal to the error term in the second stage. Hansen J tests of the over-identifying restrictions never fail to reject the hypothesis that these instruments are exogenous.

Third, I run a series of additional models that control for other covariates to ensure that omitted factors are not driving the results. These other controls are Population Growth, Economic Growth, and Political Ideology, measured as the political affiliation of the executive branch in year t.

The basic results are unchanged.

Measuring state capacity as state antiquity

As a final robustness test, I now estimate a pooled regression via OLS but switch to a different way of measuring state capacity, State Antiquity. This is for two reasons. First, an argument can be made that state capacity is a "stock" variable, and that the metrics used to capture it thus far – Total Tax Revenues, Private Credit, International Reserve Deviations, and Military Size – do not adequately capture the historical accumulation of state capacity. Second, considering that the average date of peak oil production for wealthy OECD countries is 1986 and all others is 1994, readers might be concerned that the negative association between state capacity and oil exploration reflects a sample selection effect. Might it be the case that during this post-World War II sample period the only oil remaining to be discovered was located in low capacity states?

To address these issues, in Table 5.4, Column 6, I report the results of a regression where the dependent variable is Oil Exploration and state capacity is measured as State Antiquity. The latter captures the longevity of a state's infrastructure and bureaucracy and is available since 1930. As in the IV regressions, I also control for the full suite of controls: Oil Endowment, Years Since Peak Production, Oil Price (t–1), Oil Price (t+1), Elevation Difference, Surface Area, an OPEC dummy, region-fixed effects, and region-specific time trends. As has been the case throughout the chapter, state capacity is negative and highly significant, both substantively and statistically. If a country moves from having the oldest state in the dataset to the newest one, it decreases the number of exploratory wells drilled by a whopping 709.

Conclusion

This chapter draws on a recent generation of research and the institutions curse theory to argue and show that the oil sector is endogenous. Although a large and influential body of work in political science and economics known as the resource curse argues that oil retards modernization and breeds countless pathologies, an emerging literature is skeptical that causation runs from oil to underdevelopment. It instead suggests that state capacity might be an omitted factor that drives both oil reliance and development pathologies, including authoritarianism (e.g., Haber and Menaldo 2011a). This chapter builds on this insight, and its articulation in the institutions curse theory outlined in the previous chapter, to argue that oil exploration, extraction, exportation, taxation, and capital is not a monolithic reflection of underlying geological endowments or high oil prices.

States with low capacity lack the ability to tax their citizens. They do not have a well-functioning legal system, a competent and professional bureaucracy, or an infrastructure that sustains a large formal economy that can be monitored and audited. Oil, if discovered, provides rents that can bolster the state's foreign reserves, revenues, and borrowing ability. Therefore, greater exploration efforts and higher extraction rates should be more likely in states with lower state capacity because they are desperate for these valuable things. Moreover, weak states should be able to rely on a variety of innovative tools to finance oil exploration and production *despite their general inability to commit to their promises*. These have included colonialism, Gunboat Diplomacy, the oligopolistic structure of the market, vast asymmetries in information and power between foreign investors and host governments, and BITs.

This chapter subjects these hypotheses to empirical scrutiny. It does so in two main ways.

As a first step, I walk through a case study of Azerbaijan. The state deliberately revived the country's oil industry after its independence from the Soviet Union because it was devoid of regular tax sources. It therefore both looked for oil and drilled it at the highest rates in its history to generate easier-to-collect revenues. Additionally, this case is helpful from the perspective of causal identification because it exhibits a strong shock to state capacity that occurred unexpectedly and swiftly. Its independence from the Soviet Union threw a seemingly strong state into a perilous situation. Finding itself in a fragile and desperate situation after a war against Armenia, a huge banking crisis, and an economic collapse, the government was left with no other option than to rev up oil exploration and hasten the depletion of extant wells, despite the fact that oil discoveries had peaked. This is the story revealed, in particular, by oil exploration and production contracts penned between Azerbaijan's state-run oil company and IOCs, which entitled the state to a cascade of generous pre-exploration fees and pre-drilling bonuses.

As a second step, I use a panel dataset with global scope to find that weak states are more likely to explore for oil and produce it, export it, and tax it at high rates, as well as court higher amounts of capital to its oil sectors. The results are robust to different measures of both the dependent and independent variables. I isolate the exogenous variation in state capacity in various ways. This includes a Structure GMM approach that exploits lags in levels after first-differencing the data and exploiting geographic and historical factors that capture several dimensions of state capacity. These include the ease with which the state can project power into the periphery, administer censuses, and collect taxes, as well as whether elites have faced incentives to provide public goods, raise direct taxes, and invest in courts.

These results have important implications. Although many countries observed as oil reliant do not tax their citizens, this may *not* be because the state is content to rely on the oil sector to finance public spending after oil is discovered. Rather, it is likely that a country observed as resource reliant is as unable to tax non-resource sectors *before* oil is discovered as it is afterwards. Moreover, this chapter suggests that many oil-states' failure to democratize, uphold the rule of law, and promote growth may not be a product of their underlying oil wealth either. Rather, the real culprit is state weakness. Therefore, state weakness has been the curse that has produced considerable consternation among well-intentioned researchers and policymakers all along, not the chimerical resource curse.

In the following two chapters, I will empirically corroborate the thesis that there is a resource blessing. Given the endogeneity of natural resources, this requires that we isolate the exogenous variation in oil and mineral wealth. Once I do this, I find that oil is actually a blessing that improves taxation, democracy, institutional quality, the allocation of capital, and the provision of public goods.

6 | *The resource blessing*

If one looks back at world history, resource blessings seem to abound. This includes both the distant and more recent past. Let us consider some illuminating anecdotes.

Mining has always been an important, yet rarely remarked upon, engine of Sweden's economy. Sweden's public education system has always been characterized by aggressive government involvement in research and development centered on the natural sciences. This agenda has been driven by the country's natural resource industries, including mining and forestry, which have required advanced technical training, especially in engineering. Public investments in vocational training have driven innovation, first in the natural resource sector itself, and later in telecommunications and information technology.[1] These spillovers have helped create a highly skilled workforce that enjoys some of the highest living standards in the world, while living in one of the world's most celebrated social democracies.

This phenomenon was itself a product of the Swedish state's explicit attempt, as early as the fifteenth century, to promote mining in a bid to enhance its military and economic power. This strategy was wildly successful, as advances in the extraction and smelting of copper ore allowed Scandinavia's most celebrated monarch, Gustavus Adolphus, to amass a vast empire and enrich his kingdom.

Similarly, developing countries such as Indonesia, Malaysia, Zambia, Chile, and Peru have grown steadily throughout the 2000s on the back of spectacular natural resource booms. More impressively, they have also weathered a few sizable price declines in their exportable commodities since the dawn of the millennium. Indeed, they have often grown at rates above their regional averages during these "price corrections," the most recent of which began in 2014.

---

[1] This paragraph draws extensively on Blomström and Kokko (2007).

This is for two main reasons: first, because these countries have adopted countercyclical fiscal policies in which they save windfalls accrued during boom times and drawn down on their stashed natural resource revenues during bad times. Second, because they have successfully diversified their economies, nurtured their agricultural sectors, and invested heavily in education and healthcare. This is perhaps because these countries all belong to the world's "democracy club"; indeed, they have been members in good standing for quite some time now.

Even so-called petro states are no longer all that reliant on natural resources, despite reaping the benefits of recent price booms. In Sub-Saharan Africa, this includes Angola and Chad. In the Middle East, this includes glitzy Gulf States. Qatar is perhaps known more today for its influence over global media and ambitious foreign policy than its dwindling oil stocks. Dubai boasts the world's busiest airport, the region's busiest port, the world's tallest building, the world's largest mall, one of the world's leading airlines, and a booming service industry centered on global logistics and supply-chain management.

What do we make of these anecdotes? They definitely strike against received wisdom. As I outlined in Chapter 3, a large and vocal contingent of political scientists and economics have, for decades now, blamed natural resources for several pathologies. The extraction, transportation, and export of hydrocarbons and minerals are believed to vitiate the rule of law and jeopardize property rights. They are thought to hinder economic diversification and retard economic growth by catalyzing unproductive rent seeking and fomenting corruption. Supposedly, this fuels civil strife, promotes authoritarianism, and exacerbates gender inequality.[2]

The logic behind this resource curse was also outlined in that chapter. The driving idea is that mineral exports – and especially oil – constitute an external, unearned source of rents that can be arrogated by governments. This distorts the otherwise "natural" course of affairs that would take place in the absence of natural resources, one in which rulers tax their citizens in exchange for representation and public goods. By severing the fiscal link between rulers and the ruled, rents from natural resources render the former unaccountable to the latter. Once rulers are freed from taxing their citizens, they are freed from

---

[2] For an excellent review of this literature, see Frankel (2010).

having to solicit their input or seek their consent. Natural resource revenues therefore bolster the power of executives and the bureaucracy and create countless opportunities for rent-seeking and corruption. Paradoxically, although these rents may prolong the tenure of tyrants, they might also catalyze civil wars in a bid to capture this valuable prize.

So what should we believe? Do rents from oil and other natural resources displace non-oil revenues? Do they promote authoritarianism? Do they undermine capitalism? Or do they instead promote political and economic development? That is to say, are natural resources a blessing or a curse? And how can we figure out what the right answer is?

Given the size and importance of the natural resource sector in the developing world and the keen interest in state capacity, democracy, and capitalism expressed by scholars and policymakers alike, these are important questions. "Between 1996 and 2007, global investments in exploration by transnational private-sector corporations accounted for approximately US$2 trillion in the hydrocarbons sector and US$91 billion in the mining sector" (Bebbington and Bury 2013, p. 42). Moreover, the lion's share of this Foreign Direct Investment (FDI) was funneled into regions with fledgling, but fragile, democracies and liberalizing, but vulnerable, economies. For example, "between 1990 and 2007, Latin America received US$969 billion in FDI" (ibid., p. 41), the vast majority of it flowing to the natural resource sector. The numbers for Sub-Saharan Africa are similar, with a growing share of capital intended for that sector emanating from China – a country that is not known for exporting liberalism, democracy, and capitalism abroad.

This chapter aims to adjudicate between two competing camps that provide answers to these questions. The resource curse theory avers that oil, gas, and minerals are bad for state capacity, democracy, and market-preserving institutions, such as those that secure private property and enforce contracts. By contrast, as outlined in Chapter 3, a disparate group of researchers instead hypothesize that, at worst, natural resources make no difference to these outcomes and, at best, are a boon for state capacity, democracy, and capitalism. This chapter finds considerable evidence for the latter view. Contrary to the prevailing consensus, there is a resource blessing; and a quite robust one at that.

This chapter revisits the relationship between natural resources and several economic and political outcomes of interest. I reevaluate the relationship between resources and (1) the state's ability and willingness to tax citizens, (2) regime type, (3) the quality of a country's political and legal institutions, (4) the government's ability to credibly commit to its promises, and (5) the size and sophistication of the market economy.

In seeking to find out if there is a resource blessing or a resource curse, I take a multifaceted approach. I first evaluate the relationship between minerals and hydrocarbons over the course of Latin American history, paying particular attention to Mexico, a country that has had several pronounced mining and oil booms. I then address these questions against an original panel dataset with wide global and temporal coverage, exploiting both the data's time-series variation and exogenous variation in countries' income from hydrocarbons.

In evaluating the relationship between natural resources and the politics and economics of Latin America, I evaluate whether there is empirical support for the potential mechanisms linking natural resources to state capacity, capitalism, industrialization, and democracy. I identify the economic, fiscal, and political impacts made by the production and export of primary commodities in this region of the world – going back to these countries' independence.

This is an excellent laboratory. Sovereign Latin American nations are nearly two centuries old; they exhibit considerable variation in the importance of their natural resource sectors over time simply by virtue of how old they are. The same is true in regards to their tax systems, regime types, and development models.

I then turn to a panel dataset that observes over 150 countries since as early as 1930. I evaluate the relationship between income from hydrocarbons and non-oil taxation, regime type, institutional quality, the credibility of the government's commitment to market institutions, and the size and sophistication of the market itself. In order to militate against the possibility of omitted variable bias and reverse causation, I exploit the data's time-series variation, as well as exogenous sources of variation in hydrocarbon income. Namely, I use both the quantity of proven reserves associated with a country's giant oil fields and the total oil reserves possessed by its neighbors as instrumental variables. I also control for oil exploration efforts, which further isolates the geological signal from the political noise.

The findings in this chapter resoundingly reject the resource curse. Instead, I uncover strong evidence for a resource blessing. Oil improves the taxation of sources of ordinary revenue, promotes democracy and liberalism, is a boon for property rights, grows the public bond market and stock market, and boosts investment. In Latin America, the production and export of raw commodities in the nineteenth century revived moribund states and societies after catastrophic wars of independence. Minerals and hydrocarbons also promoted industrialization there in the twentieth century. They remain among the largest sources of FDI and generators of foreign exchange. They employ millions.

Logic of the resource blessing

How should we think about the political and economic impact of natural resources? There are several good reasons to believe that mining and hydrocarbons help to drive political and economic development.

First and foremost, natural resources may enhance state capacity by endowing a government with a laboratory in which it can "learn how to tax." While mining and hydrocarbon firms are often countries' largest employers in the developing world, they are also some of the biggest consumers of goods and services. On the one hand, mining and oil companies withhold personal income taxes from their employees. On the other hand, they often face excise and value added taxes on their consumption activities, as well as property taxes and a host of licenses and fees. These activities are almost always conducted in the formal sector, which has important knock-on effects: it induces an overall reduction in the fiscal transaction costs faced by the state. Finally, and most simply, governments may use resource rents to finance the deployment of tax collectors to sectors that were previously untaxed.

The development of natural resource sectors may also jumpstart state capacity building outside of the government's taxing efforts. States may be forced to regulate, if not participate in, the prospecting, extraction, refining, and marketing of minerals and hydrocarbons. To undertake these activities, the state might invest in the development of legal and administrative activities associated with licensing and leasing, the inspection of mines and oil wells, and the enforcement of safety and environmental regulations. Furthermore, if mining and hydrocarbon firms are nationalized, states may have no choice but to

develop indigenous engineering, infrastructure, marketing, and financial capabilities.

Several positive spillovers *vis-à-vis* other sectors of the economy may
also improve state capacity. These include the transfer of capital and
technology, including managerial expertise. Also, hydrocarbon extraction and mining may spawn upstream industries and services. This
includes construction companies, banks, and insurance companies.
They may also spawn downstream industries such as shipping companies and light manufacturing. The natural resource sector also stimu-
lates derived demand – miners and oil workers enter the market for
housing, transportation, and a range of personal services. This demand
is then met by a range of industries and service providers: home construction, automobiles, and hospitality, for example. States can then
swoop in and regulate and tax these new sectors.

By giving the government incentives to provide public goods, the
resource sector also has indirect impacts on state and fiscal capacity.
The discovery of resource stocks may encourage states to expand and
improve transportation networks to bring raw materials to market.
It may also encourage governments to assign and enforce property rights
more steadfastly – not only rights to the subsoil, but property rights
generally. For example, this is necessary if the state is to promote
unitization in order to increase oil wells' productivity, as occurred in
California, Texas, and other American oil-producing states during the
early twentieth century. And, as I argued in Chapter 4, greater security of
property rights reduces fiscal transaction costs writ large, making it
easier for the state to tax all economic sectors.

Adjudicating two views

Does oil displace non-oil revenues? Does it promote authoritarianism?
Does it undermine capitalism? Or does it do the opposite? Are natural
resources a blessing or a curse?

The rest of this chapter revisits the relationship between natural
resources and several economic and political outcomes of interest. I
first look at Latin America's political and economic history through
a mix of quantitative and qualitative evidence. While I was able to put
together several data series for a number of Latin American countries to
illustrate the relationship between resources and economic and political development, I focus particular attention on Mexico. This is for two

reasons. This case perhaps adduces the greatest variation on all relevant dimensions – not only in terms of its reliance on natural resources over time but in important economic, political, and fiscal outcomes. Second, it was usually easier for me to find raw data for Mexico that could be assembled into reliable, machine readable form.

I then reevaluate the relationship between oil and the political and economic outcomes privileged by the resource curse view using an original panel dataset with substantial time-series and cross-sectional coverage. These outcomes include the state's ability and willingness to tax citizens; regime type; the quality of countries' political and legal institutions; the government's ability to credibly commit to its pro-mises; and the size and sophistication of the market economy. I exploit the data's time-series variation, in particular, and also avail techniques that allow me to take advantage of the exogenous variation in fuel income.

The effect of natural resources in Latin America

Between 1810 and 1830, sixteen sovereign nations emerged on the world stage in Latin America. In 1822, Brazil achieved independence from Portugal. In 1818, Chile achieved independence from Spain, and Mexico soon followed in 1821. In 1823, Central America was organized as a confederation and separated from Mexico. This arrangement soon dissolved: in 1839, Guatemala, El Salvador, Honduras, Nicaragua, and Costa Rica splintered off into five separate republics. In 1830, Gran Colombia, which encompassed Venezuela, Colombia, Panama, and Ecuador, split apart. Venezuela became a separate country, as did Ecuador. Colombia, together with Panama, was known as New Granada until 1903, when Panama split off, and Colombia adopted its modern name. Peru achieved independence in 1824, and Bolivia did so a year later. Meanwhile, in the southern cone, the Viceroyalty of the River Plate splintered into Uruguay, Paraguay, and Argentina around 1810.

For both historical and geographical reasons, natural resources and raw commodities have had a disproportional impact on Latin America's history. They have often accounted for the lion's share of economic activity across the majority of Latin American countries. This is for both the period before and after independence. Therefore, this region affords us several opportunities to assess the origins of natural resource sectors, their evolution, and their effects.

Since independence, the development of mining and hydrocarbons in Latin America has been characterized by four main stages. The first is efforts to repair and reconstitute once vibrant mining sectors across the region after they had been destroyed during highly destructive wars of independence. The second is a resource boom that was induced throughout the region due to the devaluation of silver backed currencies in the late nineteenth century identified by Haber (2006, 2014). The third is a resource boom coupled to a bevy of institutional and macroeconomic reforms introduced throughout the region after World War I. The last is a resource boom first catalyzed in the 1990s on the back of several institutional and political changes that liberalized politics and economics.

The reconstitution of mining based economies

New Spain's economy was considerably diversified on the eve of the Mexican war of independence in 1810. During the late colonial era, Mexico was experiencing a shift from subsistence agriculture to greater specialization and widespread commercialization; it was also developing a more coherent internal market and industrial base (Dobado Gonzales and Marrero 2006, p. 762). At the heart of this economic dynamism was a very productive and innovative mining sector.

Its larger consequences were impressive. New Spain's urbanization rate in 1800 equaled the European average and even surpassed that of many future economic powerhouses, such as Germany and France (see DeVries et al. 1984). Table 6.1 reveals that New Spain's fiscal structure during colonialism was, accordingly, quite diversified. While revenue extraction was centered on domestic consumption (*alcabala*), and colonial authorities relied on a fair number of excise taxes – on liquor, for example – a respectable amount of direct taxation on income (*tributes*) was also levied. Given the mercantilist system the Spanish had set up, it is no surprise that permits and licenses were also popular, such as permits to practice a trade or to export goods (*patentes*). Similarly, a state monopoly on salt production (*estanco*), the sale of offices, and taxes on mining were also prevalent.

However, this would soon change. Rampant destruction, chaos, and protracted political instability were unleashed by Mexico's war of independence. The result was much the same elsewhere. Costly, protracted, and incredibly destructive wars of independence laid waste to

Table 6.1 *Mexican government revenues: colonialism vs. aftermath of independence*

Revenue source	New Spain circa 1787	Revenue source	Mexican Republic 1825
Alcabala (internal tax on commerce)	3,546,715		1,618,223
Gun Powder	451,909	*New taxes, fees, and grants*	178,546
Duties on assaying	78,292	Duties on imports and exports	2,732,995
Duties on gold	13,314	Tobacco	1,029,671
Duties on silver	1,800,546	Internal tax on tobacco	39,784
Duties on jewelry	14,161	Mail service revenues	342,533
Coinage of gold and silver	1,573,701	Lottery revenues	95,858
Alum, copper, tin, and lead	3,132	Salt mine revenues	68,382
Tributes (direct tax)	815,437	Grants from territories	16,147
Rentals	1,326	Grants from natl. properties	66,692
Trades	33,718	Revenues from ocho catedrales	529,989
Chancery fees	3,252	Revenues from the mitra	86,929
Stamped paper	59,765	Revenues from the church	8,194
Semiyearly incomes	59,530	Quota from the states	2,285,877
Duty paid in lieu of military service	19,488	Ad valorem tax	169,664
Occupation taxes	504	Tolls	47,994
Sales, purchases, and adjustments of lands	1,540		
Grocery stores	68,677		
Confiscations	3,024		
Cochineal, indigo, and vanilla	41,387		

Table 6.1 (*cont.*)

Revenue source	New Spain circa 1787	Revenue source	Mexican Republic 1825
Wine, spirits, and vinegar	57,812		
Nieve	28,823		
Leathers	4,615		
Cock-fights	42,489		
Lottery	134,096		
Ninth part of tithes	178,111		
Pulques	816,820		
Navy and *averia*	10,094		
Almojarifazgo	600,579		
Port dues	14,641		
Other port dues in Veracruz	25,025		
Salt and salt works	201,033		
Supplies	32,969		
Results of accounts	6,288		
Donations	4,818		
Unclaimed goods	352		
Totals	10,747,978		9,317,486

Notes: The figures for 1787 reflect an average year of revenue deduced from a quinquennial report from 1785–89; the figures for 1825 are estimates made by the treasury department that year.
Source: See Menaldo (2009).

most Latin American countries' capital base. This was the result of wanton destruction, sabotage, and the normal depreciation of machinery and facilities that failed to be arrested by offsetting investments.

Perhaps the most conspicuous victim of Latin America's economic and fiscal collapse was the mining sector (see Bulmer-Thomas 2003, p. 27).[3] In the large mining centers that populated Peru, Mexico, and Bolivia, almost all of the stocks of fixed capital were damaged or

---

[3] For the preeminent take on the economic consequences of independence across Latin American countries, see the various chapters in Prados de la Escosura and Amaral (1993).

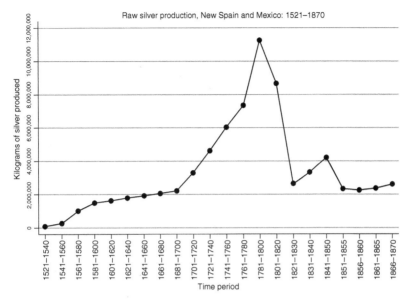

Figure 6.1 Collapse of Mexican silver mining after independence.
Source: Menaldo (2009).

destroyed (Prados de la Escosura 2007, p. 12). The result was catastrophic. When mines were abandoned and plundered they could not be easily rehabilitated. Most were flooded beyond repair (see Lewis 1999, p. 71). In Bolivia, the mining industry was left in shambles after independence; by 1840, there were 10,000 abandoned mines, resulting in rapid depopulation (Centeno 1997, p. 1583). In Mexico, the rampant destruction and abandonment of mines led to a collapse in silver production, and rapid capital flight from this sector ensued (Dobado Gonzales, and Marrero 2006).

Figure 6.1 documents the jaw-dropping collapse in silver mining observed in Mexico. It depicts the long-run trajectory of mining production from early colonialism to 1870. During the final year of coverage, the level of silver production barely surpassed its 1700 level!

This constitutes an experiment of sorts. What were the economic, fiscal, and political effects of this phenomenon? How would Mexico, a big, new, and important sovereign nation, grapple with the exigencies of state making and development in the utter absence of a mining sector?

Alas, it did not do so well. The destruction of the mining sector produced several negative spillovers. The flow of labor and supplies was brought to a halt throughout the economy. The scarcity of silver precipitated a severe contraction in the money supply (see, e.g., Cardenas 1997). This exacerbated a spiraling de-industrialization process. Mexico's second largest industry, textiles, was brought to a virtual standstill when "[r]aw materials became scarce, and the commercial routes to the north, traditionally an important market for domestic textile production, were cut [...] textile workers abandoned their looms to join the contending armies, and many died as a consequence of epidemics" (Dobado Gonzales et al. 2008, p. 767).

Table 6.1 reveals the effect that the absence of the mining sector and its associated spillovers had on the country's fiscal system. In 1825, four years after its independence from Spain, Mexico's total revenues were about 13 percent lower than in 1787. The relatively diversified tax base was gone, along with its tax administration system. For this reason, direct taxation was abandoned shortly after independence. Indeed, while only two taxes were carried over from the colonial era – the internal tax on commerce and an excise tax on powder – the revenues garnered from these sources were considerably diminished. For this reason, Mexico's post-independence government adopted a customs tax for the first time in history – and it immediately became its largest revenue source.

Any attempt by the Mexican government to improve its tax yield was complicated by the fact that the disappearance of the mining sector contributed to widespread immiseration. This adversely affected the state's ability to raise indirect taxation on consumption. While abject poverty seriously curtailed the demand for consumables, it also raised fiscal transaction costs. In other words, "[a]side from relatively few commodities, large parts of the population did not consume very much that could be easily taxed" (Centeno 1997, p. 1584). It did not help matters that wage laborers who were once miners, or who might have otherwise become miners, were left destitute.

Figure 6.2 captures this phenomenon via a scatterplot of the Mexican share of *Consumption Taxes* regressed against the *Urban, Unskilled Wage Rate* between 1823 and 1847. This graph depicts a strong, positive correlation between wages and reliance on consumption taxes. However, this graph also shows that wages and consumption taxes both declined steadily over time. Consequently, the further away we travel from Mexican independence, the lower the government's yield from sales and excise taxes.

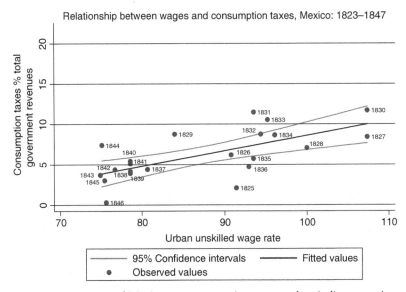

Figure 6.2 Poverty and Mexican governments' attempts to levy indirect taxation. *Notes:* Urban Wages is an index that equals 1 in 1828; calculated from urban, unskilled wage rates in Reales per day (8 Reales = 1 peso); between 1821 and 1838, an official series of wages earned by Peones; between 1838 and 1860, waged earned by Peones as recorded by records of hospitals, convents, and other institutions. Consumption Taxes is revenue from taxes on goods and services; for notes on Consumption Taxes as % Government Revenues, see Menaldo (2009). The slope coefficient from the regression is .19, the t-statistic is 3.97, and the r-squared statistic is 0.44, with an n equal to 22. *Source:* (Menaldo 2009).

This pattern was not restricted to Mexico. In Gran Colombia, colonial monopolies on mercury, playing cards, and gun powder were discontinued after independence from Spain, due to an implosion in the demand for these products. The only fiscal monopolies that – just barely – survived were salt and alcohol (see Deas 1982). Similarly, at the dawn of independence in 1830, the new Uruguayan government inherited a crushing debt of 2 million pesos with few revenues to pay for it (Reyes, Abadie, and Romero N.d, p. 337).

These fiscal problems were a direct result of the fact that between 1820 and 1870, Per Capita Income in Latin America – based on the population weighted average of Brazil, Mexico, Argentina, Uruguay, and Venezuela – only increased 7.9 percent, while in Mexico it actually decreased 11 percent. To put this in perspective, while Latin America's GDP Per Capita was 56 percent of the United States' level in 1820, it was only 31 percent in 1870.[4] Although Mexico had 44 percent of the United States' Per Capita Income in 1800 – on the eve of independence – this figure had fallen to only 13 percent in 1910, on the eve of the Mexican Revolution (Coatsworth 1978, pp. 82–83).

Given the proliferation of expenses associated with state building, this was an unfortunate phenomenon. Fledgling Latin American governments faced entirely new governance costs associated with the advent of political sovereignty.[5] Each new nation faced the need to erect sundry government ministries from scratch, pay the salaries of government officials, field national armies, and pay for the pensions awarded to recent war veterans. Moreover, the fiscal and currency fragmentation that followed colonialism meant that new countries had to adopt their own currencies and raise their own taxes.[6]

After independence, the provision of public goods, such as law enforcement and street paving, were often written into national budgets, with little money available to actually pay for these new obligations (see Prados de Escosura 2007, p. 3). For example, each of these nascent Latin American nations faced spiraling expenses when attempting to erect and run new customs houses. Moreover, these mushrooming expenses were amplified by the fact that Spain had not really invested in infrastructure within the Latin American colonies. Contrary to what had occurred in North America across the British colonies, dense networks of ports never arose; nor did a common market, neither within or between the administrative units created by Spain to rule Latin America (see North, Summerhill, and Weingast 2000, p. 42).

---

[4] These data are from Przeworski and Curvale (2005, p. 7). I hasten to note, however, that there is actually an ongoing debate regarding whether Mexico's Per Capita Income (1) deteriorated between 1800 and the mid nineteenth century, (2) remained stagnant, (3) or actually increased, albeit modestly. For the mushrooming literature on this topic, see Prados de la Escosura (2007, p. 13).

[5] On the other hand, independence from Spain meant that Latin America's former colonies were relieved from their obligation to pay Spain remittances.

[6] According to Grafe and Irigoin (2006), intra-colonial transfers were pivotal to perpetuating Spain's colonial system in Latin America (cited in Prados de la Escosura 2007, p. 2).

The common strategy pursued by Latin American governments to raise taxes in this trying context was to increase their integration with global markets. This strategy was aimed at generating revenues from tariffs and foreign exchange. This called on countries to exploit their comparative advantage in the production of primary commodities, including minerals. It also called on courting large volumes of FDI in the exploration, production, and transportation of these products. This is how entirely new natural resource sectors came into being across Latin America's new nations during the nineteenth century.

The Spanish Empire's demise had also spelled the collapse of a mercantile strategy used to generate rents and, thus, government revenues. The Spanish Crown had strategically granted monopoly rights over trans-Atlantic trade to elites in exchange for political loyalty and revenues. One of the implications of this political-fiscal strategy was that, until 1764, trade was heavily restricted across the Spanish Empire. The only trade that was authorized was between Cadiz, in Spain, and a few ports in the New World: Cartagena (Colombia), Portobelo (Panama), La Habana (Cuba), and Veracruz (Mexico).[7] Trade between colonial outposts was proscribed.

Therefore, after their wars of independence, Latin America's nascent republics were now free to trade with Europe, North America, and each other. This unleashed a steady increase in the volume of Latin American trade (see Bulmer-Thomas 2003), which was complemented by a gradual and sizable improvement in Latin American countries' terms of trade (Dobado Gonzales 2008, p. 760). In Argentina, Chile, and Uruguay, primary product exports included wool, cattle, linseed, maize, and wheat. In the tropics, including Brazil, Venezuela, and Colombia, exports included sugar, cacao, rubber, and coffee. In Mexico, Peru, Bolivia, and Chile, the major exports were silver, copper, tin, gold, lead, and nitrates.

Figure 6.3 helps to corroborate this claim. It documents the evolution of Mexican trade from immediately after independence, in 1822, to the start of the Mexican Revolution, in 1910. The picture is clear: the volume of trade (Per Capita) increased steadily after independence – and then really took off in the early 1890s. The same patterns were reproduced in the Andean countries – Bolivia, Ecuador, Venezuela,

[7] Restrictions were somewhat reduced in 1765, in an effort to maximize revenues by boosting the volume of trade (see Dobando Gonzales et al. 2008, p. 763).

Figure 6.3 Mexican trade per capita from independence to the Mexican revolution.

Notes: Per Capita Trade is the sum of exports and imports divided by population, expressed in U.S. dollars. Converted from pesos into dollars at the market exchange rate (exchange rates are yearly averages). Original source reports fiscal years (June to July) between 1855 and 1910 for imports, and 1861 – 1910, for exports. When converting fiscal years into calendar years, the calendar year is always the first year in the fiscal year dyad, for example, 1810–1811 is 1810 in calendar years. Imputation used to calculate values for some years. For imports, linear interpolation used for 1821 and 1822; 1856–1859; 1868–1871; 1875–1876; 1878–1882; between 1860 and 1867, since only the 1860–1867 average is provided by the original source, the average is imputed as the observed values during those years. For exports, linear interpolation used for 1821 and 1822; 1857–1859; 1868–1971; 1875–1876; between 1860 and 1867, since only the 1860–1867 average is provided by the original source, the average is imputed as the observed values during those years.

Source: Menaldo (2009).

Colombia, and Peru – as well as in Argentina, Chile, Brazil, and Mexico.

Therefore, this phenomenon also constitutes an experiment of sorts. What were the economic, fiscal, and political effects of the advent of natural resource sectors across Latin America?

The fiscal effect of natural resources

At first, increasing volumes of Latin American trade were taxed to the hilt by the region's governments. This fiscal strategy was not a result of the fact that tariffs were an optimal way of generating revenues; instead, it was borne out of desperation. Indeed, export taxes generate distortions and pose serious risks that can ultimately undermine revenues. Governments often fear that exporters will pass any taxes on to foreign consumers, thus endangering their country's market share by encouraging competitors to enter the international market, incentivizing domestic miners to allow otherwise extractable lower grade ores to remain stranded, or by stimulating a search for synthetic substitutes. Indeed, in Peru an exorbitantly high tax rate on silver mining threatened the revival of silver production after independence, and for this reason it was eventually ratcheted down (see Quiroz 1993).

Yet, many Latin American countries were nonetheless able to resort to relatively high export taxes when needed. Peru and Chile were able to do so in regards to nitrates in the form of guano, which was heavily taxed after independence – that is, at least until the early twentieth century, when the advent of synthetic nitrate production displaced exports of organic saltpeter throughout the world. Brazil was able to do so in regards to gold and coffee. While export tariffs in the province of Minas Gerais were only 5 percent of total revenues in 1889, they climbed to 64 percent in 1892 (Sokoloff and Zolt 2007, pp. 113–114). Finally, Argentine governments periodically leveled confiscatory taxes on soy exports over the twentieth century, without decimating domestic production. Figure 6.4 depicts this phenomenon.

Although necessary, Latin American governments' fiscal reliance on natural resources was not permanent. Gradually, several mineral- and oil-rich governments shifted away from their exaggerated dependence on export taxes and other non-tax sources of revenues centered on the natural resource sector. Notably, direct, progressive taxation was adopted during the nineteenth century in resource-rich countries such as Ecuador, Peru, and Chile – well before the United States permanently adopted progressive income taxation at the federal level through the sixteenth amendment in 1913. By 1940, income and wealth taxes were 17.9 percent of total revenues in Argentina, 10.2 percent in Brazil, 23.7 percent in Chile, 30.4 percent in Colombia, and 18.4 percent in Peru (see Sokoloff and Zolt 2007, p. 103).

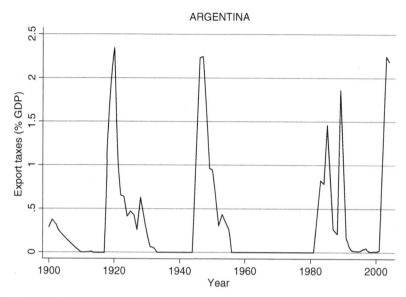

Figure 6.4 Export taxation in Argentina over the twentieth century.
Source: Menaldo (2009).

However, the quintessential example of this phenomenon is perhaps Mexico. On the heels of the adoption of its "socialist constitution" in 1917, at the tail end of the Mexican Revolution, a progressive tax law was spearheaded by Plutarco Elías Calles during his presidential term (1924–1928). Among other measures, this law ushered in a federal income tax on individual income and corporate profits at progressive rates. Figure 6.5 documents the (central) public revenues from income, profits, and capital gains collected in Mexico (as a share of GDP) – a variable that excludes any revenues from natural resources – over the twentieth century.

While this figure reveals a steady, palpable growth of direct taxation, Figure 6.6 graphs the Mexican government's fiscal reliance on revenues from natural resources (% total revenues) during the same period. Mexico's reliance on revenues from natural resources has oscillated in accordance with two distinct oil booms that bookend the twentieth century – illustrated in Figure 6.7, which graphs Mexico's total income from minerals and hydrocarbons. Clearly, the country has never been entirely fiscally dependent on its natural resources.

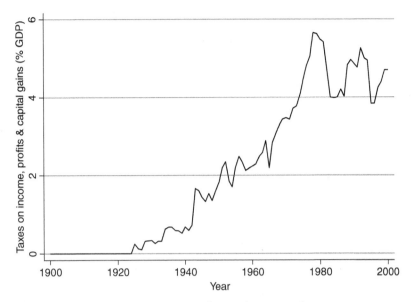

Figure 6.5 Direct taxation in Mexico during the twentieth century.
Source: INEGI.

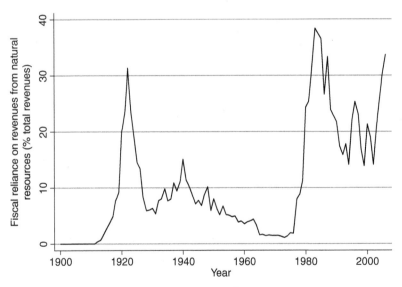

Figure 6.6 Mexico's fiscal reliance on natural resource revenues.
Source: Haber and Menaldo (2011a).

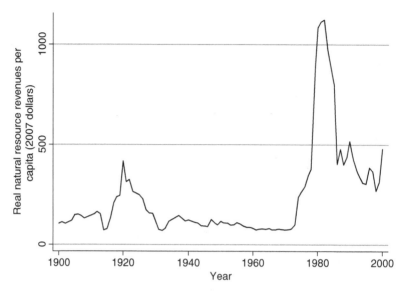

Figure 6.7 Mexico's natural resource income.
Source: Haber and Menaldo (2011a).

The effect of natural resources on the provision of public goods

During the nineteenth century, Latin American governments fastidiously courted portfolio investment and FDI to reconstitute their
mining and commodity sectors. This allowed them to finance several
backward and forward linkages, as big investments in infrastructure
and institutions were required to transport Latin America's minerals
and hydrocarbons to their ultimate destinations in the developed
world. On the supply side, first British, and then American, investors
were attracted to Latin America because of the prospects of a high rate
of return in countries that were relatively labor abundant but capital
scarce.

Much of this foreign capital was used to finance railroads dedicated
to transporting minerals and other raw commodities from Latin
American countries' interiors to their littorals, as well as build new
ports and depots (see Stallings 1987). Figures 6.8–6.10 showcase various Latin American countries' railway density, measured as the proportion of railway length in a given country to its land mass in
a given year (in kilometers), between 1850 and 1910. These graphs,
which are broken down by sub-region – Mexico and Central America,

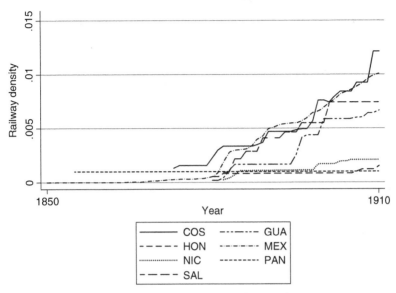

Figure 6.8 Railway construction in Mexico and Central America.
Source: Mitchell (2003).

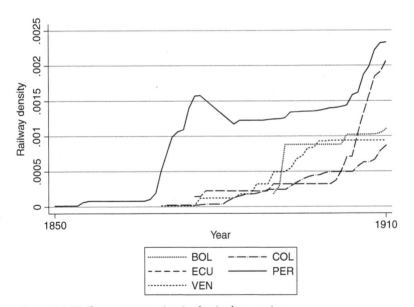

Figure 6.9 Railway construction in the Andean region.
Source: Mitchell (2003).

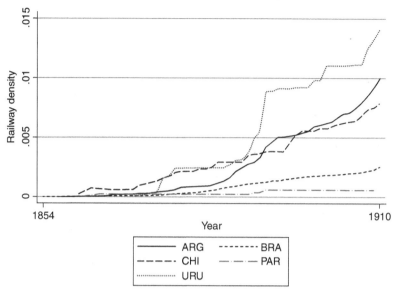

Figure 6.10 Railway construction in South America.
Source: Mitchell (2003).

the Andean countries, and the South American countries, respectively –
show a gradual, steady increase in the share of national territory
covered by railways.

To be sure, Latin America's nineteenth-century railroad boom did
not fully mitigate the isolation of the Latin American interior.
Williamson (1999, p. 106) reports that, by 1912, the length of railway
track that was laid down (per every 1,000 people) in Bolivia, Ecuador,
Paraguay, and Peru was only 1/10 that of Australia, New Zealand, and
Canada. Nonetheless, by 1850, average transport costs from Latin
America's interior to its ports had substantially fallen, even if they
remained comparatively high (Williamson 1999, p. 106; Bertola and
Williamson 2006). These railway networks eventually had a huge,
positive effect on Latin American industrialization, which will be discussed further below.

Legal reforms in the shadow of natural resources

As in the case of non-resource revenues, or the provision of public
goods, Latin America's copious natural resources and commodities
did not preclude several waves of legal and administrative reforms

from washing over the region. Between 1831 and 1916, civil and commercial codes were modernized across Latin America, as were banking, insurance, and, unsurprisingly, mining laws (Coatsworth 2008, p. 564, table 4). According to Coatsworth, this was accomplished by the full abolishment of communal properties, the expulsion of squatters, the expropriation of Church property held in mortmain, and the reform of commercial and civil codes (ibid., p. 559). Examples include the Brazilian *Lei da terra* in 1850, Mexico's *Ley Lerdo* in 1856, and Argentina's so-called desert campaign. These laws were aimed at replacing collective landholding with freeholdings and helped underpin new plantations oriented toward commodity exports. Because these reforms considerably strengthened property rights, they also incentivized the construction of a wave of new mines (see Lewis 1999, p. 76).

A second generation of reforms, aimed at further attracting foreign investment, occurred at the turn of the twentieth century. Governments across Latin America erected central banks, adopted the gold standard in order to constrain money and credit creation, and passed balanced budget laws. They also improved the administration of custom houses and domestic taxes to help defray the repayment of debts allocated to public works (see Eichengreen 1994).[8]

Both first- and second-generation reforms proved successful. This is evidenced by Figure 6.11, which graphs the total income from minerals and hydrocarbons for Colombia, Peru, Bolivia, Ecuador, Brazil, and Chile over the twentieth century. What is implied by this graph is that there was an explosion of investment in natural resources; increasingly, higher levels of income from minerals, oil, and natural gas were only made possible by a steady influx of investment into the exploration of natural resources, as well as their extraction, transformation, and transportation. While these exploration efforts were financed entirely

---

[8] These reforms were usually adopted after consultation with Edwin Kemmerer, a Princeton economist who was a strong advocate of the gold standard and central banks. However, it has been shown by several researchers that political support for these reforms, and even the blueprints aimed at implementing them, had long preceded the arrival of the "Kremmerer missions" in Latin America. Eichengreen (1994) argues that Kremmerer's role was simply to act as an imprimatur: governments used his missions to signal their preference for economic orthodoxy and to bolster the credibility of their commitment to debt repayment.

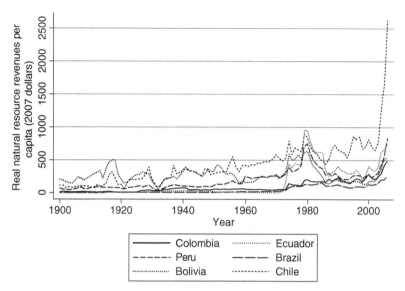

Figure 6.11 Latin American natural resources during the twentieth century.
Source: Haber and Menaldo (2011a).

by FDI during the first part of the century, they were increasingly funded by the state or through a mix of domestic and foreign funding in the wake of nationalizations of the petroleum industry – as early as Mexico's in 1938 and as late as Venezuela's in 1976.

The effect of natural resources on industrialization

By 1913–1914, and against all odds, Latin American countries had developed quite respectable industrial sectors. Brazil's value added in manufacturing had reached 19.4 percent that year, while Argentina's was 16.6 percent, and Chile's was 14.5 percent. And although Mexico's was below 10 percent, this would soon change (see Haber 2006, p. 559, who cites Albert 1988, p. 185; and Bulmer-Thomas 2003, p. 137). Mexico would soon experience a veritable industrial revolution during the rest of the twentieth century. Haber, Razo, and Maurer (2003) evince that this was the result of the steady growth of variegated industries aimed at satisfying domestic demand: steel, cement, glass, soap, dynamite, foodstuffs and beer, tobacco, clothing, appliances, and eventually cars.

Several facts and figures help convey this process. Figure 6.12 graphs Mexico's gross fixed domestic investment (% GDP) between 1900 and

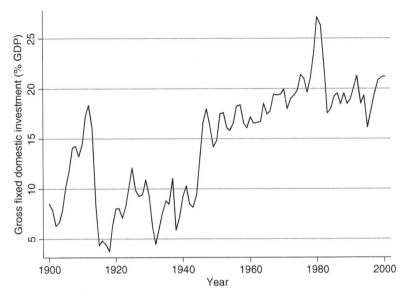

Figure 6.12 Mexican domestic capital base, twentieth century.
Source: Astorga et al. (2003).

2000, and evidences an explosion in the accumulation of capital. A large share of new investments was financed by directed credit: loans channeled by Mexican development banks at subsidized rates to protected, industrial sectors. By 1979, and buoyed by record oil prices induced by the second oil shock, a record US$6,213 pesos per person were allocated by said banks to thousands of firms serving the domestic market.[9] Figure 6.13 graphs Manufacturing Value Added (% GDP), which mirrors this story. By 1990, 28 percent of Mexico's population was employed in industry, mining, energy, and construction.[10] Figure 6.14 graphs the culmination of these processes, a nearly 10,000 percent increase in the country's real Per Capita Income over the long twentieth century.

What was the effect of natural resources on industrialization in Latin America? There is a strong case to be made that the latter was stimulated by the former, in both direct and indirect ways. Haber (2006, 2014) documents how the growth of the export sector across Latin

---

[9] These data are from Instituto Nacional de Estadística y Geografía (INEGI).
[10] These data are from INEGI.

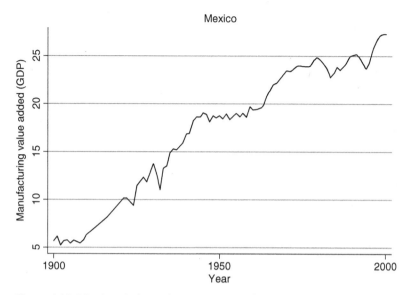

Figure 6.13 Mexican industrialization, twentieth century.
Source: Astorga et al. (2003).

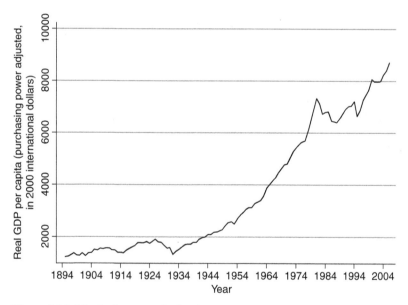

Figure 6.14 Mexico's economic development.

America was due to the depreciation of these countries' real exchange rates, which was the result of industrial nations going off of the silver standard. As outlined above, these exports were centered on raw commodities and minerals. On the one hand, this depreciation created a natural protective barrier to Latin American countries' internal markets. On the other hand, its timing corresponded to a dramatic decline in transportation costs associated with the diffusion of technology such as steamships.

According to Haber, in the wake of the rapid expansion of Latin America's tradables sector, there were several developments that favored manufacturing. First, wage earners employed in this sector stimulated demand for finished products such as clothing, foodstuffs, and appliances. Second, railroad construction consolidated internal markets and allowed import substituting firms to exploit economies of scale. Third, mining and associated smelting industries had given rise to a group of entrepreneurs who then transferred their skills to steelmaking. In short, to satisfy new consumer demands, new domestic industries leveraged the *de facto* protection implied by Latin American countries' currency depreciations, a steep reduction in transportation costs, and technological spillovers from the mining sector. Eventually, new firms received additional protection from governments in the way of import tariffs on finished goods and zero taxes on intermediate inputs needed to manufacture these goods.

The new wave of natural resources in Latin America and state capacity

There has been sustained, if not absolutely impressive, growth in Latin America's oil and mining sector in the twenty-first century. From 2004 to 2007, FDI dedicated to hydrocarbons grew by 223 percent in Brazil and 623 percent in Colombia. Over the same period, FDI allocated to mining has grown 458 percent in Brazil, 502 percent in Bolivia, and 550 percent in Mexico. Bebbington and Bury (2013, p. 16) note that these investments have financed both traditional extraction projects and entirely new ventures.

Much of this FDI can be traced to fiscal and economic crises that have plagued Latin American countries since Mexico defaulted on its sovereign debt in 1982. According to Bury and Bebbington (2013), "[w]ithin Latin America, the extractive sector was seen as a critically important driver of economic growth by policymakers seeking to overcome the economic and political crises spurred by successive oil price shocks and massive national debt burdens" (p. 38). A massive debt overhang was inherited from a statist era, and the response was swift and painful: austerity and the steady retrenchment of the state. While publicly owned companies were privatized at a rapid clip to generate much needed government revenues and foreign exchange, capital accounts were liberalized and free trade agreements were penned.

Latin American governments have since bent over backward to curry foreign investment in their natural resource sectors. This has entailed several remarkable transformations; transformations that could be labeled as big improvements in state capacity. For example, reforms have included "reorganizing and clarification of mining and hydrocarbons concessions, removal of local hiring and sourcing requirements, limitations on expropriation rights, ratification of international arbitration accords, and the creation of investment protections" (pp. 44–45); "natural resource extraction legislation was either abolished or amended to limit public interest and eminent domain, reform environmental protection, establish minimal taxation regimes, formalize mineral and hydrocarbons concession taxation and leasing, and create investment incentives" (p. 45); furthermore, Latin American countries "developed infrastructure to provide access to remote areas where new hydrocarbons and mineral deposits were being discovered" (ibid.); and "provided the necessary military and police support to ensure the safety of new extractive operations and their foreign personnel" (ibid.).

This phenomenon has not crowded out investment in other economic sectors; most importantly, it has not catalyzed de-industrialization. For example, over the last three decades, oil-rich Mexico has aggressively liberalized its economy, and become one of the most globalized countries in the world. After privatizing hundreds of industries such as telecommunications, electricity, and airlines, it has embraced fiscal and monetary discipline. It has become an export powerhouse outside of natural resources, notable for its automobiles and computers.[11]

---

[11] To be sure, Mexico experienced a relatively low level of growth in the immediate aftermath of the 2008 financial crisis. Mexico suffered through a strong recession that year. Yet, by 2009, it was registering positive growth again. And its downturn was primarily due to its interdependence with the American economy, not its fundamentals. Moreover, Mexico registered a quite decent, if not enviable, rate of growth between 2010 and 2013 – roughly 4 percent per

Copper-rich Chile has proceeded along a similar path. Its liberalizing reforms, coupled with fiscal discipline and monetary conservatism, have drastically reduced the interest rates demanded by foreign investors on its public debt. Among several beneficial outcomes to take hold, one stands out in particular: Chile's financial system has become quite large and sophisticated, fostering deep mortgage markets and allowing the homeownership rate to exceed 70 percent. It also stands out as a major exporter of wine, fruit, and fish, which together with copper has allowed it to become Latin America's richest country.

The relationship between natural resources and regime type in LATAM

As a final question to be explored in Latin America, what is the relationship between natural resource reliance and regime type? Figure 6.15 graphs Latin America's non-resource-reliant countries' average Polity Score – the most widely used continuous regime type measure, which I describe in greater detail further below – and resource reliant countries' average Polity Score. These are both graphed since 1840; resource reliance is defined and coded by Haber and Menaldo (2011a).

Figure 6.15 suggests that resource reliance has not made any difference to Latin American countries' institutional trajectory. The figure reveals that Latin America has had both waves of democratization and waves of authoritarianism. It also shows that these waves of regime change *have occurred simultaneously in both the resource-reliant and non-resource-reliant countries.* This is most obvious since the 1970s, when a palpable trend toward democracy in both countries that are resource reliant and those that are not began.

It is again instructive to zoom in on Mexico. It experienced two distinct oil booms, punctuated by a multi-decade period of decline in its oil sector. While the first boom ran from 1900 to 1924, the second one has been ongoing since 1974, after the discovery of the Cantarell supergiant oil field in the Gulf of Mexico (see Figure 6.7). Contradicting the resource curse, Mexico's reliance on oil was at historically high levels

annum. This is higher than the Latin American average during the same period and much higher than the U.S. average. However, Mexico's average growth rate did decelerate to 2.1 percent, on average, between 2013 and 2015.

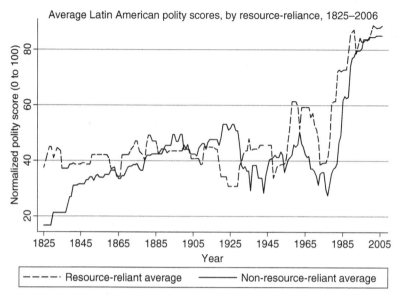

Figure 6.15 Regime type in Latin America by resource reliance over the long run.

during its protracted democratization process, which we can roughly date from 1989, when the ruling party (the PRI) began to concede state-level elections (Mexico is a federation), to 2000, when the PRI finally let go of the executive branch after losing the presidency.

First, consider that, before Mexico's first oil boom, when it was relatively resource poor, it was not the bastion of democracy that would be predicted by the resource curse. Indeed, the nineteenth century was not kind to Mexico in general. The dictator Porfirio Diaz came to power in 1876, ruling with an iron fist until 1910. The regime's repression precipitated an almost two-decade long revolution.

Before that point, things were even worse. While a gaggle of warlords controlled most of Mexico's periphery between independence in 1821 and 1876, Mexico also experienced fifty-five executives, and the average presidential tenure was less than one year. One military strongman, General Antonio López de Santa Ana, headed the executive branch on eleven different occasions, ceding more than half of Mexico's territory to the United States in 1848. As was explained above, this was in large part due to the fact that the country's mining sector was left in shambles, not a result of its natural resources.

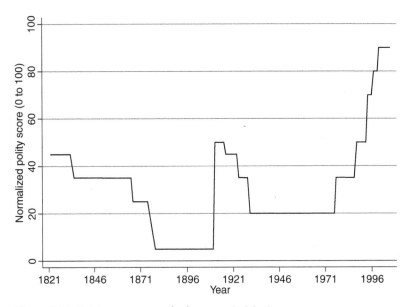

Figure 6.16 Regime type over the long run in Mexico.

Mexico's first resource boom ended circa 1925, after it had exhausted its oil reserves given the technology of the time (see Haber et al. 2003). But, as evidenced by Figure 6.16, the level of democracy did not increase in the wake of this resource bust, as would be predicted by the resource curse. Instead, Mexico saw the heyday of single party rule.

In 1929, Plutarco Elías Calles founded the National Revolutionary Party (PNR), which would later be renamed the Institutionalized Revolutionary Party (PRI), the "official" party of the "revolutionary" regime. Calles invited influential generals, regional elites, agrarian bosses, labor bosses, and the heads of small parties to join the party. These elites brought their vast networks of supporters along with them.

The party was balanced as a three-legged stool, composed of nascent industrialists, syndicated labor unions, and peasant organizations that represented rural constituents. Although a system of "corporatized" bargaining was set up to adjudicate disputes between these sectoral representatives (see Huntington 1968, pp. 318–319), any disputes that did arise were already considerably muted. Quiescence was secured by the party's strategic use of rents and patronage. To appease capitalists, the PRI used protectionism and subsidized credit, as was recounted above. To appease labor, the PRI appointed the national labor union's leader to head the ministry of Industry, Commerce, and Labor, who then ensured that increased wages and benefits would ensue for a privileged few unionized workers. To appease peasants, the PRI doled out land, seeds, fertilizer, irrigation, and other goodies. President Calles managed to redistribute over 3 million hectares of land between 1924 and 1928 alone, a number that would then grow exponentially (see Albertus and Menaldo 2012a).

The height of Mexico's authoritarian system of single party rule occurred during the nadir of its reliance on natural resources. Beginning in the late 1960s, when Mexico's oil reliance was at the lowest it had been during the twentieth century – due to rock bottom levels of export receipts from oil and minerals (see Figures 6.6 and 6.7) – PRI governments became more repressive. Roughly, one can date the beginning of this more repressive period to the crackdown of student protestors in the Tlatelolco Plaza in Mexico City, on the eve of the Olympic Games in 1968. A concerted and well-funded campaign against dissent continued after this massacre under the administration of Luis Echeverría Álvarez (1970–1976), later labeled Mexico's Dirty War. The military attempted to crush a blossoming insurgency in the state of Guerrero and perpetrated a slew of human rights violations against civilians in the process.

Mexico's second oil boom did not produce the political outcome predicted by the resource curse either. As oil rents steadily increased, the PRI gradually lost its vice-like grip on power. In the late 1970s, oil revenues exploded, launching an upward trend that continued through the start of the Ernesto Zedillo administration, in 1994. It is during this time period that Mexico gradually democratized.

The first spark was ignited after the debt crisis of 1982, when Mexico defaulted on its foreign debt obligations, inducing the López Portillo administration to commit a series of strategic blunders. On the one hand, the nationalization of the banking sector served to strengthen opposition parties on the right, especially the National Action Party (PAN), when the Mexican business community was alienated by this expropriation and came to mistrust the PRI, doubting that they would protect their property rights in the future (see Haber et al. 2008). On the other hand, fiscal austerity and an obsession with renegotiating debt repayments at the expense of social programs buoyed once marginal leftwing opposition parties, who were headed by Cuauhtémoc

Cárdenas after he defected from the PRI. As Mexico's poor fell further and further behind and inequality worsened, the Party of the Democratic Revolution (PRD), in particular, gained support.

As a result of these developments, the PRI began to surrender greater and greater ground. It accepted defeat in mayoral elections throughout the country and gradually conceded governorships in key states, beginning with Baja California in 1989, and including other economically important states in the north of the country. Moreover, the regime had to resort to widespread electoral fraud to squeak out a victory by Carlos Salinas de Gortari in the 1988 presidential elections, which further mobilized the opposition. Increased fiscal and administrative decentralization strengthened citizen groups, spurring grassroots mobilization against the PRI, and leading the PRI to lose control of the chamber of deputies (Mexico's lower house) in 1994. In short, the period between 1982 and 1994, during Mexico's second oil boom, was also the period in which the PRI lost its grip on power.

This is not to say, however, that Mexico's second oil boom has been characterized by an uninterrupted, linear increase in oil rents. Between 1980 and 1999, the oil price decreased by 76 percent, falling from US$93.08 a barrel (in real, 2007 U.S. dollars) to US$22.74 a barrel (in real, 2007 U.S. dollars). The share of Mexican government revenues attributable to oil tumbled 63 percent between 1983 and 2002, from a high of 38.4 (% Total Revenues) to 14.10 (% Total Revenues). There was then a pronounced increase in the oil price in the early 1990s associated with Saddam Hussein's invasion of Kuwait. However, it proved to be short lived; after the United States vanquished Iraq in the first Gulf War, expelling its army from Kuwait, the oil price continued its steep downward spiral. Yet, a sharp rise in oil prices later reversed this trend. It began in 2001 and lasted – albeit with an interruption in 2009 due to a plunge in demand associated with the global financial crisis – until early 2014.

It is to say, however, that even sharp reductions in the reliance of revenues from oil, due almost entirely to price collapses, do not gainsay the larger, historical pattern. During the latter part of the twentieth century, Mexico vastly increased its level of oil production, oil exports, and its reliance on oil revenues. And it was also during this time period that Mexico democratized.

In 2000, when the PRI finally lost control of the presidency, the state's fiscal reliance on oil revenues was 23 percent, in comparison to roughly 6 percent in the 1960s (see Figure 6.7). Meanwhile, its Total Resource Income Per Capita had increased six-fold, to US$478 Per Capita (in real, 2008 Dollars) (see Figure 6.7). By 2006, when Mexico held a second free and fair election, Fiscal Reliance and Total Resource Income were even higher: 37 percent and US$871 per person, respectively. Moreover, the democratically elected governments of Vicente Fox, from 2000 to 2006, and Felipe Calderón, from 2006 to 2012, financed their ambitious antipoverty (and antinarcotics) programs with petroleum taxes, helping to further consolidate Mexican democracy.

The role of oil on political development globally

The rest of this chapter systematically explores the relationship between hydrocarbons and several economic and political outcomes of interest at the global level. I reevaluate the relationship between oil and gas and (1) the state's ability and willingness to tax citizens, (2) regime type, (3) the quality of a country's political and legal institutions, (4) the government's ability to credibly commit to its promises, and (5) the size and sophistication of the market economy. I address these questions using an original panel dataset with wide cross-sectional and temporal coverage. The broadest cross-sectional coverage includes 155 countries and the broadest time-series coverage is between 1930 and 2006. To address the potential for endogeneity bias, I exploit both the data's time-series variation and several sources of exogenous variation in countries' hydrocarbon income.

Non-oil tax revenues

Measuring non-oil taxation is quite difficult. While it is relatively easy to identify total tax revenues, it is hard to identify and isolate the different streams of revenue generated by the exploration, production, transformation, transportation, and exportation of hydrocarbons. Governments can extract revenues from hydrocarbons at several points across this value chain. These include, for example, requiring firms to pay exploration licenses, levying production royalties, raising corporate taxes and other income-based taxes on oil company profits, and collecting National Oil Company (NOC) stock dividends. Yet, it is difficult for researchers to identify and expunge these revenues from total tax receipts.

There are no extant, reliable measures of the different hydrocarbon revenue streams extracted by governments that have coverage across a wide cross-section of countries or over multiple time periods.[12] Small and large oil producers, alike, sometimes tax hydrocarbons without ever disclosing these revenues; and country treasury records and similar periodicals often fail to decompose oil revenues into their constituent streams with precision. While I was able to identify these revenue streams for thirteen major oil-producing countries between 1972 and 2006 by using a slew of primary and secondary sources, I was not, alas, able to obtain reliable data across time for each of these countries. Nor is an N of 13 large enough to yield a representative sample from which one can estimate the average effect of oil income on non-oil revenues. Nevertheless, further ahead, I do use this data on natural resource taxation to evaluate the validity of the proxy I ultimately use to measure hydrocarbon revenues.

As a second best, yet feasible, approach to measuring non-oil revenues, I developed a measure of indirect taxation as a percent of GDP that I am confident is uncontaminated by hydrocarbon revenues. I constructed the measure in a way that allowed me to remove the tax revenues from hydrocarbons by default, without having to separately identify every dollar of oil that was actually taxed by the government. Specifically, by expunging all tax revenues from income, profits, capital gains, and property from the numerator, I removed, in the process, any corporate taxes on hydrocarbon firms' profits, both those produced by NOCs and International Oil Companies (IOCs). This measure also excludes dividends distributed by NOCs to governments and oil and gas royalties.[13] Most importantly, with an N of 148 and average T of

[12] Researchers who have evaluated the effect of natural resources on taxation have not always sought to isolate the component of tax revenues unrelated to the natural resource sector. Instead, they have looked at the relationship between natural resources and overall tax revenues, revenues that include taxes generated by oil and minerals. See, for example, Cheibub (1998) and Kenny and Winer (2006).

[13] To code this variable, I follow the guidelines set forth in the International Monetary Fund's *Government Finance Statistics Yearbook* (IMF-GFSY). Tax revenues are classified by this source as taxes from income, profits, and capital gains; property taxes; taxes on consumption, including sales and value added taxes; and import and export taxes. I use both primary and secondary sources to maximize data coverage while adhering to the IMF-GFSY's coding rules. The major secondary sources I avail are the IMF-GFSY, the World Bank, the Organization for Economic Cooperation and Development (OECD), and

23 – the maximum ranging from 1972 to 2006 – this variable's coverage is quite good.

The logic of this measurement strategy is as follows. Across the world, and especially in the Middle East, governments operate oil companies as quasi-independent enterprises and tax their profits, either at the regular corporate rate or at a special rate, and sometimes do so quite progressively (see Chapter 5).[14] Examples of this model include Angola, Ecuador, Kuwait, Nigeria, Norway, Oman, Trinidad and Tobago, and Venezuela.[15] In some oil-rich countries, governments also earn dividends from NOCs. These include Bahrain and Kuwait, for example. However, the most prominent method in which governments raise revenues from hydrocarbons remains collecting royalties and property taxes/licenses. Examples of this model include Bahrain, Colombia, Ecuador, Gabon, Iran, Kuwait, Malaysia, Oman, Peru, and Venezuela.

Figure 6.17 helps justify my measurement strategy. It graphs the trajectory of the average, annual share of taxes collected from income, profits, and capital gains (% GDP) for the fifty-three resource-reliant countries identified by Haber and Menaldo (2011a) against the real price of oil, expressed as its annual average, and lagged by one year.[16] The pattern is clear: changes in tax receipts from income, profits, and capital gains in oil-reliant countries closely parallel changes in the international oil price. This is because higher oil prices axiomatically boost the profits earned by oil companies.

Indeed, partially because of this fact, I am not biasing in favor of identifying a resource blessing by using this measure. I am not bestowing an artificial handicap upon the non-resource-reliant countries by omitting huge sources of tax revenues earned by their governments in the form of taxes on income and profits. To the contrary, Figure 6.18 makes clear that *it is the resource-reliant countries that have usually*

---

various IMF country profiles. See Albertus and Menaldo (2014) for all of the sources I employ on a country-by-country basis.

[14] The same is true for major mineral exporters that have nationalized production. These include Chile, Peru, Zaire, Zambia, the Dominican Republic, Guinea, Guyana, Jamaica, and Suriname.

[15] However, Mexico, Ecuador, and Norway gain revenues from oil through excise and export taxes.

[16] A country is considered to be resource reliant when its fiscal reliance on natural resources is equal to or exceeds five percent.

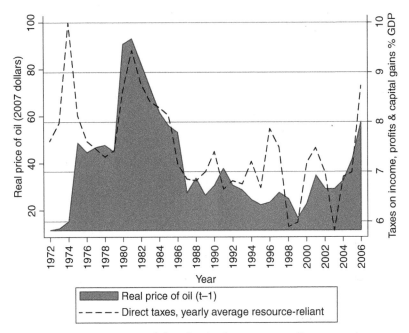

Figure 6.17 Direct taxes and the oil price for resource-reliant countries.

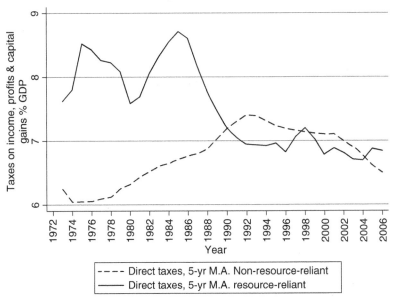

Figure 6.18 Direct taxes by resource reliance.

exhibited much higher levels of revenues from direct taxes. It graphs the five-year moving average of the (average) level of direct taxes between 1972 and 2006 by a country's resource-reliance status.

The pattern is interesting. Although the mid-1980s was marked by a precipitous decline in direct tax receipts in the resource-reliant countries, this contrasted with a steady ascent in this variable for non-resource-reliant countries. Yet, before this period, resource-reliant countries exhibited much higher levels of direct taxation. And the trend in direct taxes for the non-resource-reliant countries began to reverse its upward course in about 1992. Therefore, both groups approached parity during the 1990s and early 2000s. Moreover, during the mid-2000s, their trajectories began to diverge: the level of direct taxes for the resource-reliant countries surpassed the level for countries not reliant on resources again in 2004.

What is the reason for the apparent parity between resource-reliant countries and those not reliant on resources in the yield from direct taxation? Part of the explanation may lie with the fact that while several resource producers with high levels of direct taxation are included in the resource-reliant average, a plethora of resource-poor countries with low levels of direct taxation are included in the non-resource-reliant average. Therefore, while countries that are rich in oil and minerals quite often tax these natural resources directly, by deploying taxes on income, capital, and property, the average non-resource-reliant country does not overly rely on direct taxation to finance its expenditures.

Moreover, any noise produced by using indirect taxes to measure state capacity should be negligible. While this measurement strategy forces us to also lose information on revenues extracted from the profits and dividends earned by firms operating *outside of the resource sector*, there are only a few resource-reliant countries with relatively high levels of direct taxation on sources other than natural resources. These include Norway, the Netherlands, Malaysia, and Chile.[17] Resource-reliant countries' revenues from direct taxes are usually in line with the world average.[18]

---

[17] The average direct taxation percent GDP between 1972 and 2006 for these countries is, respectively, 16.11, 12.19, 8.77, and 4.34.

[18] Resource-reliant countries that are closer to the average include Algeria, Angola, Azerbaijan, Bolivia, Botswana, Cameroon, Gabon, Guinea, Guinea-Bissau,

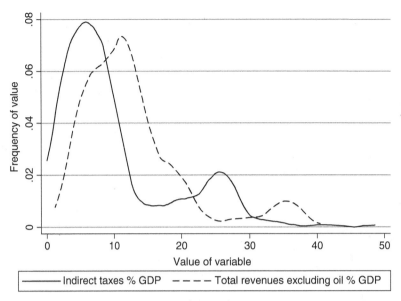

Figure 6.19 Comparing measures of non-oil revenues.

Some simple exercises can help us assess the validity of this proxy. These are centered on comparing it to the measure of non-hydrocarbon government revenues for thirteen major oil producers I alluded to above; in the case of Algeria, Bahrain, Ecuador, Gabon, Indonesia, Iran, Kuwait, Mexico, Nigeria, Norway, Oman, Venezuela, and Trinidad and Tobago I was able to separately identify each stream of hydrocarbon revenue. For each of these countries, I then subtracted the sum of these revenues from total government revenues, yielding a measure of non-oil revenues.[19] For the sample in which there is identical observation for each variable (n = 356), while the mean value for *Indirect Taxation* percent GDP is 10.03, it is 12.7 (% GDP) for *Total Revenues Excluding Oil*; and while the standard deviation for the former is 8.6, for the latter it is 7.9. As a final comparison, Figure 6.19 graphs kernel density plots for each variable;

Jamaica, Mauritania, Mexico, Mongolia, Namibia, Niger, Nigeria, Oman, Papua New Guinea, Peru, Russia, Tunisia, Vietnam, and Yemen.

[19] *Inter alia*, these revenues include taxes on the corporate profits of hydrocarbon firms, taxes on oil exports, excise taxes on oil production, dividends distributed to the treasury by state-run oil companies, and oil and gas royalties. See Haber and Menaldo (2011a) for the sources.

while Total Revenues Excluding Oil is shifted to the right, as expected, they have almost identical distributions.

Regime type

Following the rest of the literature on the political economy of natural resources that evaluates the effect of oil on democracy, I measure *Regime Type* as the Combined Polity 2 Score (Polity). This is an index of the competitiveness of political participation, the openness and competitiveness of executive recruitment, and the constraints on the chief executive (Marshall and Jaggers 2008). It is originally scaled from –10 (most autocratic) to 10 (most demo-cratic), with politically unstable years interpolated. For ease of inter-pretation, I normalize this index to run from 0 to 100. The results that follow are also robust to using Freedom House's Democracy Index and to measuring regime type as a binary variable, following Przeworski, et al. (2000) and coded by Cheibub, Gandhi, and Vreeland (2010).

Property rights, institutional quality, and credible commitments

I measure property rights security, institutional quality, the govern-ment's credible commitment to capitalist institutions, and thus the potential for state capacity, in several ways. Each of these measures captures different dimensions of the nexus between institutional qual-ity, the government's credible commitment to the rule of law, the will-ingness of private actors to make investments, and the state's ability to tax the population. The latter is possible because the former reduces fiscal transaction costs. The first variable is veto points. The second is Contract Intensive Money. The third is the value of public bonds out-standing. The fourth is stock market capitalization. The fifth is the share of GDP that is composed of investment.

Following North and Weingast (1989), Tsebelis (1995), and Henisz (2000), I measure institutional quality as the number of veto points. The logic of using this measure is that if a greater number of veto points have a say over public policy, incumbents will be rendered more accountable; their hands will be tied and their discretion limited. By the same token, veto points can also make incumbents less responsive to special interest groups bent on capturing policy to advance their narrow interests (Keefer and Stasavage 2003). Veto points may include competing branches of government with their own preferences and agendas that check and balance each other (formal institutional veto points), or partisan actors with competing preferences (political veto points). I measure *Veto Points* as the Political Constraint Index III from Henisz (2010), which subsumes both types of veto players.

I also measure property rights security and institutional quality as *Contract Intensive Money* (the CIM ratio) (see Clague et al. 1996, 1999). The CIM ratio is a metric of property rights in so far as it captures citizens' decisions regarding the form in which they choose to hold their financial assets. When there is institutional stability in banks and when the government protects property rights and enforces contracts, citizens should be more confident that banks or the government will not confiscate their deposits. As Clague et al. (1996, p. 254) aver, "[t]hose forms of money, such as currency, that rely least on the fulfillment of contractual obligations by others will be preferred when property and contractual rights are insecure, whereas other forms of money are more advantageous for most purposes in environments with secure contract-enforcement and property rights." The logic is that if the public can rely on institutional stability and third parties to enforce contracts, they will have greater confidence that banks or the government will not confiscate their deposits or investments. CIM, as in Ahlquist and Prakash (2008), is measured as $(M2-M1)/M2$, where $M2$ is "money and quasimoney," and $M1$ is money outside the banking system. The data are from the World Bank Development Indicators (WBDI).

Public Bond Capitalization, the total public domestic debt securities issued by the government (% GDP), also captures whether the government credibly commits to property rights and enforces contracts in an impartial manner. When the government is expected to pay back its loans because it can credibly commit to private debt holders' rights, it should face lower interest rates. In turn, this should incentivize the government to borrow more and spur a larger and more liquid market for public debt. This variable is from Beck, Demirgüç-Kunt, and Levine (2010).

I measure two other outcomes associated with secure property rights, the rule of law, and the government's credible commitment to a market economy, as follows. The size of the stock market is operationalized as *Stock Market Capitalization*: the value of listed shares (% GDP). A larger and more liquid stock market bespeaks that investors expect the government to respect their rights, enforce contracts, and enact prudential regulation, such as proscriptions against insider trading. This variable is from Beck, Demirgüç-Kunt, and Levine (2010). Similarly, *Investment Share of Real GDP*, from Heston, Summers, and Aten (2009), captures the cumulative value of the investments made by all economic actors throughout the economy.

Independent variables

My main measure of oil is *Fuel Income Per Capita*. It is composed of both countries' real oil income and real natural gas income (in thousands), expressed in 2007 dollars, and divided by the population. I took the natural log of this composite measure after adding 0.001 to address zero values. These data are from Haber and Menaldo (2011a).

The descriptive patterns recounted in Chapter 5 can help put this variable in perspective. An ever larger portion of the globe became populated with oil producers between the nineteenth century, when oil was first produced in Romania, North America, and several European countries, and the late 2000s. Therefore, the distinct trend in the data is one in which developing countries increasingly joined the family of established oil and gas producers from the developed world.

Addressing the endogeneity of oil flows

Treating Fuel Income Per Capita as a randomly assigned variable is problematic. The ultimate level of oil income that is produced is endogenous to countries' political and economic institutions. The latter determines the exploration of oil, as well as its discovery, production, and exports. As argued in the previous chapter, oil dependence often reflects insecure property rights and weak state capacity (see also Brunnschweiler and Bulte 2008, 2009; Dunning 2010; Luong and Weinthal 2010; Haber and Menaldo 2011a). On the one hand, poor governments with weak state capacity are often able to generate oil income to raise public revenues and produce foreign exchange in short order, even if their countries do not possess huge oil stocks. On the other hand, many rich governments with strong state capacity exhibit trivial amounts of yearly oil income, even if large oil stocks exist underground.[20] Moreover, this problem is not mitigated when the numerator is oil production instead of exports and the denominator is population (see Haber and Menaldo 2011a).

To avoid generating biased estimates of the effect of oil income that may be engendered by omitted variables or reverse causation, I take a multipronged approach. First, the regressions that follow control for country fixed effects, year fixed effects, country-specific time trends, and several time-varying covariates that are possibly correlated with oil and gas rents. These techniques allow me to expunge multiple sources of both time-invariant and time-varying omitted variables from the panel regressions. They do so by exploiting the within-country variation in both oil and the outcomes of interest.

I also take other, more muscular, steps to address causality. To help isolate the exogenous variation in oil, I hold constant the level of exploratory effort across most of the regressions estimated and reported below. I also estimate a series of Two Stage Least Squares Instrumental variables (2SLS IV) regressions where Fuel Income Per Capita is instrumented with variables designed to capture its exogenous variation. Finally, I conduct a series of statistical tests associated with these 2SLS IV models (Sargan-Hansen tests of the over-identifying restrictions) that fail to reject the hypothesis that the instruments are valid; in other words, I confirm that the exclusion restriction is satisfied – at least in a statistical sense.

While I take the opportunity here to explain how I operationalize oil exploration effort, as well as two instrumental variables that represent the exogenous variation in oil, further below I identify a series of control variables besides oil exploration effort. I also discuss the specifics of the econometric techniques employed to isolate the exogenous variation in Fuel Income Per Capita. Taken together, these steps should bolster our confidence that the results obtained in this chapter move us closer to identifying the causal effect of oil on taxation, democracy, and

---

[20] Indeed, consider that the United States, Canada, Australia, and Great Britain, which are among the world's major resource producers, are below the 5 percent threshold that divides resource-reliant and non-resource-reliant countries, while Belarus, Tajikistan, and Morocco, countries that produce trivial quantities of oil, gas, and minerals, are above the threshold.

a host of other outcomes related to institutional quality and the potential for state capacity.

Measuring oil effort

As a first step in an attempt to isolate oil income's exogenous variation, I control for *Oil Exploration* in the majority of the regressions that follow below. This is measured as the number of wildcat wells drilled (in hundreds). As explained in Chapter 5, this is a good proxy for exploration efforts. Wildcat wells are drilled *outside of known oilfields*, and are therefore located *outside of the vicinity of known oil reserves*. In other words, a wildcat well is drilled to find out if there is oil in the first place, even if seismic tests and other plausibility probes have already been conducted. Once this variable is controlled for, we can assume that the effect of income from oil and gas is largely associated with the share of oil and gas plays that lie in the most geologically obvious and accessible basins, and therefore required the least intensive exploratory efforts to unearth.

Instrumental variables

Controlling for exploratory effort is necessary but not sufficient for isolating the exogenous share of oil wealth. In the IV 2SLS regressions depicted in Table 6.2, I also instrument a country's Fuel Income with two different variables. The first is the quantity of proven reserves associated only with a country's giant oil fields. The second is the proven petroleum reserves possessed by its neighbors. This strategy follows the way in which I identified the exogenous component of a country's oil discoveries in the previous chapter.

First, a primer on proven oil reserves is in order. These are quantities of crude petroleum that can be expected, with reasonable certainty, to be recoverable from identified reservoirs at a commercially viable scale. That means that the oil reserves have already been drilled and vetted and are located in oil fields that are currently online or forthcoming. Increases in proven reserves can be the result of: new oil discoveries, the upgrading of facilities to permit a greater number of wells to be drilled, pressure depletion of extant reservoirs, and the installation of compressor modules that allow oil to be produced at lower reservoir pressures.

Geological Endowment is the cumulative total oil barrels (in billions) associated with giant oil fields from Tsui (2011). This is the most exogenous, time-varying measure of a country's underlying geological potential.[21] The reason is because happening upon these huge oil fields is much easier than discovering smaller fields, which requires considerable exploratory efforts. I take the natural log of this variable after adding .01 to address zero values. I hasten to emphasize that the results of the regressions are also robust to using the log of the running count of giant oil fields, as well as the log of cumulative total oil reserves, that is, giant well oil + regular well oil.

I also instrument Fuel Income with Neighbors' Oil Reserves, the total oil reserves possessed by a country's neighbors in the same geographic region, lagged by one period. To reduce skew, I log this variable after adding 0.01 to address zero values. This variable is from Haber and Menaldo (2011a). To appreciate the logic of using Neighbors' Oil Reserves as an instrument for oil income, consider Saudi Arabia. Like itself, Iraq and Kuwait, its northern neighbors, have sizable oil reserves, as does southwest Iran. Each of these countries' hydrocarbon endowments are a product of the areal extent of the Arabian plate's northeast (NE) margin shelf. This 2,000 km (width) X 3,000 km (length) region has experienced repeated and extensive source rock beds over geological time, bestowing it with superior carbonate and sandstone reservoirs in good juxtaposition, as well as superior regional seals and expansive anticlinal traps (see Beydoun 1998). In short, because they capture the underlying geology, the total oil reserves in Saudi Arabia's neighborhood constitute a surrogate measure of its own oil endowment.

Control variables

In the regression models in Table 6.2, where the dependent variable is non-oil taxation, I add several control variables whose omission may confound the statistical results. Several researchers have identified a positive association between Per Capita Income and the tax yield (see, e.g., Cheibub 1998). I therefore control for the log(*Per Capita Income*) in 2000 international dollars from Haber and Menaldo

---

[21] A giant oil field has at least 500 million barrels of oil that can ultimately be recovered; moreover, this measure does not depend on government self-reporting. Its correlation with the Ultimately Recoverable Reserves, from Tsui (2011), is 0.80.

Table 6.2 Panel regressions on the determinants of non-resource taxes
Autocorrelation and heteroskedasticity consistent standard errors in brackets

	1	2	3	4	5	6a	6b
Estimation strategy	OLS	OLS	OLS	OLS	OLS	IV 2SLS	IV 2SLS
Dependent variable	Non-resource taxes	Non-resource taxes	Non-resource taxes	Non-resource taxes	Non-resource taxes	P.C. Fuel Income	Non-resource taxes
log(Per capita fuel income)	-0.027*** [0.05]	0.174* [0.103]	0.382* [0.192]	0.663** [0.273]	0.292** [0.119]		3.501** [1.764]
Oil exploration			-0.0211*** [.006]	-0.029*** [.009]		0 [0.003]	-0.053*** [0.016]
log(Per capita income)					-1.386 [0.860]	1.245*** [0.211]	-7.335** [3.267]
Inflation					-0.022** [0.01]	-0.002 [0.003]	-1.340* [0.790]
Civil War					-0.738* [.185]	0.077 [0.055]	-0.079*** [0.026]
Old age ratio					0.241** [0.103]	0.181*** [0.048]	-0.474 [0.399]
Geological endowment						0.188*** [0.066]	
Neighbors' oil reserves						-0.068* [0.04]	

	(1)	(2)	(3)	(4)	(5)	(6)	(7)
Country fixed effects	NO	YES	YES	YES	YES	YES	YES
Year fixed effects	NO	NO	NO	YES	YES	YES	YES
Country-specific time trends	NO	NO	NO	YES	YES	YES	YES
Observations	3,372	3,372	1,307	1,307	2,576	1,015	1,015
Number of countries	148	148	51	51	121	47	47

* significant at 10%; ** significant at 5%; *** significant at 1%

Constant estimated across models but not reported; country fixed effects expunged the within transformation; year intercepts estimated but not reported; country-specific trends estimated but not reported. Driscoll-Kraay Standard Errors estimated with Newey West adjustments reflecting Arellano Bond tests of serial correlation.

a = First-stage regression

b = Second-stage regression

(2011a). The inflation tax is an alternative source of revenues availed by weak states to finance government deficits and might serve as a substitute for non-oil taxation. Moreover, as demonstrated in Chapter 5, weak states may be more likely to search for and extract oil. I therefore also control for *Inflation*. To maximize coverage, I use a proxy for inflation, Central Bank Assets percent GDP, from Beck, Demirgüç-Kunt, and Ross Levine (2010). To address the possibility that oil may drive civil conflict and civil conflict may affect the tax yield, I also control for *Civil War*. This variable is from Haber and Menaldo (2011a). Finally, I also control for the *Old Age Ratio*, from the WBDI, which is the percent of the population above sixty-five years of age. While countries with high levels of oil income, such as the Persian Gulf States, may attract young, migrant laborers to work in both the hydrocarbon industry and outside of it, driving this ratio down, such a demographic distribution may separately militate against taxation, since the demand for inter-generational transfers will be reduced. All of these variables are lagged by one time period.

In the Table 6.2 regressions, I also experimented with controlling for other covariates, but I do not report the results of these regressions, or discuss them, because the main findings were never affected; and these variables were never statistically significant at conventional levels. For example, some argue that ongoing inter-state rivalries and international wars may induce a state to invest in fiscal capacity and increase taxes to finance defense expenditures and war participation (Besley and Persson 2009). I therefore estimated several regressions that also included a running count of militarized interstate disputes, as well as different measures of cumulative war participation using data from the Correlates of War Project.

In the regression models in Table 6.3, where the dependent variable is, Regime Type, Veto Points, Contract-Intensive Money, Public Bond Capitalization, Stock Market Capitalization, or Investment Share of Real GDP, I introduce the control variables used in Haber and Menaldo (2011a). These are log(Per Capita Income), Civil War, and the percentage of democracies in a country's geographic-cultural region. The latter operationalizes regional democratic trends following Gleditsch and Ward (2006). The results are also robust to experimenting with other control variables that are typical in the literature on regime type and political liberalization.

Econometric models and results

My econometric strategy proceeds from the simplest to the most complex model. As a first step, I evaluate the relationship between oil and non-oil taxation measured as Indirect Taxation percent GDP by estimating a pooled regression model that exploits the data's cross-sectional and time-series variation. In this regression, however, we cannot assume that Fuel Income is exogenous. This purely correlational analysis serves as a baseline and is reported in Table 6.2, Column 1. This is followed by a series of panel fixed effects (FE) models reported in the remainder of Table 6.2. All of the regressions reported across Table 6.2 are estimated via Ordinary Least Squares (OLS) with Driscoll-Kraay standard errors, a technique that addresses heteroskedasticity, serially correlated errors, and spatial correlation.[22]

The panel FE regressions are followed by a series of Instrumental Variables Two-Stage Least Squares (IV 2SLS) regressions where Fuel Income Per Capita is instrumented with a country's geological endowments and neighbors' oil reserves. In these models, besides looking at the effect of oil on non-oil taxation, I also evaluate the effect of oil on Regime Type, Veto Points, Contract Intensive Money, Public Bond Capitalization, Stock Market Capitalization, and the Investment Share of Real GDP. These are reported in Table 6.2.

Column 1 reports the regression results obtained after estimating the baseline model that pools all of the observations – in other words, it excludes the country fixed effects, year fixed effects, country-specific time trends, and control variables. If the rentier-effect hypothesis is correct, then the coefficient should be negative: an increase in fuel income should displace non-oil taxation. As would be expected by that hypothesis, the coefficient on Fuel Income is indeed negative (although it is not statistically significant at conventional levels).

However, correlation does not equal causation. Because this is a naïve estimation strategy that does not address omitted variable bias or reverse causation, we should remain circumspect. As I have argued repeatedly in this book, treating Fuel Income as an exogenous, randomly assigned variable is unwise; especially because, as demonstrated in Chapter 5, weak state capacity might jointly determine both high levels of oil rents and low levels of non-oil taxation. In the remainder of

[22] This called on making a Newey West adjustment to the error term, the lag length of which was determined by an Arellano Bond test of serial correlation.

Table 6.2 and in Table 6.3, therefore, I estimate a series of regressions that relax this assumption. The results of these experiments reject the rentier-effect mechanism, in particular, and several of the predictions put forth by the resource curse theory, in general. Instead, I uncover evidence that strongly points to a blessing.

The FE (OLS) model that represents the unrestricted estimation in Table 6.2, Column 5, is:

$$y_{it} = \alpha_i + \lambda_t + \beta X_{it-1} + (\phi \times \alpha_i)\xi + u_{it} \tag{1}$$

in which y_{it} is the estimated value of the outcome variable of interest for country i in year t; α_i addresses time-invariant country fixed effects and λ_t addresses country-invariant year fixed effects, both potentially correlated with X, a vector of k explanatory variables lagged by one year in most cases; β are estimated parameters; ξ are estimates of country-specific time trends produced by the interaction between ϕ, a linear time trend, and α_i; and u_{it} is an error term.

In keeping with the simplest to most complex strategy, Column 2 of Table 6.2 reports a simpler version of the regression represented by equation (1), where I only control for country fixed effects. The sign on Fuel Income flips: it is now positive. It is also statistically significant at the 0.09 level. Specifically, a one-percentage point increase in Fuel Income actually leads to a 0.17 percentage point increase in non-oil tax revenues. Needless to say, this contradicts the resource curse's rentier-effect mechanism.

The rest of Table 6.2 reports several additional steps, within the OLS framework, that address endogeneity. In Column 3, I add Oil Exploration to help isolate the exogenous variation in Fuel Income. The coefficient on Fuel Income remains positive, increases in magnitude, and is now statistically significant at the 95 percent level. Oil exploration is negative and largely statistically significant. From our perspective, this is expected, since, as argued in Chapter 5, weak states are more likely to launch oil exploration efforts to generate public revenues and foreign exchange. In Column 4, I add both year fixed effects and country-specific time trends. The statistical and substantive effect of Fuel Income, which remains positive, again improves (p-value = 0.02).

Column 5 is a further robustness check. While I remove Oil Exploration, I add the time-varying control variables outlined above: Per Capita Income, Inflation, Civil War, and the Old Age Ratio. I do this to ensure that the results in Columns 3 and 4 are not being driven by the fact that Oil Exploration is only available for sixty-two major oil producers, reducing the number of observations by more than half. Moreover, as explained above, these control variables proxy for several possible reasons why a country would ratchet up its exploration, production, export, and taxation of oil, therefore compensating for the omission of Oil Exploration. The results are largely the same, which gives me confidence that controlling for Oil Exploration is not biasing the results in Columns 3 and 4 by dint of the reduced data coverage.

Isolating the exogenous portion of oil stocks

The results reported so far make clear that there is no evidence for the rentier effect after controlling for some popular explanations for non-resource taxation. Could it be the case, however, that the results reported above are biased by other time-varying, unobserved variables? Or could they be distorted by reverse causation?

   To address this possibility, I isolate the exogenous source of variation in oil stocks by estimating a series of Generalized Method of Moments (GMM) two-stage instrumental variables (IV) regressions. To help ensure that the exclusion is satisfied, I take three steps. First, I continue to include country fixed effects, year fixed effects, and country-specific time trends.[23] Second, I include the battery of control variables outlined above: Oil Exploration, Per Capita Income, Inflation, Civil War, and the Old Age Ratio. Third, I over-identify the first-stage equation by including two instruments. This allows me to estimate a test of the over-identifying restrictions: the hypothesis that the two instruments are correlated with non-oil revenues only indirectly, via their effect on fuel income. In other words, this is a test of whether fuel income is orthogonal to the error term in the second-stage equation.

   A GMM-IV approach calls for running two separate regression equations. The first-stage model estimates the determinants of Fuel Income Per Capita and includes the two instruments outlined above, Geological Endowment and Neighbors' Oil Reserves. The second-stage model estimates the determinants of non-resource direct taxation, as in

---

[23] To address heteroskedasticity and AR1 correlation, I use an Eicker-Huber-White robust covariance estimator and adjust the standard errors through the Newey-West technique.

the regressions reported so far in Table 6.2. The most important independent variable in these second-stage models is the predicted level of Fuel Income calculated from the first-stage models.

Table 6.2 Column 6a reports the coefficients calculated from the first-stage regression, where Fuel Income is the dependent variable. A 1 percent increase in a country's oil from giant fields possessed by a country's neighbors leads to a 0.19 percent increase in a country's fuel income. This result is highly statistically significant ($p < 0.01$). Surprisingly, an increase in the reserves possessed by neighbors is negatively associated with a country's fuel income ($p = 0.09$); upon further investigation, however, this is a product of the fact that the other control variables are included in the first-stage equation. If these are removed, the sign flips: as expected, neighbors' endowments are positively correlated with a country's own fuel income. A Hansen J test of the over-identifying restrictions fails to reject the hypothesis that the instrumental variables are exogenous (p-value = 0.79).

Column 6b reports the coefficients calculated from the second-stage regression, where non-oil taxation is the dependent variable. Consistent with the results obtained so far, this coefficient is positive and statistically significant. A 1 percent increase in Fuel Income maps onto an increase in taxes on non-oil sources of revenue of 3.5 percentage points (p-value = 0.05). This again ratifies the idea that, rather than oil displacing non-oil revenues, oil increases regular tax revenues. And it does so after addressing the potential for endogeneity bias in a very exacting manner. In short, there is no rentier-effect mechanism.

The effect of oil on the other dependent variables

Does income from oil and gas negatively affect a country's regime type, institutional quality, the government's commitment to market institutions, and the size and sophistication of the market itself? To find out, I now move to estimating the effect of oil on the Polity Score, Veto Points, Contract Intensive Money, Public Bond Capitalization, Stock Market Capitalization, and the Investment Share of Real GDP. As argued above, this allows us to investigate other empirical implications associated with the resource curse theory. To capture the exogenous variation in fuel income, I continue to avail the GMM-IV approach, and instrument it with a country's geological endowment and its neighbors' oil reserves. To follow the conventions in the literature, I introduce the control variables used in Haber and Menaldo (2011a). These are log(Per Capita Income), Civil War, and the percentage of democracies in a country's geographic-cultural region, to capture regional democratic trends. I also continue to control for oil exploration efforts.

The dependent variables in the second-stage regressions are as follows. The first is the Polity Score. The second is Veto Points. The third is Contract Intensive Money. The fourth is Public Bond Capitalization. The fifth is Stock Market Capitalization. The sixth is the Investment Share of Real GDP.

Table 6.3 Column 1a reports the coefficients calculated from a first-stage regression where Fuel Income is the dependent variable. A 1 percent increase in a country's oil from giant fields leads to a 0.14 percent increase in a country's fuel income. This result is highly statistically significant ($p < 0.001$). And now, unlike in Column 6a, as expected, an increase in the reserves possessed by a country's neighbors is positively associated with its fuel income ($p < 0.001$). As explained above, this is because several of the control variables employed previously have been omitted from the equation. The F-statistic of the excluded instruments is 29.63 (p-value < 0.001), well above the threshold separating weak from strong instruments.[24] And a Hansen J test of the over-identifying restrictions again fails to reject the hypothesis that the instrumental variables are exogenous (p-value $= 0.15$).

Table 6.3 Column 1b reports the coefficients calculated from the second-stage regression, where the polity score is the dependent variable. In contradiction to the resource curse, the effect of oil and gas is positive and statistically significant. A 1 percent increase in Fuel Income maps onto an increase in the democracy score of 9 points (p-value is <0.01). It is also instructive that the coefficient on oil exploration is negative and highly statistically significant. In so far as this variable captures state capacity, this result is expected. As argued in Chapter 5, countries with weak state capacity are more likely to launch exploratory efforts. It is therefore not too surprising that, once we address the potential endogeneity of oil, both by controlling for exploration and isolating the exogenous variation in oil income, there is a resource blessing.

---

[24] Staiger and Stock (1997) argue that first-stage F-tests should be greater than 10.

Table 6.3 *Instrumental variables two state least squares regressions*
Autocorrelation and heteroskedasticity consistent standard errors in brackets

Dependent Variable	1a P.C. Fuel Income	1b Polity score	2b Polity score (after 1980)	3b Veto points	4b CIM ratio	5b Public bond Cap.	6b Stock market cap.	7b Investment share GDP
log(Per capita fuel income)		9.336***	31.91*	0.111***	6.646***	0.534**	1.008***	2.214**
		[3.083]	[16.99]	[0.0271]	[2.117]	[0.222]	[0.377]	[1.059]
Oil exploration	-0.002	-0.191***	-0.015	-0.001	0.194***	-0.007	-0.012	-0.095***
	[0.002]	[0.054]	[0.082]	[0.000]	[0.071]	[0.005]	[0.018]	[0.026]
log(Per capita income)	1.368***	-9.570**	-27.19*	-0.124***	-13.56***	-0.375***	-0.443	4.412***
	[0.165]	[4.643]	[16.16]	[0.0402]	[3.527]	[0.107]	[0.368]	[1.477]
Civil War	0.108*	-2.193	0.393	-0.0356**	-0.646	0.000175	-0.0952*	-1.043
	[0.057]	[2.554]	[3.201]	[0.0172]	[1.099]	[0.0251]	[0.0575]	[0.734]
Regional democratic diffusion	0.24	0.762***	0.60***	0.004***	-0.01	-0.001	0.006**	-0.015
	[0.197]	[0.063]	[0.173]	[0.049]	[0.044]	[0.001]	[0.003]	[0.020]
Geological endowment	0.142***							
	[0.021]							
Neighbors' oil reserves	0.149***							
	[0.041]							

Country fixed effects	YES	YES	YES	YES	YES	YES	YES	YES
Year fixed effects	YES	YES	YES	YES	YES	YES	YES	YES
Country-specific time trends	YES	YES	YES	YES	YES	YES	YES	YES
Observations	2,854	2,854	1,447	2,733	1,950	436	810	2,350

Constant estimated across models but not reported; country fixed effects estimated but not reported; year intercepts estimated but not reported; country-specific trends estimated but not reported. Instrumental Variables Two Stage Least Squares estimated via a Generalized Method of Moments approach; Newey West Standard Errors estimated with 1 lag length.

a = First-stage regression; these are estimated across all IV 2SLS models but only reported for Model 1 to conserve space. b = Second-stage regression.

It is helpful to put this effect in perspective. This is the magnitude of the increase in the Polity Score experienced by Mexico between 1999 and 2000. As outlined above, this change was brought about by the fact that Vicente Fox, the candidate from Partido Acción Nacional (PAN), the chief opposition party to the PRI, won a free and fair presidential election, thus ending seventy-one years of single party dictatorship.

However, might there be scope conditions under which the relationship between oil and democracy might be negative? Andersen and Ross (2014) aver that, since 1980, there has been a resource curse. They argue that oil wealth began to hinder democratic transitions only after the oil nationalizations of the 1970s, which allowed developing country governments to recruit oil rents to prevent political reforms. In Column 2 I test this hypothesis by truncating the dataset to post 1980 observations. To conserve space, I omit the results from the first-stage regression and limit discussion to the second-stage results. Contradicting Andersen and Ross, the sign on Fuel Income remains positive and is statistically significant at the .06 level. Moreover, the substantive effect of oil increases substantially, tripling in magnitude.

In the rest of Table 6.3, I report the results for second-stage regressions in which, respectively, the dependent variables are Veto Points, the CIM ratio, Public Bond Capitalization, Stock Market Capitalization, and the Investment Share of Real GDP. The regressions are estimated on the full dataset (i.e., it is no longer truncated to post 1980 observations). I omit the first-stage regressions for reasons of space, but note that they are essentially the same as those reported in Column 1b. Across Columns 3 through 7, there is further evidence of a resource blessing. Fuel Income is positive and statistically and substantively significant in each of these models. Everything else held equal, increases in oil income make democracy, liberalism, and capitalism more likely. These findings complement the fact that oil does not displace non-oil sources of government revenues. In other words, there is compelling evidence for a resource blessing.

Conclusion

Is there a resource curse or a resource blessing? To find out, this chapter does two things.

First, I evaluate whether there is empirical support for the potential mechanisms linking natural resources to state capacity, democracy, and capitalism in Latin America. I identify the economic, fiscal, and political impacts made by the production and export of primary commodities – going back to these countries' independence. Sovereign Latin American nations are nearly two centuries old and exhibit considerable variation in the importance of their natural resource sectors. The same is true in regards to their tax systems, regime types, and development models. They therefore constitute an excellent laboratory to evaluate the relationship between natural resources and a country's politics and economics.

Second, I evaluate the relationship between fuel income and nonresource taxation, as well as between the former and regime type, the quality of a country's institutions, the government's commitment to honoring its promises, and the size and sophistication of the market. I conduct a battery of statistical analyses on a panel dataset that controls for country fixed effects, year fixed effects, country-specific time trends, and a bevy of possible confounders – chief of which is the exploratory efforts dedicated to discovering oil. I also employ instrumental variables to isolate the exogenous variation in fuel income. Across these models, I find strong evidence for a resource blessing.

Chapter 7 continues in this vein. Motivated by the puzzle of wide variation in political instability across the Middle East and North Africa (MENA) during the Arab Spring, I try to make sense of the fact that the region's monarchies largely elided turmoil and violence. The "republics" did not. I show that this has also been the case historically. Most importantly, the association between political stability and monarchy is not driven by oil wealth; nor does oil explain why monarchies have higher quality institutions, provide more public goods, and have higher levels of educational attainment and faster economic growth. I illustrate the evolution of monarchic political cultures over the history of the MENA, where I document the geographic and biogeographic underpinnings of monarchy, arguing that extreme aridity and pastoral nomadism centered on camel herding sustained a tribal social structure.

The chief policy implication suggested by the findings in this chapter and Chapter 7 is that we should not be too quick to dismiss the development potential represented by hydrocarbons and mining. While it is imperative to continue to engage in the critical debate about the negative spillovers associated with these activities, including environmental damage and greenhouse gas emissions, the tenor of the debate should change. We should focus our attention on helping to further improve political and legal institutions in the developing world, beyond the beneficial effect already engendered by natural resource sectors. And also: we should devise a way to force energy consumers in the developed world to internalize the costs of these spillovers. This can perhaps be accomplished by promoting the adoption of Pigovian taxes, the creation of markets that cap and trade carbon emissions, or command control regulation that limits the actual market supply. Each of these approaches entails tradeoffs and represents different winners and losers.

This book has so far demonstrated, however, that there may be a sharp tradeoff between a reduction in our use of fossil fuels in the developed world and political and economic development in the Global South. I hope that readers will acknowledge this tradeoff, even if the moral, political, and economic benefits of drastically reducing carbon emissions outweigh the costs. It should no longer be said that one of the incidental benefits of reducing our consumption of oil and coal is to mitigate or obviate the resource curse. And if a carbon free economy were to come to pass, we should find ways to compensate developing countries for eschewing a powerful route to political and economic development – one that many developed countries traversed. In light of the evidence, it is the right thing to do.

7 | Oil curse or monarchical exceptionalism?

Beginning in December of 2010, a wave of protests rippled across the Middle East.[1] What at first seemed like minor disturbances soon snowballed into dramatic political changes. Some long-lived rulers, including Zine El Abidine Ben Ali of Tunisia and Hosni Mubarak of Egypt, were swiftly forced from power. Others, such as Mohammed VI of Morocco, introduced major reforms. Still others were recalcitrant. Despite Western airstrikes and repeated pleas that he step down, Libya's Muammar Gaddafi was brutally murdered by rebels in the streets of his hometown, Sirte. In Syria, Bashar al-Assad viciously cracked down against protestors, unleashing a civil war that still rages on. It has claimed over 250,000 lives.

The Arab Spring has raised a lot of important questions. Why did Tunisia and Egypt erupt into popular revolutions that toppled long-lived dictators, only to see political instability unleashed in the first case and dictatorship return in the second case? Why did Yemen's largest opposition bloc join tribal groups and protestors to bring down the Saleh regime, rather than accept concessions – instigating a civil war fought along sectarian lines that has become a proxy fight between Iran and Saudi Arabia? Why did gruesome violence convulse Libya and Syria – leading to anarchy in the first case and the takeover of 50 percent of the territory by the so-called Islamic State in the second case? Why did Jordan, Kuwait, Morocco, Qatar, Saudi Arabia, Oman, and the U.A.E. manage to avoid serious unrest, if not grow stronger?

The MENA's recent history affords us the opportunity to interrogate the stories we tell about modernization, development, and democracy. It also calls into question how we view what is often considered in the

---

[1] The countries included in the MENA are Morocco, Libya, Algeria, Tunisia, Egypt, Sudan, Turkey, Lebanon, Iran, Iraq, Jordan, Saudi Arabia, Yemen, Kuwait, Bahrain, Qatar, the U.A.E., and Oman. Later, for purposes of conducting empirical tests of some of the claims introduced further below on a dataset of ethnic groups, I broaden the definition to include the Sahel.

West as one of the world's most exotic regions. A gaggle of theories have been put forth to make sense of the Arab Spring and situate it historically (see, especially, Goldstone 2011). While some researchers have advanced novel ideas that privilege the role of Islam or the pitfalls of incomplete colonialism, others have settled on a familiar trope. It is oil that explains many of the setbacks and disappointments that have afflicted the MENA since 2011, if not why these countries missed out on previous waves of political liberalization, thus making the Arab Spring possible in the first place (see, for example, Ross 2012; and Robinson 2012).

To support these claims, advocates of the resource curse point to the policies observed in the Persian Gulf states since 2010. Kuwait's sheikh, Jaber al-Sabah, dispensed cash gifts to every citizen, as well as food vouchers. In Oman, spending on welfare, social insurance, and public jobs was revved up. Abu Dhabi's crown prince, Sheikh Muhammad bin Zayedi, ordered that unemployed Emiratis be given government jobs and political activists be arrested. In Bahrain, King Hamad bin Isa al-Khalifa cracked down against thousands of protestors occupying Manama's iconic Pearl Roundabout, and then demolished it.

Yet, as this book has argued, there are theoretical and empirical reasons to be skeptical of the resource curse. When it comes to the MENA, many of these reasons are often hiding in plain sight. For example, well before anybody had ever heard of "the Arab Spring," large public investments financed by oil rents were commonplace across the Gulf. Contrary to popular belief, the billions of dollars pledged by King Abdullah to social spending in the spring of 2011 was not blood money aimed at quelling unrest. Rather, it was an installment in a larger spending package that reflected high oil prices and a budget surplus. In the Qatari case, the government reinvested 50 percent of government revenues in various projects, including off-shore natural gas production and the *Al Jazeera* television network. It only did so, however, because this is the way that public spending has always taken place there since independence.

Also contradicting the resource curse is the fact that, rather than turn to repression, many oil-rich monarchies embraced constitutionalism after 2011. In the U.A.E., isolated and small protests led to free elections for the Federal National Council and ushered in several reforms. In Kuwait, there were some peaceful protests and the boycott of elections. Shaikh Sabah al-Ahmad al-Sabah responded by reshuffling his cabinet and holding elections for parliament. In Qatar, legislative elections were held in 2011, and women were granted the franchise for municipal elections. In Oman, after protestors took to the street, Sultan Qaboos bin Said al-Said reshuffled his cabinet and created a consumer protection bureau. In Saudi Arabia, there were protests by *Shi'ites* in the Eastern, oil-producing provinces. The Abdullah regime responded by making a commitment to hold municipal elections.

Even in the case of Bahrain's infamous crackdown, the facts on the ground belie an explanation centered on Saudi oil money or the preeminence of petro politics. Al-Khalifa only attempted to restore order after protestors, having been allowed to demonstrate peacefully for over a month, illegally blocked off Manama's financial district and paralyzed the city. This was deemed a security threat by the government, triggering emergency rule and, in accordance with the Peninsular Shield Defense Treaty, the invitation of troops from Qatar, Saudi Arabia, and the U.A.E. Ultimately, although over 1,000 protestors were imprisoned, foreign troops were not involved in suffocating the protests. Instead, 5,000 foreign troops were deployed to defend key public installations, including oil refineries and ministries.

But if not oil then what is the key to understanding the Arab Spring? Ocular regression suggests a possible answer. A quick glance at the MENA map reveals that the monarchies largely avoided the turmoil. These regimes include oil-poor Morocco and Jordan, as well as oil-rich Saudi Arabia, Kuwait, Bahrain, Qatar, the U.A.E., and Oman. Meanwhile, the republics, including Tunisia, Libya, Egypt, Syria, and Yemen, have been bedeviled by the most serious unrest and violence.

Drawing on these patterns, and in keeping with the larger themes pursued in this book, this chapter challenges the idea that the MENA has been beset by a resource curse, both during the Arab Spring and before it.[2] Instead, to make sense of the region's historical development, as well as recent events, I focus on institutional legacies. I argue that, over several centuries, MENA monarchs have carefully cultivated political cultures conducive to stability and good governance. Bootstrapped norms and practices have mixed ancient traditions with modern institutions to help kings and royal families brook challenges

---

[2] Waldner (2012) also gainsays the claim that oil has made a big difference during the Arab Spring. For skeptical views that doubt the historical importance of oil *vis-à-vis* the region's politics, see Haber and Menaldo (2011b); Herb (1999); Menaldo (2012); and Okruhlik (1999).

to their rule. One of the cornerstones of monarchical rule in the region is tribalism. Kings have manipulated tribal social structures and reinforced them to legitimize rent-sharing arrangements and orchestrate succession plans.[3]

This chapter adduces abundant evidence to support monarchical exceptionalism. While places that became and remained monarchies have largely elided political instability throughout their history and promoted economic and social development, unrest has been quite common in places that eventually became "republics." So has underdevelopment.

Drawing on the factor endowment framework explicated in Chapter 4, this chapter also documents the origins of the region's monarchical exceptionalism. It does so by employing novel datasets observed at both the country and ethnic group level. I demonstrate that in the MENA there is a systematic relationship between geography, economic structure, social structure, and regime type. This allows me to document where tribalism emerged from in the first place, as well as why it has been compatible with a monarchical form of rule. By harnessing a history of nomadic pastoralism, MENA monarchs were able to co-opt entrenched tribal social structures and identities. Conversely, due to a legacy of feudalistic agriculture and stronger, more centralized, states, non-monarchs invested in nationalism and socialism.

This chapter continues as follows. First, I justify why the MENA represents a good laboratory for evaluating both the resource curse and monarchical exceptionalism. I then assess the relationship between oil and political stability in the MENA and argue that there are grounds to be skeptical of the resource curse. This is followed by an elucidation of how monarchical political cultures arise and are sustained. Next, to corroborate monarchical exceptionalism, I report and discuss the statistical relationship between monarchy and several outcomes in the MENA: political stability, institutional quality, educational attainment, and economic development. In that section, I also rule out the resource curse. Finally, following the factor endowment centered theory of political and economic development explored in Chapter 4, I empirically evaluate where and why monarchical rule emerged and survived in some places within the MENA and not others. I demonstrate that differences in geography conduced to differences in regime

---

[3] Menaldo (2012) and Woods (2012) advance similar views about monarchical norms.

types over the *longue durée*. Specifically, economic and social structures that favored nomadism, tribalism, and political decentralization eventually culminated in monarchy.

The MENA as a laboratory

The Arab Spring illustrated that the MENA is an excellent laboratory for testing theories about development. It is a region with a deep and rich history and is home to countries that exhibit vast variation on a host of political, economic, and social dimensions. The MENA is an especially good place to evaluate the resource curse and monarchical exceptionalism. On the one hand, the region is characterized by substantial variation in natural resource reliance and regime types: while some countries are monarchic, others are not. On the other hand, it also exhibits substantial variation in political stability, institutional quality, education, and growth.

Vast variation in hydrocarbons

The MENA is home to some of the countries with the greatest degree of oil wealth in the world. The Great Arid Belt of Afro-Eurasia, which stretches from North Africa (the Sahara) to Eastern Central Eurasia (the Gobi), contains the lion's share of the world's conventional hydrocarbons. There is also wide variation in oil wealth within the MENA. While Saudi Arabia possesses about one-fifth of the world's reserves and is the world's largest oil producer and exporter, Morocco, Jordan, Egypt, Lebanon, Turkey, and Syria are all net oil importers. This variation allows us to gain significant leverage on whether oil, rather than other salient factors, affects outcomes of interest in this region.

Figure 7.1 showcases both between- and within-regional variation in oil wealth. On the one hand, a series of bar plots showcase the mean level of oil wealth, as operationalized by the values of *Fuel Income Per Capita* (in 2007 dollars), by world region. On the other hand, another series of bar plots showcase this measure's standard deviation, also by region.[4]

---

[4] The data are, as in previous chapters, from Haber and Menaldo (2011a), and are graphed for 2006. The patterns are not sensitive to taking different cross-sectional slices over the 1970s, 1980s, 1990s, or 2000s; nor are they affected by calculating decade averages.

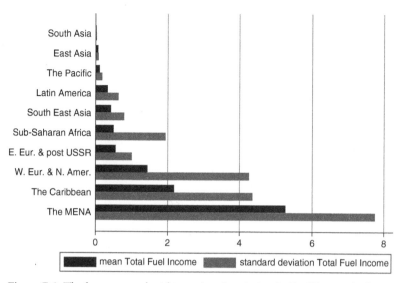

Figure 7.1 The between and within regional variation in Fuel Income in 2006.

Several patterns stand out. The MENA has both the highest mean and standard deviation of Fuel Income, clocking in, respectively, at US$5,268 and US$7,755. Indeed, the MENA dwarfs other regions on both dimensions; the region with the next highest average level of Fuel Income is the Caribbean, at US$2,181, and Western Europe and North America, at US$1,440 – a region of the world that has the second greatest degree of variance, with a standard deviation of US$4,280. Other regions rank as follows: the Eastern European and post-Soviet states and Central Asia (mean of US$553 and standard deviation of US$1,005); Sub-Saharan Africa (mean of US$489 and standard deviation of US$1,939); Southeast Asia (mean of US$421 and standard deviation of US$791); Latin America (mean of US$327 and standard deviation of US$629); the Pacific (mean of US$103 and standard deviation of US$179); East Asia (mean of US$59 and standard deviation of US$72); and South Asia (mean of US$17 and standard deviation of US$22).[5]

---

[5] These patterns are not an artifice of measuring oil wealth as Fuel Income Per Capita. If I instead perform this exercise using *Proven Oil Reserves*, from Haber and Menaldo (2011a), the MENA also exhibits the largest mean and standard deviation, and the remaining rank order is almost identical. In billions of barrels, the MENA's average level of proven reserves in 2006 is 3.05 and its standard deviation is 11.8.

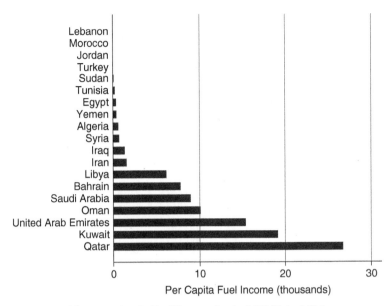

Figure 7.2 The variation in Fuel Income in the MENA in 2006.

Figure 7.2 exhibits the variation in Fuel Income among the MENA countries. It is a bar chart of oil wealth by country in 2006. Unsurprisingly, the Gulf States, with huge oil reserves and relatively small populations, have the highest amounts of Fuel Income Per Capita. Qatar leads the pack with US$26,772. Kuwait is next with US$19,159, followed by the United Arab Emirates with US$15,444. Other notable countries are Saudi Arabia, clocking in at US$8,963, Libya, with US$6,170, and Iran, with US$1,601. The relatively hydro-carbon poor MENA countries, those with Per Capita Fuel Income below $1,000, are Syria, Algeria, Yemen, Egypt, Tunisia, Sudan, Turkey, Jordan, Morocco, and Lebanon.

Vast variation in political stability

The MENA is also a place that has been characterized by vast variation in political stability. This was the case well before 2011. Consider several examples of instability that predate the Arab Spring. Sectarian strife rented Bahrain asunder during the 1980s, pitting the minority Sunni elite against the Shia majority. In Syria, this dynamic was reversed: the Alawi elite brutally persecuted the Sunni opposition and

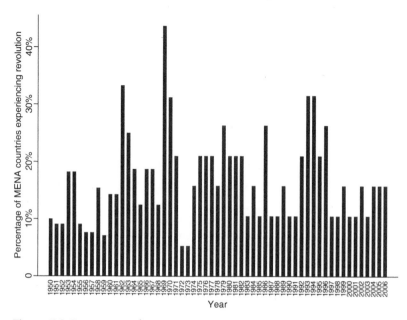

Figure 7.3 Percentage of countries experiencing revolution in the MENA, 1950–2006.

perpetrated the Hama Massacre, killing over 25,000 people. Youth riots rocked Jordan during the 1980s in response to an IMF standby agreement; a similar scenario also occurred in Morocco during that same decade. In Algeria, a civil war broke out in 1992. Saudi Arabia was beset by Islamist activism in the 1990s. In 2005, Lebanon was marked by popular demonstrations triggered by the assassination of Rafik Hariri, a popular politician. In Iran, mass protests against the rigged reelection of President Mahmoud Ahmadinejad in 2009, followed by a brutal crackdown, were dubbed the Green Revolution.

Indeed, since the end of World War II, the MENA has been the site of a raft of independence movements, revolutions, civil wars, and popular protests. Figure 7.3 graphs the percentage of MENA countries experiencing one or more revolutions, by year, from 1950 to 2006.[6] The countries included are Morocco, Libya, Algeria, Tunisia, Egypt, Sudan,

---

[6] *Revolution* is defined and coded by Banks (2009) as "any illegal or forced change in the top governmental elite, any attempt at such a change, or any successful or unsuccessful armed rebellion whose aim is independence from the central government."

Turkey, Lebanon, Iran, Iraq, Jordan, Saudi Arabia, Yemen, Kuwait, Bahrain, Qatar, U.A.E., and Oman. These countries are observed since either 1950 or their first year of independence. The dataset has 921 observations.

During each of the 57 years included, revolutions were the norm, not the exception. While Iraq experienced a revolution for 30 out of 57 years between 1950 and 2006, and Sudan had a revolution for 31 out of 47 years, Algeria is recorded as experiencing a revolution for 12 out of 40 years, Syria, 12 out of 54 years, Egypt, 8 out of 54 years, and Iran, 6 out of 57 years. On the other end of the spectrum are countries such as Oman and Jordan, both with 4 revolutionary years out of 57 total years. Qatar, Kuwait, and Bahrain each have one year of revolution.

There were several years where close to a majority of MENA countries experienced revolution. In 1969, 43 percent of the countries in the region (seven countries) experienced revolution. In both 1993 and 1994, it was 31.6 percent of countries (six countries). In 1962, 33.3 percent of MENA countries (five countries) experienced revolution. It is therefore not surprising that the mean percentage of countries experiencing a revolution during any given year in the region is 16.8 percent (the mean number of revolutions is 2.9).

The relationship between oil and political stability

What explains the variation in political stability observed historically across the MENA? The resource curse posits that oil makes all the difference. The logic is as follows. Rulers in the MENA who rely on easy-to-collect revenues, such as oil rents, are inoculated against pressures for political liberalization and representation (see Anderson 1987; Beblawi and Luciani 1987; Crystal 1990; Mahdavy 1970). They are able to deploy oil revenues to placate dissent and repress would-be revolutionaries (see Gause 1994).[7] This protracts dictators' tenure in office and lowers the odds of political instability in general.

Figure 7.4 is a preliminary exploration of the resource curse. It is a graph of the percentage of countries experiencing one or more revolutions, by year, from 1950 to 2006, juxtaposed against the regional

[7] For cross-national evidence that oil promotes regime stability, see Smith (2004).

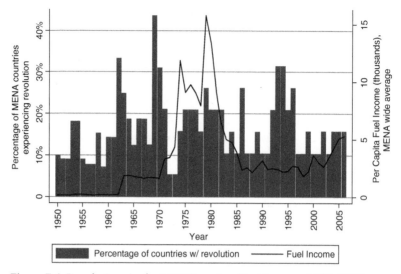

Figure 7.4 Revolutions in the MENA against Fuel Income, 1950–2006.

mean of Fuel Income Per Capita. The evidence is mixed. On the one hand, there was a 217 percent increase in the oil price in 1974, in the wake of the first oil shock. This ushered in a series of historically unprecedented year-on-year increases in Fuel Income, culminating in the data series apex in the aftermath of the second oil shock in 1979: $15,766. During this time period, the degree of political instability was less pronounced than during periods in which the level of oil income was lower. On the other hand, following a 7 percent rise in the real price of oil in 1958, and a concomitant increase in Fuel Income during the early 1960s, there was a marked increase in the proportion of countries experiencing revolution.

Although eyeballing the data yields inconclusive results, we can evaluate this question more systematically. Specifically, a Cox proportional hazards model can calculate a country's risk of succumbing to revolution as a function of its income from fuel.[8] To estimate this model, I pool the data, allowing me to exploit both its between- and

---

[8] This survival approach is preferred because it addresses right censoring, as well as time-varying covariates. Tests of the Cox proportional hazards assumption in this and succeeding models (Table 7.1, columns 2–3) based on the Schoenfeld residuals justify the proportional hazards assumption.

within-variation.[9] Robust standard errors clustered by country address heteroskedasticity and any intragroup correlation within countries.[10] Because it is significantly right-skewed, I take the natural log of Fuel Income Per Capita.[11]

Table 7.1, Column 1, discloses the results of this regression. As the resource curse theory predicts, Fuel Income is negative and statistically significant at conventional levels. The hazard rate is –0.887, with a p-value of 0.05. Figure 7.5 displays survival estimates by the level of oil income, graphing the hazard rate for countries at the 10th Percentile of log of Fuel Income (–6.908), 25th Percentile (–5.472), 50th Percentile (–1.209), 75th Percentile (1.153), and at the maximum value (4.397). For example, the cumulative revolutionary avoidance rate of countries that lie at or below the 10th Percentile drops below 40 percent in just under five years, whereas countries above the 75th Percentile only reach this rate after fifteen years. In short, it appears that in the MENA political stability is indeed bought and paid for with oil money.

Skepticism about the resource curse

Yet, this conclusion is premature. A key issue remains to be addressed. Does the relationship between oil and political stability hold after accounting for other salient differences between MENA countries? In previous chapters, this book has argued that the most important omitted factor may be political institutions.

Particularly, while regime type is correlated with oil in the MENA, the latter may be what really explains differences in political stability. The oil-poor monarchies help to make this point. Particularly, the way in which Jordan and Morocco reacted to the Arab Spring suggests that monarchy, not oil, may be what drives political resilience. In Jordan, protestors called for reforms, but not the overthrow of King Abdullah's regime. In turn, the widely popular monarch has made concessions that have further bolstered his legitimacy, including the relaxation of laws

---

[9] The results are robust, however, to introducing a frailty term that implies an unobservable and multiplicative random effect with a unit mean and variance defined by the Gamma distribution.

[10] If the models that follow are instead estimated with the standard errors clustered by year, the results are similar. Thus, they are robust to contemporaneous/spatial correlation.

[11] I add 0.001 to account for zero values. The mean of the logged version is –1.895 and the standard deviation is 3.472.

Table 7.1 *Determinants of revolution and institutional quality in the MENA*
Heteroskedasticity and autocorrelation consistent t statistics in brackets

	1	2	3	4	5	6
Dependent variable	Revolution	Revolution	Revolution	QOG index	QOG index	QOG index
log(Total fuel income PC)	-0.12	-0.087	-0.056	0.011	0.004	-0.001
	[1.93]*	[1.37]	[0.76]	[6.07]***	[1.70]	[0.22]
Monarch		-1.065	-1.125		0.133	0.134
		[4.18]***	[2.92]***		[15.05]***	[11.35]***
Economic growth			-0.018			0.002
			[1.75]*			[2.63]**
Per capita income			-0.278			0.052
			[1.39]			[4.53]***
log(Population)			-0.176			0.034
			[1.30]			[3.65]***
log(Area)			0.202			-0.021
			[2.38]**			[6.50]***
Percent Muslim			0.004			0.003
			[0.25]			[4.30]***
Ethnic fractionalization			1.851			-0.125
			[2.66]***			[5.95]***
Persian Gulf			0.418			-0.042
			[1.13]			[3.67]***

log(Distance to Istanbul)	-0.066				-0.003
	[1.23]				[0.98]
Constant			0.495	0.43	-0.457
			[33.39]***	[27.16]***	[2.63]**
Observations	921	921	429	429	429
Countries	19	19	19	19	19
r-squared			0.05	0.25	0.48

* significant at 10%; ** significant at 5%; *** significant at 1%

Columns 1–3 are pooled regressions estimated as survival models using the Cox Proportional Hazards technique. Hazard ratios reported.

Columns 4–6 are OLS regressions with Driscoll Kraay standard errors to address heteroskedasticity and spatial correlation.

A Newey West adjustment of the error term with a one lag length is made to address first-order serial correlation.

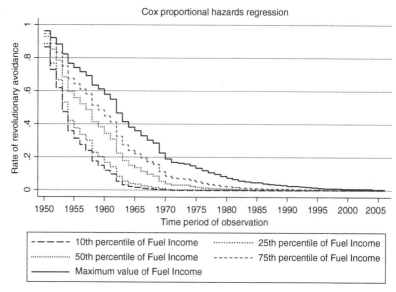

Figure 7.5 Revolutionary avoidance rate of MENA countries by oil.

restricting public gatherings and the drafting of new, more liberal, electoral laws and independent electoral commission, and the establishment of a constitutional court.[12] In Morocco, discontent was channeled into a political movement based on "transformation without violence." This ushered in a new constitution and liberalization.[13]

I also hasten to emphasize that this book is not the first place to broach the notion that the omission of regime type may confound inferences about the relationship between oil and politics in the MENA. Such an idea was articulated by Herb, over a decade ago (1999, p. 253):

It is assumed, it appears, that their oil wealth renders them stable, or at least so odd that they are beyond the pale of comparison. Rentier wealth, however, does not make monarchies stable, as the citizens of Libya have learned to their regret. If the possibility that resilience does not derive from

---

[12] A constitutional commission has floated reforms: electing a prime minister, greater freedom of speech, loosening restrictions on political parties, and a redrawing of political districts.

[13] While the new constitution imposes limits on executive power, King Muhammad proceeded to appoint a prime minister from the *Islamist and Development Party*.

oil is entertained, the survival of the Arabian monarchies is all the more puzzling. These dynasties ruled the Arabian peninsula in the days of wooden boats and camel caravans. How have they survived the utter transformation that yanked these societies into the modern age faster than virtually any other societies on the planet, and certainly with less preparation, warning or indigenous effort?

The theory of monarchical political culture

Drawing on the authoritarianism literature

Recent literature on the political economy of authoritarianism posits that elites, rather than the masses, are the pivotal actors in non-democratic regimes (Bueno de Mesquita et al. 2003; Gandhi 2008; Geddes 1999; Haber 2007; and Svolik 2009). Drawing on this assumption, several researchers argue that, while it is wise for a ruler to remain outside the reach of popular mobilization, it behooves him to remain accountable to his inner circle. If elites can trust that a dictator will protect their interests, they lack an incentive to plot against him or countenance sedition (Magaloni 2008; Myerson 2008).

Besides engendering political stability, such a dynamic also produces economic benefits. Consider Firmin-Sellers' (1995, p. 878) explanation of how tribal chiefs codified land rights in Ghana during British colonialism, therefore allowing them to exploit a growing international trade in timber, cash crops, and minerals:

[P]roperty rights will not inspire individual investment and economic growth unless the ruler wields sufficient coercive authority to silence those who advocate an alternative, more distributionally favorable property rights system and force them to accept their losses. At the same time, the ruler must credibly commit him or herself to the new property rights system. The ruler must persuade the subjects that coercive authority will not be used to violate property rights and confiscate the subjects' wealth. In Akyem Abuakwa, customary land tenure generated productive investment because Nana Ofori Atta manipulated both colonial and traditional institutions to satisfy these conditions.

How do dictators make credible commitments to property rights when they face strong incentives to abrogate limits on their authority? One way is to allow political elites to be able to coordinate to defend their interests (Gehlbach and Keefer 2011; Haber, Razo, and Maurer

2003; Haber 2007; Weeks 2008; Weingast 1997). In this scenario, a dictator is held accountable by the shadow of a retaliatory coup. While Gandhi and Przeworski (2006) argue that legislatures can help elites solve their collective action problem in order to make this happen, others point to constitutions (see Albertus and Menaldo 2012b) and ruling parties (Magaloni 2008).

Research on political culture suggests another potential avenue. According to Greif (1994, p. 915): "[p]ast cultural beliefs provide focal points and coordinate expectations, thereby influencing equilibrium selection and society's enforcement institutions."

Drawing on these insights, the rest of this section advances a theory of monarchic political culture to explain why some countries in the MENA have proven more stable and successful than others. Like other literature at the vanguard of the study of authoritarianism, it is predicated on the assumption that the best way to understand the politics of autocracies is to focus on elites, not citizens.

However, a skeptical reader might point out that the Arab Spring gainsays this assumption. The 2011 revolutions in Tunisia, Egypt, and Libya, and the ongoing civil war in Syria, suggest that one should instead focus on public opinion and popular mobilizations. After all, was it not regular citizens, rather than party apparatchiks, who put these regimes on their backs?

Upon further reflection, however, the Arab Spring actually corroborates the precept that we should keep our attention focused on political elites. Mass-based rebellions were ultimately epiphenomenal. In Tunisia, Egypt, Libya, and Syria, splits within the ruling clique allowed popular unrest to blossom into revolts in the first place. Regime opponents were keenly aware of the incoherence within the ranks of the regime and took full advantage. They smelled blood in the water. Therefore, a scenario in which citizens voiced discontent and took to the streets to let off some steam quickly evolved into organized protests centered on regime change.

The Arab Spring's revolutions were a symptom of a deeper crisis at the regime level – one in which elites failed to rally around incumbents. Had they done so, this would have preempted full-fledged crises. In Yemen, for example, a split at the elite level created two factions, each commanding its own armed forces and constituents. In Syria, several military officers, diplomats, and politicians defected. They then created the Free Syrian Army.

It is perhaps in Egypt where the events of 2011 were most clearly driven by a split between civilian insiders and the armed forces. After only eighteen days of mass demonstrations, both the coercive forces of the regime and the National Democratic Party imploded after the military pronounced it would not retaliate against the Tahrir Square protestors. Less than a month after the army and police were deployed to protect Cairo's strategic locations, Mubarak and Sulayman were purged from the ruling clique, ceding power to the Supreme Council of the Armed Forces.

This split was the culmination of a gradually deepening economic and political cleavage. Leading up to the spring of 2011, the Egyptian military had thwarted efforts by civilian elites to reform the economy in order to protect its vast holdings in the country's economic conglomerates. For their part, the armed forces chafed at the Mubarak regime's worsening corruption and nepotism (see Cook 2007 and Middle East/North Africa Report 2012).

These examples echo the literature on the micro-foundations of revolutions. Kuran (1991) argues that conflicts between regime factions that lead to splits may ignite a revolutionary bandwagon. If the military openly disobeys a dictator, or if there are defections by high-profile insiders, cracks within the regime become visible, emboldening discontented citizens to take to the streets. When regime insiders demonstrate irresolution, this reveals the underlying level of discontent, and it motivates less courageous citizens to join protests. Eventually, a tipping point is reached, precipitating a revolution.

Conversely, a unified front deters the majority of regime opponents from taking a stand. In the absence of elite defections or mixed signals put forth by the regime, potential revolutionaries tend to underestimate the prevalence of discontent. Of course grievances may abound, but they cannot be galvanized by political entrepreneurs. If there is nothing like a high-level defection, a cascade effect will never have the chance to materialize. It will never trigger other defections or embolden protestors.

Inventing and investing in a political culture

A regime's political culture is a package of informal institutions. It consists of the myths and rituals that help to stabilize and legitimize rule. As a first-order concern, the political culture establishes a clear demarcation between insiders and outsiders. It also manufactures values and beliefs that allow elites to solve their collective action problem. By transmitting information about punishment for deviations from accepted behavior, a political culture allows regime insiders to enforce their rights and interests. Yet this does not entail that a dictator will necessarily sacrifice his share of rents or be made worse off. A political culture is not tantamount to genuine pluralism and liberalism.

For a dictator to generate, disseminate, and sustain a political culture that promotes self-enforcing limits on executive authority, three things must occur. The first order of business is to make the boundaries of the ruling group less fluid. That is to say, to distinguish regime insiders from outsiders.

The second is to standardize and disseminate norms. If there is disagreement about the regime's norms, or if they are unknown, it is logically impossible for them to be enforced. Therefore, elites must recognize and uphold a uniform set of norms and come to share the same beliefs about how the ruler should comport himself. They should also agree on how they will respond if he violates their rights. In this way, the regime's norms become focal points that elites can use to coordinate their actions. And provided that they can monitor the ruler's actions, this confers them with a credible threat of punishment. The upshot is that they will be able to deter the ruler from engaging in opportunism.

Third, a political culture institutionalizes a particular distribution of benefits and opportunities. Its norms regulate who is entitled to what share of the rents.

However, norms and institutions that help produce common knowledge and monitor adherence to agreed-upon standards are public goods. Hence, they do not emerge out of thin air. Indeed, rulers are willing to provide these goods only if it suits them; they invest power and resources in the regime's political culture if they can retain the distributional upper hand. This means that elites are only able to sanction rulers when they are cheated out of a preordained share of rents, therefore preventing them from arbitrary attempts to increase their share of the pie. Elites accept a lopsided arrangement because it makes them better off: it is far better than the ruler adopting a divide-and-conquer approach that makes all attempts at coordination impossible.

Monarchical political cultures

A monarchical form of government is usually more effective than other autocratic regimes at creating and broadcasting a political culture. A monarchy's traditions and rituals, even if recently invented, foster historical memory and stability. Because they are part of a standardized routine, the king's actions are anticipated and predictable. The monarchy's pomp and circumstance ensures that his actions are visible to all relevant elites. Information about adherence to the regime's norms tends to be transparent and public, especially when the monarch furnishes collective gathering places.

Indeed, monarchies provide countless opportunities to publicize their norms. Monarchical rituals and institutions such as coronation ceremonies serve as forums that facilitate elite coordination, disseminate regime norms, and standardize beliefs. These types of ceremonies generate common knowledge. And, to boot, a coronation ceremony has an added benefit: it allows elites to jointly and publicly recognize the ruler's heir. This makes peaceful political succession more likely and predictable.

For several reasons, monarchs are also well positioned to harness a political culture to stimulate economic development. First, because a monarchic culture allows elites to coordinate, the king is deterred from predation. Second, since it is easier in a monarchy to codify a succession mechanism, and since it is in the interest of elites that he remains in power and that his official heir inherits the throne, the ruler also expects to remain in office until he dies or abdicates. He therefore expects to reap future returns associated with his investments. Third, elites are also deterred from behaving opportunistically and refrain from trying to cut the ruler out of the deal. In turn, the king does not fear that the provision of growth enhancing policies will strengthen and enrich elites in ways that threaten his own rule.

The implication is that, as a residual claimant on the gains associated with investments and growth, the monarch should impose the revenue maximizing tax rate, as well as adopt economic policies that promote economic efficiency. In other words, he should behave as an economic steward with an encompassing interest in the long run vitality of the economy (see Clague et al. 1996). Similarly, since the political culture enshrines secure property rights and a predictable sense of how future contingencies will be dealt with, the kingdom's elites are also incentivized to make optimal investment decisions over relatively long horizons.

Finally, monarchs should also be able to maintain their grip on power during difficult economic times. Once the political culture has consolidated, only an unequivocal violation of the elites' rights should motivate the latter to retaliate. The culture's focal points ensure that a mere shortfall in rents will not trigger elite coordination against the ruler – instead, only a brazen attempt to change the distribution of rents should do so.[14] This inoculates monarchical regimes against economic crises. If the absolute amount of rents decline in line with reductions in GDP, this should not threaten political stability. That is, not if the kingdom's preexisting distribution scheme is respected.

Monarchical political culture in the MENA

We can now apply the theory's logic to the MENA monarchies. Embraced by ruling families and commoners, their political cultures have been strategically cultivated over decades, if not centuries. Monarchical cultures in the region have evolved to serve several purposes. They have created and enforced boundaries between regime insiders and outsiders. They have also enshrined norms that regulate the distribution of rents, and fostered mechanisms of consultation and negotiation. Finally, although these political cultures have not entirely eliminated conflict over who should rule, they have made peaceful and regular succession the norm.

Across the MENA monarchies, settling the boundaries regarding who qualifies as a regime insider is a political process that has evolved over time. This includes elaborating clear rules about who qualifies as a member of the ruling family, as a member of the inner circle, and as a member of the government. To create coherent ruling families, monarchs have relied on intermarriage and tribal networks. Control of the executive branch in the region's monarchies has often cycled back-and-forth between different factions of these endogenous royal families.

---

[14] Compare this to the consequences of economic crises in personalist regimes. Rulers lost control of clientlistic networks during the 1980s and 1990s when economic shocks forced them to reduce benefits in the wake of demands from donors and lenders that opposed state intervention (Geddes 1999, p. 24). Austerity destabilized these regimes when regime allies deserted their leaders. This process precipitated the downfall of many of these regimes, especially across Sub-Saharan Africa.

Other regime insiders have also been constructed in similar ways. In Morocco, for example, the monarch's inner circle was institutionalized gradually. Now referred to with the honorific the *makhzen*, it has become widely respected and revered (see Maghraoui 2011). Morocco and other MENA monarchies have also elaborated detailed norms about who can serve in the cabinet, bureaucracy, and military (see Herb 1999).

The distribution of rents

Across the MENA monarchies, rents are usually allocated via informal processes enforced by cultural norms. This is true of both oil-poor and oil-rich kingdoms. On the one hand, the establishment of these norms preceded the advent of oil rents. On the other hand, these norms have been quite impervious to manipulation after the oil era. As Okruhlik (1999, p. 309) writes:

Life did not begin, as many imply, in 1973 with the quadrupling of oil prices. Rather, oil enters into an ongoing process of development and into a constellation of identities. The extent to which social forces were corporate groups before oil has indeed proven important. The receipt of oil revenues *per se* does not explain development or opposition or relations between ruler and ruled. The manner in which the rent is deployed, however, tells us much [...] Deployment is fundamentally affected by political concerns.

The Qatari monarchy embodies the endogenous evolution of practices intended to distribute oil rents among elites. In 1949, Ali al-Thani introduced the distinction between public and private revenues. He then regularized the allocation of customs receipts and introduced norms that sought to clarify how revenues should be distributed. As Crystal (1990, pp. 129–130) explains, these norms eventually evolved into detailed and explicit rules:

[T]he ruling family, and no other, was entitled to allowances [...] The next principle was that familial proximity to the Shaikh was the first criterion for financial claims [...] The relative weights of various claims were painfully sorted out [...] Allowances were calculated roughly on the degree of consanguinity with the ruler, with distinctions for seniority, different mothers, and sometimes leadership potential. Gradations were worked out among the various ranks.

To help enforce these norms, Ali's son, Ahmad, introduced a *Consultative Council* composed of members of Qatar's recognized tribes. This political body was invested with the power to make recommendations to the *emir's* cabinet, debate laws, summon hearings related to pending legislation, and review budgets for public projects. Today, these practices and institutions still facilitate consensus building among members of Qatar's ruling family.

Oil-poor MENA monarchies have cultivated similar institutions.[15] In Morocco, for example, monarchs have worked hard to achieve consensus by institutionalizing consultation between kings, regime officials, and dignitaries. The same holds true for Jordan.

The importance of stable succession

The MENA monarchies' ability to establish stable succession mechanisms is perhaps their biggest asset. Structured and predictable, these mechanisms are also quite flexible and are loosely based on a mix of political and technical qualifications. Rulers choose their successors from extended royal families only after conducting quiet political campaigns aimed at obtaining support among key elites. While monarchs seeking support for their successors use regular political offices as patronage, the candidates who are ultimately selected tend to be those who gain consensus across family factions (pp. 236–238).[16]

This contrasts with non-monarchical rulers in the MENA who have announced rudderless succession plans that ultimately fell flat because they lacked consent and legitimacy. Before the Arab Spring, many dictators had spent years grooming their sons to succeed them, but never invested in the type of political cultures that could help them achieve this objective. Needless to say, in Egypt, Libya, and Yemen these plans were thwarted by the 2011 revolutions. The last instance of dynastic succession in a non-monarchic regime was when Bashar al-Assad succeeded his father, Hafez, in 2000. Given that Syria's civil war rages on with no end in sight, it is doubtful that this example will soon be repeated.

[15] See Herb (1999, pp. 262–263) for similar claims to those advanced in this paragraph.

[16] Herb (1999) contends that the overall key to MENA monarchs' stability is their dynastic structure. He argues that this is because ruling families monopolize government institutions, including the bureaucracy and security apparatus, and govern via consensus. Herb also gives credit to an information network that allows regime insiders to make better decisions (p. 238).

How to make sense of the non-monarchies

The MENA's monarchical exceptionalism also provides a lens by which to view the region's non-monarchies. These regimes have lacked coherent and strong political cultures capable of building inter-elite consensus. This has permitted – both in 2011 and at various times in the past – popular discontent to escalate into revolutions. The question is why?

After European colonialism, anti-imperial and secular ideologies took hold across the MENA's non-monarchies. Used to define regime insiders in a way that branded outsiders as implacable enemies, they stoked polarization.[17] They encouraged competing political elites allied with military factions to fixate on mutually exclusive political visions and platforms. In turn, this fueled zeros-sum contests over power and increased the stakes of politics, inducing regime outsiders to try to defend their rights, interests, and lives through extralegal means and violence. This mentality was exemplified most stridently by the Baathists in both Iraq and Syria.[18]

Putting monarchical exceptionalism to the test

As argued above, monarchy should be negatively associated with political conflicts that draw in key elites and which can threaten the regime. Chief among these are popular revolutions. By creating self-enforcing limits on the ruler, and circumscribing the range of collective action that can be exercised by the elites, monarchism should give elites a strong stake in the regime. In turn, monarchs should be incentivized to invest in the rule of law and physical and human capital. Therefore, monarchy should also have a positive effect on economic development.

Have the MENA monarchies been less likely to experience revolutions? As a first step in addressing this question, let us take stock of the raw data. Between 1950 and 2006, while only 31 out of 409 monarch

---

[17] Lewis (2005, p. 44) blames the virulence and totalitarian tendencies of these ideologies on the influence exercised by both the Nazis during World War II – when Germany occupied France and its MENA colonies – and Stalinist-inspired Communists afterward.

[18] However, the battle lines have not necessarily been drawn according to partisanship or ideology. For example, Syria's ongoing civil war has been characterized by a sectarian divide pitting the Sunni majority against the Shia, Allawite minority. The latter have ruled the country for decades with an iron fist and severely oppressed the former.

country years exhibit a revolution (7.6%), 134 out of 512 republican country years do so (26.2%).[19] Figure 7.6 graphs the number of MENA revolutions, by year, during this time period, sorting these frequencies by regime type. While the secular trend is similar across regimes, political instability for the MENA monarchs is considerably less frequent than for the republics. The only exception is 1955 to 1957 and 1972 to 1975. Moreover, the "political stability gap" separating monarchies from non-monarchies widened over time. The gap began to expand perceptibly in 1980 and grew almost exponentially during the 1980s, 1990s, and 2000s.

This impressionistic evidence holds once I perform a statistical test of the hypothesis that the MENA monarchies are more politically stable. Specifically, if I add the variable Monarch to the Cox proportional hazards model reported in Column 1 of Table 7.1 – discussed earlier in the chapter – Fuel Income is no longer statistically significant (although it retains a negative sign) and Monarch is negative and statistically significant (the hazard ratio is 0.917 and the p-value is <0.001). Moreover, the substantive effect of Monarch is sizable. Figure 7.7 displays survival estimates by regime type, graphing the hazard rate for countries that are monarchic versus those that are not. The cumulative revolutionary avoidance rate of non-monarchies drops to 20 percent in seven years, whereas monarchies only reach this rate after nineteen years. These results therefore support monarchical exceptionalism and reject the resource curse.

To ensure that these results are robust, Column 3 controls for other determinants of political instability. Wright (2008, p. 326) finds that *Ethnic Fractionalization*, log(*Population Size*), and the *Percent of Population that is Muslim* are statistically significant correlates of monarchical rule. I therefore control for each of these variables.[20] I also control for log(*Per Capita Income*) – in real, 2000 international dollars from Haber and Menaldo (2011a) – as well as the *Growth Rate*

---

[19] *Monarch*, coded by the author, is a regime where the executive is not elected, there is a clear succession mechanism based on royal lineage, and the country's constitution recognizes a monarch as the legitimate ruler. Former monarchies include Libya (Qaddafi overthrew King Idris in 1970), Iran (Ayatollah Khomeini ousted the Shah, Mohammad Reza, in 1979); Iraq (Karrim Kassem overthrew King Faisal II in 1959), Egypt (a cadre of officers overthrew King Naguib in 1952), and North Yemen (AlBadr unseated Ibn Yahya Hamid in 1962).

[20] These variables are from Menaldo (2012).

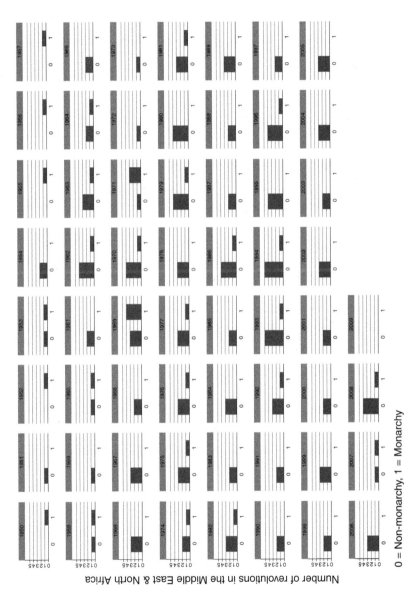

Number of revolutions in the Middle East & North Africa

0 = Non-monarchy, 1 = Monarchy

Figure 7.6 Revolutions in the MENA by regime type, 1950–2006.

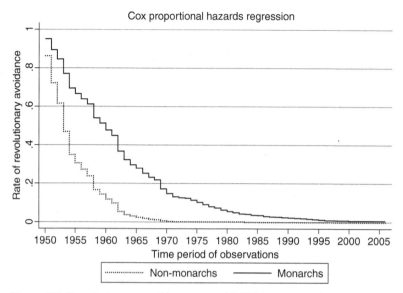

Figure 7.7 Revolutionary avoidance rate of MENA countries by regime type.

of Per Capita Income. Both variables address the modernization thesis: wealthier countries will be more likely to liberalize their political system and may experience political instability during this process.

Geography may also matter. I control for log(*Surface Area*), from the World Bank Development Indicators (WBDI), to address the possibility that monarchy is proxying for small countries in which there are fewer sources of conflict that can escalate into political violence. To capture a country's strategic importance, I control for whether the country is located in the *Persian Gulf.* The Strait of Hormuz is the major transit point for Middle Eastern oil and the U.S. Navy – and British Navy before it – therefore polices these sea-lanes. I also control for log(*Distance to Istanbul*) to test the hypothesis that countries on the periphery of the former Ottoman Empire have achieved greater political stability.[21]

The inclusion of these control variables does not materially affect the main results. Monarch is still substantively and statistically

---

[21] The Ottomans conquered Egypt in the fifteenth century and Yemen in the early sixteenth century. Although they were subsequently beat back by recalcitrant tribes, they fully established control over Yemen by the late nineteenth century, and then took over large swaths of the Persian Gulf. However, their hegemony was soon challenged – and eventually wrested away – by the British.

significant – even though it is highly correlated with many of these variables: population, country size, Persian Gulf, and Distance to Istanbul. Meanwhile, Fuel Income is even less statistically significant than before (p-value = 0.45), although it retains its negative sign.

Other robustness checks make no real difference to the bottom line. If the regressions across Columns 1 to 3 are re-estimated as probit models – with linear, quadratic, and cubic terms to address temporal dependence – the results are materially the same. This is also the case if these models are reestimated with different measures of the dependent variable, be it Government Crises, Guerilla Wars, Purges, Assassinations (all from Banks 2009), or Leadership Survival.[22] The results are also robust to controlling for other dimensions of institutional variation among autocratic regimes, including *Single Party Regime, Military Regime*, and *Personalist Regime*, as well as the *Size of the Winning Coalition* and *Selectorate*.[23] Finally, the results are robust to measuring oil as Proven Oil Reserves instead of Fuel Income Per Capita.

Other empirical implications

While I have ruled out the resource curse as an explanation for political stability in the MENA and corroborated monarchic exceptionalism, we still do not know if either of these theories account for broader patterns of political, economic, and social development. Therefore, we now move to evaluating this question. While the theory of monarchical political culture posits that monarchs should promote the rule of law, provide public goods, and encourage faster growth, the resource curse argues that oil should be negatively associated with these outcomes.

I operationalize the rule of law/lack of corruption as the *Quality of Government* (QOG Index) from the International Country Risk Guide. This is the average of a "Corruption," "Law and Order," and "Bureaucracy" index and is based on subjective perceptions about the prevalence of corruption in the public sector, respect for the rule of law,

---

[22] This was operationalized using the ARCHIGOS (2006) dataset with the leader-year as the unit of observation and coded as right-censored if the leader dies of natural causes, as the result of an accident, or if he is displaced by a foreign invasion.

[23] Geddes (1999) argues that an autocratic regime's survival prospects are affected by whether it is a single-party regime versus a military dictatorship versus a personalist regime. Bueno de Mesquita et al. (2003) focus on the size of the winning coalition and the selectorate.

and the bureaucracy's professionalism. While each of these components is measured on a six-point scale, the QOG index is normalized to run from 0 to 1, with 1 denoting the best institutions. This variable is available since 1985 (n = 429).

I operationalize public goods in two ways. The first is by measuring human capital investments as *Social Spending* (% of GDP), from Albertus and Menaldo (2014). This consists of government expenditures on education, health, and housing. These are all investments that help improve the stock of human capital over the long run, bolster productivity and, hence, spur economic growth. Social Spending (n = 353) varies between 0.865 and 16.895, with a mean of 6.83, and a standard deviation of 2.712.

The second is *Average Years of Schooling*, from Barro and Lee (2013). This is the average of years of education for the entire population that is twenty-five years of age and above. The measure includes years of primary, secondary, and tertiary education. Because Average Years of Schooling is only available every five years between 1950 and 2005 (t = 11), the models displayed across Columns 4–6 (Table 7.2) have fewer observations than the other models.

I measure *Economic Growth* as the real (logarithmic) growth rate of Per Capita Income (2,000 international dollars) per annum (expressed in percentage terms). The mean growth rate across the MENA between 1950 and 2006 (for 969 observations) is 1.5 percent, with a standard deviation of 8.7 percent.

These dependent variables – institutional quality, human capital investments, and economic growth – are all continuous. Therefore, unlike in Table 7.1, Columns 1–3, I now estimate regressions using Ordinary Least Squares (OLS).[24] However, following the previous regressions, I continue to pool the data to exploit variation both across and within countries. I note that the results are nonetheless robust to controlling for country fixed effects.

Table 7.2, Columns 4–6 and Table 7.2, Columns 1–9, report the results for each of these dependent variables. I repeat the format pursued in Table 7.1, Columns 1–3. For each dependent variable, the first set of regressions includes only Fuel Income. The second includes both Fuel Income and Monarch. The third includes Fuel Income,

---

[24] As in previous chapters, I address the potential for non-spherical errors by estimating Driscoll Kraay standard errors.

Table 7.2 Determinants of investments in human capital and economic growth in the MENA
Heteroskedasticity and autocorrelation consistent t statistics in brackets

Dependent variable	1 Social spending	2 Social spending	3 Social spending	4 Yrs. schooling	5 Yrs. schooling	6 Yrs. schooling	7 Econ. growth	8 Econ. growth	9 Econ. growth
log(Total fuel income PC)	0.08 [1.49]	0.068 [1.52]	0.083 [1.56]	0.337 [4.85]***	0.321 [4.24]***	0.158 [2.39]**	-0.205 [1.95]*	-0.244 [2.43]**	-0.172 [1.09]
Monarch		0.311 [1.05]	2.314 [5.62]***		0.691 [1.97]*	0.616 [3.38]***		1.085 [2.03]*	1.925 [2.12]**
Economic growth			-0.02 [0.89]			0.003 [0.19]			
Per capita income			0.109 [0.42]			0.769 [5.89]***			-0.172 [0.30]
log(Population)			1.227 [7.08]***			0.933 [4.72]***			-0.266 [0.68]
log(Area)			-0.66 [4.03]***			-0.67 [6.46]***			0.333 [1.36]
Percent Muslim			-0.098 [3.01]***			-0.006 [0.47]			0.017 [0.35]
Ethnic fractionalization			-8.277 [10.88]***			0.61 [.152]			-3.035 [1.88]*

Table 7.2 (*cont.*)

Dependent variable	1 Social spending	2 Social spending	3 Social spending	4 Yrs. schooling	5 Yrs. schooling	6 Yrs. schooling	7 Econ. growth	8 Econ. growth	9 Econ. growth
Persian Gulf			1.024 [1.66]			-0.896 [2.69]**			-0.369 [0.48]
log(Distance to Istanbul)			0.497 [8.51]***			0.016 [0.28]			-0.226 [2.07]*
Constant	6.922 [40.41]***	6.744 [46.95]***	2.398 [0.58]	3.517 [5.54]***	3.179 [5.10]***	-9.257 [2.63]**	1.1 [1.78]*	0.521 [0.81]	3.294 [0.41]
Observations	353	353	353	176	176	176	969	969	969
Countries	15	15	15	17	17	17	19	19	19
r-squared	0.01	0.01	0.36	0.28	0.3	0.55	0.01	0.01	0.03

* significant at 10%; ** significant at 5%; *** significant at 1%

These are pooled regressions estimated as OLS regressions with Driscoll Kraay standard errors to address heteroskedasticity and spatial correlation. A Newey West adjustment of the error term with a one lag length is made to address first-order serial correlation.

Monarch, and the control variables discussed above and included in Column 3.

According to the resource curse, oil should have a negative effect on institutional quality, investments in human capital, and economic development. The tests of these hypotheses are reported, respectively, in Table 7.1, Column 4 (where Institutional Quality is the dependent variable), Table 7.2, Column 1 (where Social Spending is the dependent variable), Table 7.2, Column 4 (where Educational Attainment is the dependent variable), and Table 7.2, Column 7 (where Economic Growth is the dependent variable).

The results are mixed. Contradicting the resource curse, oil is positively associated with institutional quality (p-value <0.001), social spending (although not at statistically significant levels), and educational attainment (p-value <0.001). Consistent with the resource curse, Fuel Income is negatively associated with economic growth (p-value = 0.07).

Models that include both oil and Monarch are reported in Table 7.1, Column 5 (where Institutional Quality is the dependent variable), Table 7.2, Column 2 (where Social Spending is the dependent variable), Table 7.2, Column 5 (where Educational Attainment is the dependent variable), and Table 7.2, Column 8 (where Economic Growth is the dependent variable).

The results are consistent with the predictions generated by the theory of monarchic political culture. Monarch is positively associated with institutional quality (p-value > 0.001), social spending (although not at conventional levels), educational attainment (p-value < 0.001), and economic growth (p-value = 0.06).

The remaining regressions add a host of control variables. Because there is a paucity of solid empirical findings on the determinants of the rule of law, investments in human capital, and economic growth *vis-à-vis* the MENA region, I take a conservative approach. Namely, I control for all of the independent variables included in Table 7.1, Column 3 (where Revolution is the dependent variable). I note, however, that adding the *Consumption Share of GDP*, the *Government Share of GDP*, and *Trade Openness* to these regressions makes no difference to the results.

The results generated by this final round of regressions support the thesis that the MENA monarchies are exceptional and challenge the resource curse. Monarch is positively associated with the QOG Index at the highest level of statistical significance (Table 7.1, Column 6). Monarch is positively associated with social spending at the highest level of statistical significance (Table 7.2, Column 3). Monarch is positively associated with Years of Schooling at the highest level (Table 7.2, Column 6). Monarch is also positively associated with economic growth at the 5 percent level (Table 7.2, Column 9). Fuel Income is no longer statistically associated with institutional quality, social spending, and economic growth.

On balance, the magnitude of the effects produced by Monarch is sizable. For example, switching from a non-monarchy to a monarchy leads to an increase of 2.3 percentage points (as a share of GDP) in spending on education, health, and housing. Most tellingly, switching from non-monarchy to monarchy increases the growth rate of Per Capita Income by 1.9 percentage points.

The deeper roots of monarchical political cultures

The theory of monarchical exceptionalism outlined above hinted at the idea that, despite the fact that the MENA's monarchical political cultures are inventions, they are underpinned by deeper historical forces. This section of the chapter will explore those forces. To do so, it will build on the factor endowment framework introduced in Chapter 4.

In that chapter, I argued that, historically, in arid places that are not particularly suited to settled agriculture, the modal economic system was pastoral nomadism and the dominant social structure was tribalism. In the MENA, this retarded the development of centralized states. In turn, it favored a monarchic form of government. This was true despite repeated imperial conquests, the spread of Islam, and more recent colonial adventures launched by European powers. Furthermore, places characterized by a tribal social structure became more clan-based and web-like over time. This is due to the fact monarchs invested in political cultures that capitalized upon tribalism and reinforced it.

The converse is also true. Places with moderate rainfall, or fertile river valleys, favored an economy that was more sophisticated than pastoral nomadism – one based on agriculture, specialization, and a class-based system. By extension, those places were associated with settled farming communities, political centralization, and weaker tribal structures. In the MENA, this took the form of oligarchic societies in which agriculture was organized along feudal lines. This pattern persisted well into the twentieth century – and in some places is still the norm. In turn, because tribal affiliations and identities were weaker, republican forms of government were favored. Indeed, if these places started out as monarchies – usually because this form of rule was imposed by the British – they invariably transitioned to non-monarchy.

I hasten to emphasize that these hypotheses are not deterministic. There are certainly examples where the relationship between pastoral nomadism and monarchy is weak. Iran is a good example. The country's vast Khorasan province, which is situated southeast of the Caspian coast, over the Alborz Mountains, was nomadic for millennia. In fact, the rulers of the Persian Empire after Alexander the Great, the Parthians, were a nomadic tribe that hailed from this region. They ruled Persia until 250 AD. Yet tribalism never really took root in Tehran. By 1979, the monarchy of Mohammad Reza Shah Pahlavi, which was imposed by Western powers after it had experimented with democracy, was swept away by the Iranian Revolution.

Or consider the case of Afghanistan. The progenitors of the Muhammadzai dynasty were Pashtun tribes that were predominantly nomadic and pastoral. Yet this monarchy ultimately failed by dint of a weak family structure and a non-existent political culture. This is attested to by several facts: a failed coup attempt in 1964, the fierce infighting between members of the ruling family that ensued, and the overthrow of the monarchy by a mild mannered politician, Mohammad Daud Khan, in 1973.

The bottom line is that, after holding everything else equal, there should be a probabilistic relationship between geography, the social structure, the economic structure, the degree of political centralization, and contemporary regime types. As we shall see shortly, Iran and Afghanistan are two exceptions that prove the rule.

Corroborating these claims empirically

To support the claims made above, the rest of this chapter takes several steps. I first demonstrate a correlation between precipitation and nomadic tribalism across MENA countries. I then corroborate these claims using ethnic group data, adducing evidence for correlations between geography, settled agriculture, and political centralization at that level of analysis. I then switch gears temporarily and summon qualitative

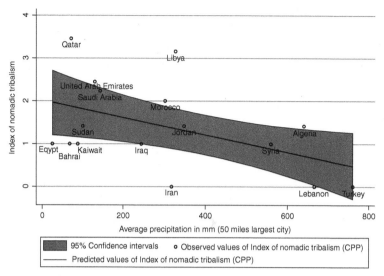

Figure 7.8 Tribalism and average precipitation in the MENA A.

evidence that supports the contention that tribalism nourished monarchical regimes and political cultures over the MENA's history. Finally, I return to the cross-national data to report and discuss the theory's chief empirical implications. First, in places where the climate and bio-geography were unfavorable to settled agriculture and instead conduced to pastoral nomadism and a strong tribal social structure, a monarchical form of government was more likely to survive.[25] Second, tribalism strengthened over time in the monarchies.

The association between geography, social structure, and political centralization

Figure 7.8 graphs a scatterplot of the nomadic tribalism index against the average annual level of precipitation for sixteen MENA countries.[26] The nomadic tribalism index is the square root of the number of times

[25] It is important to note, however, that the rulers of Bahrain, the U.A.E., and Qatar were predominantly involved in pearl fishing and pearl farming and had therefore settled along the Gulf's Eastern coast. Yet this does not necessarily challenge the claims made in this section, since the interior of these emirates were populated by nomadic, camel-herding tribes.

[26] As in Chapter 4, this average is calculated using data between 1980 and 1989 from a 50-mile radius around the country's largest city. See that chapter for the sources used and the justification behind this measurement strategy.

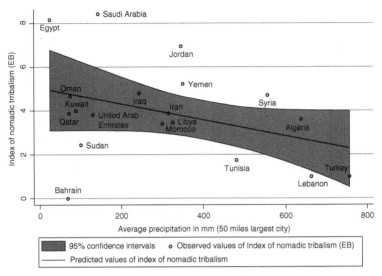

Figure 7.9 Tribalism and average precipitation in the MENA B.

that the University of Toronto Country Profiles Project (CPP) uses the words Tribe, Tribal, Clan, or Nomad to describe a country's social structure.[27] To identify the statistical relationship between these variables, the fitted values generated from a bivariate OLS regression are juxtaposed on the scatterplot and flanked by upper and lower 95 percent confidence bounds.[28] As expected, there is an inverse relationship between rainfall and nomadic tribalism. The slope of the regression line is sharply negative with relatively narrow confidence intervals.

Figures 7.9 and 7.10 suggest that this finding is not driven by the measure of nomadic tribalism employed, the omission of some MENA countries, or the equation's functional form. Figure 7.9 is identical to Figure 7.8, except for two modifications. The index of nomadic tribalism is now constructed from the Encyclopedia Britannica's (EB) Country Profiles. It uses different weights for different terms associated with a nomadic tribal social structure. Moreover, it includes all nineteen

---

[27] These cultural profiles provide an overview of the life and customs of the profiled country. They are available at http://cp-pc.ca/english/. The square root of this word count is taken to reduce skew and over-dispersion.

[28] The results are similar if a Tobit model is employed. The standard errors are robust and, thus, the confidence intervals are heteroskedasticity consistent.

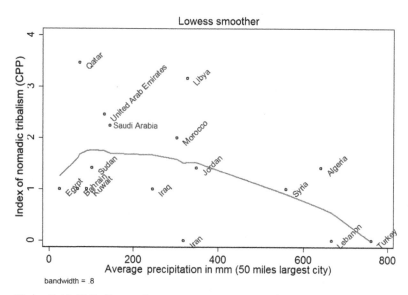

Figure 7.10 Tribalism and average precipitation in the MENA C.

MENA countries.[29] Figure 7.10 returns to using the CPP nomadic tribalism index; yet, rather than impose a linear relationship between rainfall and nomadic tribalism, the regression line is estimated via a Lowess Smoothing technique. In both figures, the basic pattern is again confirmed: rainfall is negatively correlated with tribalism.

Using the ethnic group database

The empirical exercises conducted above suggest that, in the MENA, there is a relationship at the country level between rainfall and tribalism. Yet, there are potential pitfalls to drawing inferences from these correlations using country-level data.

First, the perpetuation of tribalism is supposed to be a deep-seated historical process that occurred well before the recent formation of nation states. For example, Qatar, Bahrain, and the U.A.E. only gained independence in the 1970s. What if modern territorial borders shaped the observed prevalence of pastoral nomadism? Might national policies have explicitly shaped the quality of the soil or opportunity for

---

[29] The word counts of the following terms (in parentheses) are aggregated in the following way: square root[(tribe)/2+(tribal)+(clan)+(nomad)*3+(Bedouin)*2]. The results are not sensitive to different weighting schemes.

pasturage? Moreover, both state boundaries and the presence and strength of tribalism could have been jointly determined by country-specific and unobserved factors.

Second, even if rainfall data are collected around the vicinity of the country's largest city, it may not adequately capture the potential for settled agriculture. To be sure, in most cases this is not a problem. For example, Algeria, Lebanon, Syria, and Turkey all lie above 540 mm of annual rainfall and are relatively cool and moist. They therefore possess some of the richest soils in the MENA. Yet, there are also countries in the MENA with relatively low levels of precipitation that are home to rivers that periodically flood adjacent valleys. In Egypt and Iraq, for example, irrigation-dependent cereal production has been able to take root on the banks of the Nile and Tigris and Euphrates, respectively.[30] And some MENA countries, though semi-arid, have pockets of rain-fed agriculture. They include Tunisia, Libya, and Iran. While Tunisia and Libya are characterized by narrow strips of fertile land that straddle the southern fringe of the Mediterranean Sea, Iran is a case onto itself.[31]

Therefore, I now turn to an analysis centered on MENA's pre-colonial ethnic groups to evaluate the relationships between the suitability for agriculture, the prevalence of pastoral nomadism, and the strength of tribalism.[32] This within-country strategy allows me to address the problems outlined above. I hypothesize that ethnic groups residing in areas more suitable to agriculture have been less likely to (1) practice nomadism, (2) engage in pastoralism, and (3) exhibit tribal social structures. On the one hand, any of the correlations I uncover will be robust to omitted factors that jointly determine a society's economic organization and social structure. On the other hand,

---

[30] This is reflected in the fact that 80 million out of Egypt's 85 million people live in the narrow Nile River valley.

[31] Iran lacks fertile river valleys and, historically, the rain-fed Caspian coast – composed of the provinces of Gilan and Mazandaran – was underdeveloped, despite the fact that it is now the country's bread basket. Well before the spread of Islam, however, Persian rulers developed the so-called qanat system, a water pipeline sourced by underground reservoirs. This allowed for the irrigation of vast farmlands in the middle of the *Dahst-e Kavir Desert*.

[32] Awareness of this methodological problem and the solution proposed here, that is, one centered on an inter-ethnic group analysis using the ethnic group dataset discussed shortly, was inspired by Michalopoulos, Naghavi, and Prarolo (2012).

directly focusing on agriculture at such a fine-grained level will address
the fact that rainfall may not fully capture settled farming.

To conduct these analyses, I use the updated Ethnographic Atlas
compiled by Gray (1999). This atlas contains variables on the geographic, economic, cultural, and political traits of 1,270 ethnic groups
around the world. Because the Ethnographic Atlas lists each ethnic
group's location in terms of the centroid's latitude and longitude,
these variables can be tagged to both specific countries and geo-coded
variables. This allows me to match data on agricultural suitability at
the grid-cell level to the location of each ethnic group.

Because I am focusing on the variation within countries instead of
across them, I broaden the definition of the MENA to include several
countries in the Sahel, an African biogeographic zone where the
Saharan desert meets the Savannas. Additional countries considered
as part of the MENA now include Western Sahara, Mali, Mauritania,
Niger, Chad, Eritrea, and Somalia. The database contains 122 ethnic
groups. Each of these groups is listed in Table 7.3, along with the values
they take on for each of the variables used in the analyses.

The main independent variable that will be used is *Agricultural
Suitability*. It is the proportion of land within a 200-kilometer radius
of the centroid suitable for the cultivation of cereals such as millet,
sorghum, wheat, barley, and rye. Such a measure allows us to capture
fine-grained variation in the capacity for a sedentary lifestyle centered
on settled agriculture. This includes desert oases in which non-cereal
grains were also produced, including frankincense, myrrh, vine, dyes,
and dates. The crop suitability data are from the Food and Agricultural
Organization's *Global Agro-Ecological Zones* database (2002 version), which reports these measures for 5 arc minute by 5 arc minute
grid-cells. The mean value for this variable is 50 percent and the
standard deviation is 36 percent.

The dependent variables are each from the Ethnographic Atlas.
Unlike in the case of the cross-country analysis, I can now measure
both nomadism and pastoralism directly. I can also avail a more objective, micro-level proxy for tribalism.

Nomadism is measured as Settlement Patterns, which captures the
density of ethnic groups' settlements. This is an ordinal variable composed of the following categories: (1) nomadic or fully migratory,
(2) seminomadic, (3) semisedentary, (4) compact but impermanent
settlements, (5) neighborhoods of dispersed family homesteads,

Table 7.3 *Ethnic groups in the MENA and their economic, social, and political traits*

Ethnic group	Country	Agricultural suitability	Settlement patterns	Subsistence economy	Jurisdictional authority
ABABDA	Egypt	0	Nomadic	Pastoralism	One level
AHAGGAREN	Algeria	0	Seminomad	Pastoralism	Two levels
ALGERIANS	Algeria	0	Impermanent	Intensive Agric.	Not recorded
AMARAR	Sudan	0	Seminomad	Pastoralism	One level
ANCEGYPT	Egypt	0.01122112	Impermanent	Intensive Agric.	Four levels
ANTESSAR	Mali	0	Nomadic	Pastoralism	One level
ASBEN	Niger	0	Seminomad	Pastoralism	Two levels
AZJER	Algeria	0	Nomadic	Pastoralism	Two levels
BABYLONIA	Iraq	0.03958091	Impermanent	Intensive Agric.	Three levels
BAGIRMI	Chad	0.96778523	Impermanent	Extensive Agric.	Three levels
BAKHTIARI	Iran	0.48387097	Nomadic	Pastoralism	Two levels
BAMBARA	Mali	0.90167224	Impermanent	Intensive Agric.	One level
BARABRA	Egypt	0	Impermanent	Intensive Agric.	No levels
BAREA	Eritrea	0.24193548	Impermanent	Extensive Agric.	No levels
BARI	South Sudan	0.66643975	Dispersed Homesteads	Extensive Agric.	No levels
BASSERI	Egypt	0.0601557	Nomadic	Pastoralism	One level
BENIAMER	Sudan	0.00437158	Nomadic	Pastoralism	Two levels
BERABER	Morocco	0.75654854	Semisedentary	Intensive Agric.	Two levels
BERABISH	Mali	0	Nomadic	Pastoralism	One level
BISHARIN	Sudan	0	Seminomad	Pastoralism	One level

Table 7.3 (*cont.*)

Ethnic group	Country	Agricultural suitability	Settlement patterns	Subsistence economy	Jurisdictional authority
BODI	South Sudan	0.76565799	Hamlets	Pastoralism	One level
BOGO	Sudan	0.09980172	Seminomad	Pastoralism	One level
BONGO	South Sudan	0.6888587	Dispersed Homesteads	Extensive Agric.	One level
BOZO	Mali	0.80828323	Semisedentary	Fishing	One level
BUDUMA	Chad	0.84282277	Dispersed Homesteads	Mixed Economy	One level
CHAAMBA	Algeria	0	Seminomad	Pastoralism	Two levels
DAZA	Chad	0.02421466	Seminomad	Mixed Economy	No levels
DELIM	Western Sahara	0	Nomadic	Pastoralism	Three levels
DILLING	Sudan	0.9497319	Hamlets	Intensive Agric.	One level
DINKA	South Sudan	0.50709939	Seminomad	Pastoralism	One level
DOGON	Mali	0.58489305	Impermanent	Intensive Agric.	One level
DRAWA	Morocco	0.2686217	Not recorded	Unknown Agric.	Not recorded
DRUZE	Israel	0.47222222	Impermanent	Intensive Agric.	One level
EGYPTIANS	Egypt	0	Impermanent	Intensive Agric.	Three levels
ESA	Somalia	0.25323194	Nomadic	Pastoralism	Three levels
FAJULU	South Sudan	0.82958419	Impermanent	Extensive Agric.	No levels
FUR	Sudan	0.93507363	Impermanent	Intensive Agric.	Three levels
GIMMA	Sudan	0.5083612	Seminomad	Pastoralism	Not recorded
HABBANIA	Sudan	0.96642042	Nomadic	Pastoralism	Not recorded
HADENDOWA	Sudan	0	Not recorded	Pastoralism	Not recorded

HAMAMA	Algeria	0	Semisedentary	Pastoralism	Three levels
HAMYAN	Algeria	0.60429082	Nomadic	Pastoralism	Three levels
HASANIA	Sudan	0.34466667	Seminomad	Mixed Economy	Not recorded
HEBREWS	Israel	0.31906977	Impermanent	Intensive Agric.	Two levels
HEMAT	Chad	0.82897384	Seminomad	Mixed Economy	One level
IFORA	Mali	0	Nomadic	Pastoralism	Two levels
INGASSANA	Sudan	0.51048005	Dispersed Homesteads	Intensive Agric.	No levels
IRANIANS	Iran	0.44354839	Impermanent	Intensive Agric.	Four levels
JEBALA	Morocco	0.90707965	Impermanent	Intensive Agric.	Two levels
JORDANIAN	Jordan	0.24810997	Impermanent	Intensive Agric.	Two levels
JUR	South Sudan	0.69945726	Dispersed Homesteads	Extensive Agric.	One level
KABABISH	Sudan	0	Nomadic	Pastoralism	Two levels
KABYLE	Algeria	0.66471877	Impermanent	Intensive Agric.	Three levels
KAKWA	South Sudan	0.82958419	Impermanent	Extensive Agric.	One level
KANEMBU	Chad	0.67728758	Impermanent	Intensive Agric.	One level
KASONKE	Mali	0.72727273	Impermanent	Extensive Agric.	Two levels
KOALIB	Sudan	0.81848627	Hamlets	Intensive Agric.	One level
KORO	Niger	0	not recorded	Unknown Agric.	Not recorded
KORONGO	South Sudan	0.59864407	Hamlets	Extensive Agric.	No levels
KUKU	South Sudan	0.73297003	Dispersed Homesteads	Intensive Agric.	One level
KUNAMA	Eritrea	0.3439575	Impermanent	Extensive Agric.	No levels
KUNTA	Mali	0	Seminomad	Pastoralism	One level
KURD	Iraq	0.00290867	Semisedentary	Intensive Agric.	Two levels
LAKA	Chad	0.91694801	Impermanent	Extensive Agric.	No levels
LEBANESE	Lebanon	0.57117438	Impermanent	Intensive Agric.	Three levels
LOTUKO	South Sudan	0.74318801	Impermanent	Extensive Agric.	One level

Table 7.3 (*cont.*)

Ethnic group	Country	Agricultural suitability	Settlement patterns	Subsistence economy	Jurisdictional authority
MADAN	Iraq	0.10401891	Impermanent	Mixed Economy	Not recorded
MAMBWE	South Sudan	0.31750339	Impermanent	Extensive Agric.	One level
MASA	Chad	0.98251513	Dispersed Homesteads	Intensive Agric.	No levels
MEBAN	Sudan	0.50169722	Hamlets	Extensive Agric.	No levels
MESAKIN	Sudan	0.81879195	Hamlets	Extensive Agric.	One level
MESSIRIA	Sudan	0.90309556	Nomadic	Pastoralism	Three levels
MIDOBI	Sudan	0.45376486	Seminomad	Pastoralism	One level
MINIANKA	Mali	0.97587131	Impermanent	Extensive Agric.	Two levels
MONDARI	South Sudan	0.66123557	Semisedentary	Extensive Agric.	No levels
MORO	Sudan	0.81879195	Hamlets	Intensive Agric.	No levels
MOROCCANS	Morocco	0.82497542	Impermanent	Intensive Agric.	Four levels
MORU	South Sudan	0.90816327	Dispersed Homesteads	Extensive Agric.	One level
MUTAIR	Saudi Arabia	0	Nomadic	Pastoralism	One level
MZAB	Algeria	0.02699598	Impermanent	Intensive Agric.	No levels
NAIL	Algeria	0.40347924	Seminomad	Pastoralism	One level
NONO	Mali	0.75585284	Impermanent	Intensive Agric.	One level
NUER	South Sudan	0.3122449	Seminomad	Pastoralism	No levels
NYARO	Sudan	0.64821067	Not recorded	Unknown Agric.	Not recorded
NYIMA	Sudan	0.98660415	Hamlets	Intensive Agric.	No levels
OTORO	Sudan	0.81848627	Hamlets	Intensive Agric.	One level
PARI	South Sudan	0.62151123	Not recorded	Unknown Agric.	Not recorded

QASHGAI	Iran	0.22178478	Nomadic	Pastoralism	Two levels
REGEIBAT	Mauritania	0	Seminomad	Pastoralism	Three levels
RIFFIANS	Morocco	0.90924512	Impermanent	Intensive Agric.	One level
RWALA	Syria	0.26810293	Nomadic	Pastoralism	One level
SAADI	Egypt	0.00407056	Seminomad	Pastoralism	One level
SAHEL	Tunisia	0.57123656	Impermanent	Intensive Agric.	Three levels
SANUSI	Libya	0.2125	Seminomad	Pastoralism	Three levels
SARA	Chad	0.97774781	Dispersed Homesteads	Extensive Agric.	No levels
SERER	Mali	0.84860558	Dispersed Homesteads	Extensive Agric.	Two levels
SHAWIYA	Algeria	0.7058011	Semisedentary	Intensive Agric.	Not recorded
SHILLUK	Sudan	0.42489851	Hamlets	Extensive Agric.	One level
SHLUH	Morocco	0.17484177	Hamlets	Intensive Agric.	One level
SHUWA	Chad	0.84282277	Nomadic	Pastoralism	Two levels
SIWANS	Egypt	0	Complex settlements	Intensive Agric.	One level
SOMALI	Somalia	0.16609939	Nomadic	Pastoralism	Two levels
SONGHAI	Mali	0.02761341	Impermanent	Intensive Agric.	Three levels
SONINKE	Niger	0.69225678	Impermanent	Extensive Agric.	Two levels
SURI	South Sudan	0.63265306	Impermanent	Extensive Agric.	One level
SYRIANS	Syria	0.81841432	Impermanent	Intensive Agric.	Two levels
TAZARAWA	Niger	0.95418327	Impermanent	Extensive Agric.	Two levels
TEDA	Chad	0	Seminomad	Intensive Agric.	One level
TEKNA	Morocco	0.00087336	Semisedentary	Intensive Agric.	One level
TIGON	Niger	0.05373526	Impermanent	Extensive Agric.	No levels
TIGRE	Eritrea	0.05913978	Seminomad	Pastoralism	One level
TIRA	Sudan	0.81879195	Hamlets	Intensive Agric.	One level
TOPOTHA	South Sudan	0.6827774	Semisedentary	Pastoralism	One level

Table 7.3 (*cont.*)

Ethnic group	Country	Agricultural suitability	Settlement patterns	Subsistence economy	Jurisdictional authority
TRARZA	Mauritania	0.00838415	Seminomad	Pastoralism	Three levels
TULLISHI	Sudan	0.98660415	Hamlets	Extensive Agric.	One level
TUNISIANS	Tunisia	0.91442155	Impermanent	Intensive Agric.	Four levels
TURKS	Turkey	0.82967667	Impermanent	Intensive Agric.	Three levels
UDALAN	Mali	0.21776316	Nomadic	Intensive Agric.	Two levels
YEMENI	Yemen	0	Impermanent	Intensive Agric.	Three levels
ZEKARA	Morocco	0.53880407	Semisedentary	Mixed Economy	Two levels
ZENAGA	Mauritania	0.21377518	Seminomad	Pastoralism	Two levels
ZERMA	Niger	0.99598662	Impermanent	Intensive Agric.	Two levels

(6) separated hamlets, forming a single community, (7) compact and relatively permanent settlements, and (8) complex settlements. While 36 percent of MENA ethnic groups are coded as nomadic or seminomadic, 56 percent are coded as sedentary.

Pastoralism is measured as Animal Husbandry. This is an index based on the percentage of subsistence coming from animal husbandry for each ethnicity at colonization. For example, the index equals 0 when there is 0%–5% dependence and 9 when there is 86%–100% dependence. According to the Ethnographic Atlas's Subsistence Economy variable, 33.6 percent of the MENA's ethnic groups are coded as having a predominantly pastoral economy. In the MENA, the vast majority of this pastoralism has centered on camel herding, as was discussed in Chapter 4.

Tribalism is measured as Jurisdictional Hierarchy Beyond the Local Community. This is a metric of political complexity that is inversely correlated with how tribal the ethnic group's social structure is. This variable ranges from 0 to 4 and reveals how many jurisdictional levels exist in each group beyond the local level. 0 denotes fully stateless societies, 1 denotes petty chiefdoms, 2 denotes large chiefdoms, 3 denotes states, and 4 denotes large states.

Figures 7.11 through 7.13 are added variable plots that visually represent the results of OLS regressions which evaluate the relationship between Agricultural Suitability and Nomadism, Pastoralism, and Tribalism, respectively. Each regression controls for country-fixed effects by introducing a series of dummy variables for twenty-three MENA countries.[33] Therefore, the Y-axes measure the residuals of the dependent variable regressed against the country dummies and the X-axes measure the residuals of Agricultural Suitability regressed against the country dummies.[34]

The results of these analyses are consistent with those obtained from the country-level regressions (Figures 7.8–7.10). Agricultural Suitability is positively correlated with more settled communities – and, hence, less nomadism – *within* MENA countries. It is also negatively correlated with a greater reliance on animal husbandry – and, hence, less

---

[33] A dummy variable that codes South Sudan is also included. Because of missing data on the dependent variables, the number of ethnic groups is reduced below 122 across these regressions.

[34] The standard errors are clustered by country to address heteroskedasticity and the possibility that these variables are systematically correlated within countries.

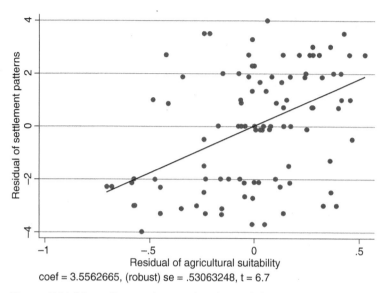

coef = 3.5562665, (robust) se = .53063248, t = 6.7

Figure 7.11 Nomadism and agricultural suitability among MENA ethnic groups.

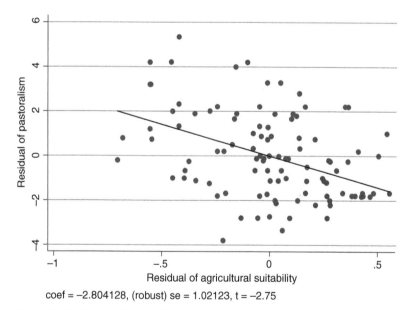

coef = −2.804128, (robust) se = 1.02123, t = −2.75

Figure 7.12 Pastoralism and agricultural suitability among MENA ethnic groups.

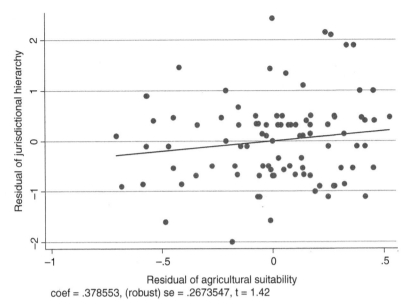

Figure 7.13 Tribalism and agricultural suitability among MENA ethnic groups.

pastoralism. Finally, Agricultural Suitability is positively correlated with political centralization and, thus, less tribalism. In short, in places in which settled agriculture is infeasible, pastoral nomadism and tribalism is more likely. This conclusion adds confidence to the inter-country correlations between precipitation and tribalism outlined above.

The importance of tribalism

Before testing the relationship between rainfall, tribalism, and monarchy, let us briefly consider the reasons *why* the creation and consolidation of monarchical political cultures should be strengthened by tribal social structures. A tribe is a kinship group, extended family, or coalition of families (Lapidus 1990, p. 26). Tribes are also political entities. They are alliances forged among fractionalized rural populations with identifiable ruling structures. Tribal authority is often based on consensus and moral authority (Eleftheriadou 2012, p. 8). Representative councils are deputized to make collective decisions. Tribal chiefs, who achieve their status and legitimacy on the basis of descent, bellicosity, or spiritual *bona fides*, sit at the pinnacle of these organizations. In the MENA monarchies, tribalism remains the basis of group identity, as well as the lifeblood of the social and political system.

The MENA monarchies have capitalized on this fact. Tribal membership regulates interactions within and outside of royal families. Consider Saudi Arabia, where "the royal family has become a cluster of tribal segments; it is heavily intermarried and bound by its elite interests" (Khoury and Kostiner 1990, p. 16). While the Saudi royal family is itself a relatively recent construction, it is based on networks of Bedouin tribes that predate Islam. Similarly, in Morocco the Alawite dynasty, which dates back to 1660, is vested in ancient Berber tribes – albeit ones that were substantially Arabicized during the spread of Islam.

Royal families have also exploited the salience of tribal pedigree to generate legitimacy and allegiance. Ruling elites claim to descend from so-called pure tribes (*asil*), and the distinction between pure and impure tribes is rooted in ancient differences between Bedouin nomads. Whereas higher status camel breeders are lionized, lower status sheep herders are derided. These status distinctions have endured long after sedentarization. Rural and less educated tribes continue to occupy the lower rungs of the ladder and defer to higher status tribes.

Finally, state building efforts across the MENA's monarchic regimes were often centered on the mobilization and co-optation of ancient tribes. Tribal chiefs played an active role during British rule and operated as parallel governments.[35] They were instrumental in consolidating rule and legitimizing central authority. Tribes helped maintain law and order in the hinterland, assisted governments in collecting taxes, and guaranteed the safe passage of government convoys. Without relinquishing their special political status, tribal chiefs also helped new states gradually take shape in the wake of colonialism. They helped monarchs assert control over security, employment, education, welfare, and dispute resolution.

The participation in state building by MENA tribes has had lingering effects. Jordan's legislative council is still organized according to tribal membership. This allows *shaykhs* to monopolize the representation of their respective tribes in any dealings with the government (Alon 2005, p. 223). In Saudi Arabia, tribal leaders have been elected to local

---

[35] This paragraph builds on Alon (2005, pp. 212–228).

government positions and act as spokesmen (*sayyid*) for their respective tribes. In both countries the armed forces are also organized along tribal lines.

Tribalism also became more clan-based and web-like over time. The reason is that monarchs incentivized a tribal social structure. A relevant example is Jordan. King Abdullah strengthened tribal identities and values by observing tribal traditions. He projected himself as a tribal chief, camped with Bedouin caravans across the country, and exchanged gifts and tribal hospitality with his subjects (see Alon 2005).

MENA non-monarchies and modernization

Conversely, in the MENA's non-monarchies tribalism was gradually replaced by nationalism. Variegated reforms launched by the Ottomans during the nineteenth century helped to modernize militaries, governance structures, and economies. Ironically, these reforms helped to plant the seeds of the empire's destruction when the British later allied with Arab armies to expunge the Turks from the MENA.[36] After World War II, urban elites undertook state-building projects centered on socialism under the aegis of Soviet military, political, and financial support.

One of the objectives of these enterprises was to stamp out tribal allegiances. In Turkey, Egypt, and Persia, local rulers (sultans, khedives, and shahs, respectively) introduced modernizing reforms during the nineteenth century in a concerted effort to narrow the gap with the West (see Kuran 2008). This came at the expense of their connections to a tribal past. Lewis (2005, p. 42) writes that:

Modernizing meant introducing Western systems of communication, warfare, and rule, inevitably including the tools of domination and repression. The authority of the state vastly increased with the adoption of instruments of control, surveillance, and enforcement far beyond the capabilities of earlier leaders [...] [the] result of modernization was the

---

[36] The ancestors of some of today's monarchs directly helped the British expel the Ottomans. Sharif Hussein bin Ali, who headed the Hashemite dynasty, and had curated several tribal alliances in the western Arabian Peninsula (the *Hejaz*), proved eminently useful to the British in providing manpower and support. His reward: after the Ottoman withdrawal at the end of World War I, Hussein's sons were crowned the heads of two newly liberated territories: Faisal governed Iraq and Abdullah ruled Transjordan.

abrogation of the intermediate powers in society – the landed gentry, the city merchants, the tribal chiefs, and others – which in the traditional order had effectively limited the authority of the state. These intermediate powers were gradually weakened and mostly eliminated, so that [...] the state was getting stronger and more pervasive.

After World War II, tribes were persecuted and subjugated (see Alon 2005, p. 235). This was especially pronounced under the *Baaths* in Syria and Iraq, Nasser in Egypt, and Bourguiba and Ben Ali in Tunisia (Eleftheriadou 2012, p. 3). In Iran, the Qajar and Pahlavi governments deployed the army to terrorize tribal groups (Khoury and Kostiner 1990, p. 14).

In the absence of a strong tribal social structure, monarchies were eventually dismantled in Iran, Iraq, and Egypt. These monarchical collapses came on the heels of anticolonial and independence movements that sought to mobilize urban constituents who were receptive to nationalistic, socialist, and pan-Arab appeals. In Egypt, General Nasser ousted King Farouk and put an end to indirect British military control and political influence. He promptly nationalized the Suez Canal and pursued many public works with Soviet support. Egypt and Syria then merged in 1958 to form the Arab Republic. Motivated by these events, Arab nationalists perpetrated a coup against King Faisal II in Iraq and the Yemeni monarchy in 1962.

The relationship between geography, tribalism, and monarchy

Having reviewed the logic at the heart of monarchical exceptionalism, we can now evaluate the rest of the causal mechanism empirically. First, I expect to find a relationship between the geographical conditions that make tribalism possible – rainfall – and monarchy. Second, I also expect to find a relationship between tribalism and monarchy.

Figure 7.14 plots bar graphs that depict MENA countries' average annual level of precipitation by regime type. As expected, the eight contemporary monarchies have considerably lower levels of rainfall than the non-monarchies. The average level of rainfall for the monarchies is only 153.9; for the non-monarchies it is 407.3. Moreover, the standard deviation for the monarchies is only 110.1, while it is 236.5 for the non-monarchies. The latter are countries that experienced settled agriculture for millennia and had built more sophisticated social and political structures than countries such as Morocco, Jordan, and the Gulf monarchies.

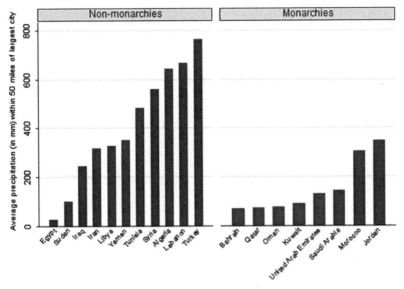

Figure 7.14 Precipitation in MENA countries, by regime type.

The data also bear the second claim out. Figure 7.15 plots bar graphs that depict MENA countries' nomadic tribalism index (using the CPP version) by regime type. Generally, the contemporary monarchies have higher levels of nomadic tribalism than the non-monarchies. While the average nomadic tribal score for the monarchies is 1.9 (with a standard deviation of 0.89), for the non-monarchies it is 1 (with a standard deviation of 1). The results are similar if nomadic tribalism is instead measured as the EB index. The average nomadic tribal score for the monarchies using this measure is 4.4 (with a standard deviation of 2.5); for non-monarchies it is 3.6 (with a standard deviation of 2.1).

Self-reinforcing monarchy

To test the claim that tribalism has been reinforced over time, Figure 7.16 depicts a scatterplot of sixteen MENA countries' contemporary EB nomadic tribalism index against a nineteenth century nomadic tribalism index. The EB index is used because the EB contains descriptions of both countries' contemporary social structures and their (recent) historical social structures. Arrayed on the Y-axis are the country values for the contemporary index of nomadic tribalism. Arrayed on the X-axis are the historical country values for a cognate

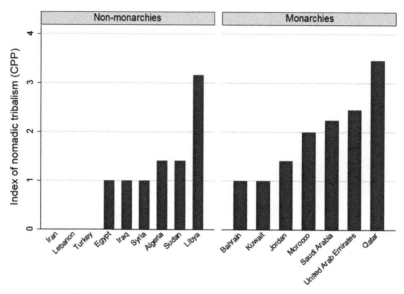

Figure 7.15 Tribalism in MENA countries, by regime type.

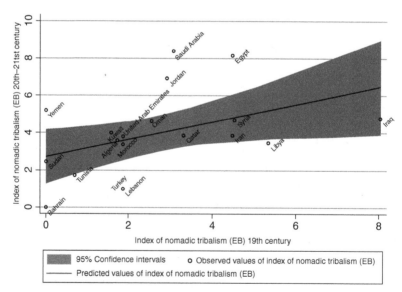

Figure 7.16 Contemporary tribalism against historical tribalism.

index of nomadic tribalism that captures countries' social structure during the nineteenth century.[37] The fitted values generated from a bivariate OLS regression of the contemporary nomadic tribalism index against the nineteenth-century nomadic tribalism index is juxtaposed on top of this scatterplot. They are flanked by upper and lower 95 percent confidence bounds.[38]

The relationship between countries' social structure in the nineteenth century and their contemporary social structure supports the idea that tribalism has been reinforced over time by monarchical regimes. The slope of the regression line is sharply positive with relatively narrow confidence intervals. Moreover, for six out of eight monarchies, nomadic tribalism has become a more salient way of describing the social structure today versus the nineteenth century. These countries are Jordan, Kuwait, Oman, Qatar, Saudi Arabia, and the U.A.E. Also consistent with the theory is the fact that, in the vast majority of cases, the republic's contemporary tribalism scores are *lower* than their historical scores.

Conclusion

This chapter helps gain purchase on the political instability that buffeted the MENA during the Arab Spring. The region's monarchies largely elided turmoil and violence. The "republics" did not. This chapter shows that this has been the case historically too. Furthermore, the association between political stability and monarchy is not driven by oil wealth; nor does it explain why monarchies have higher quality institutions, greater educational attainment, and faster economic growth.

To help understand why there is a correlation between monarchy and these outcomes in the MENA, this chapter introduces a theory about how an invented, yet historically rooted, political culture can solve a ruler's credible commitment problem, thus securing the rights

---

[37] The weighting scheme of the historical nomadic tribalism index is identical to the contemporary one. The word counts of the following terms (in parentheses) are aggregated as follows: square root[(tribe)/2+(tribal)+(clan)+(nomad)*3+(Bedouin)*2].

[38] The standard errors/confidence intervals are heteroskedasticity consistent (estimated using White robust standard errors). The results are similar with a Tobit approach.

and interests of the elite. It illustrates the evolution of this political culture over the MENA's history. I document the geographic and biogeographic underpinnings of monarchy, arguing that aridity and pastoral nomadism sustained a tribal social structure over millennia, despite imperialism, the spread of Islam, and European colonialism.

However, many important questions are left unanswered. Perhaps the most important one is whether the MENA monarchies, many of which have experienced significant political reforms since the Arab Spring, will eventually democratize. Any firm prediction is elusive. In the Gulf's hydrocarbon rich demesnes, for example, the highest standards of living on earth go hand-in-hand with strong tribal identities and pre-modern values. In Morocco, they still adore their king.

What about the prospects for democracy in the region's non-monarchies? In Syria, Egypt, and Algeria, secularism and nationalism continue to predominate – notwithstanding major inroads made by the Muslim Brotherhood in the Egyptian case and the recent success of the Islamic State in Syria. Yet this chapter showed that these modernizing tendencies are often coupled with polarization and the seeds of political instability. Moreover, these are relatively poor countries. Therefore, it is quite hard to predict how things will play out in these regimes as well. As with everything else: only time will tell.

8 | *Conclusions*

This book was inspired by three big puzzles. Each of them challenges the resource curse, the theory that oil and minerals harm state capacity, democracy, and economic development. The first is that state building and industrialization in the Western world was, to a large extent, ignited by the exploration and production of coal, minerals, and oil. The second puzzle is that, after the 1973 oil shock, new oil producers in the developing world registered big improvements in key political, economic, and social indicators. The third is that hydrocarbon-reliant countries in the Middle East are no worse off today than they were before they discovered oil and are no worse off than their oil-poor neighbors.

Notwithstanding these puzzles, resource reliance is correlated with several pathologies in the developing world. Consider the following data points. Oil-dependent Venezuela is bedeviled by rampant poverty, as well as political and social unrest. Oil-dependent Nigeria is afflicted by environmental degradation, corruption, and political violence. Oil- and gas-dependent Russia is a nasty kleptocracy that increasingly threatens its neighbors, if not world peace. Saudi Arabia, the world's largest oil producer, is ruled as a quasi-theocracy; it is one of the few places on earth where citizens have no say over their political destiny and women live under an Apartheid-like system. Angola, Iran, and Congo, all heavily dependent on natural resources, are poster children for human rights abuses and repression.

What has not been convincingly shown hitherto is if these correlations are causal. Without resorting to an explanation where the causal arrow runs from the former to the latter, this book attempted to make sense of the cross-national association between natural resources and underdevelopment. I explored the idea that, rather than a resource curse, what oil- and mineral-reliant countries suffer from is an institutions curse. Resource reliance is not an unmediated result of oil and minerals that fall like manna from heaven. It is instead endogenous to weak states with low-quality institutions. And it is these institutions that attract capital to natural-resource sectors and incentivize the exploration and production of oil and minerals, as well as its taxation and exportation. Weak state capacity also explains why many developing countries indulge in regressive taxation on inelastic consumer goods and crony capitalism, whether they are resource abundant or not.

This book argued that underlying political institutions, ultimately rooted in climate and agricultural legacies, are the real explanation for contemporary differences in development. Legacies endemic to Western Europe and their settler offshoots were rooted in grain agriculture practiced at a small scale. By endowing states with credibility and by reducing fiscal transaction costs, they nurtured political, administrative, and economic development. Conversely, many developing countries inherited a different set of legacies, which were often rooted in large plantations or the absolute lack of settled agriculture. By engendering thorny commitment problems and raising the transaction costs of taxing the economy, they ultimately encouraged elites to cultivate their natural-resource sectors. While these institutions foreclosed modern and diversified economies, they fomented authoritarianism, economic stagnation, state weakness, and other ills unduly attributed to minerals and oil. This book demonstrated that several victims of this institutions curse can still be found in Latin America and the Middle East.

Yet, this book also argued that natural resources can play an integral role in stimulating state capacity, capitalism, industrialization, and democracy, even if resources are themselves often a symptom of underdevelopment. Once one neutralizes the confounding effect of institutions, the resource curse disappears. Oil rents do not displace ordinary government revenues, nor are they causally associated with the underprovision of public goods, dictatorship, poor institutional quality, and barriers to capitalism. In fact, it is the opposite; despite being cursed by their institutions, which induces them to focus on natural resources in the first place, weak states are subsequently blessed by oil.

The stakes involved in the debate between the resource curse and the alternative view of development advanced in this book could not be higher. Natural resources are among the most capital intensive sectors on earth, and billions of people depend on the rents and foreign exchange generated by the export of hydrocarbons and minerals to survive. Yet, because of the mistaken belief that natural resources are exogenous, empirical research on the impact of minerals and oil on political and economic development has all too often been centered on unsound inferences. A burgeoning consensus that resources are a curse quickly endowed anecdotes and correlations with law-like qualities usually reserved for findings in the natural sciences. The resource curse is taken as a self-evident truth at multilateral aid organizations, presented as a robust fact in popular books and disseminated widely in the media.

In adducing evidence for both an institutions curse and a resource blessing, perhaps this book will offset some of the unfounded phobia about the metals and fuels that subsidize our modern lifestyles. Or perhaps it might at least trigger a much needed debate. I also hope that this book can open up frontiers for further research into the causes and consequences of development. Future investigations can proceed from two puzzles intimated by the book's argument and key findings.

New frontiers in the study of development

The first puzzle relates to whether multinational firms involved in the extractive industry can continue to engage in a race-to-the-bottom: locate in tax and pollution havens in a bid to protect their interests and bolster their profits. Do countries that are cursed by their institutions, but that subsequently modernize because of their natural resources, graduate beyond their reliance on an oil- and mineral-intensive economy? When these states grow stronger, do extractive industries eventually leave town, moving onto weaker states where they can exploit laxer fiscal and regulatory regimes? And does this eventually prompt yet another exit by oil and mining firms to browner pastures once the resource blessing kicks in again? If so, what will happen when these firms one day run out of weak states?

The second puzzle is about how to make sense of the venerable, but potentially flawed, fiscal contract paradigm. The resource curse derives from the idea that democracy, the rule of law, and public goods are exchanged by rulers for tax revenues and nationalistic loyalty. The strong version of this theory postulates that the constant threat of war drove European state development and democratization, and that the lack of wars in other continents is responsible for their political and economic underdevelopment. This chapter broaches several reasons why this view of the world, although quite popular, might be wrongheaded.

Ultimately, this chapter does not attempt to give definitive answers to these puzzles. Rather, it fleshes them out in great detail and offers a few insights to help guide future research.

Graduating up the production chain?

Do oil and mineral producers that grow wealthier and more democratic over time and that develop better legal institutions eventually outgrow their dependence on natural resources? What does this mean for multinational firms involved in extractive industries? Do they exploit a race-to-the-bottom dynamic in which states that grow stronger are abandoned for weaker ones?

Future research that addresses these questions might take the Environmental Kuznets Curve (EKC) hypothesis as its point of departure. This is the contention that the world's poorest countries tend to prioritize economic growth over environmental protection and thus pass through a resource intensive growth phase; yet, as they develop, they eventually switch gears and pursue growth models that are less likely to produce environmental damage and negative spillovers.

This hypothesis has received substantial empirical corroboration. For example, while Grossman and Krueger (1995) uncover an inverted U-shaped relationship between Per Capita Income and urban air pollution and water pollution, Selden and Song (1994) discover the same pattern for sulfur dioxide, suspended particulate matter, and carbon monoxide (see also Hilton and Levinson 1998 for evidence regarding other emissions). More appositely, Bimonte (2001) identifies a Kuznets Curve in the case of the proportion of protected land and protected biospheres as a share of total national territory.

This book also weighed in on why there might be an EKC. As Chapter 5 argued, mining and oil firms actively seek to do business in weak states in a bid to better protect their rights and bolster their profits. Chapter 6 made clear that the countries that host these firms may eventually undergo legal reforms and policy improvements by dint of their natural resources. Fearing higher taxes and more stringent environmental, safety, and labor regulations, multinational corporations operating in jurisdictions that experience resource blessings might therefore relocate to weaker states at earlier phases of resource extraction. Extractive firms' constant search for reliable tax and pollution havens may help explain why, beyond a certain threshold, there is a negative relationship between Per Capita Income and environmental damage and pollution.

Indeed, one might say that this is the story of how international oil and mining companies abandoned many developed countries, beginning in the mid-to-late twentieth century. Seeking to protect their rights and interests in light of more demanding publics who pined for greener and healthier landscapes and policymakers who sought to extract higher revenues from hydrocarbon and mining, these firms escaped to the browner pastures and smoke stacks of the developing world (see Potoski and Prakash 2013). It is partly for this reason that the majority of extractive activities now occur in the Global South.

A related reason for the EKC may be that oil and mineral producers may actively seek to graduate up the resource value chain. They might therefore eschew the production of raw commodities. For example, countries may instead seek to specialize in exporting refined minerals. Such is the case of Indonesia.[1] In January of 2014, the Indonesian government banned the exports of mineral ores – mostly copper, nickel, and bauxite – while still allowing processed minerals to be sold abroad. This was an explicit attempt to court investment in smelters and refiners; the Indonesian state's overriding objective is to both add value to its exports and encourage greater economic linkages. Indeed, consider that aluminum adds approximately 94 percent of final value to bauxite; the refining and smelting of ores requires processing plants, power plants, ports, and roads. In the Indonesian case, billions of dollars have already poured in from abroad to defray the costs of building these new smelting plants and their associated infrastructure.

By the same token, mineral producers often seek to diversify their economy further away from mining, while also reducing their reliance on coal and petroleum. This is usually only after their natural resources have helped them improve their legal and political institutions, however, as well as bolster their physical and human capital. While past examples of this dynamic include the United States, a contemporary example is China, which is pursuing investments that will dramatically reduce the share of energy it derives from coal and is working on

---

[1] This section draws extensively from *The Economist*, January 18, 2014.

making its electricity grid more efficient. Meanwhile, the construction of high-speed rail and subway systems continues at a break neck pace and the Chinese government is pressing forward with a campaign to expand cap-and-trade throughout the country (see Gross 2014).

What does this have to do with the EKC? Because countries that have experienced the resource blessing also tend to grow wealthier, this mechanism may help account for the inverted U-shaped relationship between Per Capita Income and environmental stewardship. This intuition accords with a more nuanced version of the theory. Whereas an earlier generation of work on the EKC held that improvements in production technologies account for the reduction in pollution as countries become richer, newer research argues that political institutions might be the channel by which higher levels of Per Capita income map onto a cleaner environment. Countries that become more democratic and better governed over time are willing and able to translate the public's desire for a greener nation into action (see Frankel and Rose 2005).

This excursus on the EKC cannot tell us whether it is inevitable that multinational firms involved in extractive industries will continue to seek out weak states to do business in. Let alone whether they will one day run out of weak states. Even so, any race-to-the-bottom dynamic in today's world is complicated by a host of factors. If international mining and oil companies would indeed like to head for the exits in natural resource producing states that have grown stronger over time, it is not clear that they will be able to continue to do so indefinitely.

Taking a proactive stance

Developing countries dedicated to the production and export of natural resources are not necessarily waiting for a resource blessing to kick in. Instead, they are busy attempting to promote transparency and accountability even in the face of serious political, legal, and administrative weaknesses. Specifically, many developing countries have signed up to the Extractive Industries Transparency Initiative (EITI) and adopted laws that promote corporate social responsibility and foster local development.

The EITI is a voluntary, multilateral system that strives to cultivate an institutional framework to properly manage natural resources. Its nuts and bolts include espousing the adoption of seemingly simple things such as computerized license and cadastral systems and record-keeping, revenue-management systems, and the training of government employees.[2]

To be designated as EITI compliant, a country must satisfy twenty-one requirements, each of them quite stringent. These include completing a validation audit within two and a half years of becoming a candidate and undergoing validation every five years after becoming a candidate. The validation process is overseen by a multi-stakeholder consortium that guarantees that EITI standards are met. Participation also requires both firms and member countries to publish EITI reports in a timely manner. While extractive industry companies publish what they pay in revenues to host governments, governments disclose the revenues they receive. EITI participation also calls on contract disclosure in general, which helps government agencies, citizens, and NGOs monitor and inspect extractive sectors in the developing world.

Several anecdotes speak to the EITI's success. Member countries such as Sierra Leone have set up detailed websites that disclose information on mining licenses and revenues. This has allowed multiple stakeholders to identify any discrepancies between the minerals that are produced and the ultimate taxes that are collected. This information has also encouraged some states to adopt new mining taxes. Moreover, resource revenue transparency has increasingly been taken seriously because of EITI at the local, national, and global levels. While several members have passed national laws requiring the transparent management of natural resource revenues, EITI standards have been extrapolated to other resource sectors like forestry. And, in places like Liberia, Sao Tome, Nigeria, and Ghana, EITI has brought together diverse stakeholders who may not otherwise have come together. In turn, this has helped cauterize tensions in post-conflict contexts and fostered debates on transparent governance.

Similar to EITI are laws adopted by mineral-rich countries that promote social betterment and environmental safeguards. These laws

---

[2] There are many possible motives that influence membership. Donors and civil society organizations often pressure poor states to join, and these groups are often located in the developed world (see Aaronson 2011). This is consistent with the vast literature on how stakeholders in the Global North scrutinize the behavior of their national firms abroad to promote environmental protection and other social goods that they value (see Prakash and Potoski 2007). This may help explain why trade can sometimes help importers in OECD countries transmit environmental standards to exporters in the developing world (Perkins and Neumyaer 2012).

often take the form of Community Development Requirements (CDR). Since 2000, thirty-two countries have passed new CDR laws or amended existing ones. Several others are in the midst of adopting these laws.[3]

Written into national mining codes, CDRs are aimed at ensuring that local communities affected by extractive operations benefit from these activities. They often prescribe firms – and in some cases, local or national governments – to carry out development projects in mining areas. These projects include infrastructure and social services.[4] CDR laws sometimes mandate that firms develop community-development plans themselves and submit them to governments when applying for mining licenses.

CDR laws involve two types of agreements: *Mineral or Mining Development Agreements* and *Community Development Agreements*. *Mineral or Mining Development Agreements* are legally binding contracts between governments and mining firms that outline the mineral rights that the latter is entitled to along with its responsibilities to community development and environmental clean-up. *Community Development Agreements* are private agreements between mining firms and local communities. They are sometimes legally binding.

Ghana is a representative example of what CDR laws can potentially achieve. Ghanaian law encourages mining firms to build infrastructure in the locations in which they operate and to promote social development. Also, the country's environmental protection agency rates these firms' corporate social performance. In the past, two domestic mining companies, Prestea Sankofo Gold Limited and Ghana Bauxite Company, have been graded as "inadequate." Conversely, several major multinational mining firms that were found to fully comply with Ghanaian law earned a so-called gold rating. This system has helped to promote accountability.

Yet, the jury is still out on whether EITIs and CDR laws can and should arrest race-to-the-bottom dynamics in the developing world. Fulfilling EITI's auditing requirements is costly, and donor states have set aside insufficient funding for EITI technical assistance programs. Additionally, EITI is not equipped to directly reduce corruption in the

---

[3] See Dupuy (2015) for a diffusion-based explanation, in which the dissemination of social responsibility norms at the global level occurs via international institutions, actors, and financial flows.

[4] This section draws heavily on Dupuy (2014).

extractives sector. It does not govern the allocation of exploration and mining rights to companies, nor how contracts are written and who they benefit. Moreover, EITI does not address revenue collection problems, such as corrupt and incompetent tax bureaucracies.

Finally, while CDR laws might look great on paper, it is often difficult for weak states to implement them in ways that actually benefit the people who are most needy at the local level. On the one hand, this may mean monitoring the behavior of multibillion dollar corporations operating in territorial peripheries that only care about obtaining good publicity but not following through with their obligations. Alas, these firms usually possess better information than national governments about what is actually going on there. On the other hand, the benefits of development and infrastructure programs may be captured by local elites.

Future research is required to address these issues. While their normative and policy implications are straightforward, the list of possible answers is no longer as clear. The idea that natural resources are a curse should no longer suffice as an adequate lens by which to evaluate these questions. New theoretical and empirical approaches will have to take its place.

Whither the fiscal contract?

The second outstanding puzzle summoned by this book is centered on the fiscal contract paradigm of state building and democracy. The resource-curse theory is predicated on the axiom that oil and minerals are anathema to the fiscal contract that typically characterizes the relationship between rulers and their citizens. The logic put forth is that hydrocarbon extraction and mining is centered on fixed assets that generate unearned revenues. That these rents can be captured rather easily by government means that resource-reliant countries miss out on a powerful state-building engine, as well as an important catalyst of democratization. Namely, the bargaining process whereby rulers reciprocate the revenues they collect from citizens with rights and benefits, such as the provision of public goods and political representation. This is especially true when capital is mobile and investors have the option of exiting political jurisdictions that offer inadequate concessions in exchange for the taxes they are compelled to pay.

Irrespective of what it has to say about the political and economic effects of natural resources, the fiscal contract paradigm is quite popular (see, for example, Bates and Lien 1985; Beard and Lewis 1932; Dincecco 2009; Levi 1988; and Tilly 1975). There are several potential reasons why. One of them is that it takes as its starting point the genesis of these social compacts. Over the *longue durée*, bargaining between rulers and the ruled was sparked by the preparation for and the waging of wars. Specifically, political entrepreneurs who sought to conquer and govern territory in Western Europe in the aftermath of feudalism had to resort to taxing their subjects to finance military campaigns. The same held true for sovereigns who were less acquisitive, but nonetheless found themselves amassing large armies to defend their realms against interlopers.

Another possible reason why the fiscal contract paradigm is popular is that it is a structural argument that can subsume a variety of different motives. Europe's variegated city states and kingdoms faced a Darwinian struggle. Those states that were more adept at raising revenues, and which could therefore finance large and formidable armies, tended to be those that survived – either because they acquired strategically valuable territory or because they deterred unwanted invasions. More often than not, however, this was not a function of military acumen, as much as fortuitous experimentation: if tax revenues were exchanged for the right mix of concessions, this tended to improve fiscal compliance, if not persuade citizens to enlist in their nation's armed forces and fight and die for newly constituted states. Political units that could not find a way to do this – or do it as effectively – were eventually weeded out of the international system. In short, permanent taxation on a mass scale proved to be the preeminent military advantage, but this consequence may not have been fully anticipated.

Yet another reason for the popularity of the fiscal contract view is that it potentially explains contemporary variation in state capacity and democratization between different world regions. If the story outlined above explains why the European continent was the birthplace of capable and eventually democratic states after the Peace of Westphalia, the reverse image is often summoned as the reason for the inveterate administrative weakness and democratic deficit that characterizes other regions. Consider Centeno's (2002) analysis of state building in Latin America. He argues that during their creation and consolidation phase, the region's states avoided European style "total wars." Although Latin American nations were the scene of myriad rebellions and civil wars, these conflicts were not associated with the type of political and military mobilization that requires permanent taxation and conscription. In turn, this obviated the fiscal bargains between rulers and ruled that strengthen state capacity and democracy. Financial and personal sacrifices were never demanded from citizens, so citizens never demanded anything from their sovereigns.

There is anecdotal evidence that seems to support the fiscal contract paradigm. Bismarck viewed the extension of suffrage to the lower classes as a powerful weapon against Austria (see Przeworski 2009, p. 305). In Sweden, debates about enfranchisement at the turn of the twentieth century were centered on national defense. Political elites believed that conscription would be more palatable if it was accompanied by political rights. The slogan coined by the Social Democratic Party "one man, one vote, one gun" embodied this sentiment. Similarly, "English soldiers returning from World War I won the right to vote and even welfare benefits in 'a land fit for heroes' " (Downing 1992, p. 253).

Other evidence is more systematic. Kiser and Linton (2001) provide quantitative evidence for the relationship between wars and tax revenues for both France and England between the fourteenth and sixteen centuries. Scheve and Stasavage (2012) argue that increased fiscal capacity among European countries, fueled by taxes levied on the wealthiest citizens, was a direct result of the mobilization for war during World War I. There is even evidence that war-making fueled state building in the developing world, albeit in a more limited fashion (for example, Thies 2005; Lu and Thies 2013).

Yet, upon further evaluation, the fiscal contract view might not fully stand up to empirical scrutiny. First, consider the evidence uncovered in this book. There are no grounds to infer a negative relationship between natural resource rents and regular tax revenues, nor between the former and democratic government. Indeed, it is the opposite. In Chapter 6, I adduced evidence that exogenous increases in oil income bolster regular taxation and strengthen democracy.

Moreover, anecdotal evidence suggests that the idea that war strengthened state building and political representation in Western Europe may be wanting. Consider the canonical case that researchers who are partial to the fiscal contract view have in mind about rulers conceding representation for taxation – England after the Glorious Revolution. Upon further interrogation this is not, in fact, an example of said phenomenon. The British Crown, as North and Weingast (1989) make clear, did not trade anything in exchange for revenues – it demanded forced loans and confiscated property to fund foreign wars. It was only *after* a protracted civil war that a coalition of nobles and merchants foisted constraints upon the crown to prevent their wealth from being stolen. Higher tax revenues were only an incidental consequence of the strengthened legislature and judiciary. They were a byproduct of more secure property rights that did not precede greater representation but lagged it considerably (see Stasavage 2003). In this case, if there was a fiscal contract to speak of, it was imposed from above, and it was not intended to raise revenues *per se*.

Other cases that patently contradict the fiscal contract paradigm are Russia, China, Iran, and Turkey. These are states and empires that fought dozens and dozens of war, both against each other and against other polities. Yet they never evolved anything that resembles a fiscal contract in which rulers reciprocated citizens' tax revenues and patriotism with political representation and public goods.

Consider Russia. It was only after fighting in fifty wars since 1500 – including big and protracted struggles such as the Seven Years War (1756–63) and the Crimean War (1853–56) – that representative institutions finally arrived in 1906, when Tsar Nicolas II inaugurated the Duma. This experiment was short lived, however, as the Russian legislature was disbanded less than a year later, and was only convened again three more times until the revolution. And although Vladimir Lenin and the Bolsheviks convoked elections with universal adult suffrage in December of 1917, in the aftermath of World War I, they rigged them. Moreover, these proved to be a one-off event: the Soviet Union subsequently abandoned popular elections.

I should also note that democratic backsliding has occurred across Europe in the shadow of continent-wide warfare on several occasions – a phenomenon not anticipated by the fiscal contract paradigm (see Ticchi and Vindigni 2009). For example, in the wake of the Napoleonic Wars (1803–15) and French invasion of Spain (1823), elected governments throughout Europe faced a reactionary backlash. After the Concert of Vienna, conservatives scuttled liberal revolutions and tried to restore erstwhile monarchies under the aegis of the Holy

Alliance. This occurred in Austria, Prussia, Spain, Portugal, and Italy. Similarly, in the aftermath of World War I, fascist governments were swept into power in Spain, Portugal, Italy, and Germany, and they proceeded to dismantle representative institutions. By 1941, there were only eleven democracies left in the entire world.

Skepticism about the fiscal contract paradigm goes beyond these anecdotes. Using regression analysis, Stasavage (2010) finds that between 1250 and 1750, only relatively small states erected and maintained representative assemblies in Europe due to high transportation costs. And while this might have helped these polities survive, larger states managed to do so as well, without relying on legislatures. Indeed, Stasavage argues that it was only until the late eighteenth century that the continent's larger polities really began to adopt representative institutions. Similarly, Przeworski (2009, p. 305) does not find systematic evidence that war participation is correlated with suffrage extensions per se, although a global wave of female enfranchisement did occur in the wake of World War I.

Moreover, the fiscal contract paradigm's logic might not be completely airtight either. In a situation in which the military-cum-existential threat posed by a state's neighbors is quite high, such as that which characterized Europe's international system between circa 1500 AD and the fall of the Berlin Wall, it might be *more likely* that citizens will acquiesce to taxation *without* expecting concessions in return. After all, the incentives of the rulers and ruled are aligned: their shared objective is to repel a common enemy. Indeed, Stasavage (2010, p. 629) floats this idea to explain his finding that it was primarily Europe's smaller states that adopted and sustained legislatures before the nineteenth century.

Or consider Latin America. Contrary to popular belief, these nations were born insecure. Their governments faced constant threats to their territorial sovereignty. Consequently, they fought a lot of wars. This helps explain why military spending consumed over 70 percent of Latin American countries' budgets during most of the nineteenth century.

There are numerous examples of big, bloody, and protracted wars in this region. Between 1810 and 1870, Argentina was involved in four international conflicts, Bolivia three, Brazil three, Chile three, Colombia three, Ecuador two, Mexico five, Paraguay two, Peru four, Uruguay four, and Venezuela one. Some notable examples include Brazil's wars against Uruguay between 1825 and 1828, against

Argentina between 1851 and 1852, and against Paraguay between 1865 and 1870. Meanwhile, Mexico had to ward off an invasion by Spain in 1829, and fought against the United States between 1846 and 1848, and then against France between 1862 and 1867. Peru fought Bolivia in 1835. Chile fought against Bolivia and Peru between 1838 and 1839 and then again between 1879 and 1883 (see Coatsworth and Williamson 2004, p. 216).

Yet Latin America's rulers *ultimately failed* to engage in full-scale mobilization and permanent taxation. Instead "[w]eak governments, under attack from within and without, abandoned internal taxes that required an extensive and loyal bureaucracy and concentrated tax collection efforts instead on a few ports and mines" (Coatsworth and Williamson 2004, p. 217). The way in which these governments financed their costly and bloody wars speaks to the institutions curse theory introduced in this book. Despite persistent threats of international war, the fiscal transaction costs of direct taxation cannot simply be eliminated with the stroke of a pen by elected officials who are otherwise eager to tax their citizens, and may be entirely willing to bargain with them to extract greater revenues.

Conclusion

This book strongly implies that, besides conceptualizing state capacity as the monopolization of violence, the establishment of legitimate authority, or the erection of a modern bureaucracy, another important dimension is the provision of inclusive and secure property rights. It is only then that a country's institutions will underpin a formal economy and mature financial system capable of underwriting the low fiscal transaction costs that make modern revenue collection possible. The latter includes invasive practices and norms that both deter tax evasion and secure compliance.

Of course, achieving this equilibrium in places where there has been only political and economic backwardness may be easier said than done. Yet this book has pointed to a potential way forward. Even when countries have been cursed by their institutions, they can turn things around after being blessed by their natural resources. Whether the fiscal contract paradigm's most renowned – and troubling – empirical implication can also be debunked remains to be seen: there may or may not be a systematic relationship between the preparation for and waging of war and political, fiscal, and economic development. I hope that this book has offered good reasons to subject this thesis to renewed scrutiny.

Even if it has not, the fact that many pundits attribute some of the world's current ills to the recent dearth of mass mobilizing wars is reason enough to reconsider the fiscal contract paradigm.[5] In reevaluating the resource curse, this book has attempted to debunk it. Perhaps future research will do the same in regards to the hypothesis that war is the answer to chronic underdevelopment and stagnation.

---

[5] For example, Tyler Cowen wrote a recent Opinion Editorial for the New York Times that argues that economic sluggishness in the developed world may be due to the lack of wide-scale preparation for war that was pervasive during the Cold War (see Cowen 2014).

References

Aaronson, Susan. 2011. "Limited Partnership: Business, Government, Civil Society, and the Public in the Extractive Industries Transparency Initiative (EITI)." *Public Administration and Development* 31(1): 50–63.

Abba, Kolo, and Thomas Wälde. 2008. "Coverage of Taxation under Modern Investment Treaties." In Peter Muchlinski, Federico Ortino, and Christoph Schreuer, eds., *The Oxford Handbook of International Investment Law*. Oxford: Oxford University Press, pp. 305–362.

ABC Azerbaijan. 2009. "SOCAR-Total PSA on Absheron Block in Caspian Sea Put into Force." *ABC Azerbaijan*, May 30. Available at: http://abc .az/eng/news/35342.html.

Acemoglu, Daron, Simon Johnson, and James Robinson. 2001. "The Colonial Origins of Comparative Development: an Empirical Investigation." *American Economic Review* 91(5): 1369–1401.

2002. "Reversal of Fortune: Geography and Institutions in the Making of the Modern World Income Distribution." *Quarterly Journal of Economics* 117(4): 1231–1294.

2005. "Institutions as the Fundamental Cause of Long-Run Growth." In Philippe Aghion, and Stephen Durlauf, eds., *Handbook of Economic Growth*. London: Elsevier, pp. 385–472.

Acemoglu, Daron, and James Robinson. 2006. *Economic Origins of Dictatorship and Democracy*. New York: Cambridge University Press.

Ahlquist, John, and Aseem Prakash. 2008. "The Influence of Foreign Direct Investment on Contracting Confidence in Developing Countries." *Regulation & Governance* 2(3): 316–339.

Aidt, Toke, and Peter Jensen. 2009. "The Taxman Tools Up: an Event History Study of the Introduction of the Personal Income Tax." *Journal of Public Economics* 93(1): 160–175.

Albert, Bill. 1988. *South America and the First World War: The Impact of the War on Brazil, Argentina, Peru, and Chile*. New York: Cambridge University Press.

Albertus, Michael, and Victor Menaldo. 2012a. "If You're Against Them You're with Us: The Effect of Expropriation on Autocratic Survival." *Comparative Political Studies* 45(8): 973–1003.

2012b. "Dictators as Founding Fathers: The Role of Constitutions under Autocracy." *Economics and Politics* 24(3): 279–306.

2012c. "Coercive Capacity and the Prospects for Democratization." *Comparative Politics* 44(2): 151–169.

2014. "Gaming Democracy: Elite Dominance during Transition and the Prospects for Redistribution." *British Journal of Political Science* 44(3): 575–603.

Alexeev, Michael, and Robert Conrad. 2009. "The Elusive Curse of Oil." *The Review of Economics and Statistics* 91(3): 586–598.

Allen, Larry. 2005. *The Global Economic System Since 1945*. London: Reaktion Books.

Alm Jim, Jorge Martinez-Vazquez, and Friedrich Schneider. 2004. "'Sizing' the Problem of the Hard-to-Tax." In James Alm, Jorge Martinez-Vazquez, and Sally Wallace, eds., *Taxing the Hard-to-Tax: Lessons from Theory and Practice*. London: Elsevier, pp. 11–75.

Alon, Yoav. 2005. "The Tribal System in the Face of the State-Formation Process: Mandatory Transjordan, 1921–46." *International Journal of Middle East Studies* 37(2): 213–240.

Altstadt, Audrey. 1992. *The Azerbaijani Turks: Power and Identity under Russian Rule*. Stanford: Hoover Institution Press.

Andersen, Jørgen, and Michael Ross. 2014. "The Big Oil Change: a Closer Look at the Haber-Menaldo Analysis." *Comparative Political Studies* 47(7): 993–1021.

Anderson, Gary, and Peter Boettke. 1997. "Soviet Venality: a Rent-Seeking Model of the Communist State." *Public Choice* 93(1–2): 37–53.

Anderson, Lisa. 1987. "The State in the Middle East and North Africa." *Comparative Politics* 20(1): 1–18.

1991. "Absolutism and the Resilience of Monarchy in the Middle East." *Political Science Quarterly* 106: 1–15.

Aslaksen, Silje. 2010. "Oil and Democracy – More than a Cross-Country Correlation?" *Journal of Peace Research* 47(4): 421–431.

Astorga, Pablo, Ame Bergés, and Edmund VK FitzGerald. 2003. *The Oxford Latin American Economic History Database (OxLAD)*. The Latin American Centre, Oxford: Oxford University.

Auriol, Emmanuelle, and Michael Warlters. 2005. "Taxation Base in Developing Countries." *Journal of Public Economics* 89(4): 625–646.

Babali, Tuncay. 2005. "Implications of the Baku-Tbilisi-Ceyhan Main Oil Pipeline Project." *Perceptions* Winter: 29–59.

Bagirov, Sabit. 1996. "Azerbaijan Oil: Glimpses of a Long History." *Journal International Affairs* 1(2): 22–36.

2006. "Azerbaijan's Oil Revenues: Ways of Reducing the Risk of Ineffective Use." Working Paper. Central European University. Budapest, Hungary.

Banks, Arthur. 2009. "Cross-National Time-Series Data Archive." SUNY Binghamton. New York: Binghamton.

Bardhan, Pranab. 1993. "Symposium on Democracy and Development." *Journal of Economic Perspectives* 7(3): 45–49.

Barma, Naazneen, Kai Kaiser, and Tuan Minh Le. 2012. *The Political Economy of Natural Resource-Led Development*. Washington, DC: World Bank Publications.

Barro, Robert, and Jong-Wha Lee. 2013. "A New Dataset of Educational Attainment in the World, 1950–2010." *Journal of Development Economics* 104(September): 184–198.

Barth, James, Gerard Caprio Jr., and Ross Levine. 2006. *Rethinking Bank Regulation: Till Angels Govern*. Cambridge: Cambridge University Press.

Bates, Robert. 1981. *Markets and States in Tropical Africa*. Berkeley: University of California Press.

1991. "The Economics of Transitions to Democracy." *PS: Political Science and Politics* 24(1): 24–27.

Bates, Robert, Avner Greif, and Smita Singh. 2002. "Organizing Violence." *Journal of Conflict Resolution* 46(5): 599–628.

Bates, Robert, and Da-Hsiang Lien. 1985. "A Note on Taxation, Development, and Representative Government." *Politics and Society* 14(1): 53–70.

Baunsgaard, Thomas. 2001. "A Primer on Mineral Taxation." IMF Working Paper. Washington, DC: International Monetary Fund.

Beard, Charles, and John Lewis. 1932. "Representative Government in Evolution." *American Political Science Review* 26(2): 223–240.

Bebbington, Anthony, and Jeffrey Bury, eds. 2013. *Subterranean Struggles: New Dynamics of Mining, Oil, and Gas in Latin America*. Austin: Texas University Press.

Beblawi, Hazem, and Giacomo Luciani. 1987. "Introduction." In Hazem Beblawi, and Giacomo Luciani, eds., *The Rentier State*. London: Croom Helm, pp. 1–21.

Becerra, Oscar, Eduardo Cavallo, and Carlos Scartascini. 2012. "The Politics of Financial Development: The Role of Interest Groups and Government Capabilities." *Journal of Banking & Finance* 36(3): 626–643.

Beck, Nathaniel, Simon Jackman, and Howard Rosenthal. 2006. "Presidential Approval: The Case of George W. Bush." Unpublished Manuscript.

Beck, Thorsten, Aslı Demirgüç-Kunt, and Ross Levine. 2010. "Financial Institutions and Markets across Countries and over Time: the Updated Financial Development and Structure Database." *The World Bank Economic Review* 24(1): 77–92.

Beck, Thorsten, Ross Levine, and Norman Loayza. 2000. "Finance and the Sources of Growth." *Journal of Financial Economics* 58(1–2): 261–300.

Bell, Duran. 2004. "Evolution of Middle Eastern Social Structures: a New Model." *Social Evolution and History* 3(2): 25–54.

Bell, Imogen, ed. 2002. *Eastern Europe, Russia and Central Asia 2003*. London: Taylor & Francis.

Benson, Bruce. 1990. *The Enterprise of Law: Justice without the State*. San Francisco: Pacific Research Institute for Public Policy.

1994. "Emerging from the Hobbesian Jungle: Might Takes and Makes Rights." *Constitutional Political Economy* 5(2): 129–158.

Bentham, Richard. 1988. *State Petroleum Companies: Legal and Organizational Structure*. Dundee: CPMLPI.

Berkey, Jonathan. 2003. *The Formation of Islam: Religion and Society in the Near East, 600–1800*. New York: Cambridge University Press.

Bernstein, Peter. 2000. *The Power of Gold: the History of an Obsession*. New York: John Wiley & Sons.

Bertola, Luis, and Jeffrey Williamson. 2006. "Globalization in Latin America Before 1940." In Victor Bulmer-Thomas, John Coatsworth, and Roberto Cortes Conde, eds., *Cambridge Economic History of Latin America: the Colonial Era and the Short Nineteenth Century*. Cambridge: Cambridge University Press, pp. 11–56.

Besley, Timothy, and Torsten Persson. 2009. "The Origins of State Capacity: Property Rights, Taxation and Politics." *American Economic Review* 99(4): 1218–1244.

2012. *Pillars of Prosperity*. Princeton: Princeton University Press.

Beydoun, Ziad. 1998. "Arabian Plate Oil and Gas: Why So Rich and So Prolific?" *Episodes* 21(2): 74–81.

Bimonte, Salvatore. 2001. "Model of Growth and Environmental Quality: a New Evidence of the Environmental Kuznets Curve." Unpublished Manuscript.

Blomström, Magnuson, and Ari Kokko. 2007. "From Natural Resources to High-tech Production: the Evolution of Industrial Competitiveness in Sweden and Finland." In Daniel Lederman, and William Maloney, eds., *Natural Resources, Neither Curse nor Destiny*. Washington, DC: World Bank Publications, pp. 213–258.

Bockstette, Valerie, Areendam Chanda, and Louis Putterman. 2002. "States and Markets: the Advantage of an Early Start." *Journal of Economic Growth* 7(4): 347–369.

Bohn, Henning, and Robert Deacon. 2000. "Ownership Risk, Investment, and the Use of Natural Resources." *The American Economic Review* 90(3): 526–549.

Bräutigam, Deborah. 2008a. "Contingent Capacity: Export Taxation and State-building in Mauritius" In Deborah Bräutigam, Odd-Helge Fjeldstad, and Mick Moore, eds., *Taxation and State-Building in*

Developing Countries: Capacity and Consent. Cambridge: Cambridge University Press, pp. 135–159.

2008b. "Taxation and Governance in Africa: Take a Second Look." *Development Policy Outlook* 1(April): 1–6.

Broadhead, Susan Herlin. 1979. "Beyond Decline: the Kingdom of the Kongo in the Eighteenth and Nineteenth Centuries." *The International Journal of African Historical Studies* 12(4): 615–650.

Broadman, Harry. 1985. "Incentives and Constraints on Exploratory Drilling for Petroleum in Developing Countries." *Annual Review of Energy* 10(1): 217–249.

Brownlee, Jason. 2011. "Executive Elections in the Arabic World: When and How Do They Matter?" *Comparative Political Studies* 44(7): 807–828.

Bruckner, Markus, Antonio Ciccone, and Andrea Tesei. 2012. "Oil Price Shocks, Income and Democracy." *Review of Economics and Statistics* 94(2): 389–399.

Brunnschweiler, Christa. 2008. "Cursing the Blessings? Natural Resource Abundance, Institutions, and Economic Growth." *World Development* 36(3): 399–419.

Brunnschweiler, Christa, and Erwin Bulte. 2008. "The Resource Curse Revisited and Revised: a Tale of Paradoxes and Red Herrings." *Journal of Environmental Economics and Management* 55(3): 248–264.

2009. "Natural Resources and Violent Conflict: Resource Abundance, Dependence, and the Onset of Civil Wars." *Oxford Economic Papers* 61(4): 651–674.

Bucks, Brian, Arthur Kennickell, and Kevin Moore. 2009. "Recent Changes in U.S. Family Finances from 2004 to 2007: Evidence from the Survey of Consumer Finances." *Federal Reserve Bulletin* 95(February): 1–56.

Bueno de Mesquita, Bruce, Alastair Smith, Randolph Siverson, and James Morrow. 2003. *The Logic of Political Survival*. Cambridge: MIT Press.

Bulmer-Thomas, Victor. 2003. *The Economic History of Latin America since Independence*. Vol. 77. Cambridge: Cambridge University Press.

Cai, Hongbin, and Daniel Treisman. 2005. "Does Competition for Capital Discipline Governments? Decentralization, Globalization, and Public Policy." *American Economic Review* 95(3): 817–830.

Calomiris, Charles, and Stephen Haber. 2014. *Fragile by Design: the Political Origins of Banking Crises and Scarce Credit*. Princeton: Princeton University Press.

Cardenas, Enrique. 1997. "A Macroeconomic Interpretation of Nineteenth Century Mexico." In Stephen Haber, ed., *How Latin America Fell Behind*. Stanford: Stanford University Press, pp. 65–92.

Carneiro, Robert. 1970. "A Theory of the Origin of the State." *Science* 169 (August): 733–738.

Centeno, Miguel. 1997. "Blood and Debt: War and Taxation in Nineteenth-Century Latin America." *American Journal of Sociology* 102(6): 1565–1605.

2002. *Blood and Debt: War and the Nation-State in Latin America.* University Park: Pennsylvania State University Press.

Centro de Estudios de Minería y Desarrollo (CEMYD). 1990. *Desempeño y Colapso de la Minería Nacionalizada.* La Paz: CEMYD.

Chanda, Areendam, and Louis Putterman. 2007. "Early Starts, Reversals and Catch-up in the Process of Economic Development." *The Scandinavian Journal of Economics* 109(2): 387–413.

Chaney, Eric. 2012. "Democratic Change in the Arab World, Past and Present." Brookings Papers on Economic Activity: 363–414.

Chaudhry, Kiren Aziz. 1994. "Economic Liberalization and the Lineages of the Rentier State." *Comparative Politics* 27(1): 1–25.

Cheibub, José Antonio. 1998. "Political Regimes and the Extractive Capacity of Governments: Taxation in Democracies and Dictatorships." *World Politics* 50(3): 349–376.

Cheibub, José Antonio, Jennifer Gandhi, and James Raymond Vreeland. 2010. "Democracy and Dictatorship Revisited." *Public Choice* 143(1): 67–101.

Cheung, Yan-Leung, Raghavendra Rau, and Aris Stouraitis. 2011. Which Firms Benefit from Bribes, and by how Much? Evidence from Corruption Cases Worldwide. Working Paper.

Chevallier, Jérôme, and Kai Kaiser. 2010. "The Political Economy of Mining in the Democratic Republic of Congo (DRC)". Unpublished Manuscript. World Bank, Washington, DC.

Ciaretta, Aitor, and Shahriyar Nasirov. N.d. "Analysis of Azerbaijan Oil and Gas Sector." Unpublished Manuscript.

Clague, Christopher, Philip Keefer, Stephen Knack, and Mancur Olson. 1999. "Contract-Intensive Money." *Journal of Economic Growth* 4 (2): 185–211.

Clague, Christopher, Philip Keefer, and Mancur Olson. 1996. "Property and Contract Rights in Autocracies and Democracies." *Journal of Economic Growth* 1(2): 243–276.

Coase, Ronald. 1937. "The Nature of the Firm." *Economica* 4(3): 386–405.

Coatsworth, John. 1978. "Obstacles to Economic Growth in Nineteenth-Century Mexico." *The American Historical Review* 83(1): 80–100.

2008. "Inequality, Institutions and Economic Growth in Latin America." *Journal of Latin American Studies* 40(3): 545–569.

Coatsworth, John, and Jeffrey Williamson. 2004. "Always Protectionist? Latin American Tariffs from Independence to Great Depression." *Journal of Latin American Studies* 36(2): 205–232.

Cohen, Youssef, Brian Brown, and Abramo F.K. Organski. 1981. "The Paradoxical Nature of State Making: the Violent Creation of Order." *American Political Science Review* 75(4): 901–910.

Collier, Paul. 2010. *The Plundered Planet: Why We Must – and How We Can – Manage Nature for Global Prosperity.* Oxford: Oxford University Press.

Conley, John, and Akram Temini. 2001. "Endogenous Enfranchisement When Groups Preferences Conflict." *Journal of Political Economy* 109(1): 79–102.

Cook, Steven. 2007. *Ruling but Not Governing: the Military and Political Development in Egypt, Algeria and Turkey.* Baltimore: The Johns Hopkins University Press.

Cordesman, Anthony. 2004. "Current MENA Energy Developments: the Trends by Sub-region and Country." Center for Strategic and International Studies. Washington, DC.

Cornell, Svante. 2011. *Azerbaijan Since Independence.* Armonk: M.E. Sharpe.

Cotet, Anca, and Kevin Tsui. 2010. "Oil and Conflict: What Does the Cross-Country Evidence Really Show?" Unpublished Manuscript.

Cowen, Tyler. 2014. "The Lack of Major Wars May Be Hurting Economic Growth." The New York Times: www.nytimes.com/2014/06/14/upshot/the-lack-of-major-wars-may-be-hurting-economic-growth.html?_r=0

Cox, Gary, Douglass North, and Barry Weingast. 2013. "The Violence Trap." Unpublished Manuscript.

Crystal, Jill. 1990. *Oil and Politics in the Gulf: Rulers and Merchants in Kuwait and Qatar.* New York: Cambridge University.

David, Paul, and Gavin Wright. 1997. "Increasing Returns and the Genesis of American Resource Abundance." *Industrial and Corporate Change* 6(2): 203–245.

Deas, Malcom. 1982. "The Fiscal Problems of Nineteenth-Century Colombia." *Journal of Latin American Studies* 14(2): 287–328.

Demirgüç-Kunt, Asli, and Ross Levine. 2009. "Finance and Inequality: Theory and Evidence." In NBER Working Papers. Cambridge, MA: National Bureau of Economic Research.

Dercon, Stefan. 1998. "Wealth, Risk and Activity Choice: Cattle in Western Tanzania." *Journal of Development Economics* 55(1): 1–42.

DeVries, Jan, S. K. Datta, J. B. Nugent, J. K. Van Ginneken, A. S. Muller, A. M. Voorhoeve, and H. Kawabe. 1984. "European Urbanization 1500–1800." *Population Studies* 38(3): 507–509.

Dincecco, Mark. 2009. "Fiscal Centralization, Limited Government, and Public Revenues in Europe, 1650–1913." *The Journal of Economic History* 69(1): 48–103.

Dobado Gonzales, Rafael, Aurora Gomez Galvarriato, and Jeffrey Williamson. 2008. "Mexican Exceptionalism: Globalization and De-Industrialization, 1750–1877." *The Journal of Economic History* 68(3): 758–811.

Dobado Gonzales, Rafael, and Gustavo Marrero. 2006. "Mining-Led Growth in Bourbon Mexico, the Role of the State, and the Economic Cost of Independence." The David Rockefeller Center for Latin American Studies. Working Paper on Latin America.

Downing, Brian. 1992. *The Military Revolution and Political Change: Origins of Democracy and Autocracy in Early Modern Europe.* Princeton: Princeton University Press.

Drelichman, Mauricio, and Hans-Joachim Voth. 2008. "Institutions and the Resource Curse in Early Modern Spain." In Elhanan Helpman, ed., *Institutions and Economic Performance.* Cambridge: Harvard University Press, pp. 120–147.

Driscoll, Jesse. 2015. *Warlords and Coalition Politics in Post-Soviet States.* Cambridge: Cambridge University Press.

Dunning, Thad. 2008. *Crude Democracy: Natural Resource Wealth and Political Regimes.* New York: Cambridge University Press.

2010. "Endogenous Oil Rents." *Comparative Political Studies* 43(3): 379–410.

Dupuy, Kendra. 2014. "Community Development Requirements in Mining Laws." *The Extractive Industries and Society* 1(2): 200–215.

Dupuy, Kendra. 2015. "Managing the Resource Curse: New Governance Initiatives." Ph.D. Dissertation, University of Washington.

Easterly, William. 2007. "Inequality Does Cause Underdevelopment: Insights from a New Instrument." *Journal of Development Economics* 84(2): 755–776.

Easterly, William, and Ross Levine. 2003. "Tropics, Germs, and Crops: How Endowments Influence Economic Development." *Journal of Monetary Economics* 50(1): 3–39.

Eichengreen, Barry. 1994. "House Calls of the Money Doctor: The Kemmerer Missions to Latin America, 1917–1931." In Paul Drake, ed., *Money Doctors, Foreign Debts, and Economic Reforms in Latin America from the 1890s to the Present.* Wilmington: Scholarly Resources, pp. 110–132.

Eifert, Benn, Alan Gelb, and Nils Borje Tallroth. 2002. "The Political Economy of Fiscal Policy and Economic Management in Oil-Exporting Countries." Policy Research Working Paper 2899. Washington, DC: The World Bank.

Ekelund, Robert, and Rorbert Tollison. 1981. *Mercantilism as a Rent-Seeking Society: Economic Regulation in Historical Perspective.* College Station: Texas A&M University Press.

Eleftheriadou, Marina. 2012 "Tribes: a Back to the Future Perspective on the Arab Spring." *Middle East Bulletin* 23(June): 2–7.

Engemann, Kristie, Michael Owyang, and Howard Wall. 2014. "Where is an Oil Shock?" *Journal of Regional Science* 54(2): 169–185.

Engerman, Stanley, and Kenneth Sokoloff. 1997. "Factor Endowments, Institutions, and Differential Paths of Growth among New World Economies: a View from Economic Historians of the United States." In Stephen, Haber. ed., *Latin America Fell Behind: Essays on the Economic Histories of Brazil and Mexico, 1800–1914*. Stanford: Stanford University Press, pp. 260–306.

Erkan, Mustafa. 2011. *International Energy Investment Law: Stability through Contractual Clauses*. Amsterdam: Walters Kluwer.

Fabian, Bornhorst, Sanjeev Gupta, and John Thornton. 2009. "Natural Resource Endowments and the Domestic Revenue Effort." *European Journal of Political Economy* 25(4): 439–446.

Fandy, Mamoun. 1994. "Tribe vs. Islam: The Post-colonial Arab State and the Democratic Imperative." *Middle East Policy* 3(2): 40–51.

Fearon, James. 2005. "Primary Commodity Exports and Civil War." *Journal of Conflict Resolution* 49(4): 483–507.

Fearon, James, and David Laitin. 2003. "Ethnicity, Insurgency, and Civil War." *American Political Science Review* 97(1): 75–90.

Firmin-Seller, Kathryn. 1995. "The Politics of Property Rights." *American Political Science Review* 89(4): 867–881.

Fisman, Raymond, and Inessa Love. 2003. "Financial Development and Growth in the Short and Long Run." In NBER Working Papers. Cambridge, MA: National Bureau of Economic Research.

Flores-Macías, Francisco. 2010. "Explaining the Behavior of State Owned Enterprises: Mexico's PEMEX in Comparative Perspective". Ph.D. Dissertation. MIT: Cambridge, MA.

Frankel, Jeffrey. 2010. "The Natural Resource Curse: a Survey." Working Paper No. 15836. Cambridge, MA: National Bureau of Economic Research.

Frankel, Jeffrey, and Andrew Rose. 2005. "Is Trade Good or Bad for the Environment? Sorting out the Causality." *Review of Economics and Statistics* 87(1): 85–91.

Freeman, John, and Dennis Quinn. 2012. "The Economic Origins of Democracy Reconsidered." *American Political Science Review* 106(1): 58–80.

Frieden, Jeff. 1989. "The Economics of Intervention: American Overseas Investments and Relations with the Underdeveloped Areas, 1890–1950." *Comparative Studies in Society and History* 31(1): 55–80.

1994. "International Investment and Colonial Control: a New Interpretation." *International Organization* 48(4): 559–593.

Fukuyama, Francis. 2011 *The Origins of Political Order: from Prehuman Times to the French Revolution.* New York: Profile Books.

Gadano, Nicolas. 2010. "Urgency and Betrayal: Three Attempts to Foster Private Investment in Argentina's Oil Industry." In William Hogan, and Federico Sturzenengger, eds., *The Natural Resources Trap.* Cambridge: MIT Press, pp. 369–404.

Gandhi, Jennifer, and Adam Przeworski. 2006. "Cooperation, Cooptation, and Rebellion Under Non-Democratic Leaderships." *Economics and Politics* 18(1): 1–26.

Gantz, David. 1977. "The Marcona Settlement: New Forms of Negotiation and Compensation for Nationalized Property." *The American Journal of International Law* 71(3): 474–493.

Gaus, Gregory. 1994. "Oil Monarchies: Domestic and Security Challenges in the Arab Gulf States." New York: *Council on Foreign Relations.*

Geddes, Barbara. 1999. "What Do We Know about Democratization after Twenty Years?" *Annual Review of Political Science* 2(1): 115–144.

Gehlbach, Scott. 2008. *Representation through Taxation: Revenue, Politics, and Development in Postcommunist States.* Cambridge: Cambridge University Press.

Gehlbach, Scott, and Phil Keefer. 2011. "Investment without Democracy: Ruling Party Institutionalization and Credible Commitment in Non-Democracies." *Journal of Comparative Economics* 39(2): 123–139.

Gelb, Alan. 1988. *Oil Windfalls: Blessing or Curse?* Oxford: Oxford University Press.

Genschel, Philipp, and Thomas Plumper. 1997. "Regulatory Competition and International Co-Operation." *Journal of European Public Policy* 4(4): 626–642.

Gervasoni, Carlos. 2010. "A Rentier Theory of Subnational Regimes." *World Politics* 62(2): 302–340.

Gillis, Malcom. 1982. "Evolution of Natural Resource Taxation in Developing Countries." *Natural Resources Journal* 22(June): 619–648.

Gleditsch, Kristian, and Michael Ward. 2006. "Diffusion and the International Context of Democratization." *International Organization* 60(4): 911–933.

Global Investment Center. 2012. *Azerbaijan Mineral & Mining Sector Investment and Business Guide.* Washington, DC: USA International Business Publications.

Goldberg, Ellis. N.d.a "Global Energy Shifts: Socialism and American Hegemony in the 20th Century." Unpublished Manuscript.

Goldberg, Ellis. N.d.a "Saudi Arabia and Aramco: Evolution of an Agreement." Unpublished Manuscript.

Goldstone, Jack. 2011. "Understanding the Revolutions of 2011: Weakness and Resilience in Middle Eastern Autocracies." *Foreign Affairs* 90(5): 8–16.

Gordon, Roger, and Wei Li. 2005. "Tax Structures in Developing Countries: Many Puzzles and a Possible Explanation." Working Chapter 11267. National Bureau of Economic Research. Cambridge, MA.

Grafe, Regina, and Maria Alejandra Irigoin. 2006. "The Spanish Empire and its Legacy: Fiscal Redistribution and Political Conflict in Colonial and Post-Colonial Spanish America". *Journal of Global History* 1(2): 241–267.

Grant, Oliver. 2005. *Migration and Inequality in Germany*. New York: Oxford University Press.

Gray, Patrick. 1999. "A Corrected Ethnographic Atlas." *World Cultures* 10(1): 24–136.

Greenwald, Gerald. 1988. "Encouraging Natural Gas Exploration Policies." In Nicky Beredjick and Thomas Walde, eds., *Petroleum Investment Policies in Developing Countries*. London: Graham and Trotman, pp. 175–188.

Greif, Avner. 1994. "Cultural Beliefs and the Organization of Society: a Historical and Theoretical Reflection on Collectivist and Individualist Societies." *Journal of Political Economy* 102(4): 912–950.

Greif, Avner, and David Laitin. 2004. "A Theory of Endogenous Institutional Change." *American Political Science Review* 98(4): 633–652.

Greif, Avner, Paul Milgrom, and Barry Weingast. 1994. "Coordination, Commitment and Enforcement: the Case of the Merchant Guild." *Journal of Political Economy* 102(4): 745–776.

Gross, Daniel. 2014. "Can China be Green?" Slate. June 19th: www.slate.com/articles/technology/the_juice/2014/06/can_china_be_green_a_case_for_china_becoming_a_leader_in_developing_a_low.html.

Grossman, Gene, and Alan Krueger. 1995. "Economic Growth and the Environment." *Quarterly Journal of Economics* 110(2): 353–377.

Guiso, Luigi, Paola Sapienza, and Luigi Zingales. 2008. "Trusting the Stock Market." *Journal of Finance* 63(6): 2557–2600.

Gustafson, Thane. 1989. *Crisis amid Plenty: The Politics of Soviet Energy under Brezhnev and Gorbachev*. Princeton: Princeton University Press. 2012. *Wheel of Fortune*. Cambridge: Harvard University Press.

Haber, Stephen. 2006. "It Wasn't All Prebisch's Fault: the Political Economy of Latin American Industrialization." In Victor Bulmer-Thomas, John Coatsworth, and Roberto Cortes Conde, eds., *The Cambridge Economic*

History of Latin America: Volume 2, The Long Twentieth Century. New York: Cambridge University Press, pp. 537–584.

2007. "Authoritarian Government." In Barry Weingast and Donald Wittman, eds., *The Oxford Handbook of Political Economy.* Oxford: Oxford University Press, pp. 693–708.

2011. "Differential Paths of Financial Development, Evidence from New World Economies." In Dora Costa and Naomi Lamoreaux, eds., *Understanding Long-Run Economic Growth: Geography, Institutions, and the Knowledge Economy.* Chicago: University of Chicago Press, pp. 89–120.

2012a. "Politics and Banking Systems." In Stanley Engerman, Kenneth Sokoloff, Elisa Mariscal, and Eric Zolt, eds., *Economic Development in the Americas Since 1500.* New York: Cambridge University Press, pp. 245–298.

2012b. "Climate, Technology, and the Evolution of Economic and Political Institutions." Working Paper.

2014. "Resource Booms and Industrial Development: Evidence from the Economic History of Latin America." Working Paper.

Haber, Stephen, Armando Razo, and Noel Maurer. 2003. *The Politics of Property Rights: Political Instability, Credible Commitments, and Economic Growth in Mexico, 1876–1929.* New York: Cambridge University Press.

Haber, Stephen, Herb Kline, Noel Maurer, and Kevin Middlebrook. 2008. *Mexico Since 1980.* Cambridge: Cambridge University Press.

Haber, Stephen, Douglass North, and Barry Weingast, eds., 2008. *Political Institutions and Financial Development.* Stanford: Stanford University Press.

Haber, Stephen, and Victor Menaldo. 2011a. "Does Oil Fuel Authoritarianism?: a Reevaluation of the Resource Curse." *American Political Science Review* 105(1): 1–26.

2011b. "Rainfall, Human Capital, and Democracy." Working Paper.

Haggard, Stephan, and Sylvia Maxfield. 1996. "The Political Economy of Financial Internationalization in the Developing World." *International Organization* 50(1): 35–68.

Halbouty, Michael. 1993. "Reflections After 62 Years of Exploration." *United States Geological Survey.* Professional Paper 1570.

Hanson, Jonathan, and Rachel Sigman. 2011. "Measuring State Capacity: Assessing and Testing the Options." Unpublished Manuscript.

Hamilton, Kirk, and Michael Clemens. 1999. "Genuine Savings Rates in Developing Countries." *The World Bank Economic Review* 13(2): 333–356.

Hechter, Michael, and William Brustein. 1980. "Regional Modes of Production and Patterns of State Formation in Western Europe." *American Journal of Sociology* 85(5): 1061–1094.

Heilbrunn, John. 2014. *Oil, Democracy, and Development in Africa.* Cambridge: Cambridge University Press.

Hendricks, Kenneth, and Robert Porter. 1996. "The Timing and Incidence of Exploratory Drilling on Offshore Wildcat Tracts." *The American Economic Review* 38(6):388–407.

Hendrix, Cullen. 2010. "Measuring State Capacity: Theoretical and Empirical Implications for the Study of Civil Conflict." *Journal of Peace Research* 47(3): 273–285.

Henisz, Witold. 2000. "The Institutional Environment for Multinational Investment." *Journal of Law, Economics, and Organization* 16(2): 334–364.

2010. "Political Constraint Index (POLCON)." *Wharton School of the University of Pennsylvania.*

Henisz, Witold, and Oliver Williamson. 1999. "Comparative Economic Organization – Within and Between Countries." *Business and Politics* 1(3): 261–277.

Herb, Michael. 1999. *All in the Family.* Albany: SUNY Press.

2003. "Taxation and Representation." *Studies in Comparative International Development* 38(3): 3–31.

2005. "No Representation without Taxation? Rents, Development, and Democracy." *Comparative Politics* 37(3): 297–316.

Herbst, Jeffrey. 2000. *States and Power in Africa: Comparative Lessons in Authority and Control.* Princeton: Princeton University Press.

Heston, Alan, Robert Summers, and Bettina Aten. 2009. Penn World Table Version 6.3. *Center for International Comparisons of Production, Income and Prices at the University of Pennsylvania.*

Hibbs, Douglas, and Ola Olsson. 2004. "Geography, Biogeography and Why Some Countries are Rich & Others Poor." *Proceedings of National Academies of Sciences* 101(10): 3715–3720.

Hilton, F. G., and Arik Levinson. 1998. "Factoring the Environmental Kuznets Curve: Evidence from Automotive Lead Emissions." *Journal of Environmental Economics and Management* 35(2): 126–141.

Hoffman, Philip, David Jacks, Patricia Levin, and Peter Lindert. 2002. "Real Inequality in Europe Since 1500." *The Journal of Economic History* 62(2): 322–355.

Hoffman, Philip, Gilles Postel-Vinay, and Jean-Laurent Rosenthal. 2007. *Surviving Large Losses: Financial Crises, the Middle Class, and the Development of Capital Markets.* Cambridge: Harvard University Press.

Hogan, William, Federico Sturzenengger, and Laurence Tai. 2010. "Contracts and Investment in Natural Resources." In William Hogan, and Federico Sturzenengger, eds., *The Natural Resources Trap*. Cambridge: MIT Press, pp. 1–44.

Humphries, Marc. 2013. "Rare Earth Elements: the Global Supply Chain". *Congressional Research Service*.

Huntington, Samuel. 1968. *Political Order in Changing Societies*. New Haven: Yale University Press.

Ibrahimov, Rovshan. N.d. "Azerbaijan Production as a Main Locomotive of State Economy." *Çankiri Karatekin Üniversitesi Uluslar arasi Avrasya Strateji Dergisi* 1(1): 61–74.

2010. "Azerbaijan Energy Strategy and the Importance of Diversification of Exported Transport Routes." *Journal of Qafqaz University* 29 (November): 23–29.

INEGI. Various Years. Instituto Nacional de Estadística y Geografía. *Estadisticas Históricas de México*. Mexico City: Instituto Nacional de Estadística y Geografía.

International Energy Agency. 2014. "World Energy Investment Outlook 2014 Factsheet." International Energy Agency. Paris, France.

International Monetary Fund (IMF). 1997. "Staff Country Report 97/001 Azerbaijan: Recent Economic Report." Washington, DC: IMF.

Jackson, Robert. 1990. *Quasi-States: Sovereignty, International Relations and the Third World*. Cambridge: Cambridge University Press.

Jacoby, Henry. 1973. *The Bureaucratization of the World*. Berkeley: University of California Press.

Jalan, Jyotsna, and Martin Ravallion. 2001. "Behavioral Responses to Risk in Rural China." *Journal of Development Economics* 66(1): 23–49.

Jensen, Nathan, and Leonard Wantchekon. 2004. "Resource Wealth and Political Regimes in Africa." *Comparative Political Studies* 37(7): 816–841.

Jensen, Nathan, and Noel Johnston. 2011. "Political Risk, Reputation, and the Resource Curse." *Comparative Political Studies* 44(6): 662–668.

Kantchev, Georgi. 2015. "Oman to Use Solar Power to Extract Oil." The Wall Street Journal. July 9th, B5.

Karl, Terry Lynn. 1997. *The Paradox of Plenty: Oil Booms and Petro-States*. Berkeley: University of California Press.

Kato, Junko, and Seiki Tanaka. 2014. "Representation with Regressive Taxation: State Revenue Production and Democratization Revisited." Working Paper.

Kau, James, and Paul Rubin. 2002. "The Growth of Government: Sources and Limits." *Public Choice* 113(3–4): 389–402.

Keefer, Philip. 2004. "What Does Political Economy Tell us about Economic Development – and Vice-Versa?." *Annual Review of Political Science* 7: 247–272.

Keefer, Philip, and David Stasavage. 2003. "The Limits of Delegation: Veto Players, Central Bank Independence, and the Credibility of Monetary Policy." *American Political Science Review* 97(3): 407–423.

Keefer, Philip, and Razvan Vlaicu. 2007. "Clientelism, Credibility, and the Policy Choices of Young Democracies." *American Journal of Political Science* 51(4): 804–821.

   2008. "Democracy, Credibility, and Clientelism." *Journal of Law, Economics, and Organization* 24(2): 371–406.

Kemp, Alexander. 1992. "Petroleum Policy Issues in Developing Countries." *Energy Policy* 20(2): 104–115.

Kennedy, Hugh. 1998. "Egypt as a Province in the Islamic Caliphate." *Cambridge History of Egypt*, 1: 62–85.

Kennedy, Ryan, and Lydia Tiede. 2013. "Economic Development Assumptions and the Elusive Curse of Oil." *International Studies Quarterly* 57(4): 760–771.

Kenny, Lawrence, and Stanley Winer. 2006. "Tax Systems in the World: an Empirical Investigation into the Importance of Tax Bases, Administration Costs, Scale, and Political Regime." *International Tax and Public Finance* 13(2): 181–215.

Kerner, Andrew, and Jane Lawrence. 2014. "What's the Risk? Bilateral Investment Treaties, Political Risk and Fixed Capital Accumulation." *British Journal of Political Science* 44(1): 107–121.

Khoury, Philip Shukry, and Joseph Kostiner. 1990. "Introduction: Tribes and the Complexities of State Formation in the Middle East." In Philip Shukry Khoury, and Joseph Kostiner, eds., *Tribes and State Formation in the Middle East.* Berkeley: University of California Press, pp. 1–24.

King, Gary. 1988. "Statistical Models for Political Science Event Counts: Bias in Conventional Procedures and Evidence for the Exponential Poisson Regression Model." *American Journal of Political Science.* 32(3): 838–863.

Kiser, Edgar, and April Linton. 2001. "Determinants of the Growth of the State: War and Taxation in Early Modern France and England." *Social Forces* 80(2): 411–448.

Kobrin, Stephen. 1984. "Expropriation as an Attempt to Control Foreign Firms in LDCs." *International Studies Quarterly* 28(3): 329–348.

Kocher, Matthew. 2010. "State Capacity as a Conceptual Variable." *Yale Journal of International Affairs* 5(Spring/Summer): 137–145.

Kolstad, Ivar, and Arne Wiig. 2009. "Is Transparency the Key to Reducing Corruption in Resource-Rich Countries?" *World Development* 37(3): 521–532.

Kressel Gideon. 1996. *Ascendancy Through Aggression: the Anatomy of a Blood Feud Among Urbanized Bedouins.* Wiesbaden: Otto Harrassowitz Verlag.

Krishnan, Malavika. 2014. "Canadian Mining in Latin America: Exploitation, Inconsistency, and Neglect." Council on Hemispheric Affairs. June 11, 2014.

Krueger, Anne. 1974. "The Political Economy of the Rent-Seeking Society." *The American Economic Review* 64(3): 291–303.

Krylov, N.A., A.A. Boksernan, and E.P. Stavrovsky. 1998. *Oil Industry of the Former Soviet Union: Reserves, Extraction, and Transportation.* Amsterdam, Holland: Gordon and Breach Science Publishers.

Kuran, Timur. 1991. "Now Out Of Never: the Element of Surprise in the East European Revolution of 1989." *World Politics* 44(1): 7–48.

——— 2008. "Institutional Causes of Economic Underdevelopment in the Middle East: a Historical Perspective." In János Kornai, László Mátyás, and Gérard Roland, eds., *Institutional Change and Economic Behavior.* New York: Palgrave-Macmillan, pp. 64–76.

La Croix, Sumner. 1992. "Property Rights and Institutional Change During Australia's Gold Rush." *Explorations in Economic History* 29(2): 204–227.

Laherrère, Jean. 2003. "Future of Oil Supplies." *Energy, Exploration & Exploitation* 21(3): 227–267.

Laeven, Luc, and Fabian Valencia, 2008. "Systemic Banking Crises: A New Database." Washington, DC: IMF Working Paper.

Lake, David, and Michael Baum. 2001. "The Invisible Hand of Democracy: Political Control and the Provision of Public Services." *Comparative Political Studies* 34(6): 587–621.

Landes, David. 1969. *The Unbound Prometheus: Technological Change and Industrial Development in Western Europe from 1750 to the Present.* Cambridge: Cambridge University Press.

Lane, Philip, and Gian Maria Milesi-Ferretti. 2007. "The External Wealth of Nations Mark II." *Journal of International Economics* 73(2): 223–250.

Lapidus, Ira. 1990. "Tribes and State Formation in Islamic History." In Philip Shukry Khoury, and Joseph Kostiner, eds., *Tribes and State Formation in the Middle East.* Berkeley: University Of California Press, pp. 25–47.

Layish, Aharon. 2004. "The Transformation of the Sharia from Jurists' Law to Statutory Law in the Contemporary Muslim World." *Die Welt des Islams* 44(1): 85–112.

Lederman, Daniel, and William Maloney. 2008. "In Search of the Missing Resource Curse." *Economía* 9(1): 1–57.

Levi, Margaret. 1988. *Of Rule and Revenue*. Berkeley: The University of California Press.

2002. "The State of the Study of the State." In Ira Katznelson, and Helen Milner, eds., *Political Science: The State of the Discipline*. New York: W.W. Norton, pp. 33–55.

Levi, Margaret, and Victor Menaldo. 2015. "The New Economic Institutionalism in Historical Perspective." In Jennifer Gandhi and Rubén Ruiz, eds., *Routledge Handbook on Political Institutions*. New York: Routledge Press, pp. 15–30.

Levine, Ross, Norman Loayza, and Thorsten Beck. 2000. "Financial Intermediation and Growth: Causality and Causes." *Journal of Monetary Economics* 46(1): 31–77.

Lewis, Bernard. 2005. "Freedom and Justice in the Modern Middle East." *Foreign Affairs* 84(3): 36–51.

Lewis, Colin. 1999. The Economics of the Latin American State: Ideology, Policy and Performance, c. 1820–1945. In David Smith, Dorothy Solinger, and Steven Topik, eds., *States and Sovereignty in the Global Economy*. London: Routledge Press, pp. 99–119.

Lieberman, Evan. 2002. "Taxation Data as Indicators of State-society Relations: Possibilities and Pitfalls in Cross-national Research." *Studies in Comparative International Development* 36(4): 89–115.

Liou, Yu-Ming, and Paul Musgrave. 2014. "Refining the Oil Curse: Country-Level Evidence From Exogenous Variations in Resource Income." *Comparative Political Studies* 47(11): 1584–1610.

Lizzeri, Alessandro, and Nicola Persico. 2004. "Why Did the Elites Extend the Suffrage? Democracy and the Scope of Government, with an Application to Britain's 'Age of Reform'". *The Quarterly Journal of Economics* 119(2): 707–765.

Llavador, Humberto, and Robert Oxoby. 2005. "Partisan Competition, Growth, and the Franchise Franchise." *The Quarterly Journal of Economics* 120 (3): 1155–1189.

Lingyu, Lu, and Cameron Thies. 2013. "War, Rivalry and State Building in the Middle East." *Political Research Quarterly* 66(2): 239–253.

Luciani, Giacomo. 1987. "Allocation versus Production States: A Theoretical Framework." In Hazem Beblawi and Giacomo Luciani, eds., *The Rentier State*. New York: Croom Helm, pp. 63–82.

Lücke, Matthias. 2010. "Stabilization and Savings Funds to Manage Natural Resource Revenues: Kazakhstan and Azerbaijan vs. Norway." Kiel Working Paper No. 1652.

Luong, Pauline Jones, and Erika Weinthal. 2010. *Oil is Not a Curse: Ownership Structure and Institutions in Petroleum-Rich Soviet Successor States*. Cambridge: Cambridge University Press.

Lynch, Martin. 2002. *Mining in World History*. London: Reaktion Books.

Magaloni, Beatriz. 2008. "Credible Power-Sharing and the Longevity of Authoritarian Rule." *Comparative Political Studies* 41(4–5): 715–741.

Maghraoui, Driss. 2011. "Constitutional Reforms in Morocco: Between Consensus and Subaltern Politics." *The Journal of North African Studies* 16(4): 679–699.

Mahdavy, Hossein. 1970. "The Patterns and Problems of Economic Development in Rentier States: The Case of Iran." In M.A. Cook, ed., *Studies in the Economic History of the Middle East*. London: Oxford University Press: 428–467.

Manzano, Osmel, and Francisco Monaldi. 2008. "The Political Economy of Oil Production in Latin America." *Economía* 9(1): 59–98.

Marcel, Valerie. 2005. "Good Governance of the National Oil Company." Position paper for the Workshop on Good Governance of the National Petroleum Sector.

Mares, David. 2011. "Oil Policy Reform in Resource Nationalist States: Lessons for Mexico." James A. Baker III Institute for Public Policy, Rice University 29.

Mares, Isabela. 2015. *From Open Secrets to Secret Voting: Democratic Electoral Reforms and Voter Autonomy*. Cambridge, UK: Cambridge University Press.

Mariscal, Elisa, and Ken Sokoloff. 2000. "History Lessons: Institutions, Factors Endowments, and Paths of Development in the New World." *The Journal of Economic Perspectives* 14(3): 217–232.

Marshall, Monty, and Keith Jaggers. 2008. "Polity IV Project: Political Regime Characteristics and Transitions, 1800–2006." University of Maryland.

Matsen, Egil, Gisle Natvik, and Ragnar Torvik. 2014. "Petro Populism." Working Paper.

Maurer, Noel. 2011. "The Empire Struck Back: Sanctions and Compensation in the Mexican Oil Expropriation of 1938." *Journal of Economic History* 71(3): 590–615.

2013. *The Empire Trap: The Rise and fall of U.S. Intervention to Protect American Property Overseas, 1893–2013*. Princeton: Princeton University Press.

McGuire, Martin, and Mancur Olson. 1996. "The Economics of Autocracy and Majority Rule: The Invisible Hand and the Use of Force." *Journal of Economic Literature* 34(1): 72–96.

McPherson, Charles. 2003. "National Oil Companies: Evolution, Issues, Outlook." In Jeffrey Davis, Rolando Ossowski, and Annalisa Fedelino, eds., *Fiscal Policy Formulation and Implementation in Oil-Producing Countries*. Washington, DC: International Monetary Fund, pp. 184–203.

Mehlum, Halvor, Karl Moene, and Ragnar Torvik. 2006. "Institutions and the Resource Curse." *The Economic Journal* 116(508): 1–20.

Menaldo, Victor. 2009. "Banking on Redistribution in Latin America: Transaction Costs, Democracy, and Fiscal Redistribution in Latin America from 1808 to 2008." Ph.D. Dissertation: Stanford University.

2012. "The Middle East and North Africa's Resilient Monarchs." *Journal of Politics* 74(3): 707–729.

2016. "The Fiscal Roots of Financial Underdevelopment." *American Journal of Political Science*. 60(2): 456–471.

Menaldo, Victor, and Nora Webb-Williams. 2015. "Judicial Supremacy: Explaining False Starts and Surprising Successes." In James Melton and Robert Hazell, eds., *How the Magna Carta Matters: Reflecting on the Legacy of the Great Charter*. Cambridge: Cambridge University Press, pp. 169–193.

Michalopoulos, Stelios, Alireza Naghavi, and Giovanni Prarolo. 2012. "Trade and Geography in The Origins and Spread of Islam." No. 18438. Washington, DC: *National Bureau of Economic Research*.

Middle East/North Africa Report. 2012. "Lost in Transition: The World According to Egypt's Scaf." *Middle East/North Africa Report* 121 (April): 1–31.

Midlarsky, Manu. 1998. "Democracy and Islam: Implications for Civilizational Conflict and the Democratic Peace." *International Studies Quarterly* 42(3): 485–511.

Migdal, Joel 1988. *Strong Societies and Weak States*. Princeton: Princeton University Press.

Mikdashi, Zuhayr. 1985. "Oil Funding and International Financial Arrangements." *Natural Resources Forum* 9(4): 283–291.

Mitchell, Brian. 2003. *International Historical Statistics: The Americas 1750–2000*. New York: Palgrave MacMillan.

Monaldi, Francisco. 2002. "Government Commitment Using External Hostages." Mimeo.

Moore, Barrington. 1966. *Social Origins of Dictatorship and Democracy: Lord and Peasant in the Making of the Modern World*. Boston: Beacon Press.

Moran, Theodore. 1998. "Lessons in the Management of International Political Risk from the Natural Resource and Private Infrastructure Sectors." In Theodore Moran, ed., *Managing International Political Risk*. Malden: Blackwell, pp. 70–79.

Morris, Ian. 2010. *Why the West Rules–for Now: the Patterns of History and What They Reveal About the Future.* London: Profile Books.

2014. *War! What is it Good for? Conflict and the Progress of Civilization from Primates to Robots.* London: Profile Books.

Morrison, Kevin. 2009. "Oil, Nontax Revenue, and the Redistributional Foundations of Regime Stability." *International Organization* 63(1): 107–138.

Myerson, Roger. 2008. "The Non-Democratic Leader's Credibility Problem and Foundations of the Constitutional State." *American Political Science Review* 102(1): 125–139.

Neumayer, Eric, and Laura Spess. 2005. "Do Bilateral Investment Treaties Increase Foreign Direct Investment to Developing Countries?" *World Development* (33)10: 1567–1585.

Newby, Gordon Darnell. 1988. *A History of the Jews of Arabia.* Columbia: University of South Carolina Press.

North, Douglass. 1981. *Structure and Change in Economic History.* New York: Norton.

1990. *Institutions, Institutional Change, and Economic Performance.* Cambridge: Cambridge University Press.

2005. *Understanding the Process of Economic Change.* Princeton: Princeton University Press.

North, Douglass, and Barry Weingast. 1989. "Constitutions and Commitment: The Evolution of Institutional Governing Public Choice in Seventeenth-Century England." *Journal of Economic History* 49(4): 803–832.

North, Douglass, William Summerhill, and Barry Weingast. 2000. "Order, Disorder and Economic Change: Latin America vs. North America". In Bueno de Mesquita, and Hilton Root, eds., *Governing for Prosperity.* New Haven: Yale University Press, pp. 17–58.

North, Douglass, John Joseph Wallis, and Barry Weingast. 2009. *Violence and Social Orders: a Conceptual Framework for Interpreting Recorded Human History.* Cambridge: Cambridge University Press.

Okruhlik, Gwenn. 1999. "Rentier Wealth, Unruly Law, and the Rise of Opposition: the Political Economy of Oil States." *Comparative Politics* 31(3): 295–315.

Olson, Mancur. 1993. "Dictatorship, Democracy and Development." *American Political Science Review* 87(3): 567–576.

Olson, Bradley, and Erin Ailworth. 2015. "Low Prices Catch up with U.S. Oil Patch." The Wall Street Journal. November 21–22, A2.

O'Rourke, Kevin, and Jeff Williamson. 2002. "After Columbus: Explaining Europe's Overseas Trade Boom, 1500–1800." *The Journal of Economic History* 62(2): 417–456.

Otto, James, Craig Andrews, Fred Cawood, Michael Doggett, Pietro Guj, Frank Stermole, John Stermole, and John Tilton. 2006. *Mining Royalties: A Global Study of their Impact on Investors, Government, and Civil Society.* World Bank, Washington, DC.

Papaioannou, Elias, and Gregorios Siourounis. 2008. "Economic and Social Factors Driving the Third Wave of Democratization." *Journal of Comparative Economics* 36(3): 365–387.

Perkins, Richard, and Eric Neumayer. 2012. "Does the 'California Effect' Operate Across Borders?" *Journal of European Public Policy* 19(2): 217–237.

Petri, Martin, Günther Taube, and Aleh Tsyvinski. 2002. "Energy Sector Quasi-Fiscal Activities in the Countries of the Former Soviet Union." Washington, DC: IMF Working Paper.

Pierson, Paul. 2000. "Increasing Returns, Path Dependence, and the Study of Politics." *American Political Science Review* 94(2): 251–267.

Pomeranz, Kenneth. 2009. *The Great Divergence: China, Europe, and the Making of the Modern World Economy.* Princeton: Princeton University Press.

Potoski, Matthew, and Aseem Prakash. 2004. "The Regulation Dilemma: Cooperation and Conflict in Environmental Governance." *Public Administration Review* 64(2): 152–163.

2013. "Green Clubs: Collective Action and Voluntary Environmental Programs." *Annual Review of Political Science.* 16: 399–419.

Prados de la Escosura, Leandro. 2007. "Lost Decades? Independence and Latin America's Falling Behind, 1820–1870." Working Papers in Economic History. Universidad Carlos III de Madrid.

Prados de la Escosura, Leandro, and Samuel Amaral. 1993. *La Independencia Americana: Consecuencias Económicas.* Madrid: Alianza Editorial.

Prakash, Aseem and Matthew Potoski. 2007. "Investing Up: FDI and the Cross-Country Diffusion of ISO 14001 Management Systems." *International Studies Quarterly* 51(3): 723–744.

Prichard, Wilson, Alex Cobham, and Andrew Goodall. 2014. "The ICTD Government Revenue Dataset." International Centre for Tax and Development. Brighton, United Kingdom.

Przeworski, Adam. 2009. "Conquered or Granted? A History of Suffrage Extensions." *British Journal of Political Science* 39(2): 291–321.

Przeworski, Adam, Michael Alvarez, José Antonio Cheibub, and Fernando Limongi. 2000. *Democracy and Development.* New York: Cambridge University Press.

Przeworski, Adam, and Carolina Curvale. 2005. "Does Politics Explain the Economic Gap between the United States and Latin America." Unpublished Manuscript. New York University, Department of Politics.

Putterman, Louis, and David Weil. 2010. "Post-1500 Population Flows and the Long-Run Determinants of Economic Growth and Inequality." *The Quarterly Journal of Economics* 125(4): 1627–1682.

Quiroz, A.W. 1993. "Consequencias Economicas y Financieras del Proceso de la Independencia en el Peru, 1800–1850." In Prados de la Escosura and Amaral, eds., *Independencia Americana: Consecuencias Economicas.* Madrid: Alianza Editorial, pp. 124–146.

Radnitz, Scott. 2012. "Oil in the Family: Managing Presidential Succession in Azerbaijan." *Democratization* 19(1): 60–77.

Rajan, Raghuram, and Luigi Zingales. 1998. "Financial Dependence and Growth." *American Economic Review* 88(3): 559–586.

Ramsay, Kristopher. 2011. "Revisiting the Resource Curse: Natural Disasters, the Price of Oil, and Democracy." *International Organization* 65(3): 507–529.

Razo, Armando. 2008. *Social Foundations of Limited Dictatorship: Networks and Private Protection during Mexico's Early Industrialization.* Stanford: Stanford University Press.

Reizman, Raymond, and Joel Slemrod. 1987. "Tariffs and Collection Costs." *Review of World Economics* 123(3): 545–549.

Reyes Abadie, Washington, and A. Vazquez Romero. N.d. *Cronica General del Uruguay, Volume 3: El Uruguay del Siglo XIX.* Montevideo: Ediciones de la Banda Oriental.

Robinson, Glenn. 2012. "Oil States, Rentier States, and the Arab Spring." In Marc Lynch, ed., *Arab Uprisings: New Opportunities for Political Science.* Washington, DC: Project On Middle East Political Science, pp. 53–55.

Roeder, Philip. 1993. *Red Sunset: The Failure of Soviet Politics.* Princeton: Princeton University Press.

Root, Hilton. 1989. "Tying the King's Hands: Credible Commitment and Royal Fiscal Policy during the Old Regime." *Rationality and Society* 1(2): 240–258.

Ross, Michael. 1999. "The Political Economy of the Resource Curse." *World Politics* 51(2): 297–322.

2001. "Does Oil Hinder Democracy?" *World Politics* 53(3): 325–361.

2012. *The Oil Curse: How Petroleum Wealth Shapes the Development of Nations.* Princeton: Princeton University Press.

Rosser, Andrew. 2007. "Escaping the Resource Curse: The Case of Indonesia." *Journal of Contemporary Asia* 37(1): 38–58.

Rostoum, Elly. 2014. "Dissecting China's $1 Trillion in Investments Globally." Foreign Policy Association.

Rothkopf, David. 2012. *Power, Inc.: The Epic Rivalry between Big Business and Government – and the Reckoning That Lies Ahead.* New York: Macmillan.

Sachs, Jeffrey, and Andrew Warner. 2001. "The Curse of Natural Resources." *European Economic Review* 45(4): 827–838.

Scheve, Ken, and David Stasavage. 2012. "Democracy, War, and Wealth: Lessons from Two Centuries of Inheritance Taxation." *American Political Science Review* 106(1): 81–102.

Schrad, Mark. 2014. *Vodka Politics: Alcohol, Autocracy, and the Secret History of the Russian State*. Oxford: Oxford University Press.

Schultz, Kenneth, and Barry Weingast. 2003. "The Democratic Advantage: Institutional Foundations of Financial Power in International Competition." *International Organization* 57(1): 3–42.

Selden, Thomas, and Daqing Song. 1994. "Environmental Quality and Development: Is There a Kuznets Curve for Air Pollution Emissions?" *Journal of Environmental Economics and Management* 27(2): 147–162.

Siegelbaum, Paul, Khaled Sherif, Michael Borish, and George Clarke. 2002. *Structural Adjustment in the Transition: Case Studies from Albania, Azerbaijan, Kyrgyz Republic, and Moldova*. Washington, DC: World Bank.

Skaperdas, Stergios. 1992. "Cooperation, Conflict, and Power in the Absence of Property Rights." *The American Economic Review* 82(4): 720–739.

Skocpol, Theda. 1979. *States and Social Revolutions: A Comparative Analysis of France, Russia & China*. Cambridge: Cambridge University Press.

Smith, Alastair. 2008. "The Perils of Unearned Income." *Journal of Politics* 70(3): 780–793.

Smith, Benjamin. 2004. "Oil Wealth and Regime Survival in the Developing World, 1960–1999." *American Journal of Political Science* 48(2): 232–246.

Smith, Benjamin. 2007. *Hard Times in the Lands of Plenty: Oil Politics in Iran and Indonesia*. Cornell: Cornell University Press.

Smith, Brock 2015. "The Resource Curse Exorcised: Evidence from a Panel of Countries." *Journal of Development Economics* 116(4): 57–73.

Snyder, Richard, and Ravi Bhavnani. 2005. "Blood, Diamonds, and Taxes: Lootable Wealth and Political Order in Sub-Saharan Africa." *Journal of Conflict Resolution* 49(4): 563–97.

Soares de Oliveira, Ricardo. 2007. "Business Success, Angola-Style: Postcolonial Politics and the Rise of Sonangol." *Journal of Modern African Studies* 45(4): 595–619.

Sokoloff, Kenneth, and Eric Zolt. 2007. "Inequality and the Evolution of Institutions of Taxation: Evidence from the Economic History of the Americas." In Sebastian Edwards, Gerardo Esquivel, and Graciela Marquez, eds., *The Decline of Latin American Economies: Growth, Institutions, and Crises*. Chicago: University of Chicago Press, pp. 83–138.

Solnick, Steven. 1988. *Stealing the State: Control and Collapse in Soviet Institutions*. Cambridge: Harvard University Press.

Sornarajah, Muthucumaraswamy. 2010. *The International Law on Foreign Investment*. Cambridge: Cambridge University Press.

Spector, Regine. 2012. "The Impact of Energy Resources on Nation- and State-Building: The Contrasting Cases of Azerbaijan and Georgia." In Brenda Shaffer, and Taleh Ziyadov, eds., *Beyond the Resource Curse*. College Station, PA: University of Pennsylvania Press, pp. 225–258.

Spiegel Online. 2011. "Interview with Mikhail Gorbachev: They Were Truly Idiots." Hamburg, Germany. August 16th: Available at: www.spiegel .de/international/world/spiegel-interview-with-mikhail-gorbachev-they-were-truly-idiots-a-780526.html.

Spruyt, Hendrik. 1994. *The Sovereign State and its Competitors: an Analysis of Systems Change*. Princeton: Princeton University Press.

Staiger, Douglas, and James Stock. 1997. "Instrumental Variables Regression with Weak Instruments." *Econometrica* 65(3): 557–586.

Stallings, Barbara. 1987. *Banker to the Third World: U.S. Portfolio Investment in Latin America, 1900–1986*. Berkeley: University of California Press.

Stasavage, David. 2003. *Public Debt and the Birth of the Democratic State*. Cambridge: Cambridge University Press.

2010. "When Distance Mattered: Geographic Scale and the Development of European Representative Assemblies." *American Political Science Review* 104(4): 625–643.

2011. *States of Credit: Size, Power, and the Development of European Polities*. Princeton: Princeton University Press.

Steckel, Richard. 2004. "New Light on the 'Dark Ages': The Remarkably Tall Stature of Northern European Men during the Medieval Era." *Social Science History* 28(2): 211–229.

Stijns, Jean-Philippe. 2006. "Natural Resource Abundance and Human Capital Accumulation." *World Development* 34(6): 1060–1083.

Strayer, Joseph. 2005. *On the Medieval Origins of the Modern State*. Princeton: Princeton University Press.

Sunnevåg, Kjell. 2002. "Auctions Combined with Ex Post Taxation – Expected Revenue When Three Parties Want a Piece of the Cake." *Resources Policy* 28(1): 49–59.

Suny, Ronald. 1996. *Armenia, Azerbaijan, and Georgia*. Washington, DC: DIANE Publishing.

Svolik, Milan. 2009. "Power Sharing and Leadership Dynamics in Authoritarian Regimes." *American Journal of Political Science* 53(2): 477–494.

Swietochowski, Tadeusz. 1995. *Russia and Azerbaijan: a Borderland in Transition*. New York: Columbia University Press.

Thies, Cameron. 2005. "War, Rivalry, and State Building in Latin America." *American Journal of Political Science* 49(3): 451–465.

The Economist. 2013. "Supermajordämmerung." August, 3rd: http://www .economist.com/news/briefing/21582522-day-huge-integrated-inter national-oil-company-drawing.

   2014. "Smeltdown." January 18th: www.economist.com/news/business/ 21594260-government-risks-export-slump-boost-metals-processing-in dustry-smeltdown.

   2014. The North Sea: Running on Fumes. March 1st: www.economist.com /news/britain/21597890-scottish-nationalists-are-right-charge-britain- has-mismanaged-north-sea-oil-unionists.

   2015. Nodding Donkeys: Some Oil Majors are Still Ducking the Issue of Global Warming. November 14th: www.economist.com/news/busi ness/21678219-some-oil-majors-are-still-ducking-issue-global-warm ing-nodding-donkeys.

Thornton, John. 2001. "The Origins and Early History of the Kingdom of Kongo, c. 1350–1550." *The International Journal of African Historical Studies* 34(1): 89–120.

Ticchi, Davide, and Andrea Vindigni. 2009. "War and Endogenous Democracy." Unpublished Manuscript.

Tijerina Guajardo, José, and José Pagan. 2003. "Government Spending, Taxation, and Oil Revenues in Mexico." *Review of Development Economics* 7(1): 152–164.

Tilly, Charles. 1975. *The Formation of National States in Western Europe*. Princeton: Princeton University Press.

   1992. *Coercion, Capital, and European States, AD 990–1990*. Cambridge: Blackwell.

Tordo, Silvana, Brandon Tracy, and Noora Arfaa. 2011. "National Oil Companies and Value Creation." World Bank Working Paper 218.

Tortella, Gabriel, and Francisco Comin. 2001. "Fiscal and Monetary Institutions in Spain." In Bordo, Michael, and Roberto Cortés-Conde, eds., *Transferring Wealth and Power from the Old to the New World: Monetary and Fiscal Institutions in the 17th through the 19th Centuries*. Cambridge: Cambridge University Press, pp. 140–86.

Tracy, Joseph, Henry Schneider, and Sewin Chan. 1999. "Are Stocks Overtaking Real Estate in Household Portfolios?" *Current Issues in Economics and Finance* 5(5): 1–6.

Tsebelis, George. 1995. "Decision Making in Political Systems: Veto Players in Presidentialism, Parliamentarism, Multicameralism and Multipartyism." *British Journal of Political Science* 25(3): 289–325.

Tsui, Kevin. 2011. "More Oil, Less Democracy: Evidence from Worldwide Crude Oil Discoveries." *Economic Journal* 121(551): 89–115.

UNCTAD. 2012. "World Investment Report." Geneva, Switzerland: United Nations Publications.

UNCRET. 1980. *State Petroleum Enterprises in Developing Countries.* New York: Pergamon Press.

UNESCAP. 2001. *Azerbaijan. Accession to the World Trade Organization: Issues and Recommendations for Central Asian and Caucasian Economies in Transition.* Bangkok: United Nations Publications.

Vagts, Detlev. 1978. "Coercion and Foreign Investment Rearrangements." *American Journal of International Law* 72(1): 17–36.

Van der Ploeg, Frederick. 2011. "Natural Resources: Curse or Blessing?" *Journal of Economic Literature* 49(2) 366–420.

Van Meurs, Pedro. 1988. "Financial and Fiscal Arrangements for Petroleum Development – an Economic Analysis." In Nicky Beredjick and Thomas Walde, eds., *Petroleum Investment Policies in Developing Countries.* London: Graham and Trotman, pp. 47–79.

Vanhanen, Tatu. 2000. "A New Dataset for Measuring Democracy, 1810–1998." *Journal of Peace Research* 37(2): 251–265.

Vardy, Felix. 2010. "The Increasing Marginal Returns of Better Institutions." *Background paper for the 2010 Annual Flagship Report, The World Bank.*

Vernon, Raymond. 1971. *Sovereignty at Bay: the Multinational Spread of U. S. Enterprises.* New York: Basic Books.

Vogel, David. 2014. "Why the Golden State Became Green: the Political Origins of Environmental Protection in California" Working Paper.

Wacziarg, Romain. 2012. "The First Law of Petropolitics." *Economica* 79(316): 641–657.

Wade, Nicholas. 2014. *A Troublesome Inheritance: Genes, Race and Human History.* New York: Penguin Books.

Waelde, Thomas. 1978. "Revision of Transnational Investment Agreements in the Natural Resource Industries." *Law Americas* 10(2): 265–298.

1988. "Investment Policies in the International Petroleum Industry – Responses to the Current Crisis." In Nicky Beredjick and Thomas Waelde, eds., Petroleum Investment Policies in Developing Countries. London: Graham and Trotman, pp. 7–27.

1996. "International Energy Investment." *Energy Law Journal* 17: 191–213.

Waldner, David. 2012. "An Agenda for a Post-Arab Spring Political Economy of the Middle East." In Marc Lynch, ed., *Arab Uprisings: New Opportunities for Political Science.* Washington, DC: Project on Middle East Political Science, pp. 59–60.

Waldner, David, and Benjamin Smith. 2014. "Rentier States and State Transformations." In Stephan Leibfried, Evelyne Huber, Matthew

Lange, Jonah Levy, Frank Nullmeier, and John Stephens, eds., *Oxford Handbook on Transformations of the State*. Oxford: Oxford University Press, pp. 714–729.

Webb, Steven. 2010. "Managing Mineral Wealth in Middle-Income Countries: Political Economy in Five Examples from Latin America." Working Paper. The World Bank.

Weeks, Jessica. 2008. "Autocratic Audience Costs: Regime Type and Signalling Resolve." *International Organization* 62(1): 35–64.

Weingast, Barry. 1995. "The Economic Role of Political Institutions: Market-Preserving Federalism and Economic Development." *Journal of Law, Economics and Organization* 11(Spring): 1–31.

1997. "The Political Foundations of Democracy and the Rule of Law." *American Political Science Review* 91(2): 245–263.

Weinthal, Erika, and Pauline Jones Luong. 2006. "Combating the Resource Curse: an Alternative Solution to Managing Mineral Wealth." *Perspectives on Politics* 4(1): 35–53.

Williamson, Jeffrey. 1999. "Real Wages, Inequality and Globalization in Latin America Before 1940." *Revista de Historia Economica*. XVII, Special Edition.

Wittfogel, Karl. 1957. *Oriental Despotism: a Comparative Study of Total Power*. New Haven: Yale University Press.

Woods, Dwayne. 2012. "Patrimonialism (Neo) and the Kingdom of Swaziland: Employing a Case Study to Rescale a Concept." *Commonwealth and Comparative Politics* 50(3): 344–366.

Woolcock, Michael, Lant Pritchett, and Jonathan Isham. 2001 "The Social Foundations of Poor Economic Growth in Resource-Rich Countries." In Richard Auty, ed., *Resource Abundance and Economic Development*. New York: Oxford University Press, pp. 76–92.

Wooldridge, Jeffrey. 2006. *Introductory Econometrics*. Mason: Thompson South-Western.

Wright, David, and Czelusta, Jesse. 2007. "Resource-Based Growth Past and Present." In Daniel Lederman, and William Maloney, eds., *Natural Resources, Neither Curse nor Destiny*. Washington, DC: World Bank Publications, pp. 183–212.

Wright, Joseph. 2008. "Do Authoritarian Institutions Constrain?" *American Journal of Political Science* 52(2): 322–343.

Wright, Joseph, Erica Frantz, and Barbara Geddes. 2015. "Oil and Autocratic Regime Survival." *British Journal of Political Science* 45(2): 287–306.

Wrigley, Edward. 1988. *Continuity, Chance and Change*. Cambridge: Cambridge University Press.

Zeitlin, Irving. 2013 *The Historical Muhammad*. Cambridge: Polity Press.

Author index

Subject index